enVisionmath 2.0

SCOTT FORESMAN · ADDISON WESLEY

Volume 2 Topics 9-15

Authors

Randall I. Charles
Professor Emeritus
Department of Mathematics
San Jose State University
San Jose, California

Jennifer Bay-Williams
Professor of Mathematics Education
College of Education and Human
Development
University of Louisville
Louisville, Kentucky

Robert Q. Berry, III
Associate Professor of
Mathematics Education
Department of Curriculum,
Instruction and Special Education
University of Virginia
Charlottesville, Virginia

Janet H. Caldwell
Professor of Mathematics
Rowan University
Glassboro, New Jersey

Zachary Champagne
Assistant in Research
Florida Center for Research in Science,
Technology, Engineering, and
Mathematics (FCR-STEM)
Jacksonville, Florida

Juanita Copley
Professor Emerita, College of Education
University of Houston
Houston, Texas

Warren Crown
Professor Emeritus of Mathematics
Education
Graduate School of Education
Rutgers University
New Brunswick, New Jersey

Francis (Skip) Fennell
L. Stanley Bowlsbey Professor
of Education and Graduate and
Professional Studies
McDaniel College
Westminster, Maryland

Karen Karp
Professor of Mathematics Education
Department of Early Childhood and
Elementary Education
University of Louisville
Louisville, Kentucky

Stuart J. Murphy
Visual Learning Specialist
Boston, Massachusetts

Jane F. Schielack
Professor of Mathematics
Associate Dean for Assessment and
Pre K-12 Education, College of Science
Texas A&M University
College Station, Texas

Jennifer M. Suh
Associate Professor for
Mathematics Education
George Mason University
Fairfax, Virginia

Jonathan A. Wray
Mathematics Instructional Facilitator
Howard County Public Schools
Ellicott City, Maryland

Glenview, Illinois   Boston, Massachusetts   Chandler, Arizona   Hoboken, New Jersey

Mathematicians

Roger Howe
Professor of Mathematics
Yale University
New Haven, Connecticut

Gary Lippman
Professor of Mathematics and
Computer Science
California State University, East Bay
Hayward, California

ELL Consultants

Janice R. Corona
Independent Education Consultant
Dallas, Texas

Jim Cummins
Professor
The University of Toronto
Toronto, Canada

Common Core State Standards Reviewers

Debbie Crisco
Math Coach
Beebe Public Schools
Beebe, Arkansas

Kathleen A. Cuff
Teacher
Kings Park Central School District
Kings Park, New York

Erika Doyle
Math and Science Coordinator
Richland School District
Richland, Washington

Susan Jarvis
Math and Science Curriculum Coordinator
Ocean Springs Schools
Ocean Springs, Mississippi

Velvet M. Simington
K–12 Mathematics Director
Winston-Salem/Forsyth County Schools
Winston-Salem, North Carolina

PEARSON

ISBN-13:   978-0-328-82743-5
ISBN-10:   0-328-82743-6

17   19

You'll be using these digital resources throughout the year!

Digital Resources

Go to PearsonRealize.com

 MP

Math Practices Animations to play anytime

 Solve

Solve & Share problems plus math tools

Learn

Visual Learning Animation Plus with animation, interaction, and math tools

A-Z **Glossary**

Animated Glossary in English and Spanish

 Tools

Math Tools to help you understand

Assessment

Quick Check for each lesson

Help

Another Look Homework Video for extra help

Games

Math Games to help you learn

eText

Student Edition online

ACTIVe-book

Student Edition online for showing your work

PEARSON realize. Everything you need for math anytime, anywhere

Contents

KEY

● Major Cluster

● Supporting Cluster

● Additional Cluster

The content is organized to focus on Common Core clusters.

For a list of clusters, see Volume 1 pages F15–F18.

Digital Resources at PearsonRealize.com

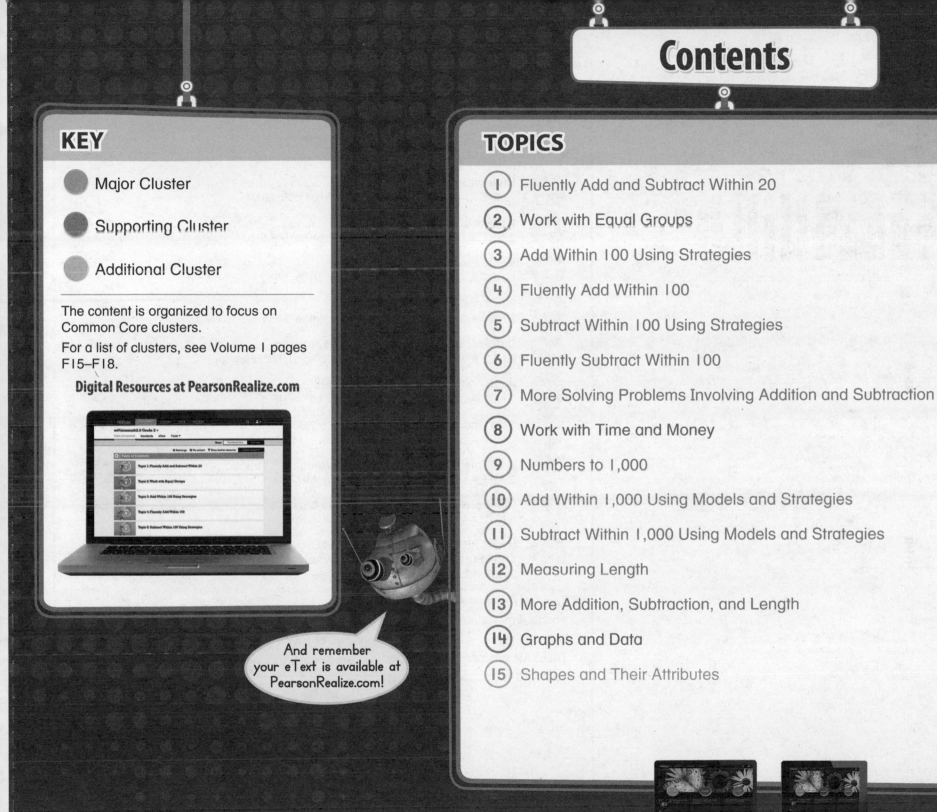

And remember your eText is available at PearsonRealize.com!

TOPICS

This shows how you can make 259 using place-value blocks.

TOPIC 9
Numbers to 1,000

This shows how you can draw models and regroup to find 173 + 244.

Hundreds	Tens	Ones		Hundreds	Tens	Ones
				1	7	3
			+	2	4	4
				4	1	7

TOPIC 10
Add Within 1,000 Using Models and Strategies

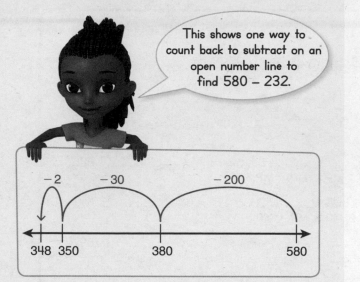

This shows one way to count back to subtract on an open number line to find 580 − 232.

$$-2 \qquad -30 \qquad -200$$

348 350   380   580

TOPIC 11
Subtract Within 1,000 Using Models and Strategies

© Pearson Education, Inc. 2

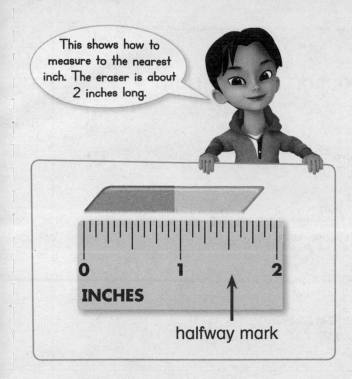

This shows how to measure to the nearest inch. The eraser is about 2 inches long.

INCHES

halfway mark

TOPIC 12
Measuring Length

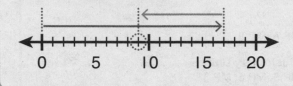

This shows how you can represent whole numbers as lengths on a number line.

Amelia walks 17 blocks before dinner. She walks 8 blocks after dinner.

How many more blocks does she walk before dinner than after dinner?

TOPIC 13
More Addition, Subtraction, and Length

© Pearson Education, Inc. 2

Contents

This picture graph shows data and can be used to solve problems.

Favorite Ball Games

Baseball	⚇ ⚇
Soccer	⚇ ⚇ ⚇ ⚇ ⚇ ⚇ ⚇
Tennis	⚇ ⚇ ⚇ ⚇

Each ⚇ = 1 student

TOPIC 14
Graphs and Data

This shows a way you can draw a cube.

TOPIC 15
Shapes and Their Attributes

Contents

STEP UP to Grade 3

These lessons help prepare you for Grade 3.

© Math Practices and Problem Solving Handbook

Math practices are ways we think about and do math.

Math practices will help you solve problems.

Math Practices

 MP.1 Make sense of problems and persevere in solving them.

 MP.2 Reason abstractly and quantitatively.

 MP.3 Construct viable arguments and critique the reasoning of others.

 MP.4 Model with mathematics.

 MP.5 Use appropriate tools strategically.

 MP.6 Attend to precision.

MP.7 Look for and make use of structure.

 MP.8 Look for and express regularity in repeated reasoning.

There are good Thinking Habits for each of these math practices.

MP.1 Make sense of problems and persevere in solving them.

Good math thinkers know what the problem is about. They have a plan to solve it. They keep trying if they get stuck.

My plan is to use counters as trucks. I can act out the problem.

A store has some toy trucks.
Mike buys 2 of the trucks.
Now the store has 3 trucks.
How many trucks did the store have at the start?

5 – 2 = 3
5 trucks

Thinking Habits

What do I need to find?

What do I know?

What's my plan for solving the problem?

What else can I try if I get stuck?

How can I check that my solution makes sense?

MP.2 Reason abstractly and quantitatively.

I completed a part-part-whole model. It shows how things in the problem are related.

Good math thinkers know how to think about words and numbers to solve problems.

Tony has 10 apples. 6 are red. The rest are green. How many apples are green?

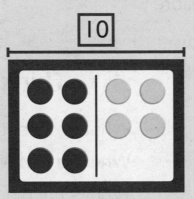

$10 - 6 = 4$

4 apples are green.

Thinking Habits

What do the numbers stand for?

How are the numbers in the problem related?

How can I show a word problem using pictures or numbers?

How can I use a word problem to show what an equation means?

F18

© Pearson Education, Inc. 2

Math Practices and Problem Solving Handbook

MP.3 Construct viable arguments and critique the reasoning of others.

I can use place-value blocks to check Paula's thinking. My explanation is clear and complete.

Good math thinkers use math to explain why they are right. They talk about math that others do, too.

Paula added 34 + 5.
She says she had to regroup the ones.
Is she correct? Show how you know.

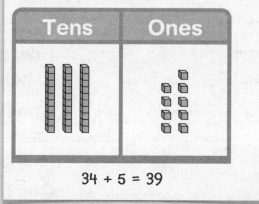

34 has 4 ones.

4 ones and 5 ones are 9 ones.

Paula is incorrect.

You do not need to regroup ones.

Tens	Ones

34 + 5 = 39

Thinking Habits

How can I use math to explain my work?

Am I using numbers and symbols correctly?

Is my explanation clear?

What questions can I ask to understand other people's thinking?

Are there mistakes in other people's thinking?

Can I improve other people's thinking?

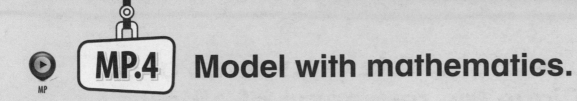
Good math thinkers
use math they know to show
and solve problems.

I can use
ten-frames and counters
to show the problem.

14 dogs are playing at a park.
9 dogs go home.
How many dogs are still at the park?

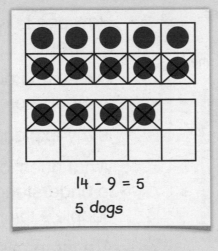

$14 - 9 = 5$

5 dogs

Thinking Habits

How can I use the math I know
to help solve this problem?

Can I use a drawing, diagram,
table, graph, or objects
to show the problem?

Can I write an
equation to show
the problem?

Math Practices and Problem Solving Handbook

MP.5 Use appropriate tools strategically.

Good math thinkers know how to pick the right tools to solve math problems.

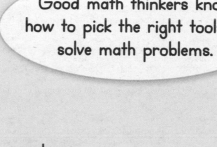

I chose connecting cubes to solve the problem.

Kai and Maddie each pick 6 apples.
Then Maddie picks 1 more apple.
How many apples do they pick in all?

6 + 7 = 13
13 apples

Thinking Habits

Which tools can I use?

Is there a different tool I could use?

Am I using the tool correctly?

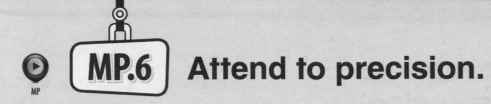

MP.6 Attend to precision.

Good math thinkers are careful about what they write and say, so their ideas about math are clear.

I can use the definition of a cube to help me describe what it looks like.

Circle each cube below.

Describe what a cube looks like.

A cube has 6 flat surfaces.

Each flat surface is the same size.

A cube has 12 edges.

Thinking Habits

Am I using numbers, units, and symbols correctly?

Am I using the correct definitions?

Is my answer clear?

Math Practices and Problem Solving Handbook

MP.7 | Look for and make use of structure.

It is hard to add three numbers at once. I can add any two numbers first. I added 6 + 4 first to make the problem easier.

Good math thinkers look for patterns in math to help solve problems.

Jeff saw 6 brown frogs, 3 green frogs, and 4 spotted frogs.
How many frogs did Jeff see in all?

Show your work and explain your answer.

$$⑥ + 3 + ④ = 13$$
10

I made 10 then added 3 to make the problem easier.

Thinking Habits

Is there a pattern?

How can I describe the pattern?

Can I break the problem into simpler parts?

MP.8 Look for and express regularity in repeated reasoning.

Good math thinkers look for things that repeat in a problem. They use what they learn from one problem to help them solve other problems.

I can compare the tens first. If the tens are the same, I can compare the ones.

Compare each pair of numbers. Write <, >, or =. Tell how you will compare each pair of numbers.

57 $<$ 75   49 $<$ 52

36 $>$ 34   61 $=$ 61

Thinking Habits

Does something repeat in the problem?

How can the solution help me solve another problem?

Math Practices and Problem Solving Handbook

Problem Solving Guide

> Math practices can help you solve problems.

Make Sense of the Problem

Reason
- What do I need to find?
- What given information can I use?
- How are the quantities related?

Think About Similar Problems
- Have I solved problems like this before?

Persevere in Solving the Problem

Model with Math
- How can I use the math I know?
- How can I show the problem?
- Is there a pattern I can use?

Use Appropriate Tools
- What math tools could I use?
- How can I use those tools?

Check the Answer

Make Sense of the Answer
- Is my answer reasonable?

Check for Precision
- Did I check my work?
- Is my answer clear?
- Is my explanation clear?

Some Ways to Show Problems

- Draw a Picture
- Draw a Number Line
- Write an Equation

Some Math Tools

- Objects
- Rulers
- Technology
- Paper and Pencil

This sheet helps you organize your work.

Name Mary

Teaching Tool 1

Problem Solving Recording Sheet

Problem:
John bikes for 17 miles on Monday.
He bikes for 15 miles on Tuesday.
How many miles does John bike in all?

MAKE SENSE OF THE PROBLEM

Need to Find	Given
I need to find how many miles John bikes in all.	John bikes 17 miles on Monday and 15 miles on Tuesday.

PERSEVERE IN SOLVING THE PROBLEM

Some Ways to Represent Problems
☑ Draw a Picture
☐ Draw a Number Line
☑ Write an Equation

Some Math Tools
☐ Objects
☐ Rulers
☐ Technology
☑ Paper and Pencil

Solution and Answer

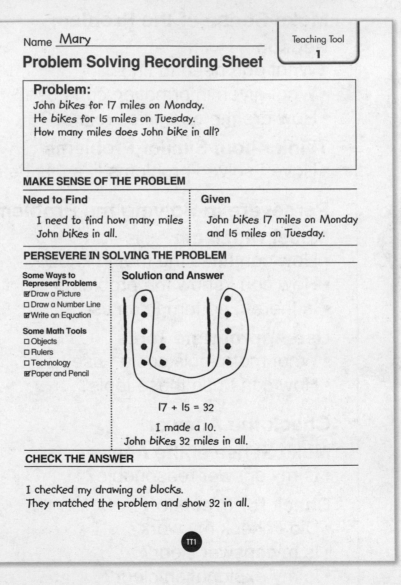

$17 + 15 = 32$

I made a 10.
John bikes 32 miles in all.

CHECK THE ANSWER

I checked my drawing of blocks.
They matched the problem and show 32 in all.

TT1

Numbers to 1,000

Essential Question: How can you count, read, and show numbers to 1,000?

Digital Resources

Solve Learn Glossary

Tools Assessment Help Games

Math and Science Project: Breaking Apart and Putting Together

Find Out Collect sets of building blocks. Take turns and work together. Use the blocks to build a model. Then take that model apart and use the same blocks to build a different model.

Journal: Make a Book Show your models in a book. In your book, also:

- Tell how many pieces you used to build your models.

- Show how to use place-value blocks to model different names for the same number.

Name _____

Review What You Know

Vocabulary

1. Circle the coin with the **least value**. Put a square around the coin with the **greatest value**.

2. Circle the number that has 5 **ones** and 4 **tens**.

54

45

40

5

3. Tom is having breakfast. The minute hand on the clock shows **half past 7 o'clock**. Circle the time on the clock.

7:15 a.m.

7:30 a.m.

7:15 p.m.

7:30 p.m.

Counting Money

4. Circle coins that total 83¢.

Breaking Apart Numbers

5. Break apart each number into tens and ones.

23 = _____ + _____

47 = _____ + _____

96 = _____ + _____

Math Story

6. Howie has $13. A backpack costs $30. How much more money does Howie need to buy the backpack?

$ _____

© Pearson Education, Inc. 2

My Word Cards

Study the words on the front of the card.
Complete the activity on the back.

A-Z Glossary

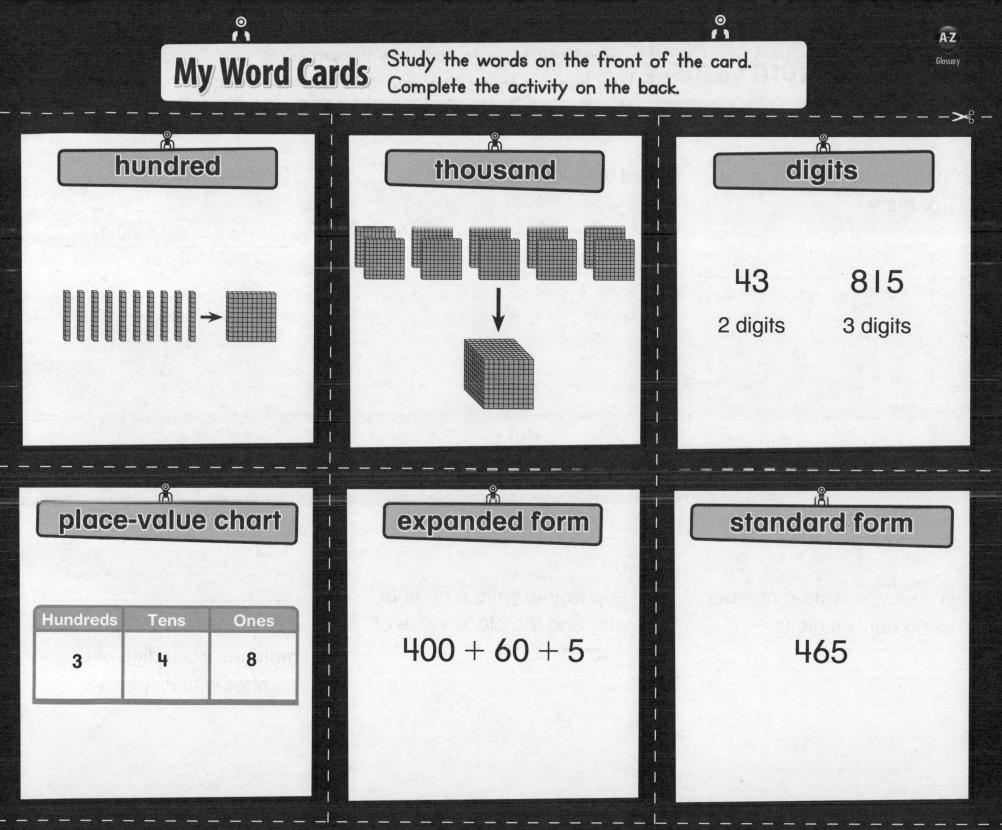

hundred

thousand

digits

43   815

2 digits   3 digits

place-value chart

Hundreds	Tens	Ones
3	4	8

expanded form

400 + 60 + 5

standard form

465

My Word Cards

Use what you know to complete the sentences.
Extend learning by writing your own sentence using each word.

Numbers are made up of 1 or more

_____.

10 hundreds make 1

_____.

10 tens make 1

_____.

_____

is a way to write a number using only its digits.

_____

is a way to write a number showing the place value of each digit.

A _____

_____

matches each digit of a number with its place.

My Word Cards

Study the words on the front of the card.
Complete the activity on the back.

---

word form

four hundred
sixty-five

---

compare

$>$ $<$ $=$

---

greater than (>)

$325 > 299$

---

less than (<)

$411 < 438$

---

equals (=)

$75 = 75$

---

increase

$224 \rightarrow 324 \rightarrow 424$

increase by 100

My Word Cards

Use what you know to complete the sentences.
Extend learning by writing your own sentence using each word.

325 is _____

_____ 299.

When you _____ numbers, you find out if a number is greater than, less than, or equal to another number.

_____ is a way to write a number using only words.

Numbers that _____ become greater in value.

75 _____ 75.

411 is _____

_____ 438.

My Word Cards

Study the words on the front of the card.
Complete the activity on the back.

A-Z
Glossary

decrease

$$424 \rightarrow 324 \rightarrow 224$$

decrease by 100

My Word Cards

Use what you know to complete the sentences.
Extend learning by writing your own sentence using each word.

Numbers that

_____

become lesser in value.

Solve

☆ Solve & Share

What is another way to show 100? Draw a picture and explain.

I can ...
understand place value and count by hundreds to 1,000.

© **Content Standards** 2.NBT.A.1a, 2.NBT.A.1b
Mathematical Practices MP.2, MP.4, MP.5, MP.7

Way 1

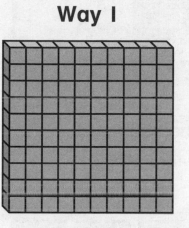

Way 2

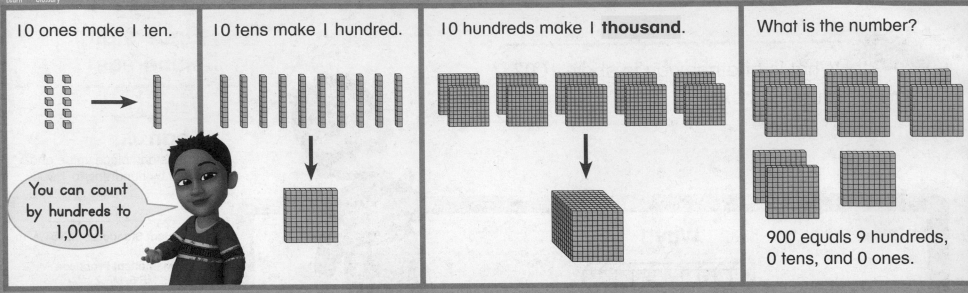

10 ones make I ten.

You can count by hundreds to 1,000!

10 tens make I hundred.

10 hundreds make I **thousand**.

What is the number?

900 equals 9 hundreds, 0 tens, and 0 ones.

Do You Understand?

Show Me! 10 ones make I ten. 10 tens make I hundred. 10 hundreds make I thousand. Do you see a pattern? Explain.

⭐ **Guided Practice** ⭐ Complete each sentence. Use models if needed.

1. _600_ equals _6_ hundreds, _0_ tens, and _0_ ones.

2. _____ equals _____ hundreds, _____ tens, and _____ ones.

⭐ Independent Practice ⭐ Complete each sentence. Use models if needed.

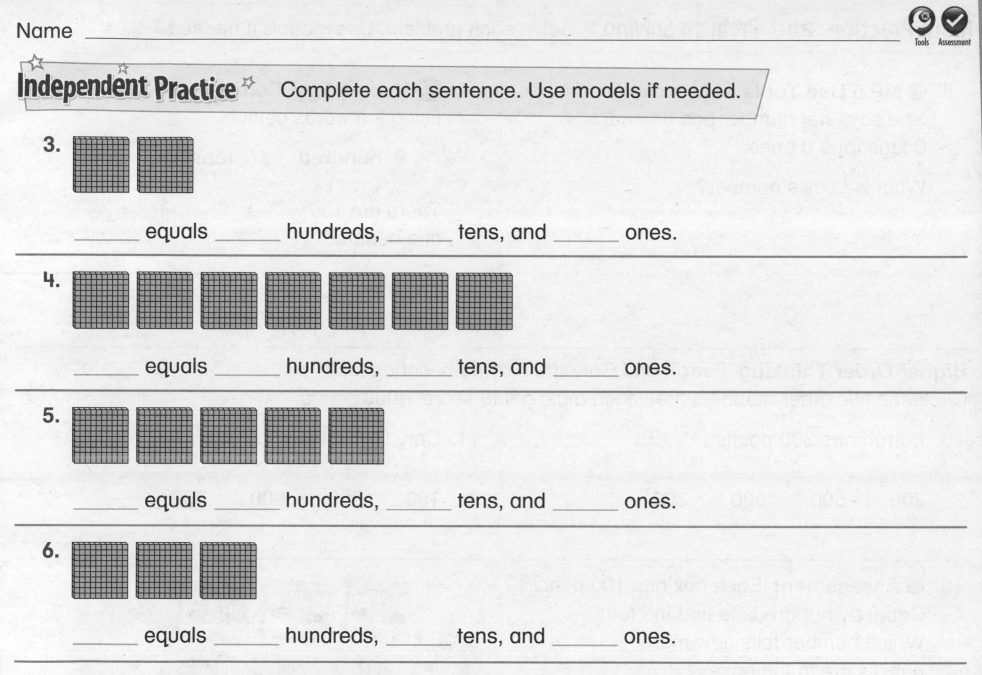

3.

_____ equals _____ hundreds, _____ tens, and _____ ones.

4.

_____ equals _____ hundreds, _____ tens, and _____ ones.

5.

_____ equals _____ hundreds, _____ tens, and _____ ones.

6.

_____ equals _____ hundreds, _____ tens, and _____ ones.

7. **Number Sense** Complete the pattern.

| 100 | 200 | 300 | | 500 | | 700 | 800 | 900 | |

8. © **MP.5 Use Tools** Lucy picked a number. She says her number has 8 hundreds, 0 tens, and 0 ones.

What is Lucy's number?

_____

9. A-Z **Vocabulary** Complete the sentences using the words below.

hundred   **tens**   **ones**

There are 100 _____ in one hundred.

There are 10 _____ in one _____.

Higher Order Thinking Farrah and Cory are playing beanbag toss.
Circle the two other numbers they each must get to score 1,000 points.

10. Farrah has 300 points.

    200   500   600   300

11. Cory has 500 points.

    100   200   400   700

12. © **Assessment** Each box has 100 pencils.
Count by hundreds to find the total.
Which number tells how many
pencils are in the boxes?

    Ⓐ 170   Ⓒ 800

    Ⓑ 700   Ⓓ 900

Name _____

Another Look! You can show hundreds with models.

Circle the models to show 500.

500 equals ___5___ hundreds, 0 tens, and 0 ones.

Count by 100s to find 500.

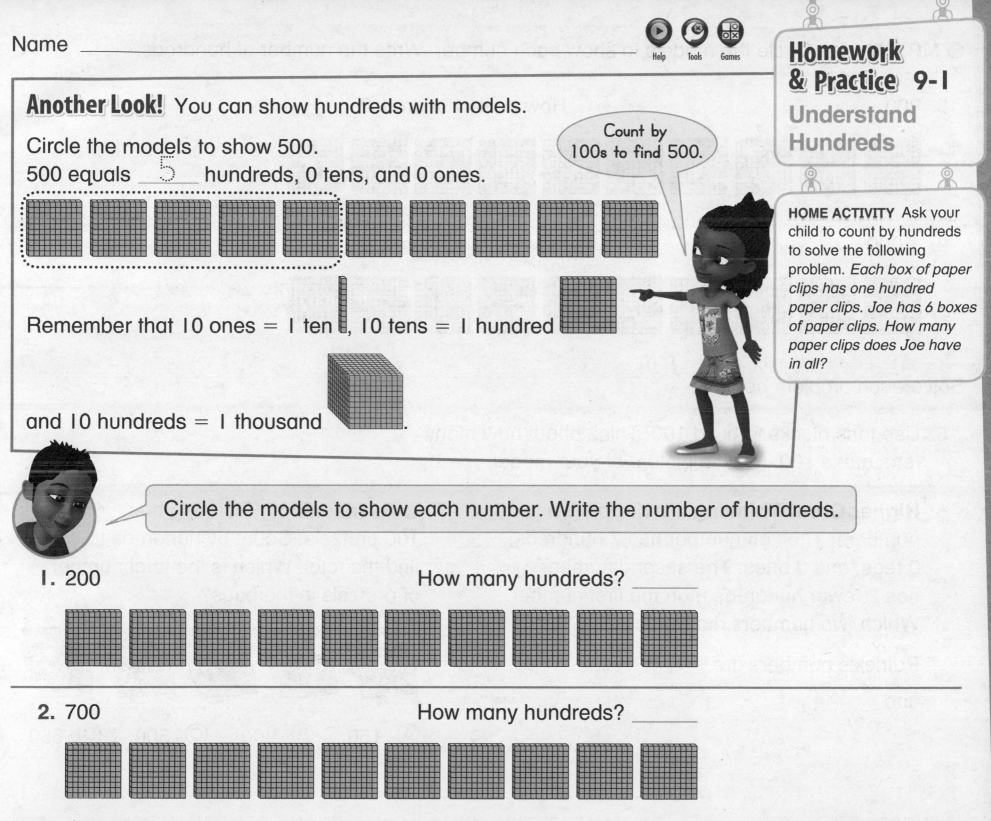

Remember that 10 ones = 1 ten , 10 tens = 1 hundred

and 10 hundreds = 1 thousand .

HOME ACTIVITY Ask your child to count by hundreds to solve the following problem. *Each box of paper clips has one hundred paper clips. Joe has 6 boxes of paper clips. How many paper clips does Joe have in all?*

Circle the models to show each number. Write the number of hundreds.

1. 200   How many hundreds? _____

2. 700   How many hundreds? _____

3. 900   How many hundreds? _____

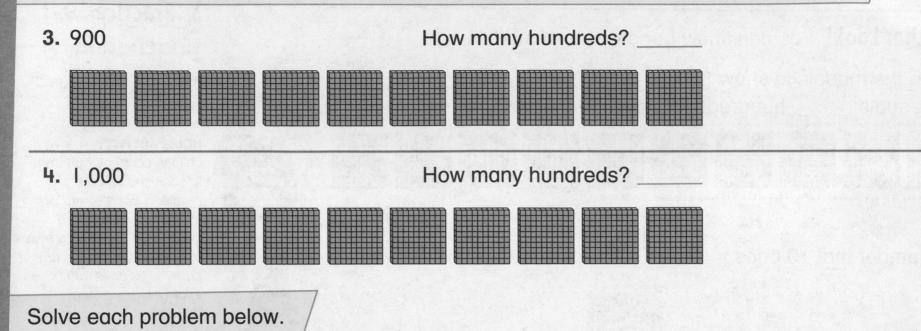

---

4. 1,000   How many hundreds? _____

Solve each problem below.

5. Use tens blocks to build 100. Think about how many tens make 100. Draw a picture of your model.

---

6. Higher Order Thinking Patrick picked two numbers. The first number has 7 hundreds, 0 tens, and 0 ones. The second number has 2 fewer hundreds than the first number. Which two numbers did Patrick pick?

Patrick's numbers are _____

and _____.

7. © **Assessment** Each bag has 100 pretzels. Count by hundreds to find the total. Which is the total number of pretzels in the bags?

Ⓐ 150   Ⓑ 400   Ⓒ 500   Ⓓ 550

Name _____

How can you use place-value blocks to show 125? Explain.

Draw your blocks to show what you did.

I can ...
use place-value blocks and drawings to model and write 3-digit numbers.

© **Content Standards** 2.NBT.A.1, 2.NBT.A.3
Mathematical Practices MP.1, MP.2, MP.4, MP.5

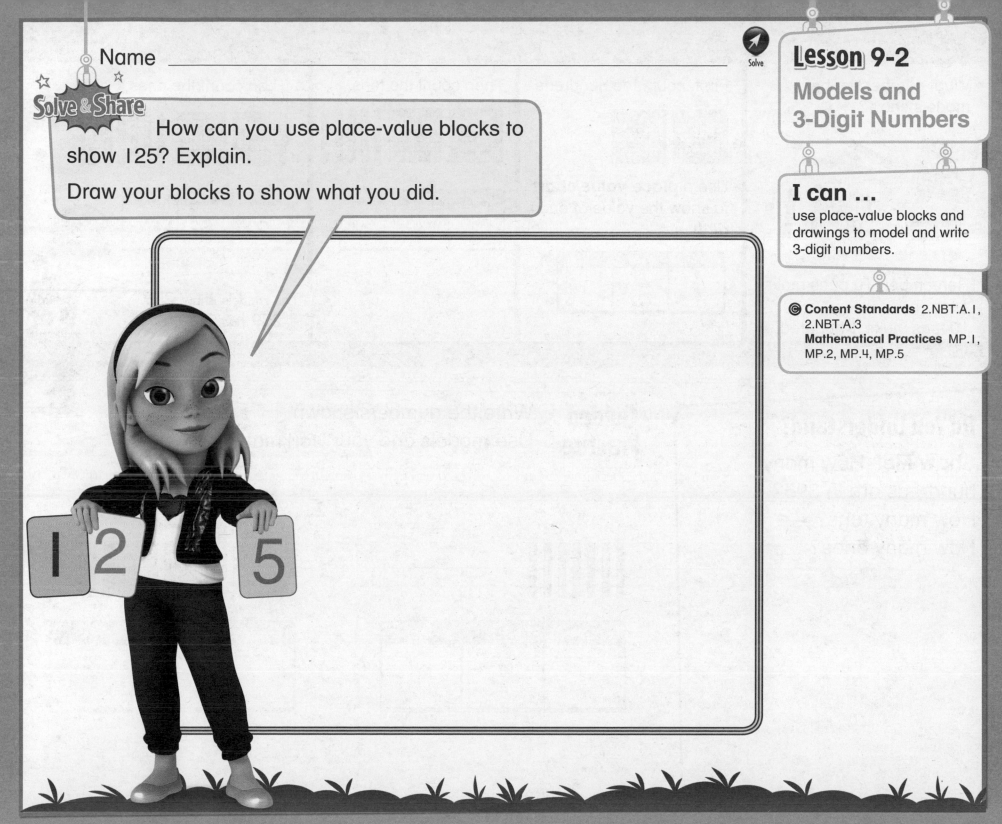

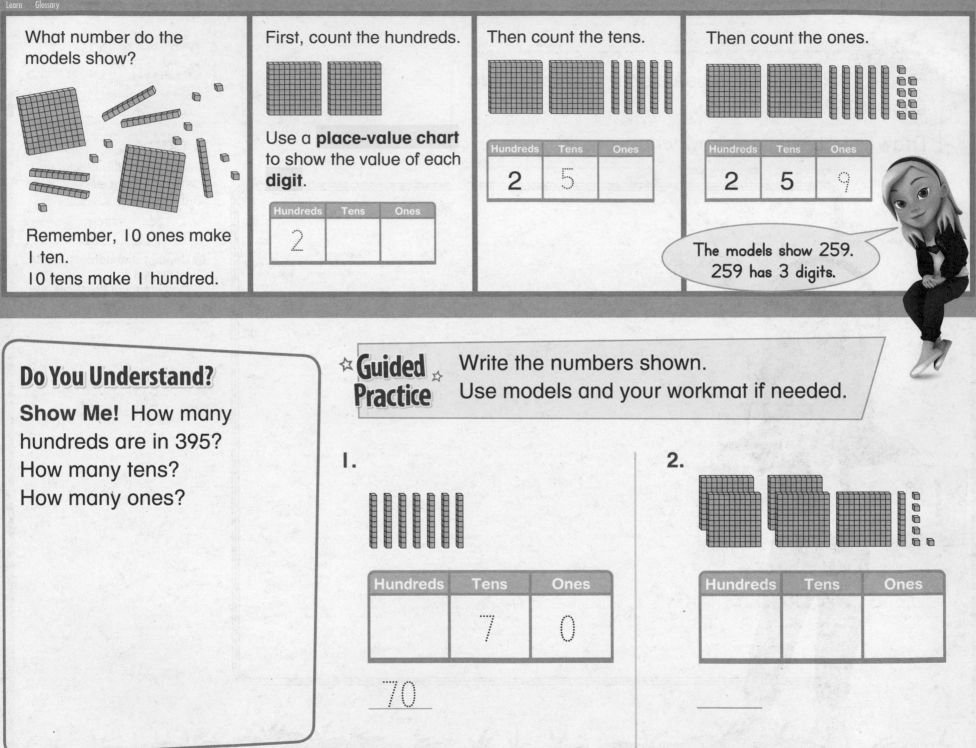

What number do the models show?

Remember, 10 ones make 1 ten.
10 tens make 1 hundred.

First, count the hundreds.

Use a **place-value chart** to show the value of each **digit**.

Hundreds	Tens	Ones
2		

Then count the tens.

Hundreds	Tens	Ones
2	5	

Then count the ones.

Hundreds	Tens	Ones
2	5	9

The models show 259. 259 has 3 digits.

Do You Understand?

Show Me! How many hundreds are in 395? How many tens? How many ones?

☆ Guided Practice ☆

Write the numbers shown.
Use models and your workmat if needed.

1.

Hundreds	Tens	Ones
	7	0

70

2.

Hundreds	Tens	Ones

___

Name _____

Independent Practice ☆ Write the numbers shown. Use models and your workmat if needed.

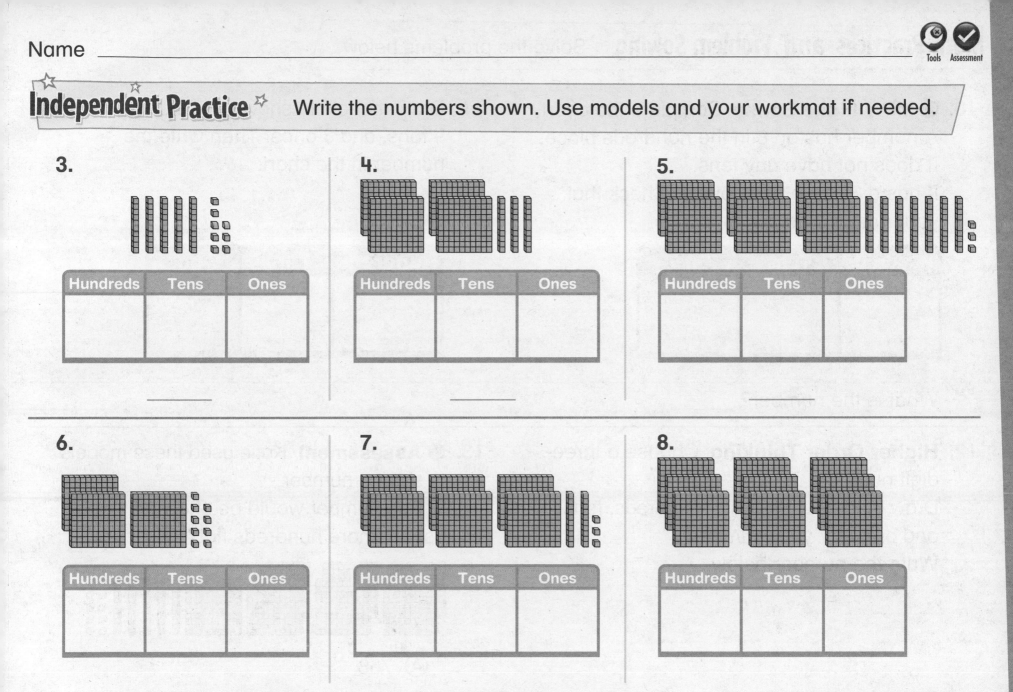

3.

Hundreds	Tens	Ones

_____

4.

Hundreds	Tens	Ones

_____

5.

Hundreds	Tens	Ones

_____

6.

Hundreds	Tens	Ones

_____

7.

Hundreds	Tens	Ones

_____

8.

Hundreds	Tens	Ones

_____

9. Higher Order Thinking Find the number. It has 5 hundreds.
The digit in the tens place is between 5 and 7. The number of
ones is 2 less than 4. _____

10. © **MP.1 Make Sense** Complete the chart.
A number has an 8 in the hundreds place.
It does not have any tens.
It has a 3 in the ones place. Check that
your answer makes sense.

Hundreds	Tens	Ones

What is the number? _____

11. Draw models to show the 1 hundred,
4 tens, and 3 ones. Then write the
number in the chart.

Hundreds	Tens	Ones

12. **Higher Order Thinking** Choose a three-
digit number.
Draw models to show the hundreds, tens,
and ones for your number.
Write the number below.

_____

13. © **Assessment** Katie used these models
to show a number.
Which number would be shown if Katie
used 1 more hundreds flat?

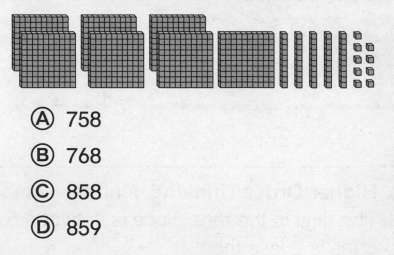

Ⓐ 758

Ⓑ 768

Ⓒ 858

Ⓓ 859

   Topic 9 | Lesson 2

Name _____

Another Look! Use models and your workmat to sort and count.

First, put the hundreds flats on your mat. Next, put the tens rods on your mat. Last, put the ones cubes on your mat.

Write the number of hundreds, tens, and ones.

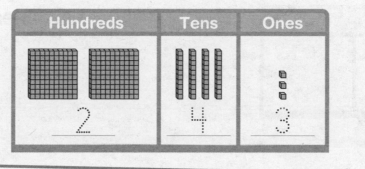

Hundreds	Tens	Ones
2	4	3

HOME ACTIVITY Give your child 50 paper clips or other small, countable objects. Ask your child how many ones make 5 tens.

Write the numbers.
Use models and your workmat if needed.

1.

Hundreds	Tens	Ones

2.

Hundreds	Tens	Ones

Solve each problem. Use models and your workmat if needed.

3. © **MP.4 Model** Write the number based on the model shown.

Hundreds	Tens	Ones

4. **Number Sense** Use the clues to solve the number puzzle.

I have a 5 in my ones place.
The digit in my tens place is 3 plus the digit in my ones place. The digit in my hundreds place is 2 less than the digit in my ones place. What number am I?

_____

5. **Higher Order Thinking** Look back at Item 4. Write your own place-value number puzzle. Give it to a friend to solve.

_____

_____

_____

_____

6. © **Assessment** Which number is shown?

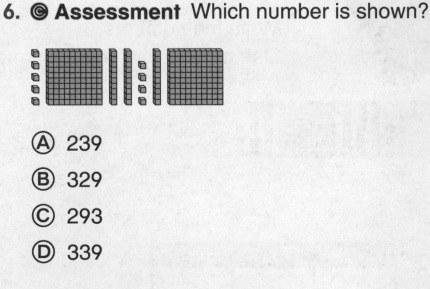

Ⓐ 239

Ⓑ 329

Ⓒ 293

Ⓓ 339

© Pearson Education, Inc. 2

Solve & Share

Jake says the 3 in 738 has a value of 3. He shows this with 3 ones blocks. Do you agree with Jake? Explain. Use the chart to help.

I can ...
tell the value of a digit by where it is placed in a number.

© **Content Standards** 2.NBT.A.1, 2.NBT.A.3
Mathematical Practices MP.3, MP.4, MP.5, MP.8

Hundreds	Tens	Ones

_____

_____

_____

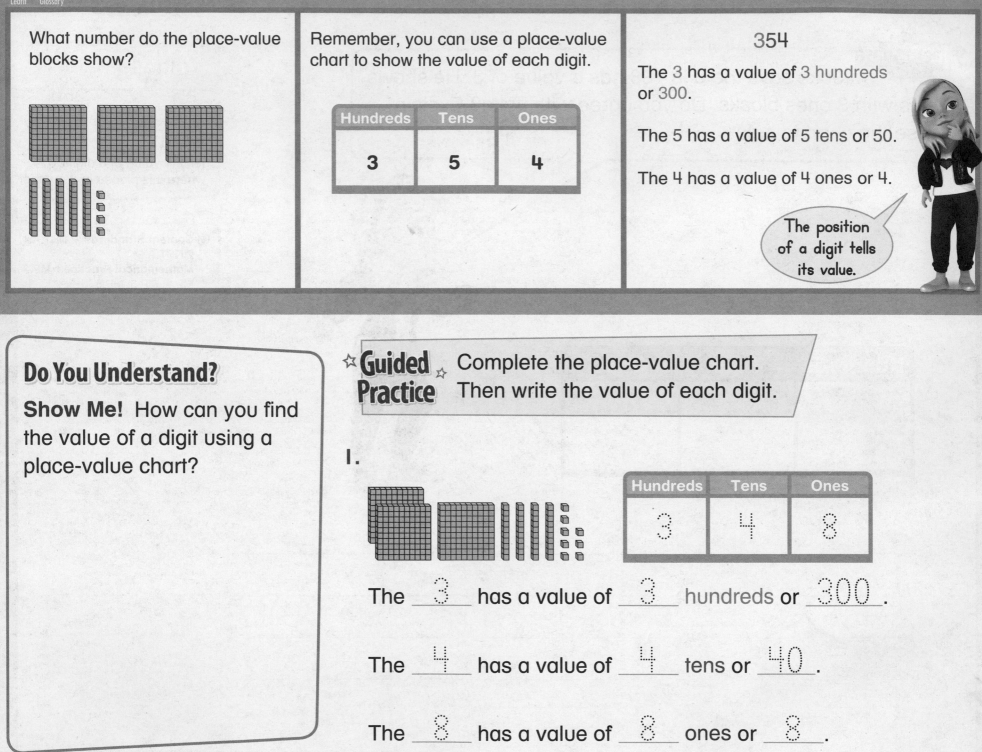

What number do the place-value blocks show?

Remember, you can use a place-value chart to show the value of each digit.

Hundreds	Tens	Ones
3	5	4

354

The 3 has a value of 3 hundreds or 300.

The 5 has a value of 5 tens or 50.

The 4 has a value of 4 ones or 4.

The position of a digit tells its value.

Do You Understand?

Show Me! How can you find the value of a digit using a place-value chart?

☆ Guided Practice ☆ Complete the place-value chart. Then write the value of each digit.

1.

Hundreds	Tens	Ones
3	4	8

The ___3___ has a value of ___3___ hundreds or ___300___.

The ___4___ has a value of ___4___ tens or ___40___.

The ___8___ has a value of ___8___ ones or ___8___.

© Pearson Education, Inc. 2

Tools Assessment

Independent Practice ☆ Circle the correct values for the underlined digit in each number.

2.	17<u>3</u>	3	30	3 hundreds	3 ones	3 tens
3.	<u>4</u>39	4 tens	4 hundreds	4	40	400
4.	6<u>6</u>1	6 hundreds	60	6 tens	600	6 ones
5.	<u>5</u>18	500	5 tens	5 hundreds	5	50
6.	742	20	200	2	2 tens	2 ones

7. Use the number to answer each question.

902

What is the value of the 9?

_____

What is the value of the 0?

_____

What is the value of the 2?

_____

8. Higher Order Thinking Write the number that has the following values.

- The tens digit has a value of 70.

- The ones digit has a value of 5 ones.

- The hundreds digit has a value of 8 hundreds.

9. Complete the chart to find the number.

The number has 9 hundreds.
It has 5 tens
It has 8 ones.

Hundreds	Tens	Ones

What is the number? _____

10. © **MP.4 Model** Courtney drew a picture of place-value blocks to show the number 793. Draw the blocks to show what Courtney's picture may have looked liked.

11. Higher Order Thinking A class needs to build the number 123 with place-value blocks but does **NOT** have any hundreds blocks. How can they build 123 using other place-value blocks?

_____

_____

_____

12. © **Assessment** What is the value of the 6 in the number 862?

Ⓐ 6

Ⓑ 10

Ⓒ 60

Ⓓ 600

Name _____

Another Look! You can find the value of each digit of a number by its place.

Hundreds	Tens	Ones
2	4	3

The value of the 2 is _2 hundreds_ or __200__.

The value of the 4 is _4 tens_ or _40_.

The value of the 3 is _3 ones_ or __3__.

HOME ACTIVITY Choose two three-digit numbers. Ask your child to name the values of each digit in each number.

Use the number in the place-value chart. Write the value of each digit.

1.

Hundreds	Tens	Ones
8	2	1

The value of the 8 is _____ hundreds or _____.

The value of the 2 is _____ tens or _____.

The value of the 1 is _____ one or _____.

2.

Hundreds	Tens	Ones
5	7	9

The value of the 5 is _____ hundreds or _____.

The value of the 7 is _____ tens or _____.

The value of the 9 is _____ ones or _____.

3. Complete the chart to find the number.

The number has 0 ones.
It has 7 hundreds.
It has 8 tens.

Hundreds	Tens	Ones

What is the number? _____.

4. Ⓒ **MP.3 Explain** Stacy says the 4 in 643 has a value of 4 tens or 40. Do you agree with Stacy's reasoning? Explain. Use pictures, words, or numbers in your answer.

5. **Higher Order Thinking** Kayla wrote a three-digit number. The value of the digit in the hundreds place is 6 hundreds. The digit in the tens place is 3 less than the digit in the hundreds place. The sum of all three digits is 12. What is Kayla's number?

Kayla's number is _____.

6. Ⓒ **Assessment** What is the value of the 7 in the number 763?

Ⓐ 7

Ⓑ 70

Ⓒ 100

Ⓓ 700

Name _____

⭐ **Solve & Share**

What is another way to write the number 231?
Explain.

I can ...
read and write 3-digit numbers in expanded form, standard form, and word form.

© **Content Standards** 2.NBT.A.3, 2.NBT.A.1
Mathematical Practices MP.2, MP.4, MP.6, MP. 7

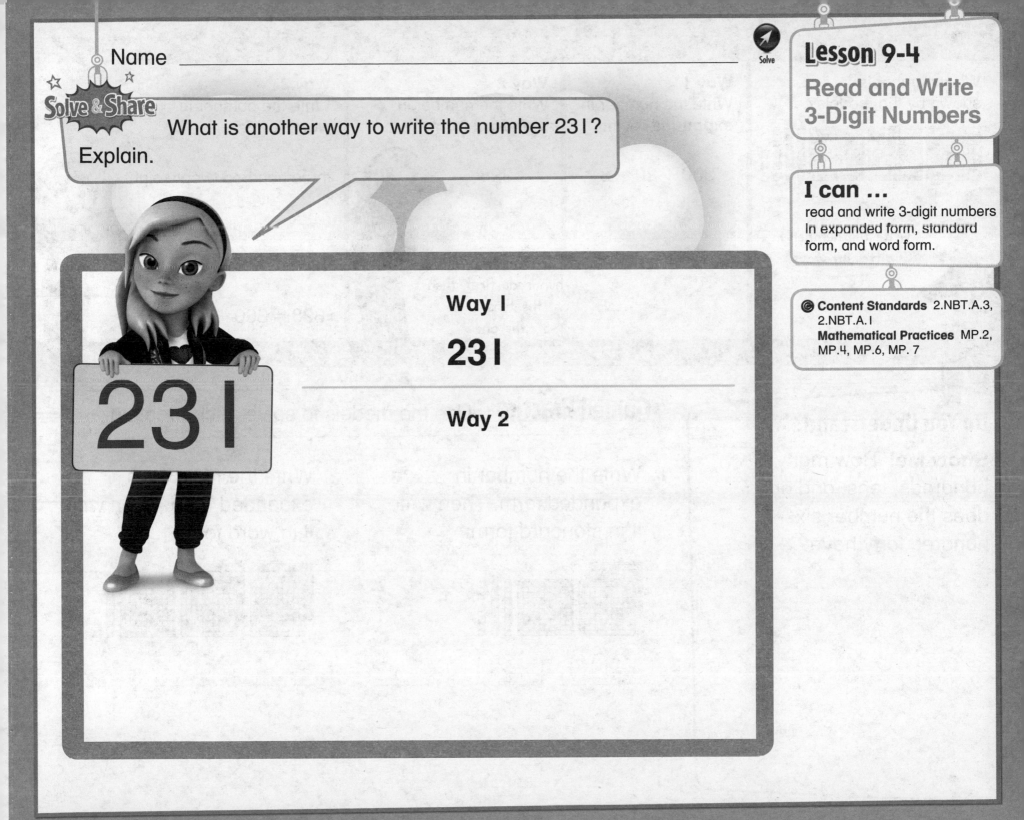

Way 1

231

Way 2

231

What number is shown by the models?

You can write the number in different ways.

Way 1
Write the number in **expanded form**.

$300 + 20 + 8$

Way 2
Write the number in **standard form**.

328

Write the hundreds first, then the tens, then the ones.

Way 3
Write the number in **word form**.

three hundred twenty-eight

All three ways show the same number!

$328 = 300 + 20 + 8$

Do You Understand?

Show Me! How many hundreds, tens, and ones does the number six hundred forty have?

☆ Guided Practice   Use the models to solve each problem.

1. Write the number in expanded form. Then write it in standard form.

$\underline{300} + \underline{20} + \underline{5}$

$\underline{325}$

2. Write the number in expanded form. Then write it in word form.

$\underline{} + \underline{} + \underline{}$

_____

_____

© Pearson Education, Inc. 2

Topic 9 | Lesson 4

Independent Practice ✭ Write the number in word form and standard form.

3. 300 + 80 + 2

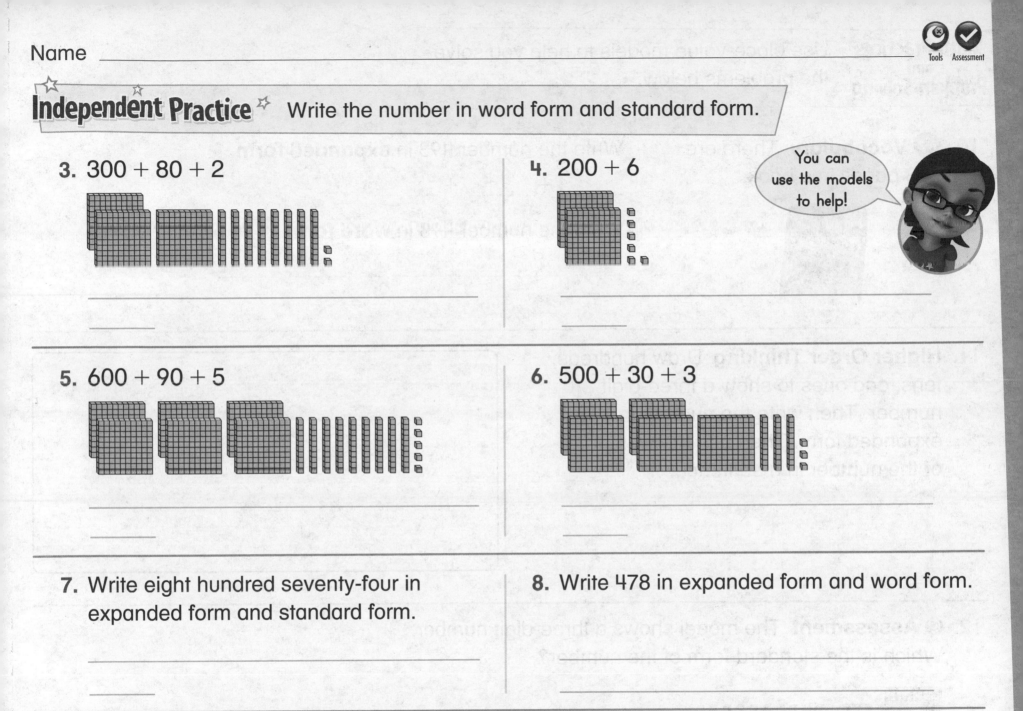

_____

You can use the models to help!

4. 200 + 6

_____

5. 600 + 90 + 5

_____

6. 500 + 30 + 3

_____

7. Write eight hundred seventy-four in expanded form and standard form.

_____

8. Write 478 in expanded form and word form.

_____

9. **Higher Order Thinking** Write the number in two different ways. It has 5 hundreds. The tens digit is 1 less than the hundreds digit. The ones digit is 2 more than the hundreds digit.

Standard form: _____   Expanded form: _____

10. **A-Z Vocabulary** There are 493 pages in a book.

Write the number 493 in **expanded form**.

_____ + _____ + _____

Write the number 493 in **word form**.

_____

11. **Higher Order Thinking** Draw hundreds, tens, and ones to show a three-digit number. Then write the number in expanded form. Then use the word form of the number in a sentence.

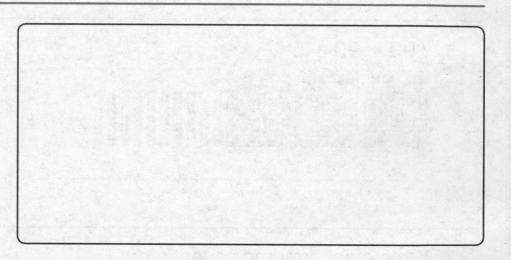

12. **© Assessment** The model shows a three-digit number. Which is the standard form of the number?

Ⓐ 300 + 80 + 6　　Ⓑ 386　　Ⓒ 300 + 90 + 7　　Ⓓ 397

Name _____

Another Look! You can write and show numbers in different ways.

Expanded form uses plus signs to show hundreds, tens, and ones.

$200 + 60 + 4$

You can draw models to show the expanded form.

The **word form** is two hundred sixty-four.

The **standard form** is

264 .

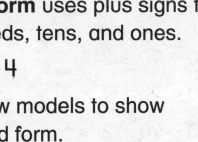 Solve each problem.

1. Draw models to show the expanded form. Write the number in standard form.

$400 + 30 + 8$

four hundred thirty-eight

_____

2. Write the number in expanded form and standard form.

three hundred fifty-four

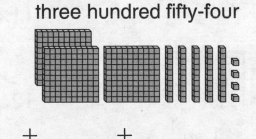

_____ + _____ + _____

_____

3. **A-Z Vocabulary** Write the number in **standard form**. Then write it in **word form**.

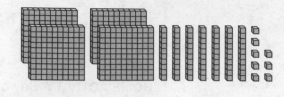

$$400 + 70 + 8$$

_____

4. **© Assessment** 329 cars and 293 trucks are parked in a parking lot.

Which is the expanded form of the number of cars parked?

Ⓐ $200 + 90 + 3$

Ⓑ $300 + 20 + 9$

Ⓒ $300 + 90 + 2$

Ⓓ $600 + 20 + 2$

Higher Order Thinking Use the clues to complete the number puzzle.

Across

5. $500 + 20 + 3$

7.

9. $400 + 20 + 9$

10.

13. Two hundred sixty-nine

Down

6. $300 + 40 + 7$

7. Three hundred ninety-seven

8. $500 + 60 + 9$

11.

12. Four hundred thirty-eight

© Pearson Education, Inc. 2

Topic 9 | Lesson 4

Name _____

Solve & Share

Use place-value blocks. Show two ways to make 213. Then draw each way. Tell how your ways are alike and different.

Make your models here.

I can ...
make and name a number in different ways to show the same value.

Content Standards 2.NBT.A.3, 2.NBT.A.1a
Mathematical Practices MP.2, MP.3, MP.4, MP.5, MP.6

Draw your models here.

Way 1	**Way 2**

You can show 123 in different ways. Here is one way.

Or break apart the hundred to make 10 tens.

Or break apart a ten to make 10 ones.

$123 = 100 + 20 + 3$

$123 = 120 + 3$

$123 = 100 + 10 + 13$

Do You Understand?

Show Me! How can you show that 5 hundreds and 4 tens has the same value as 4 hundreds and 14 tens?

☆ **Guided Practice** ☆ Use place-value blocks to count the hundreds, tens, and ones. Show two other ways to make the number.

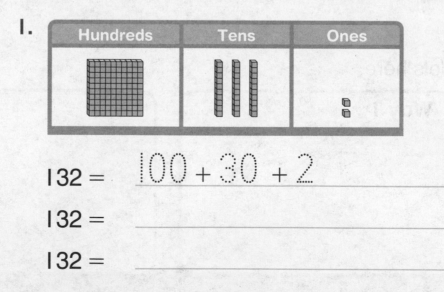

1.

Hundreds	Tens	Ones

$132 =$ $100 + 30 + 2$

$132 =$ _____

$132 =$ _____

© Pearson Education, Inc. 2

Tools Assessment

Independent Practice

Use place-value blocks to count the hundreds, tens, and ones. Then show two other ways to make the number.

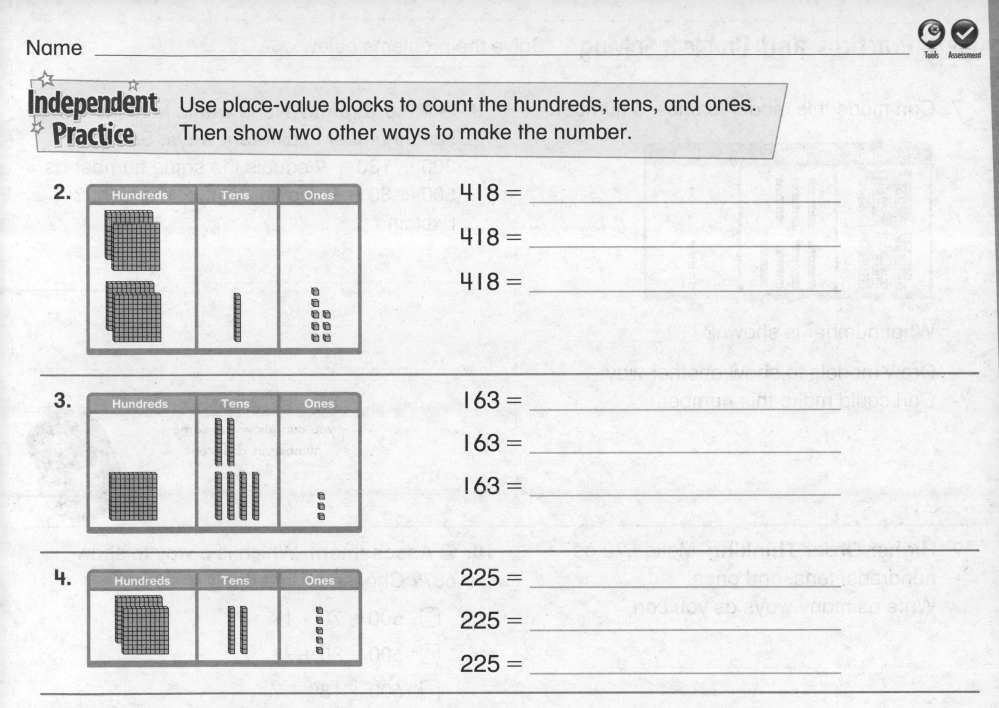

2.

Hundreds	Tens	Ones

418 = _____

418 = _____

418 = _____

3.

Hundreds	Tens	Ones

163 = _____

163 = _____

163 = _____

4.

Hundreds	Tens	Ones

225 = _____

225 = _____

225 = _____

Algebra Write the missing number.

5. $698 = 500 + \underline{\hspace{1cm}} + 8$

6. $939 = 900 + 20 + \underline{\hspace{1cm}}$

7. Carl made this model to show a number.

Hundreds	Tens	Ones

What number is shown? _____

Draw models to show another way Carl could make this number.

8. ⓒ MP.3 Explain Neha wants to make the same number in different ways. She says $300 + 130 + 9$ equals the same number as $500 + 30 + 9$. Do you agree with Neha? Explain.

_____

_____

_____

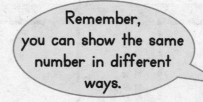

Remember, you can show the same number in different ways.

9. Higher Order Thinking Make 572 as hundreds, tens, and ones. Write as many ways as you can.

_____

_____

_____

10. ⓒ Assessment Which is a way to show 687? Choose all that apply.

☐ $600 + 70 + 17$

☐ $600 + 80 + 7$

☐ $600 + 180 + 7$

☐ $500 + 180 + 7$

Name _____

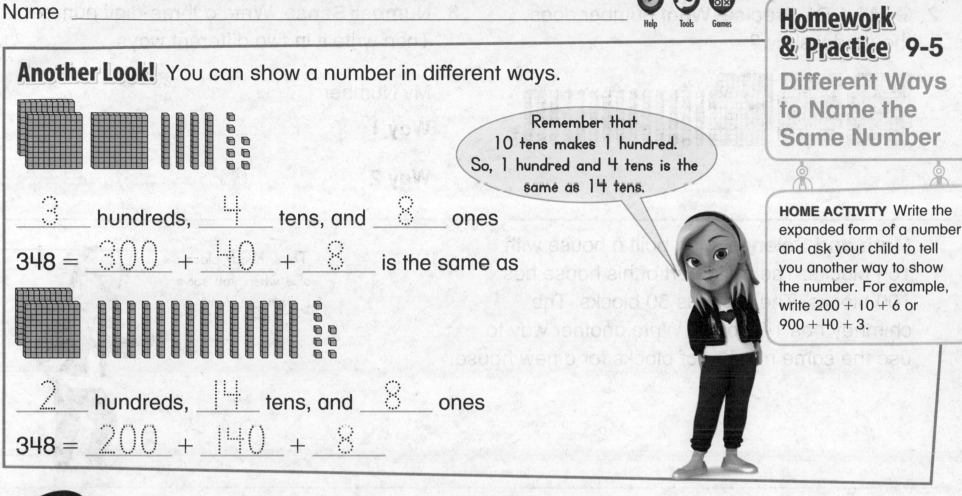

Help Tools Games

Another Look! You can show a number in different ways.

Remember that 10 tens makes 1 hundred. So, 1 hundred and 4 tens is the same as 14 tens.

___3___ hundreds, ___4___ tens, and ___8___ ones

$348 = $ ___300___ $+$ ___40___ $+$ ___8___ is the same as

___2___ hundreds, ___14___ tens, and ___8___ ones

$348 = $ ___200___ $+$ ___140___ $+$ ___8___

HOME ACTIVITY Write the expanded form of a number and ask your child to tell you another way to show the number. For example, write $200 + 10 + 6$ or $900 + 40 + 3$.

Show two different ways to name the number. You can use place-value blocks to help.

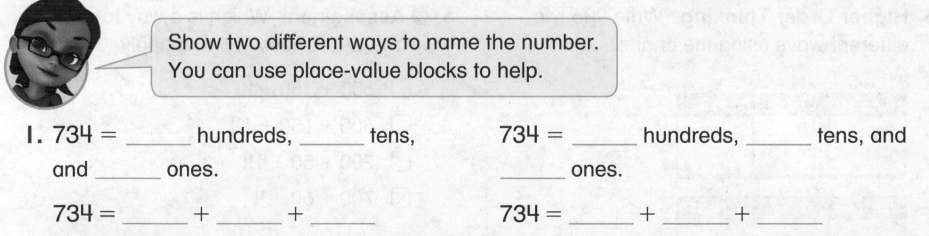

1. $734 = $ _____ hundreds, _____ tens, and _____ ones.

$734 = $ _____ $+$ _____ $+$ _____

$734 = $ _____ hundreds, _____ tens, and _____ ones.

$734 = $ _____ $+$ _____ $+$ _____

2. **© MP.6 Be Precise** What number does the model show?

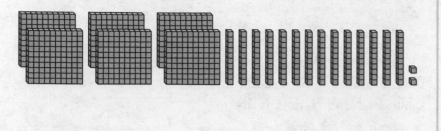

_____

3. **Number Sense** Write a three-digit number. Then write it in two different ways.

My Number _____

Way 1 _____

Way 2 _____

4. **Math and Science** Matt built a house with 164 blocks. The main part of his house has 100 blocks. The roof has 50 blocks. The chimney has 14 blocks. Write another way to use the same number of blocks for a new house.

Think about place value when you solve this problem.

5. **Higher Order Thinking** Write 936 two different ways using the charts.

Hundreds	Tens	Ones

Hundreds	Tens	Ones

6. **© Assessment** Which is a way to show 764? Choose all that apply.

☐ 600 + 150 + 4

☐ 600 + 150 + 14

☐ 700 + 50 + 14

☐ 700 + 60 + 4

© Pearson Education, Inc. 2

Solve & Share

Write the missing numbers in the chart.
Be ready to explain how you found the missing numbers.

I can ...
use place-value patterns to
mentally count by 1s and 10s
from a given number.

© **Content Standards** 2.NBT.A.2,
2.NBT.B.8
Mathematical Practices MP.3,
MP.5, MP.7, MP.8

51	52	53	54	55	56	57	58	59	60
61	62	63	64	65	66	67	68	69	70
71	72	73	74	75	76	77	78	79	80
	82	83		85				89	
91			94		96	97	98		100
101	102	103	104	105	106	107	108	109	110
111	112	113	114	115	116	117	118	119	120
	122	123		125				129	
131			134				138		

You can use place-value patterns and mental math to count by 1s and 10s to 100.

37, 38, 39, 40, 41!

31	32	33	34	35	36	37
41	42	43	44	45	46	47
51	52	53	54	55	56	57

The ones digits go up by 1 from left to right.
The tens digits go up by 1 from top to bottom.

You can also use place-value patterns and mental math to count by 1s and 10s to 1,000.

537, 547, 557, 567!

531	532	533	534	535	536	537
541	542	543	544	545	546	547
551	552	553	554	555	556	557

The ones digits go up by 1 from left to right.
The tens digits go up by 1 from top to bottom.

Do You Understand?

Show Me! Use mental math and place-value patterns to write each missing number.

536, 537, _____, 539, 540

531, 541, _____, 561, 571

☆ Guided Practice ☆ Use place-value patterns and mental math to find the missing numbers.

1.

784	785	786	787	788	789	790
794	795	796	797	798	799	800
804	805	806	807	808	809	810

2.

412		414		416		418
422			425		427	
432	433		435	436	437	

© Pearson Education, Inc. 2

Name _____

Independent Practice

Use place-value patterns and mental math to find the missing numbers.

3.

884			887		889
	895			898	
904	905		907	908	

4.

	146	147			150
155				159	
	166	167		169	170

5. 456, 457, 458, _____, _____,

461, 462, _____, _____,

6. 620, 630, 640, _____, 660, _____,

680, 690, _____, 710,

7. 232, 242, _____, 262, _____,

_____, 292, 302, _____, _____

8. 175, 176, _____, _____, 179,

_____, 181, _____, 183, _____

Number Sense Describe each number pattern.

9. 130 ⟶ 230 ⟶ 330 ⟶ 430 ⟶ 530

_____

_____

10. 320 ⟶ 330 ⟶ 340 ⟶ 350 ⟶ 360

_____

_____

11. © **MP.7 Look for Patterns** Sally sees a pattern in these numbers. Describe the pattern.

> 500, 501, 502, 503, 504, 505

_____

_____

12. © **MP.7 Look for Patterns** Yoshi sees a pattern in these numbers. Describe the pattern.

> 341, 351, 361, 371, 381, 391

_____

_____

13. **Higher Order Thinking** Write your own three-digit numbers. Describe the number pattern for your numbers.

_____, _____, _____, _____, _____

_____

_____

14. © **Assessment** Use the numbers on the cards. Write the missing numbers in the number chart.

210	211	212	213		215
220	221		223		225
230		232	233	234	235

Help Tools Games

Another Look! The digits in numbers can help you find patterns.

975	976	977	978	979	980
985	986	987	988	989	990
995	996	997	998	999	1,000

1,000 comes after 999.

Pick a row in the chart. Read the numbers across the row.

The ones digits go up by _____.

Pick a column in the chart and read the numbers from top to bottom.

The tens digits go up by _____.

HOME ACTIVITY Write a three-digit number such as 120. Ask your child to write four more numbers after it, counting by 1s. Then ask your child to start at the number and write four more numbers below it, counting by 10s.

Use place-value patterns and mental math to find the missing numbers.

1.

633		635		637	
	644			647	648
653			656	657	

2.

	285	286			289
294	295		297		299
304			307		

3. © **MP.3 Explain** Manuel thinks the tens digit goes up by 1 in these numbers. Do you agree? Explain.

460, 470, 480, 490, 500, 510

_____

_____

_____

4. © **MP.3 Explain** Maribel thinks the tens digit goes up by 1 in these numbers. Do you agree? Explain.

864, 865, 866, 867, 868, 869

_____

_____

_____

5. **Higher Order Thinking** Write 5 three-digit numbers. From left to right, the ones digit in your numbers should go up by 1.

_____, _____, _____, _____, _____

Write 5 three-digit numbers. From left to right, the tens digit in your numbers should go up by 1.

_____, _____, _____, _____, _____

6. © **Assessment** Use the numbers on the cards. Write the missing numbers in the number chart.

557 539 545 547

535	536	537	538		540
555	546		548	549	550
555	556		558	559	560

Name _____

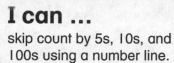
Solve

Solve & Share

Use the number line to skip count by 5s, starting at 0. Write the two missing numbers. Describe any patterns you see.

I can ...
skip count by 5s, 10s, and 100s using a number line.

© **Content Standard** 2.NBT.A.2
Mathematical Practices MP.2, MP.4, MP.7, MP.8

0   5   10   15   20   ☐   ☐

_____

_____

_____

This number line shows skip counting by 5s.

I see a pattern in the ones digits!

400 405 410 415 420 425 430

This number line shows skip counting by 100s.

I see a pattern in the hundreds digits!

400 500 600 700 800 900 1,000

Do You Understand?

Show Me! How could you use the number line in the first box above to skip count by 10s starting at 400?

☆ **Guided Practice** ☆ Skip count on the number line. Write the missing numbers.

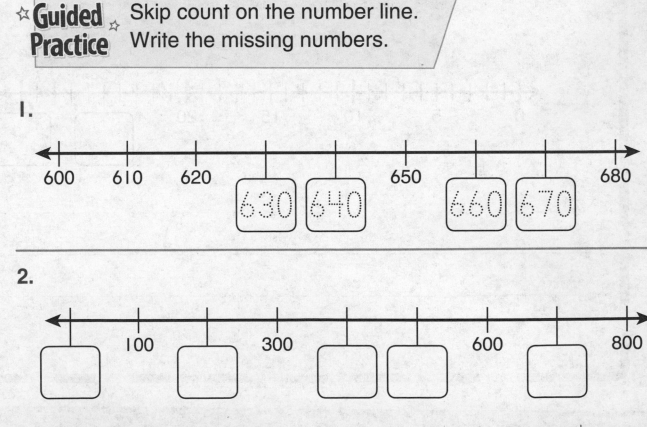

1.

600 610 620 [630] [640] 650 [660] [670] 680

2.

[   ] 100 [   ] 300 [   ] [   ] 600 [   ] 800

© Pearson Education, Inc. 2

Name _____

Independent Practice Skip count on the number line.
Write the missing numbers.

3.

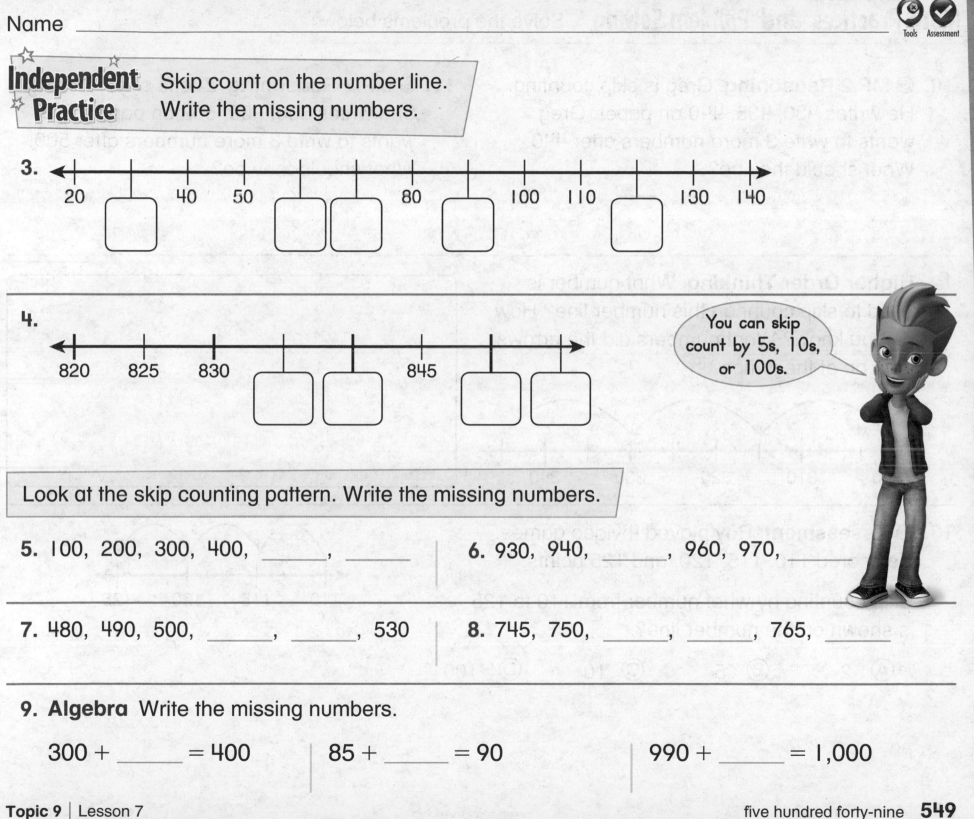

20   40 50   80   100 110   130 140

4.

820   825   830   845

You can skip count by 5s, 10s, or 100s.

Look at the skip counting pattern. Write the missing numbers.

5. 100, 200, 300, 400, _____, _____

6. 930, 940, _____, 960, 970, _____

7. 480, 490, 500, _____, _____, 530

8. 745, 750, _____, _____, 765, _____

9. Algebra Write the missing numbers.

300 + _____ = 400 | 85 + _____ = 90 | 990 + _____ = 1,000

10. © **MP.2 Reasoning** Greg is skip counting. He writes 430, 435, 440 on paper. Greg wants to write 3 more numbers after 440. What should they be?

_____, _____, _____

11. © **MP.2 Reasoning** Zoe is skip counting. She writes 300, 400, 500 on paper. Zoe wants to write 3 more numbers after 500. What should they be?

_____, _____, _____

12. Higher Order Thinking What number is used to skip count on this number line? How do you know? What numbers did the arrows land on at the jumps?

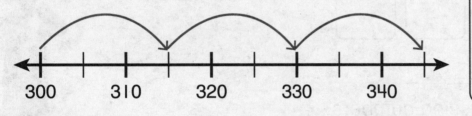

13. © **Assessment** Roy played 4 video games. He scored 110, 115, 120, and 125 points.

Skip counting by what number from 110 to 125 is shown on the number line?

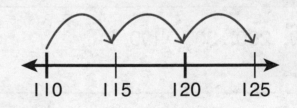

Ⓐ 2 Ⓑ 5 Ⓒ 10 Ⓓ 100

Name _____

Another Look! Skip count on the number line. Write the missing numbers.

We are skip counting by 10s!
160, 170, 180, 190...

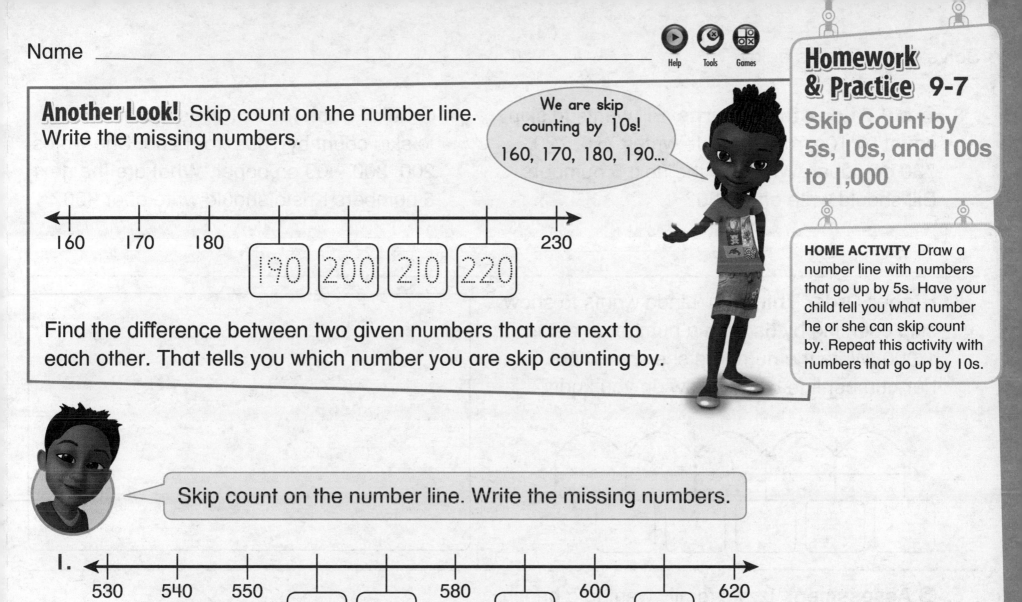

160   170   180   190 200 210 220   230

Find the difference between two given numbers that are next to each other. That tells you which number you are skip counting by.

HOME ACTIVITY Draw a number line with numbers that go up by 5s. Have your child tell you what number he or she can skip count by. Repeat this activity with numbers that go up by 10s.

Skip count on the number line. Write the missing numbers.

1.
530   540   550   ☐   ☐   580   ☐   600   ☐   620

2.
100   200   ☐   400   ☐   ☐   ☐   800   ☐   ☐

Solve the problems below.

3. © **MP.7 Look for Patterns** Bill wants to skip count by 10s from 710. He writes 710, 720, 730 on paper. What are the next 5 numbers Bill should write after 730?

_____, _____, _____, _____, _____

4. © **MP.7 Look for Patterns** Krista wants to skip count by 100s from 200. She writes 200, 300, 400 on paper. What are the next 5 numbers Krista should write after 400?

_____, _____, _____, _____, _____

5. **Higher Order Thinking** Linda wants to show skip counting by 5s from a number to get to 1,000. Write the numbers she should put on her number line below. How do you know?

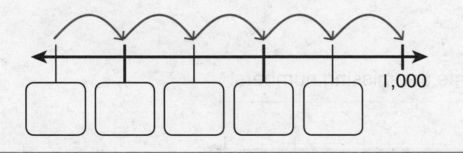

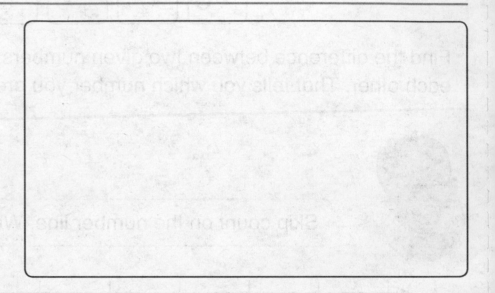

6. © **Assessment** Izzy's family went to a beach 4 times. On their trips, they collected 120, 130, 140, and 150 shells.

Skip counting by what number from 120 to 150 is shown on the number line?

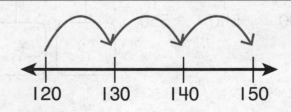

Ⓐ 2   Ⓑ 5   Ⓒ 10   Ⓓ 100

© Pearson Education, Inc. 2

Name _____

Solve & Share

Joy and Zach flipped three number cards. Then they each made a number. Joy made 501 and Zach made 510.

Who made the greater number? How do you know? Use place-value blocks to help you solve.

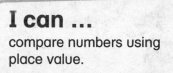

Hundreds	Tens	Ones

_____ is greater than _____.

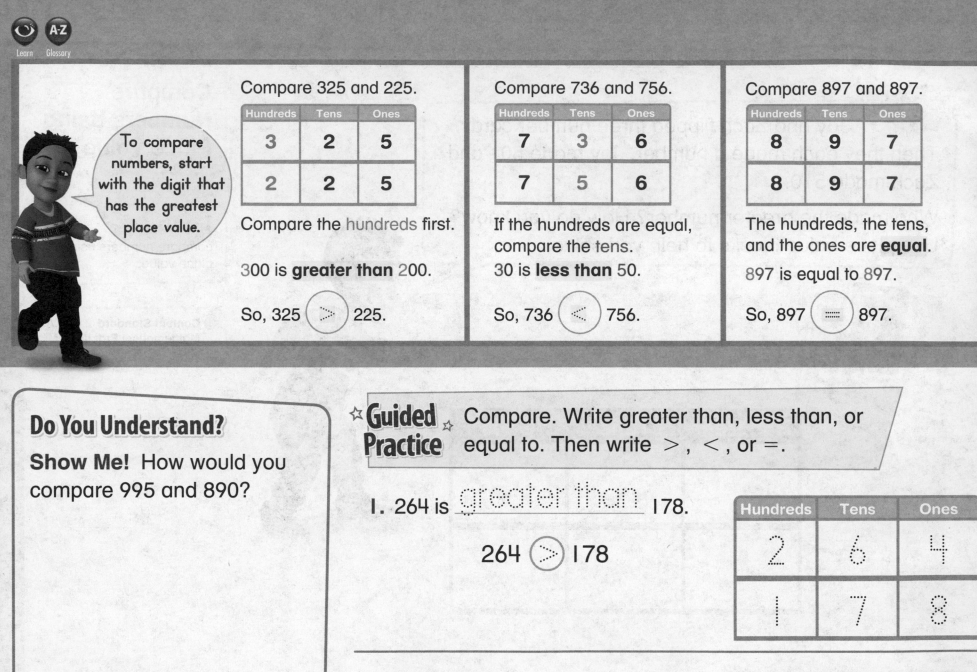

To compare numbers, start with the digit that has the greatest place value.

Compare 325 and 225.

Hundreds	Tens	Ones
3	2	5
2	2	5

Compare the hundreds first.

300 is **greater than** 200.

So, 325 ⊃ 225.

Compare 736 and 756.

Hundreds	Tens	Ones
7	3	6
7	5	6

If the hundreds are equal, compare the tens.

30 is **less than** 50.

So, 736 ⊂ 756.

Compare 897 and 897.

Hundreds	Tens	Ones
8	9	7
8	9	7

The hundreds, the tens, and the ones are **equal**.

897 is equal to 897.

So, 897 ═ 897.

Do You Understand?

Show Me! How would you compare 995 and 890?

☆Guided Practice☆

Compare. Write greater than, less than, or equal to. Then write $>$, $<$, or $=$.

1. 264 is ___greater than___ 178.

264 ⊃ 178

Hundreds	Tens	Ones
2	6	4
1	7	8

2. 816 is _____ 819.

816 ◯ 819

Hundreds	Tens	Ones

Name _____

Independent Practice

Compare. Write greater than, less than, or equal to.
Then write >, <, or =.

3.
572 is _____ 577.

572 ◯ 577

4.
256 is _____ 243.

256 ◯ 243

5.
837 is _____ 837.

837 ◯ 837

6.
486 is _____ 468.

486 ◯ 468

7.
208 is _____ 208.

208 ◯ 208

8.
936 is _____ 836.

936 ◯ 836

9.
821 is _____ 821.

821 ◯ 821

10.
347 is _____ 437.

347 ◯ 437

11.
286 is _____ 189.

286 ◯ 189

12. Higher Order Thinking Find one number that will make
all three comparisons true.

_____ < 111   _____ > 109   _____ = 110

13. © MP.2 Reasoning Ming sells 319 tickets.
Josie sells 315 tickets.
Who sells more tickets?

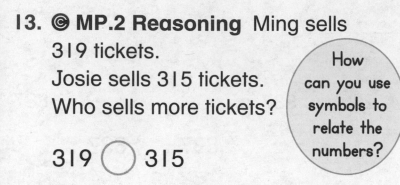

How can you use symbols to relate the numbers?

319 ◯ 315

_____ sells more tickets.

14. © MP.2 Reasoning Jared earned 189 pennies doing chores.
Tara earned 200 pennies doing chores.
Who earned more pennies?

189 ◯ 200

_____ earned more pennies.

15. **Higher Order Thinking** Compare the numbers 298 and 289. Write the comparison two ways. Then explain your thinking.

_____ ◯ _____

_____ ◯ _____

_____

_____

_____

_____

16. © **Assessment** Solve the riddle to find the number of coins in the second chest. Then compare the numbers.

The two numbers have the same digits.
The hundreds digits are the same.
The tens and ones digits are in different orders.

556 coins

? coins

Ⓐ 556 < 665

Ⓑ 556 > 565

Ⓒ 556 = 565

Ⓓ 556 < 565

Name _____

Another Look! To compare two numbers, first compare the digits with the greatest place value.

If the hundreds are equal, compare the tens.
If the tens are equal, compare the ones.

Use models to help!

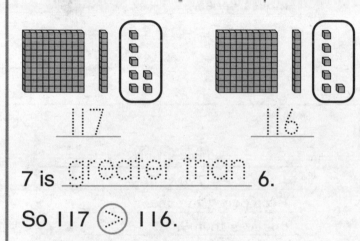

117   116

Hundreds	Tens	Ones
1	1	7
1	1	6

7 is _greater than_ 6.

So 117 ⟩ 116.

> means greater than.
< means less than.
= means equals.

HOME ACTIVITY Ask your child if 540 is greater than or less than 524. Then have your child explain his or her answer.

Compare. Write >, <, or =. Use place-value blocks to help if needed.

1. 341 ◯ 432

2. 990 ◯ 290

3. 621 ◯ 639

4. 890 ◯ 880

5. 546 ◯ 546

6. 999 ◯ 995

© MP.1 Make Sense Use the numbers in the triangles as digits. Write a number that will make each comparison true.

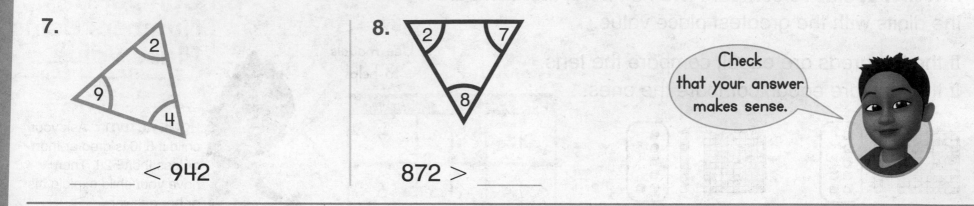

7.

2
9
4

_____ < 942

8.

2   7
8

872 > _____

Check that your answer makes sense.

---

9. Nyla compared 790 and 709. Her work is shown at the right.

Is Nyla's comparison correct? If not, correct her mistake.

_____

_____

_____

Nyla's work
790 < 709
I compared the ones.
0 is less than 9.
So, 790 < 709.

---

10. **Higher Order Thinking** A number is less than 200 and greater than 100. The ones digit is 5 less than 10. The tens digit is 2 more than the ones digit. What is the number?

_____

11. **© Assessment** This week, 161 fans watched a soccer game. Last week, 116 fans watched a soccer game. Which correctly compares the number of soccer fans in these two weeks?

Ⓐ 116 = 116   Ⓒ 116 > 161

Ⓑ 161 < 116   Ⓓ 116 < 161

© Pearson Education, Inc. 2

Name _____

Solve & Share

This number line shows only one number. Name a number that is greater than 256. Then, name a number that is less than 256. Show your numbers on the number line and explain why you are correct.

Lesson 9-9
Compare Numbers on the Number Line

I can ...
compare and write a three-digit number that is greater than or less than another three-digit number.

© **Content Standard** 2.NBT.A.4
Mathematical Practices MP.2, MP.3, MP.4, MP.7, MP.8

←————————————————|————————————————→
                              256

_____ is greater than 256.

_____ is less than 256.

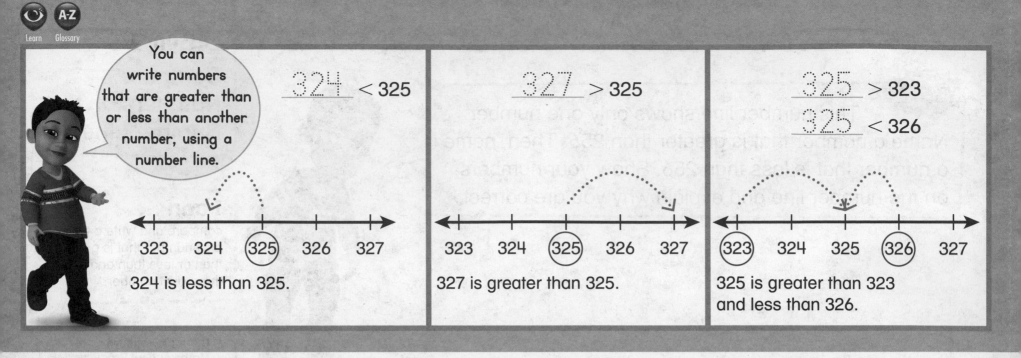

You can write numbers that are greater than or less than another number, using a number line.

324 < 325

323 324 **325** 326 327

324 is less than 325.

327 > 325

323 324 **325** 326 327

327 is greater than 325.

325 > 323
325 < 326

323 324 325 **326** 327

325 is greater than 323 and less than 326.

Do You Understand?

Show Me! Can you write a number that is less than 325, and that is not shown on the number line above? Explain.

☆ Guided ☆ Practice

Write a number to make each comparison correct. Draw a number line to help if needed.

1. __461__ < 467

2. _____ < 470

3. 132 < _____

4. 263 < _____

5. 675 > _____

6. 684 = _____

© Pearson Education, Inc. 2

Name _____

Independent Practice

Write a number to make each comparison correct. Draw a number line to help if needed.

7. 421 > _____

8. _____ < 884

9. 959 < _____

10. _____ < 619

11. 103 = _____

12. 566 > _____

13. 394 < _____

14. _____ < 417

15. _____ > 789

Write <, >, or = to make each comparison correct.

16. 107 ◯ 106

17. 630 ◯ 629

18. 832 ◯ 832

19. **Higher Order Thinking** Write a number to make each comparison correct. Place the numbers on the number lines.

_____ < 780 < _____

← ────────┼──────── →
               780

_____ > 457 > _____

← ────────┼──────── →
               457

20. **© MP.2 Reasoning** Kim is thinking of a number.
It is greater than 447.
It is less than 635.
What could the number be?

_____

21. **© MP.2 Reasoning** Don is thinking of a number.
It is less than 982.
It is greater than 950.
What could the number be?

Think about how the numbers relate.

_____

22. **Higher Order Thinking** Monty picked a number card. The number is greater than 282. It is less than 284. What is the number? _____

Explain how you know.

23. **© Assessment** What number is neither greater than nor less than the number shown? Explain how you know.

Name _____

Another Look! Think about the order of numbers.

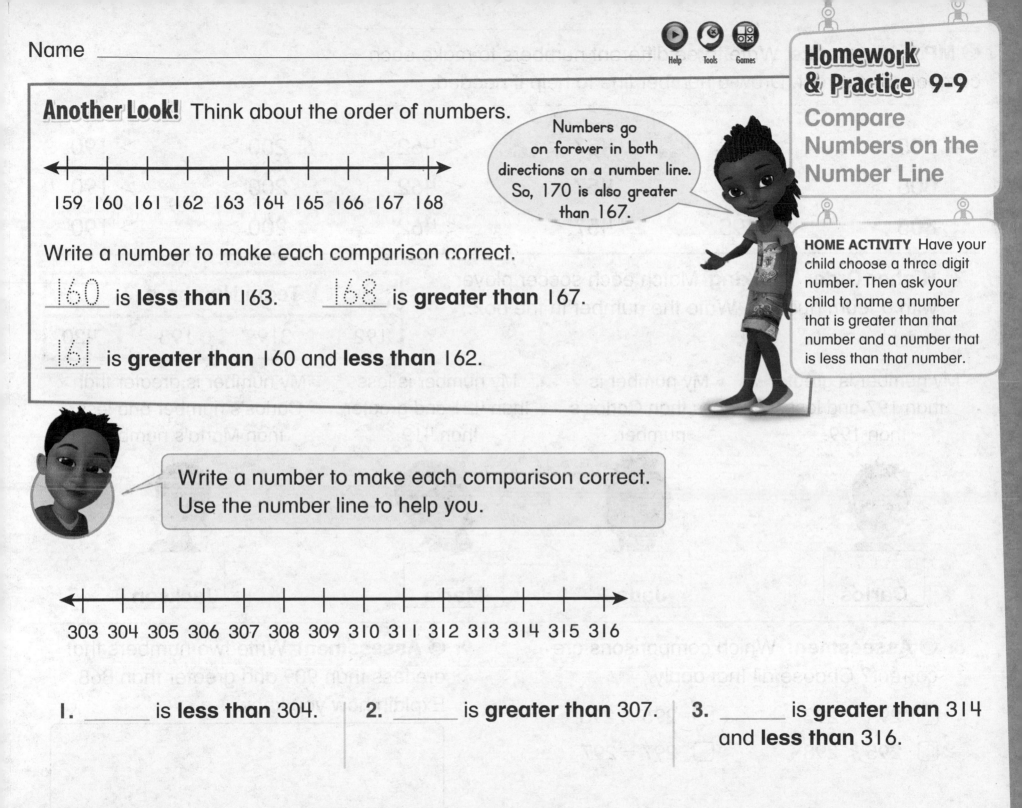

Numbers go on forever in both directions on a number line. So, 170 is also greater than 167.

159 160 161 162 163 164 165 166 167 168

HOME ACTIVITY Have your child choose a three digit number. Then ask your child to name a number that is greater than that number and a number that is less than that number.

Write a number to make each comparison correct.

160 is **less than** 163.   168 is **greater than** 167.

161 is **greater than** 160 and **less than** 162.

Write a number to make each comparison correct. Use the number line to help you.

303 304 305 306 307 308 309 310 311 312 313 314 315 316

1. _____ is **less than** 304.

2. _____ is **greater than** 307.

3. _____ is **greater than** 314 and **less than** 316.

© **MP.8 Generalize** Write three different numbers to make each comparison correct. Draw a number line to help if needed.

4. 805 > _____ > 795

   805 > _____ > 795

   805 > _____ > 795

5. 457 < _____ < 462

   457 < _____ < 462

   457 < _____ < 462

6. 200 > _____ > 190

   200 > _____ > 190

   200 > _____ > 190

7. **Higher Order Thinking** Match each soccer player with a team number. Write the number in the box.

Team Numbers			
192	319	198	420

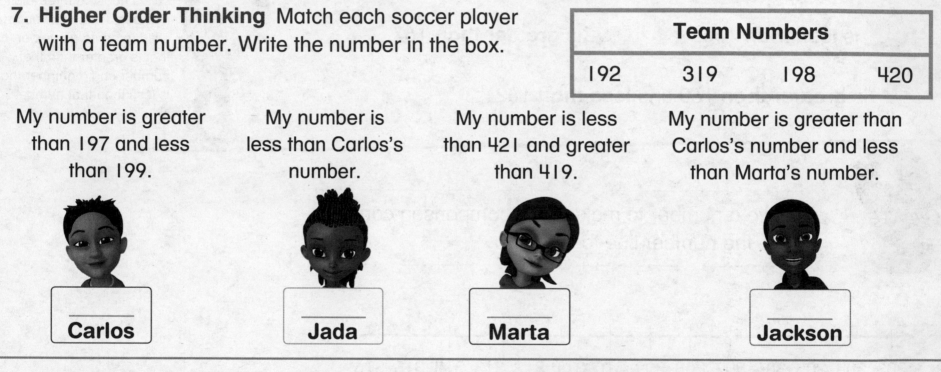

My number is greater than 197 and less than 199.

My number is less than Carlos's number.

My number is less than 421 and greater than 419.

My number is greater than Carlos's number and less than Marta's number.

Carlos

Jada

Marta

Jackson

8. © **Assessment** Which comparisons are correct? Choose all that apply.

   ☐ 294 < 293

   ☐ 295 < 298

   ☐ 296 > 295

   ☐ 297 = 297

9. © **Assessment** Write two numbers that are less than 909 and greater than 868. Explain how you know.

Name _____

Solve & Share

Sort the numbers 500, 800, 600, 400, and 700 from least to greatest.
Describe any number patterns that you see.
Are there any other numbers that fit the pattern?

I can ...
look for patterns to help me solve problems.

© **Mathematical Practices**
MP.7 Also MP.1, MP.2, MP.3
Content Standards 2.NBT.A.2, 2.NBT.B.8, 2.NBT.A.4

Number patterns

Thinking Habits

Are there things in common that help me?

Is there a pattern? How does it help?

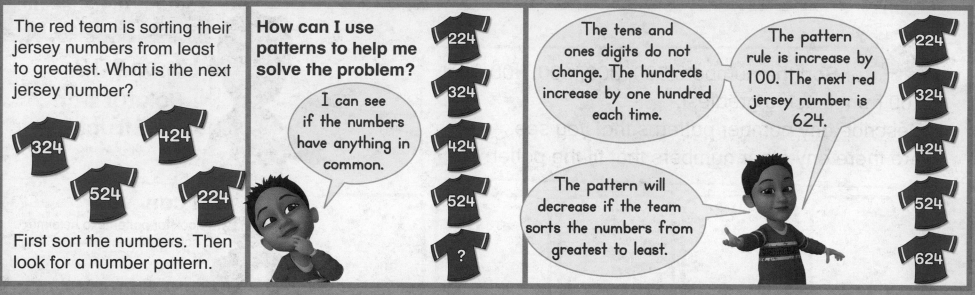

Do You Understand?

Show Me! How can you use the pattern to find the next three red jersey numbers?

⭐ **Guided Practice**   Look for a pattern to solve each problem.

1. The yellow team is sorting their uniforms.

420   440   410   430   ?

Sort the first four jersey numbers from least to greatest.

_____, _____, _____,

2. Look for a pattern in the sorted jersey numbers. What is the pattern rule?

_____

3. What is the next greatest yellow jersey number?

Name _____

Independent Practice   Break the problem into simpler parts to solve. Use a hundreds chart, a number line, or place value chart if you need to.

4. The blue team wants to sort their jersey numbers from greatest to least. After they sort the numbers, what number would come next?

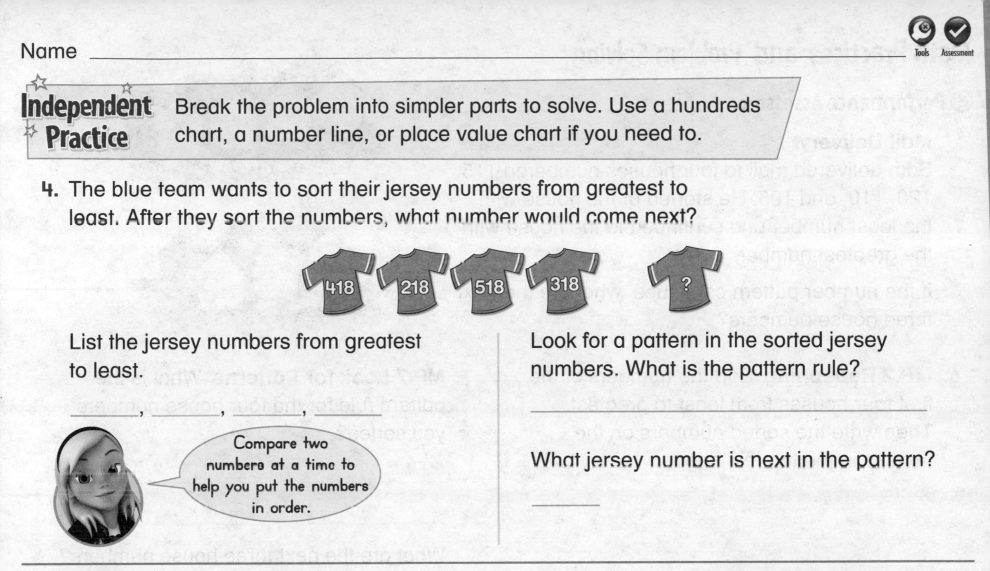

418   218   518   318   ?

List the jersey numbers from greatest to least.

_____, _____, _____, _____

Compare two numbers at a time to help you put the numbers in order.

Look for a pattern in the sorted jersey numbers. What is the pattern rule?

_____

What jersey number is next in the pattern?

_____

5. A librarian sorted these books. Find the missing book number. _____
Describe one pattern you notice.

_____

_____

860   850   ?   830   820

Math Practices and Problem Solving

© **Performance Assessment** _____

Mail Delivery

Sam delivered mail to four houses numbered 115, 120, 110, and 105. He started at the house with the least number and continued to the house with the greatest number.

If the number pattern continues, what are the next three house numbers?

6. **MP.2 Reasoning** Sort the numbers of the first four houses from least to greatest. Then write the sorted numbers on the houses in the top row above.

_____

7. **MP.7 Look for Patterns** What is the pattern rule for the four house numbers you sorted?

_____

_____

What are the next three house numbers?

_____

Write the numbers of the houses in the bottom row of houses above.

8. **MP.3 Explain** Why do you sort the numbers before looking for a pattern? Explain.

_____

_____

Name _____

Another Look! Sam needs to paint his taxi number on his taxi.
His number is the next greatest number in the pattern.
What is Sam's taxi number?

First sort the numbers from least to greatest.

400, 405, 410, 415

Then look for a pattern and name the pattern rule.

The hundreds digit stays the same. The numbers increase by 5 each time.

The pattern rule is increase by 5! Sam's taxi number is 420.

Look for a number pattern to solve.

1. James wants to sort the numbers on his teddy bears from greatest to least. After he sorts the numbers, what number would come next?

   First sort the numbers from greatest to least.

   _____, _____, _____, _____

   Then look for a pattern and name the pattern rule.

   _____

   What number is next in the pattern? _____

Bicycle Race

Jack and Sara join the purple team for the bike race. Their bike numbers will be the next two greater numbers in the pattern.

Help them find their bike numbers.

2. **MP.2 Reasoning** List the bike numbers from least to greatest.

_____, _____, _____, _____, _____

3. **MP. 7 Look for Patterns** Look for a pattern and name the pattern rule. What are Jack's and Sara's bike numbers?

_____

_____

_____

_____

4. **MP.7 Look for Patterns** Suppose new bike numbers are given in decreasing order. Then what numbers would Jack and Sara be given? Explain.

_____

_____

_____

Follow the Path

Color a path from **Start** to **Finish**. Follow the sums and differences that are even numbers. You can only move up, down, right, or left.

Start								
66 − 28	15 + 12	64 − 27	57 + 36	99 − 66	53 − 14	23 + 46	75 − 22	52 + 13
15 + 35	59 − 28	57 + 22	87 − 74	56 − 12	78 − 52	61 + 15	42 − 29	29 + 16
53 + 43	44 + 39	90 − 18	47 − 23	61 + 39	61 − 36	24 + 38	15 + 58	73 − 52
85 − 39	56 + 17	43 − 11	25 + 26	81 − 28	61 + 14	53 − 37	33 + 38	45 − 18
33 + 57	78 − 52	56 + 12	87 − 32	16 + 45	93 − 24	63 + 15	26 + 44	27 − 19
								Finish

A-Z Glossary

Word List
- compare
- decrease
- digits
- equals (=)
- expanded form
- greater than (>)
- hundred
- increase
- less than (<)
- ones
- place-value chart
- standard form
- tens
- thousand
- word form

Understand Vocabulary

Write *standard form*, *expanded form*, or *word form*.

1. $400 + 30 + 7$

_____

2. four hundred thirty-seven

_____

3. 437

_____

Label each picture. Use terms from the Word List.

4.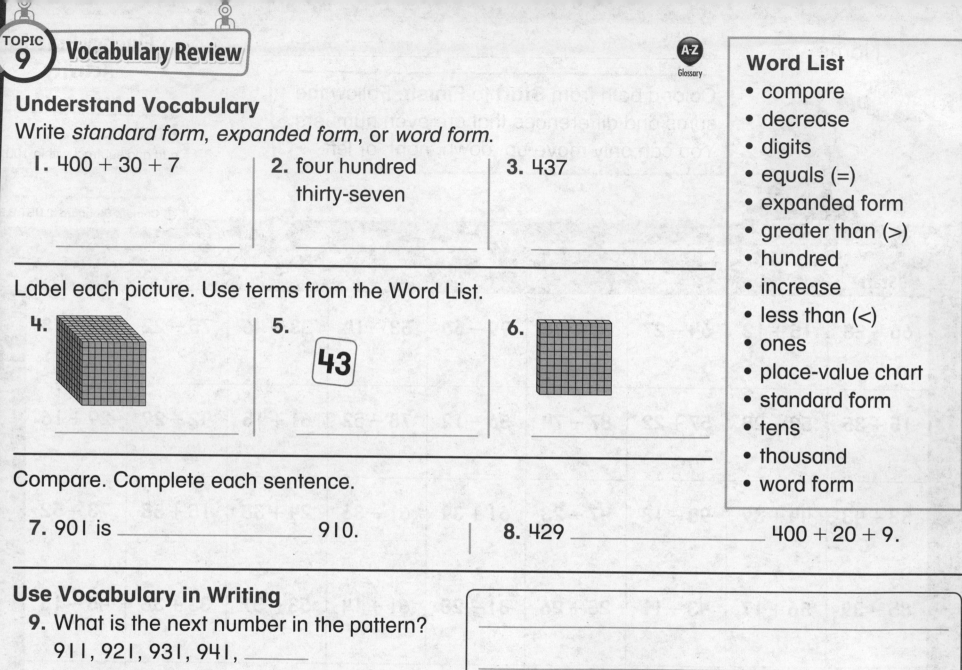

_____

5. 43

_____

6.

_____

Compare. Complete each sentence.

7. 901 is _____ 910.

8. 429 _____ $400 + 20 + 9$.

Use Vocabulary in Writing

9. What is the next number in the pattern?
911, 921, 931, 941, _____

Explain how you solved the problem.
Use terms from the Word List.

_____

_____

_____

_____

_____

Name _____

Set A

10 tens make 1 hundred.
You can count by hundreds.

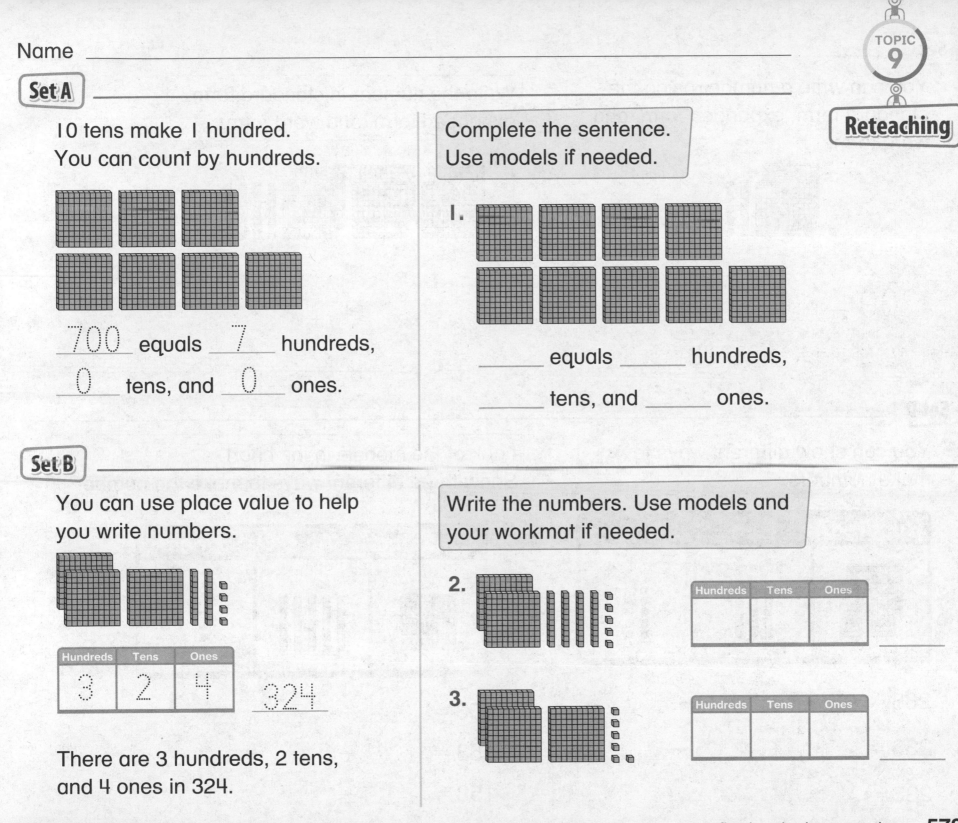

__700__ equals __7__ hundreds,

__0__ tens, and __0__ ones.

Complete the sentence.
Use models if needed.

1.

_____ equals _____ hundreds,

_____ tens, and _____ ones.

Set B

You can use place value to help
you write numbers.

Hundreds	Tens	Ones
3	2	4

324

There are 3 hundreds, 2 tens,
and 4 ones in 324.

Write the numbers. Use models and
your workmat if needed.

2.

Hundreds	Tens	Ones

_____

3.

Hundreds	Tens	Ones

_____

You can write a number using the standard form, expanded form, and word form.

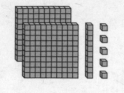

215

$\underline{200} + \underline{10} + \underline{5}$

two hundred fifteen

Write the number in standard form, expanded form, and word form.

4.

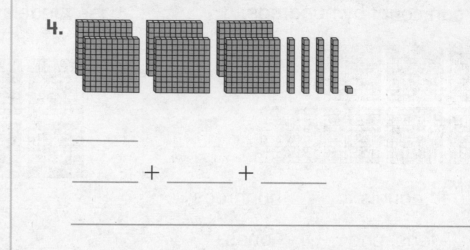

_____

_____ + _____ + _____

_____

You can show different ways to make numbers.

Hundreds	Tens	Ones
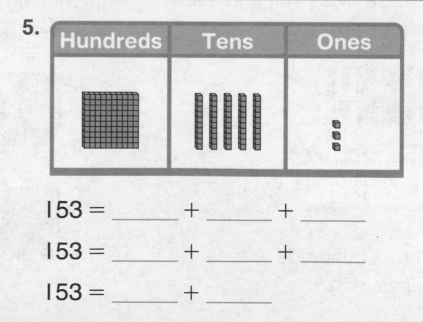		

$238 = \underline{200} + \underline{30} + \underline{8}$

$238 = \underline{200} + \underline{20} + \underline{18}$

$238 = \underline{230} + \underline{8}$

Look at the models in the chart.
Show three different ways to make the number.

5.

Hundreds	Tens	Ones

$153 = \underline{} + \underline{} + \underline{}$

$153 = \underline{} + \underline{} + \underline{}$

$153 = \underline{} + \underline{}$

Set E

You can look for patterns with numbers on a hundreds chart.

342	343	344	345	346	347
352	353	354	355	356	357
362	363	364	365	366	367

From left to right, the __ones__ digit goes up by 1.

From top to bottom, the __tens__ digit goes up by 1.

Reteaching
Continued

Use place-value patterns to find the missing numbers.

6.

574		576	577	578	
584		586		588	589
	595	596	597		

7.

	222		224	225	
	232		234	235	236
241	242			244		246

Set F

You can skip count by 5s, 10s, and 100s on a number line.

Skip count on the number line. Write the missing numbers.

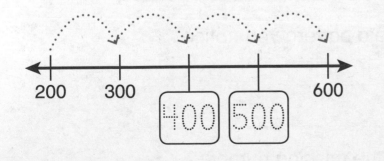

200   300   400   500   600

8.

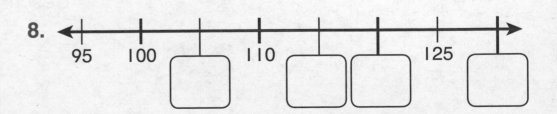

95   100   110   125

You can use place value to compare numbers.

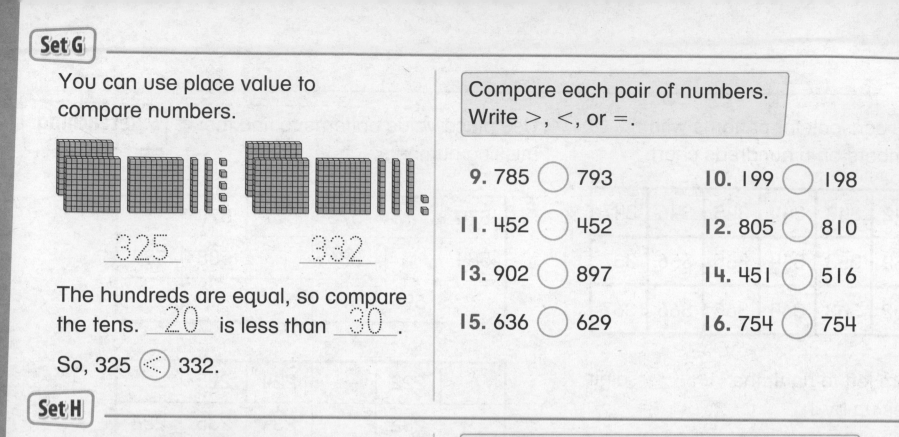

325   332

The hundreds are equal, so compare the tens. _20_ is less than _30_.

So, 325 $<$ 332.

Compare each pair of numbers. Write >, <, or =.

9. 785 ◯ 793   10. 199 ◯ 198

11. 452 ◯ 452   12. 805 ◯ 810

13. 902 ◯ 897   14. 451 ◯ 516

15. 636 ◯ 629   16. 754 ◯ 754

Set H

Thinking Habits

Look for and Use Structure

Are there things in common that help me?

Is there a pattern? How does it help?

Look for a pattern to solve the problem.

17. These tags are in a drawer.

175 275 375 ? 575

Describe a pattern you notice.

_____

_____

What is the missing number? _____

© Pearson Education, Inc. 2

Name _____

1. Each box has 100 crayons.
Count by hundreds to find the total.
Which number tells how many crayons
are in all of the boxes?

Ⓐ 600

Ⓑ 700

Ⓒ 800

Ⓓ 900

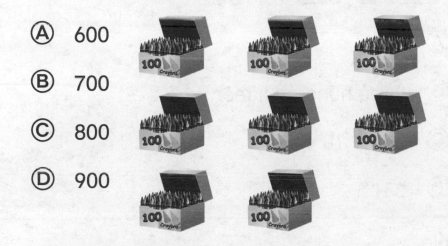

2. Danny made this model.
Write the number in three
different forms.

Ⓒ Assessment

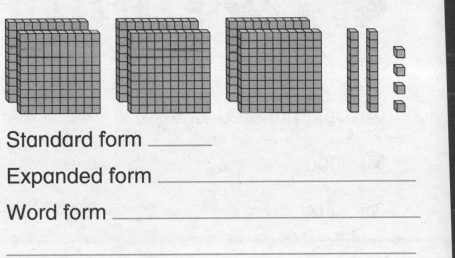

Standard form _____

Expanded form _____

Word form _____

_____

3. Write the number the model shows.
Use the chart.

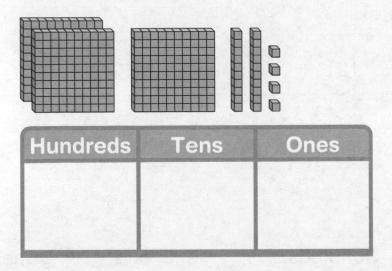

Hundreds	Tens	Ones

4. Which is the value of the 8 in the
number 789?

Ⓐ 8

Ⓑ 10

Ⓒ 80

Ⓓ 800

5. Which is the word form of the number shown by the blocks?

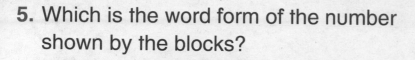

(A) four hundred fifty-six

(B) four hundred forty-six

(C) 400 + 40 + 6

(D) 446

6. Which is the standard form of the number shown by the blocks?

(A) 315

(B) three hundred fifteen

(C) 300 + 10 + 5

(D) 351

7. Draw a line from each number form to its example.

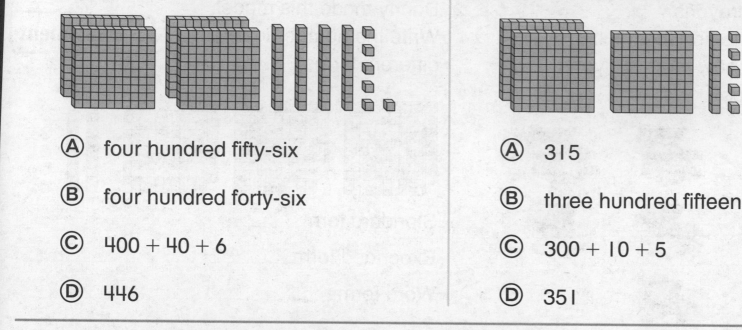

expanded form   standard form   word form

one hundred twenty-one   100 + 20 + 1   121

8. Kate made this model. What number does it show? Write the number and complete the sentence.

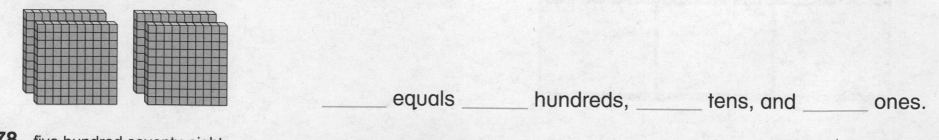

_____ equals _____ hundreds, _____ tens, and _____ ones.

Name _____

9. Lee and Maria collect pennies.
Lee has 248 pennies.
Maria has 253 pennies.
Who has more pennies?

_____

Write $>$, $<$, or $=$ to compare
the number of pennies.

248 ◯ 253

10. Jeff is thinking of a number.
The number has 2 hundreds.
It has more ones than tens.
It has 7 tens.

Which could be the number?
Choose all that apply.

☐ 276   ☐ 279

☐ 278   ☐ 289

11. Compare. Write $>$, $<$ or $=$.

429 ◯ 294   849 ◯ 984

12. Write a number that makes the
comparison correct.

327 $<$ _____   716 $>$ _____

13. There are 367 girls and 326 boys at a school. Which is
the expanded form for the number of boys?

Ⓐ $200 + 30 + 6$ Ⓑ $300 + 20 + 6$ Ⓒ $300 + 60 + 2$ Ⓓ $300 + 60 + 7$

14. Which is a way to show 576? Choose all that apply.

☐ $500 + 60 + 16$ ☐ $500 + 70 + 6$ ☐ $500 + 6$ ☐ $400 + 170 + 6$

15. Use the numbers on the cards. Write the missing numbers in the number chart.

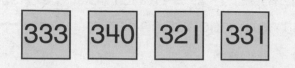

| 333 | 340 | 321 | 331 |

320		322	323	324
330		332		334
	341	342	343	344

16. Candy counts 405, 410, 415, 420, 425, 430. By what number does Candy skip count?

Ⓐ 2

Ⓑ 5

Ⓒ 10

Ⓓ 100

17. Skip count on the number line. Write the missing numbers.

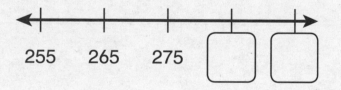

255   265   275

18. Is the statement true? Choose Yes or No.

576 < 675	◯ Yes	◯ No
435 > 354	◯ Yes	◯ No
698 < 896	◯ Yes	◯ No
899 < 799	◯ Yes	◯ No

Name _____

Reading Record

These students love to read!
These books show the number of pages
each student has read so far this year.

512 pages — Ken

493 pages — Luisa

427 pages — Ruth

378 pages — Tim

I. Write the number of pages Tim read
in expanded form.

_____ + _____ + _____

Write the number in word form.

_____

2. Complete the place-value chart
to show the number of pages
Ruth read.

Hundreds	Tens	Ones

Show two other ways to write the number.

_____ + _____ + _____

_____ + _____ + _____

3. Show two ways to compare the number of pages
that Luisa read with the number of pages that
Ruth read. Use > and <.

_____ ◯ _____

_____ ◯ _____

4. This number line shows the total number of minutes Diane read each week for 3 weeks.

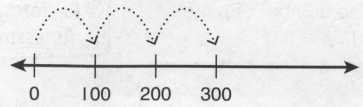

```
  0   100   200   300
```

How many minutes did she read after the first week? _____ minutes

After the second week? _____ minutes

After the third week? _____ minutes

How many minutes did she read each week? Explain how you know.

5. Diane reads the same number of minutes each week. How many minutes does she read after 4 weeks? After 5 weeks? Skip count on the number line above to find the answers.

After 4 weeks: _____ minutes

After 5 weeks: _____ minutes

6. The table shows how many pages Jim read in three different months. If he follows the pattern, how many pages will Jim read in April and May?

Number of Pages Read	
January	210
February	220
March	230
April	?
May	?

Part A

What pattern do you see in the table?

Part B

How many pages will Jim read in April and May?

Add Within 1,000 Using Models and Strategies

Essential Question: What are strategies for adding numbers to 1,000?

Look at all the tall buildings!

It takes a lot of planning to build a tall building. Would you like to try?

Wow! Let's do this project and learn more.

Math and Science Project: Building Up to 1,000

Find Out Use spaghetti sticks and mini marshmallows. The total for both cannot be more than 1,000. First, decide how many of each to use. Then share. Build the tallest buildings you can.

Journal: Make a Book Describe your building in a book. In your book, also:

- Tell how many spaghetti sticks and mini marshmallows you used.

- Tell how you would make a better building if you did it again.

Name _____

Review What You Know

A-Z Vocabulary

1. Circle all of the **hundreds digits** in the numbers below.

    5 0 2

    5 8

    1,0 0 0

2. Write the **expanded form** of the number.

    846

    _____

3. Write the **word form** of the number.

    265

    _____

    _____

Open Number Lines

4. Use the open number line to find the sum.

    <--------------------------->

    54 + 13 = _____

Mental Math

5. Use mental math to find each sum.

    40 + 37 = _____

    6 + 77 + 4 = _____

Partial Sums

6. Use partial sums to add.

$$\begin{array}{r} 46 \\ +53 \\ \hline \end{array} \qquad \begin{array}{r} 29 \\ +61 \\ \hline \end{array}$$

Name _____

Solve & Share

Forest Park has 565 trees.
Lake Park has 10 trees. Sunset Park has 100 trees.

How many trees do Forest Park and Lake Park have in all?

How many trees do Forest Park and Sunset Park have in all?

Use mental math. Be ready to explain how.

I can ...
add 10 or 100 mentally using what I know about place value.

© **Content Standards** 2.NBT.B.8, 2.NBT.B.9
Mathematical Practices MP.3, MP.4, MP.7, MP.8

$565 + 10 =$ _____

$565 + 100 =$ _____

Topic 10 | Lesson 1
Digital Resources at PearsonRealize.com
five hundred eighty-five **585**

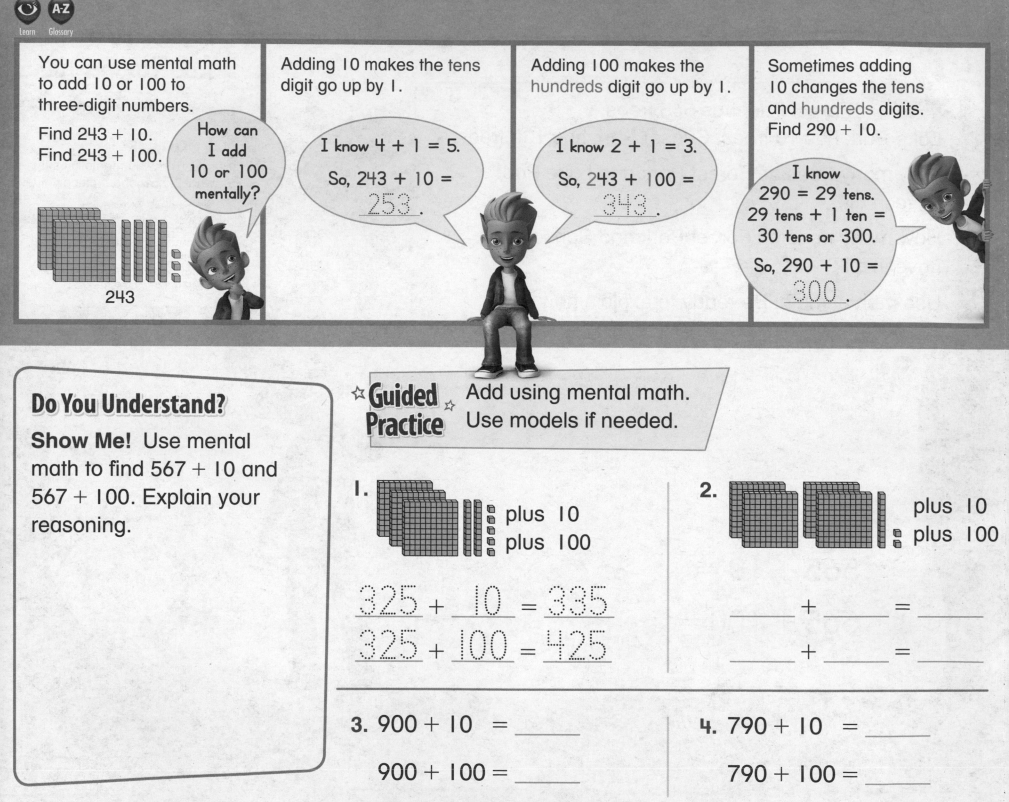

You can use mental math to add 10 or 100 to three-digit numbers.

Find 243 + 10.
Find 243 + 100.

How can I add 10 or 100 mentally?

243

Adding 10 makes the tens digit go up by 1.

I know 4 + 1 = 5.
So, 243 + 10 = 253 .

Adding 100 makes the hundreds digit go up by 1.

I know 2 + 1 = 3.
So, 243 + 100 = 343 .

Sometimes adding 10 changes the tens and hundreds digits. Find 290 + 10.

I know 290 = 29 tens.
29 tens + 1 ten = 30 tens or 300.
So, 290 + 10 = 300 .

Do You Understand?

Show Me! Use mental math to find 567 + 10 and 567 + 100. Explain your reasoning.

★ **Guided Practice** ★ Add using mental math. Use models if needed.

1. plus 10
   plus 100

   $325 + 10 = 335$
   $325 + 100 = 425$

2. plus 10
   plus 100

   ___ + ___ = ___
   ___ + ___ = ___

3. $900 + 10 =$ _____

   $900 + 100 =$ _____

4. $790 + 10 =$ _____

   $790 + 100 =$ _____

© Pearson Education, Inc. 2

Topic 10 | Lesson 1

Tools Assessment

Independent Practice ☆ Add using mental math. Use models if needed.

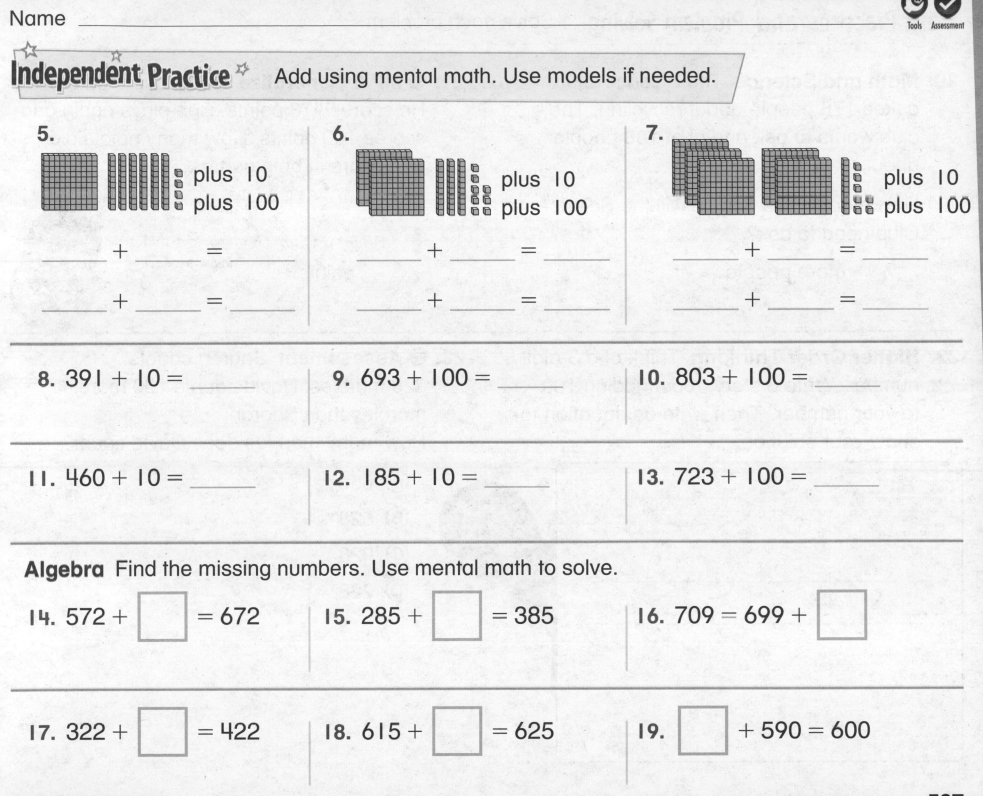

5.

plus 10
plus 100

_____ + _____ = _____

_____ + _____ = _____

6.

plus 10
plus 100

_____ + _____ = _____

_____ + _____ = _____

7.

plus 10
plus 100

_____ + _____ = _____

_____ + _____ = _____

8. 391 + 10 = _____

9. 693 + 100 = _____

10. 803 + 100 = _____

11. 460 + 10 = _____

12. 185 + 10 = _____

13. 723 + 100 = _____

Algebra Find the missing numbers. Use mental math to solve.

14. 572 + ⬜ = 672

15. 285 + ⬜ = 385

16. 709 = 699 + ⬜

17. 322 + ⬜ = 422

18. 615 + ⬜ = 625

19. ⬜ + 590 = 600

20. Math and Science The Science Club asked 178 people about recycling. The club wants to ask a total of 188 people about recycling.

How many more people will the Science Club need to ask?

_____ more people

21. © MP.8 Generalize Bob plays a game. He scores 473 points. Bob plays again and scores 100 points. How many points did Bob score in both games?

_____ points

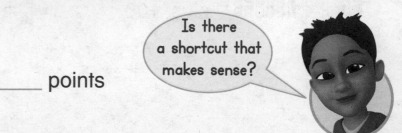

Is there a shortcut that makes sense?

22. Higher Order Thinking Think of a 3-digit number. Write a story about adding 100 to your number. Then write an equation to show your solution.

_____

_____

_____

_____

____ + ____ = ____

23. © Assessment Sharon counts 328 marbles. David counts 100 more marbles than Sharon.
How many marbles does David count?

Ⓐ 656

Ⓑ 528

Ⓒ 428

Ⓓ 228

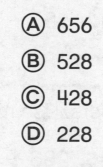

Name _____

Another Look! Use mental math to add 10 or 100 to three-digit numbers.
Find $315 + 10$ and $315 + 100$.

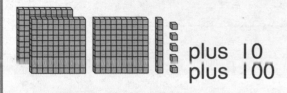 plus 10
plus 100

The tens digit goes up by 1 when you add 10.

$315 + 10 = 3\boxed{2}5$

The hundreds digit goes up by 1 when you add 100.

$315 + 100 = \boxed{4}15$

Place value can help you add 10 or 100 mentally.

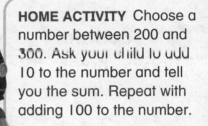

Add using mental math. Use models if needed.

1. 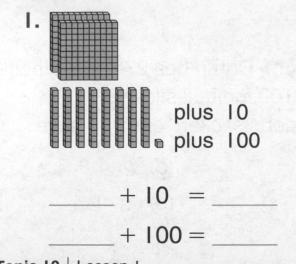 plus 10
plus 100

____ + 10 = ____

____ + 100 = ____

2. 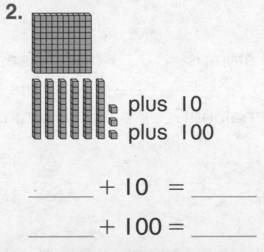 plus 10
plus 100

____ + 10 = ____

____ + 100 = ____

3. 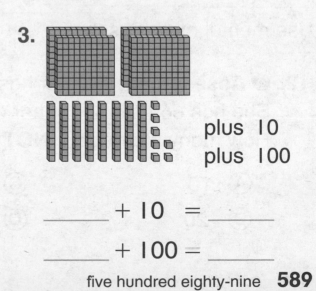 plus 10
plus 100

____ + 10 = ____

____ + 100 = ____

© **MP.7 Look for Patterns** Use mental math. Write the missing digit.

4. $100 + \boxed{}00 = 200$

5. $223 + \boxed{}00 = 323$

6. $10 + 351 = 3\boxed{}1$

A-Z Vocabulary Use mental math. Write the missing digit.
Then complete the sentence with **addend** or **sum**.

7. $6\boxed{}3 + 10 = 683$

683 is the _____.

8. $\boxed{}35 + 100 = 535$

The _____ is 535.

9. $802 + 10 = 81\boxed{}$

802 is an _____.

Higher Order Thinking Write the missing digits.

10. $22\boxed{} + 100 + 105 = 4\boxed{}8$

11. $\boxed{}12 + 205 + 10 = 32\boxed{}$

Use mental math to solve.

12. © **Assessment** Tanner has 679 stamps.
She has 669 stamps in her album.
How many stamps are **NOT** in her album?

Ⓐ 10   Ⓒ 100

Ⓑ 20   Ⓓ 689

13. © **Assessment** Darrin has 274 basketball
stickers and 100 football stickers.
How many sports stickers does he have?

Ⓐ 174   Ⓒ 284

Ⓑ 184   Ⓓ 374

© Pearson Education, Inc. 2

Name _____

Solve & Share

Use the open number line to find 598 + 123. Explain your work.

I can ...
use an open number line to add 3-digit numbers.

© **Content Standards** 2.NBT.B.7, 2.NBT.B.9
Mathematical Practices MP.2, MP.3, MP.4, MP.5

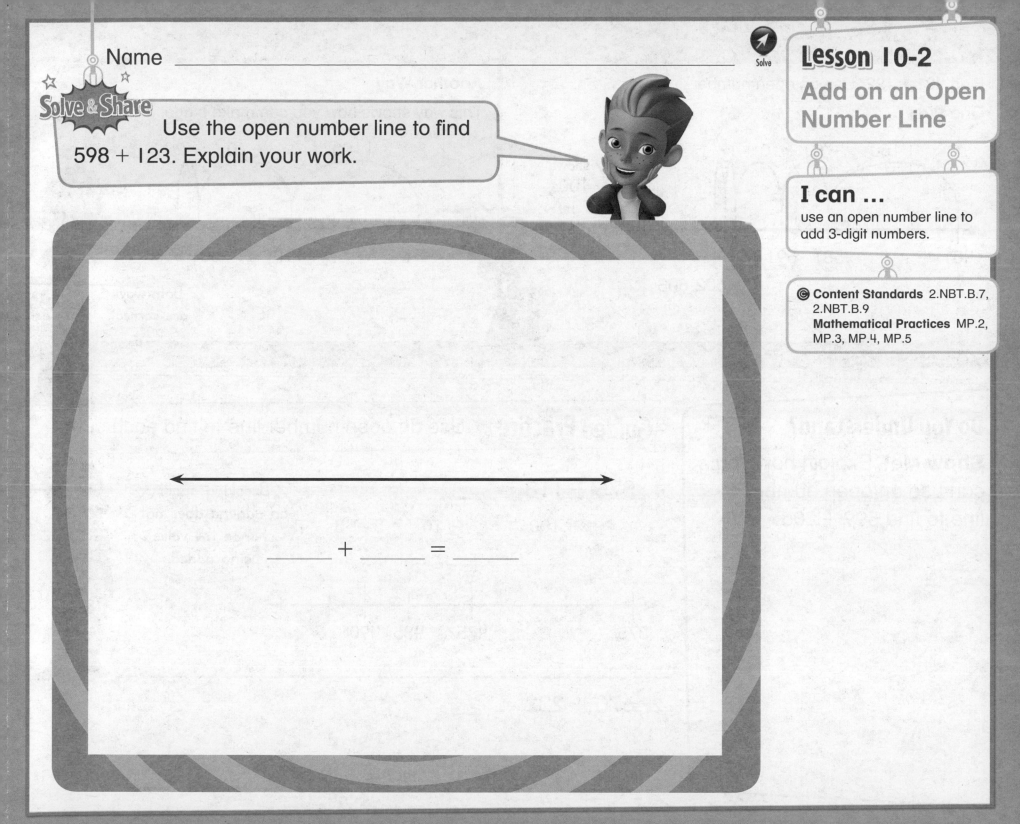

_____ + _____ = _____

Find 481 + 122. Use an open number line.
One Way

+100 +10 +10 +1 +1

481   581 591 601
                      602 603

This way shows jumps by 100s, 10s, and 1s.

481 + 122 = 603

Another Way
This way shows how you can make bigger jumps.

+100   +20 +2

481   581   601 603

Both ways are correct.

Do You Understand?

Show Me! Explain how you can use an open number line to find 599 + 205.

☆ **Guided Practice** Use an open number line to find each sum.

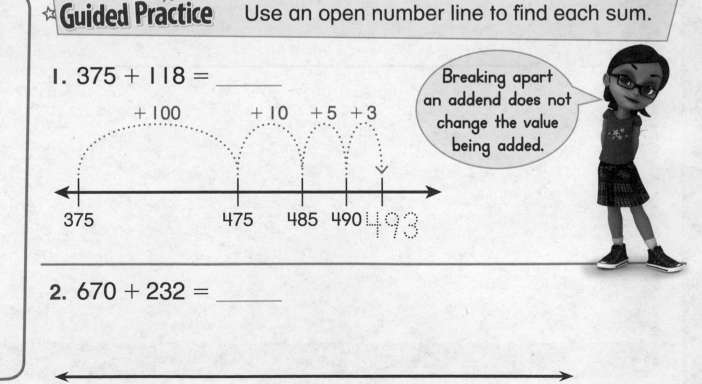

1. 375 + 118 = _____

+100   +10 +5 +3

375   475 485 490 493

Breaking apart an addend does not change the value being added.

2. 670 + 232 = _____

   Topic 10 | Lesson 2

Independent Practice ☆   Use an open number line to find each sum.

3. $278 + 152 =$ _____

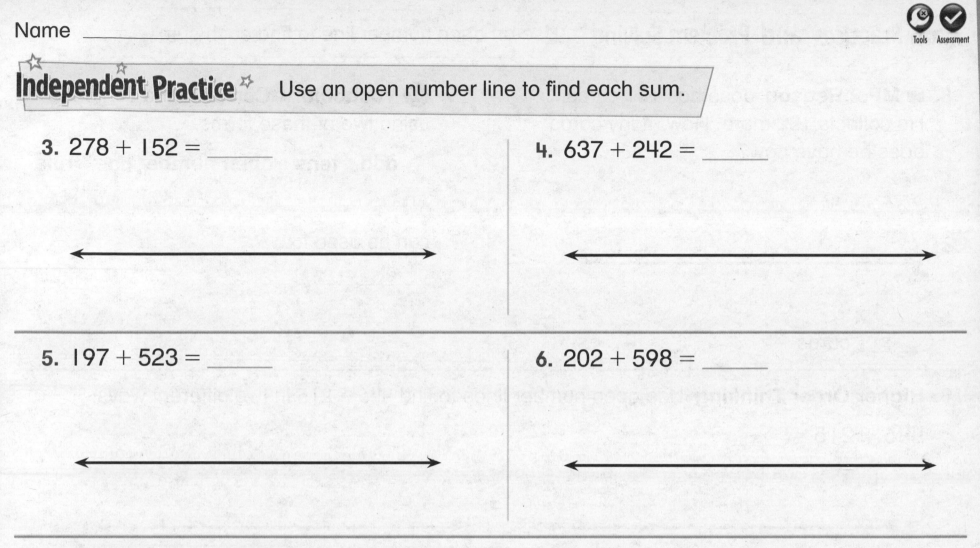

4. $637 + 242 =$ _____

5. $197 + 523 =$ _____

6. $202 + 598 =$ _____

7. Higher Order Thinking Lisa finds $550 + 298$
using the open number line below.
Is her work correct? Explain.

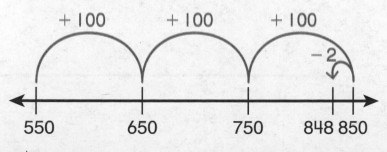

8. © **MP.2 Reason** Jose has 181 cards. He collects 132 more. How many cards does he have now?

⟵———————————————⟶

_____ cards

9. ⒜⒵ **Vocabulary** Complete the sentence using two of these terms.

add   tens   open number line   rule

An _____

can be used to

_____.

---

10. Higher Order Thinking Use open number lines to find $446 + 215$ in two different ways.

$446 + 215 =$ _____

⟵———————————————⟶   ⟵———————————————⟶

---

11. © **Assessment** Mary uses an open number line to find $286 + 137$. All of the jumps she draws are greater than 1. Draw what Mary could have done. Write the sum.

$286 + 137 =$ _____

                                 ⟵———————————————⟶

Name _____

Another Look! Find 284 + 231.

I can add by 100s, 10s, and 1s or make bigger jumps to find 284 + 231.

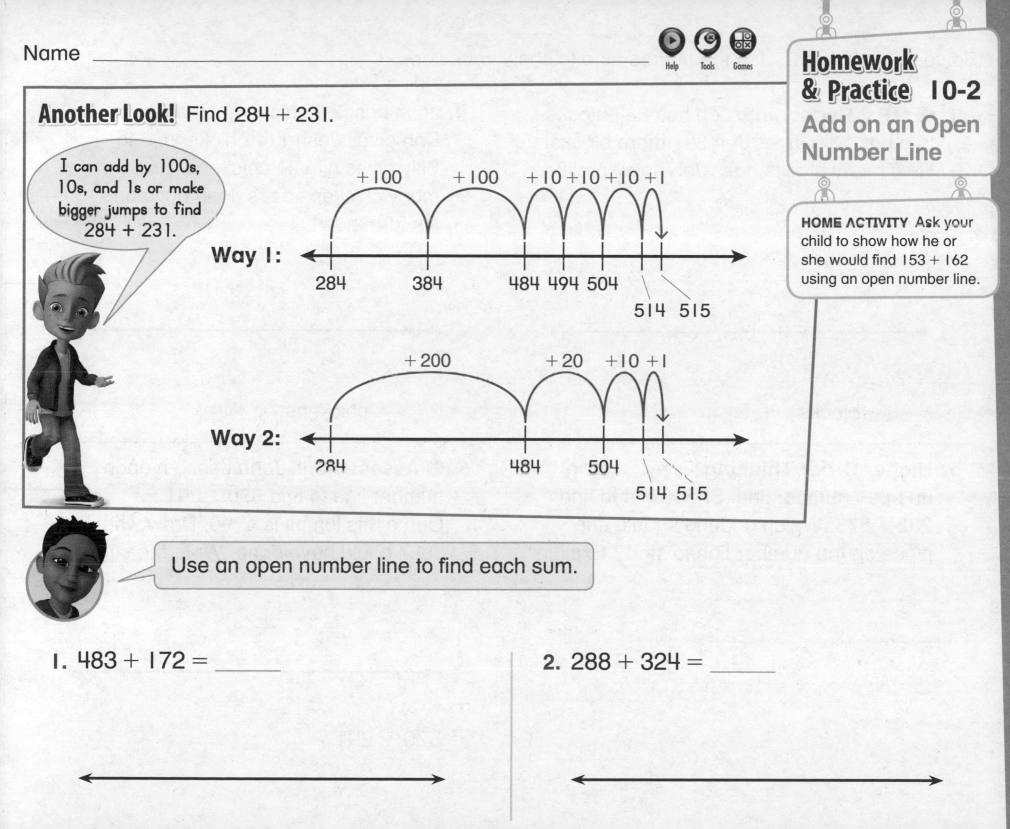

HOME ACTIVITY Ask your child to show how he or she would find 153 + 162 using an open number line.

+100   +100   +10 +10 +10 +1

Way 1: ←——————————————————→

284   384   484 494 504   514 515

+200   +20   +10 +1

Way 2: ←——————————————————→

284   484   504   514 515

Use an open number line to find each sum.

1. 483 + 172 = _____

2. 288 + 324 = _____

←——————————————————→   ←——————————————————→

Solve each problem. Use the number line to show your work.

3. © **MP.2 Reasoning** Jeb has 264 blocks in a box. Mia gives Jeb 341 more blocks. How many blocks does Jeb have in all?

_____ blocks

4. Josh has 509 chickens on his farm. Bob gives Josh 111 chickens, and Billy gives him 21 chickens. How many chickens does Josh have on his farm now?

_____ chickens

5. **Higher Order Thinking** Zoey is using an open number line. She wants to find $232 + 578$. Which addend should she place on the number line to start? Explain.

_____

_____

_____

6. © **Assessment** John uses an open number line to find $570 + 241$. One of his jumps is $+ 40$. Draw what John could have done. Write the sum.

$570 + 241 =$ _____

Solve & Share

On Monday, 248 people visit the museum.
On Tuesday, 325 people visit the museum.
How many people visit the museum on Monday and Tuesday?
Solve any way you choose. Be prepared to explain your thinking.

Solve

Lesson 10-3
Add Using Mental Math

I can ...
add 3-digit numbers using mental math strategies.

© **Content Standard** 2.NBT.B.7
Mathematical Practices MP.1,
MP.2, MP.6, MP.7

_____ people

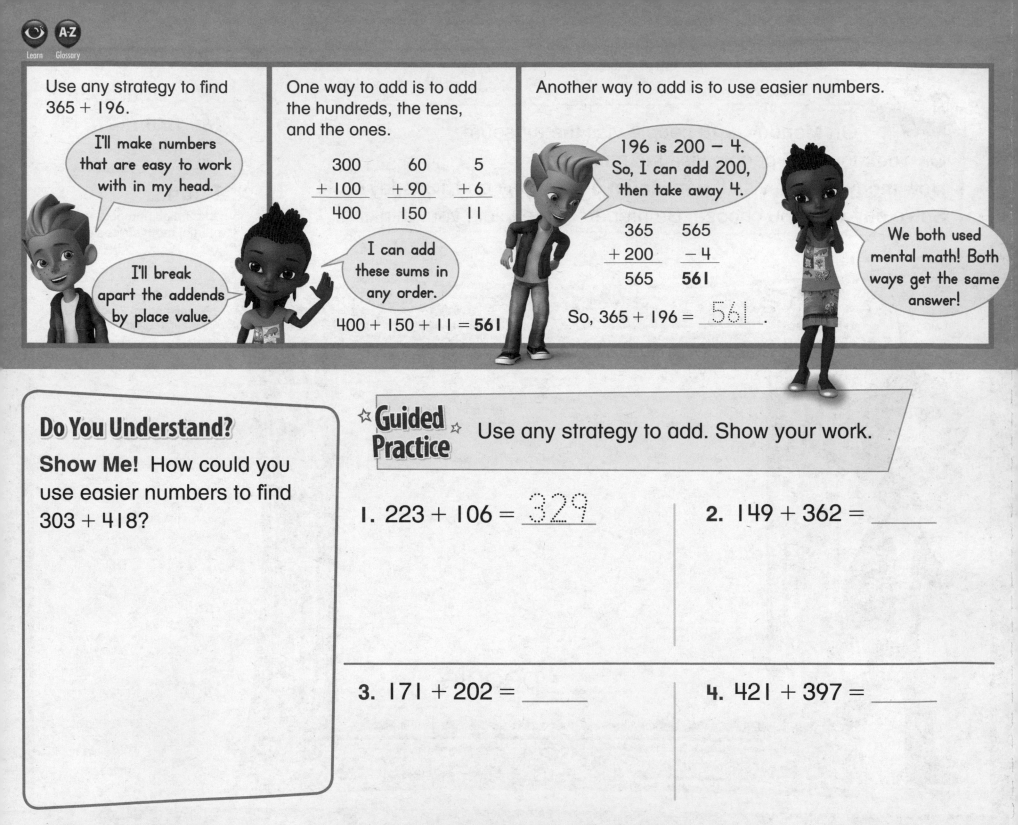

Use any strategy to find 365 + 196.

I'll make numbers that are easy to work with in my head.

I'll break apart the addends by place value.

One way to add is to add the hundreds, the tens, and the ones.

$$
\begin{array}{ccc}
300 & 60 & 5 \\
+100 & +90 & +6 \\
\hline
400 & 150 & 11
\end{array}
$$

I can add these sums in any order.

400 + 150 + 11 = **561**

Another way to add is to use easier numbers.

196 is 200 − 4. So, I can add 200, then take away 4.

$$
\begin{array}{cc}
365 & 565 \\
+200 & -4 \\
\hline
565 & \mathbf{561}
\end{array}
$$

So, 365 + 196 = __561__.

We both used mental math! Both ways get the same answer!

Do You Understand?

Show Me! How could you use easier numbers to find 303 + 418?

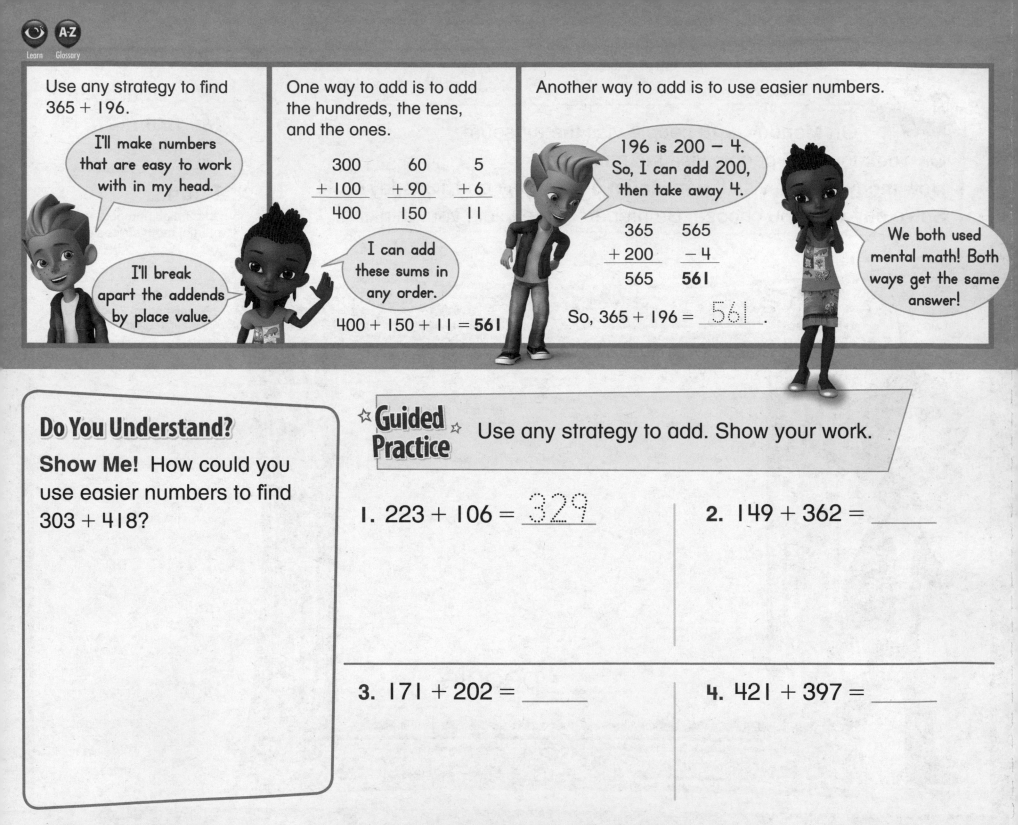
☆ **Guided Practice** ☆ Use any strategy to add. Show your work.

1. 223 + 106 = __329__

2. 149 + 362 = _____

3. 171 + 202 = _____

4. 421 + 397 = _____

Independent Practice ☆ Use any strategy to add. Show your work.

5. $151 + 324 =$ _____

6. $250 + 298 =$ _____

7. $258 + 109 =$ _____

8. $187 + 246 =$ _____

9. $236 + 318 =$ _____

10. $432 + 365 =$ _____

11. **Number Sense** Jamal says that the sum of $183 + 198$ is less than 300. Is Jamal's answer reasonable? Why or why not?

> Both addends are close to 200.

_____

_____

Math Practices and Problem Solving

Use any strategy to solve each problem. Show your work.

12. © **MP.2 Reasoning** 156 children in a school are girls. 148 children in that school are boys. How many children go to that school?

How do numbers in the problem relate to each other?

_____ children

13. **Higher Order Thinking** Write an addition problem about stickers. Use 3-digit numbers. Then solve the problem.

_____

_____

_____

14. © **Assessment** Maggie collects stickers. She gives 129 stickers to her friend. Now she has 268 stickers left.

How many stickers does Maggie have before she gives some away?

Ⓐ 292

Ⓑ 294

Ⓒ 389

Ⓓ 397

Remember! You can use a model to help.

© Pearson Education, Inc. 2

Topic 10 | Lesson 3

Name _____

Another Look! Use any strategy to find $358 + 213$.
One Way You can add the hundreds, the tens, and the ones.

Add hundreds.	Add tens.	Add ones.
300	50	8
$+ 200$	$+ 10$	$+ 3$
500	60	11

Add the partial sums.
$500 + 60 + 11 = 571$

So, $358 + 213 = \underline{571}$.

Or you can use easier numbers to find $358 + 213$.

Another Way

358 is $360 - 2$.

$360 + 213 = 573$

Take away 2.

$573 - 2 = 571$

HOME ACTIVITY Ask your child to show you how to add $305 + 497$. Have your child explain how he or she does the addition.

Use any strategy to solve each problem.
Show your work.

1. $248 + 455 =$ _____

2. $209 + 376 =$ _____

3. $597 + 122 =$ _____

Algebra Write each missing number.

4. 285 + 507 = _____

5. _____ = 378 + 142

6. 802 = _____ + 431

© **Be Precise** Find the total number of buttons for each.
Use the chart. Add any way you choose.

Are you using numbers and symbols correctly?

Button	Number
animal	378
sport	142
fruit	296
holiday	455

7. Mrs. Jones buys all of the animal and fruit buttons.

_____ + _____ = _____

_____ buttons

8. Mr. Frost buys all of the sport and holiday buttons.

_____ + _____ = _____

_____ buttons

---

9. Higher Order Thinking A theater wants to add 140 seats. Then the theater will have a total of 375 seats. How many seats does the theater have now?

_____ seats

10. © **Assessment** Rob has 225 marbles. Jake has 69 more marbles than Rob. How many marbles do they have in all?

294   509   519   529

Ⓐ   Ⓑ   Ⓒ   Ⓓ

© Pearson Education, Inc. 2

Solve & Share

Use place-value blocks to find 243 + 354. Tell which place value you added first and why. Then draw a picture to show your work.

Hundreds	Tens	Ones

$$243 + 354 = \underline{\hspace{1.5cm}}$$

Find 518 + 327.

Use place value. First, add the hundreds.

Then add the tens. Then add the ones.

	Hundreds	Tens	Ones
	5	1	8
+	3	2	7
Hundreds:	8	0	0
Tens:		3	0
Ones:		1	5
Sum =	8	4	5

Add the partial sums to find the sum.

Here is how you can write out the addition.

```
  5 1 8
+ 3 2 7
  8 0 0
    3 0
    1 5
  8 4 5
```

So, 518 + 327 = 845.

Do You Understand?

Show Me! Explain why you can use partial sums to find 281 + 276. Find the sum.

★ **Guided Practice** ★ Add. Use partial sums. Show your work. Use place-value blocks if needed.

1. 425 + 148 = 573

	Hundreds	Tens	Ones
	4	2	5
+	1	4	8
Hundreds:	5	0	0
Tens:		6	0
Ones:		1	3
Sum =	5	7	3

2. 394 + 276 = _____

```
  3 9 4
+ 2 7 6
```

Keep place values in line when you write each partial sum.

© Pearson Education, Inc. 2

Independent Practice ☆ Add. Use partial sums. Show your work.

3.   347
     |2|2

4.   193
     +243

5.   281
     +406

6.   367
     +423

7.   508
     +347

8. **Higher Order Thinking** Mark found the sum of 127 and 345. Explain his mistake. What is the correct sum?

_____

_____

_____

Mark's Work

$$\begin{array}{r} 127 \\ +\ 345 \\ \hline \end{array}$$

Hundreds: 400

Tens: 6

Ones: + 12

418

9. **Number Sense** Find the sum of 137 + 324. Then write the sum two different ways.

Way 1 _____

Way 2 _____

You can write numbers in different forms.

10. © **MP.7 Look for Patterns** 349 people are on a boat. 255 people are on another boat. How many people are on both boats?

You can use place value and partial sums to add.

_____ people

11. 163 students are in first grade. 217 students are in second grade. How many students are in both grades?

_____ students

12. **Higher Order Thinking** Choose a number between 100 and 400. Add 384 to your number. What is the sum? Show your work.

Explain the steps you took to find the sum.

_____

_____

_____

13. © **Assessment** Which is the same amount as 238 + 164? Choose all that apply.

☐ 200 + 190 + 12   ☐ 300 + 90 + 12   ☐ 402   ☐ 400 + 10 + 2

Name _____

Another Look! You can use place value to add 2 three-digit numbers.

$164 + 253 = \underline{\ ?\ }$

Hundreds	Tens	Ones
[blocks]	[blocks]	[blocks]
[blocks]	[blocks]	[blocks]

Find the partial sums. Then add the partial sums to find the sum.

1. Add the hundreds.
2. Add the tens.
3. Add the ones.
4. Add the partial sums.

Hundreds	Tens	Ones
1	6	4
+ 2	5	3
3	0	0
1	1	0
		7
4	1	7

So, $164 + 253 = \underline{417}$.

Add. Use partial sums. Show your work. Use place-value blocks if needed.

1. $218 + 136$

Hundreds	Tens	Ones
2	1	8
+ 1	3	6
Hundreds: 3	0	0
Tens:	4	0
Ones:	1	4
Sum =		

2. $365 + 248$

Hundreds	Tens	Ones
3	6	5
+ 2	4	8
Hundreds:		
Tens:		
Ones:		
Sum =		

3. 714
   +135

4. 168
   +423

5. 266
   +592

6. 474
   +238

7. 567
   +137

8. **Higher Order Thinking** Fill in the missing numbers to make the addition problem true.

	Hundreds	Tens	Ones
	2	☐	8
+	☐	7	☐
Hundreds:	☐	0	0
Tens:		☐	0
Ones:		☐	☐
Sum =	8	9	0

9. © **Assessment** Which is the same amount as 462 + 253? Choose Yes or No.

600 + 11 + 5   ○ Yes ○ No

600 + 110 + 5   ○ Yes ○ No

600 + 100 + 15   ○ Yes ○ No

715   ○ Yes ○ No

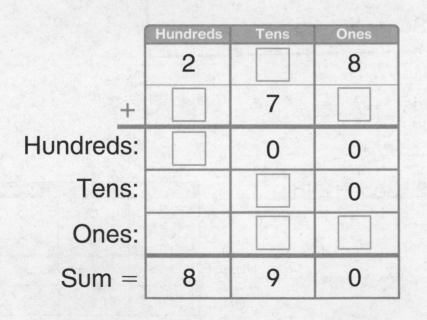

There is more than one way to write a sum.

© Pearson Education, Inc. 2

Solve & Share

Oak School has 256 students. Pine School has 371 students. How many students do the schools have in all?
Use place-value blocks to help. Draw your blocks below and solve.

I can ...
use models to add 3-digit numbers.

© **Content Standards** 2.NBT.B.7, 2.NBT.B.9
Mathematical Practices MP.3, MP.4, MP.5, MP.7

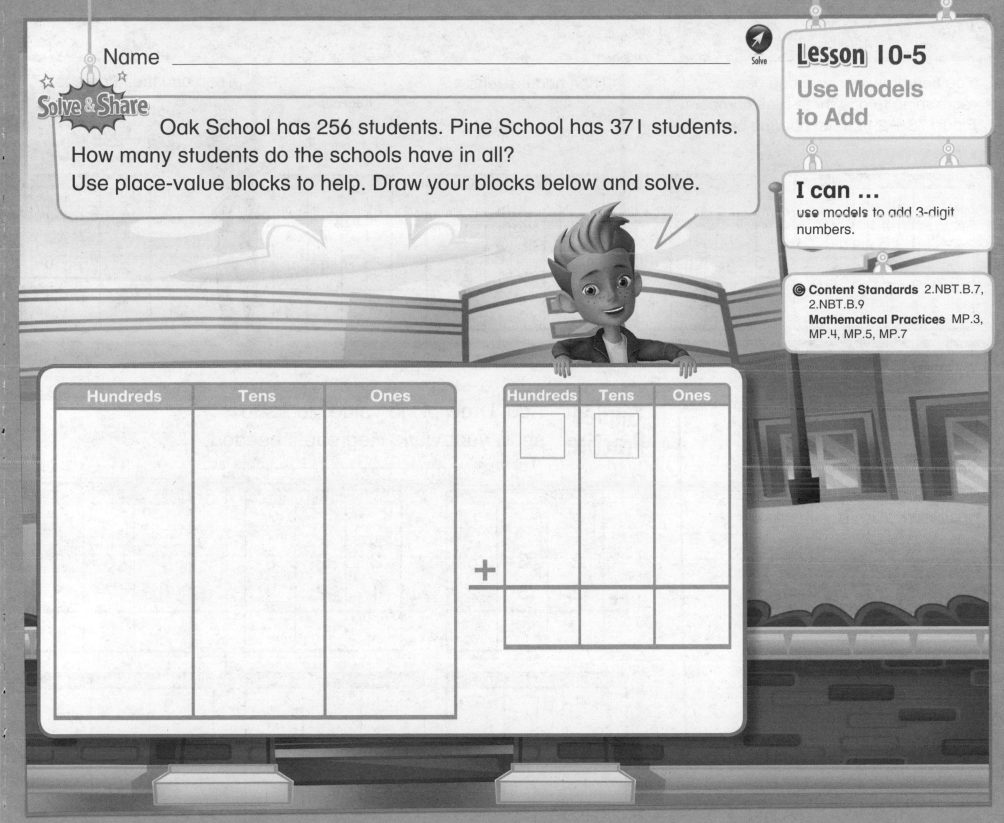

Hundreds	Tens	Ones

Hundreds	Tens	Ones

+

You can draw a model and use regrouping to add three-digit numbers. Find 173 + 244. First add the ones.

Then add the tens.

Regroup 10 tens to make 1 hundred!

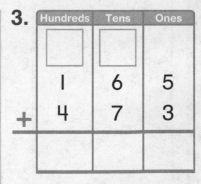

Then add the hundreds.

So, 173 + 244 = 417.

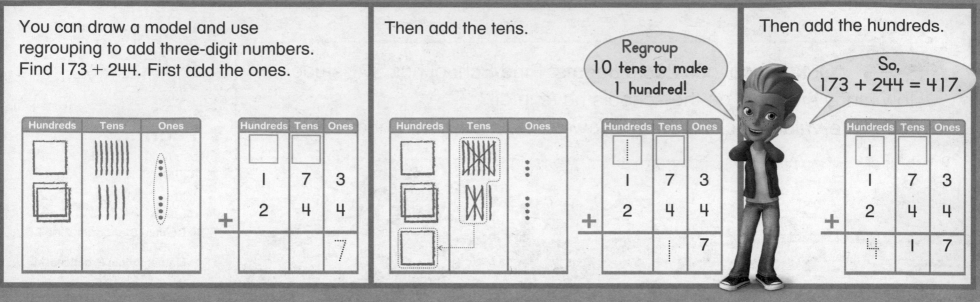

Hundreds	Tens	Ones
1	7	3
+ 2	4	4
		7

Hundreds	Tens	Ones
1		
1	7	3
+ 2	4	4
	1	7

Hundreds	Tens	Ones
1		
1	7	3
+ 2	4	4
4	1	7

Do You Understand?

Show Me! Explain why regrouping works in the problem above.

☆ Guided Practice ☆

Add. Draw place-value blocks to show your work. Regroup if needed.

1.
Hundreds	Tens	Ones
2	3	6
+ 2	5	2
4	8	8

2.
Hundreds	Tens	Ones
3	2	8
+ 1	2	4

Hundreds	Tens	Ones

3.
Hundreds	Tens	Ones
1	6	5
+ 4	7	3

Hundreds	Tens	Ones

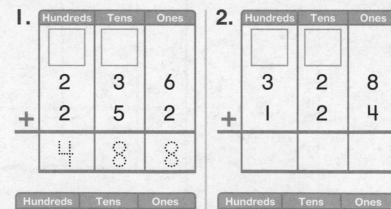

© Pearson Education, Inc. 2

Name _____

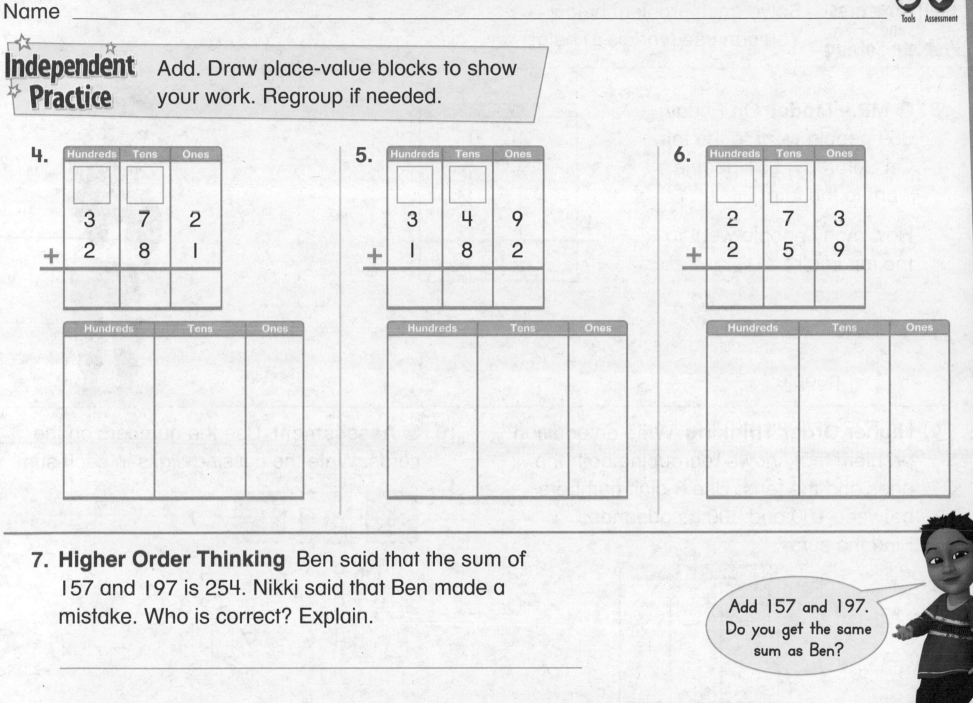

Independent Practice — Add. Draw place-value blocks to show your work. Regroup if needed.

4.

Hundreds	Tens	Ones
3	7	2
+ 2	8	1

Hundreds	Tens	Ones

5.

Hundreds	Tens	Ones
3	4	9
+ 1	8	2

Hundreds	Tens	Ones

6.

Hundreds	Tens	Ones
2	7	3
+ 2	5	9

Hundreds	Tens	Ones

7. **Higher Order Thinking** Ben said that the sum of 157 and 197 is 254. Nikki said that Ben made a mistake. Who is correct? Explain.

_____

_____

Add 157 and 197. Do you get the same sum as Ben?

Solve each problem below.
You can use models to help.

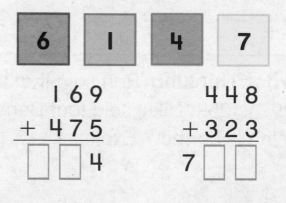

You can use or draw place-value blocks to model the problem.

8. © **MP.4 Model** On Friday, 354 people went to the fair. On Saturday, 551 people went to the fair.

How many people went to the fair in all?

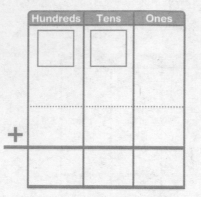

Hundreds	Tens	Ones
☐	☐	
+		

_____ people

9. **Higher Order Thinking** Write an addition problem that shows regrouping both the ones and the tens. Use 3-digit numbers between 100 and 400 as addends. Find the sum.

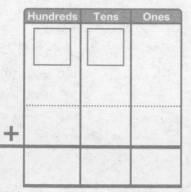

Hundreds	Tens	Ones
☐	☐	
+		

10. © **Assessment** Use the numbers on the cards. Write the missing digits in each sum.

6	1	4	7

```
  169          448
+ 475        + 323
 ☐ ☐ 4        7 ☐ ☐
```

Name _____

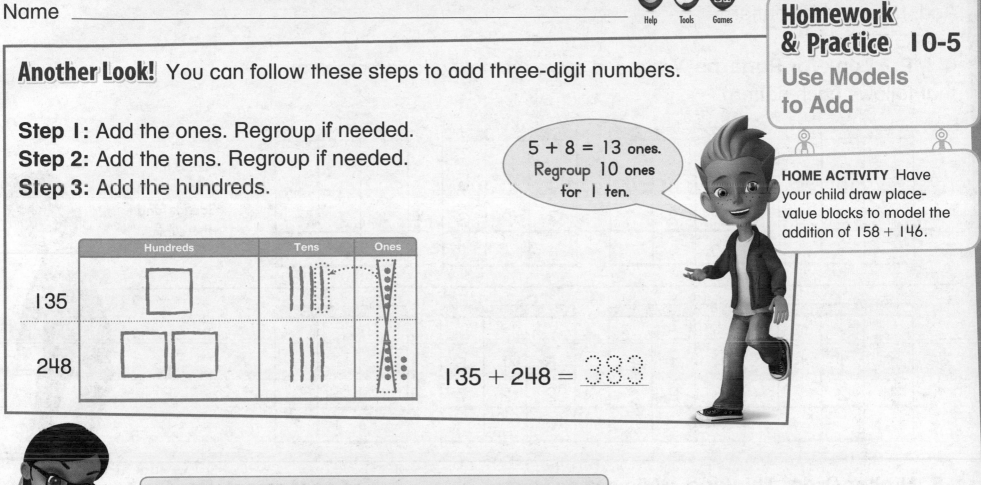

Another Look! You can follow these steps to add three-digit numbers.

Step 1: Add the ones. Regroup if needed.
Step 2: Add the tens. Regroup if needed.
Step 3: Add the hundreds.

5 + 8 = 13 ones. Regroup 10 ones for 1 ten.

HOME ACTIVITY Have your child draw place-value blocks to model the addition of 158 + 146.

Hundreds	Tens	Ones
135		
248		

$135 + 248 = \underline{383}$

Add. Regroup if needed. Draw models to help.

1. $341 + 127 = \underline{\hspace{1cm}}$

Hundreds	Tens	Ones

2. $524 + 249 = \underline{\hspace{1cm}}$

Hundreds	Tens	Ones

Add. Look for the pattern.

© **MP.7 Look for Patterns** Write and solve the next addition problem that follows each pattern.

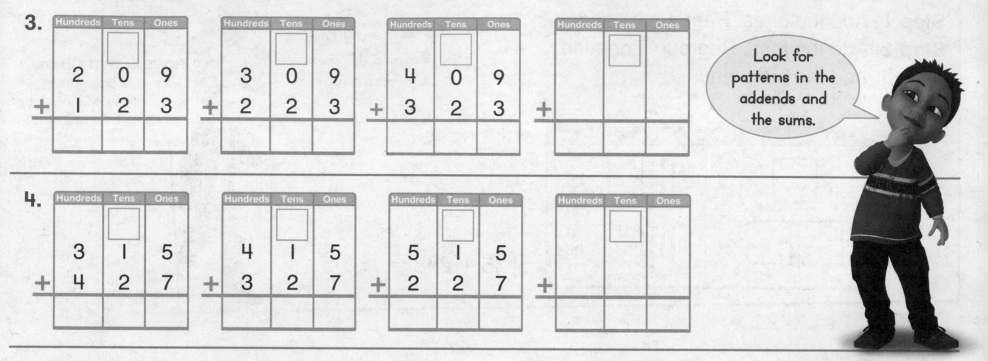

3.
Hundreds	Tens	Ones
2	0	9
+ 1	2	3

Hundreds	Tens	Ones
3	0	9
+ 2	2	3

Hundreds	Tens	Ones
4	0	9
+ 3	2	3

Hundreds	Tens	Ones
+		

Look for patterns in the addends and the sums.

4.
Hundreds	Tens	Ones
3	1	5
+ 4	2	7

Hundreds	Tens	Ones
4	1	5
+ 3	2	7

Hundreds	Tens	Ones
5	1	5
+ 2	2	7

Hundreds	Tens	Ones
+		

5. **Higher Order Thinking** Write and solve an addition story for 482 + 336.

_____

_____

_____

6. © **Assessment** Use the numbers on the cards. Write the missing digits in each sum.

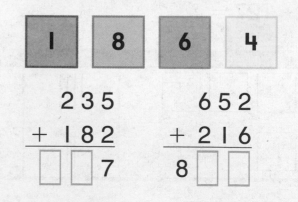

1	8	6	4

```
  2 3 5
+ 1 8 2
⬚ ⬚ 7
```

```
  6 5 2
+ 2 1 6
8 ⬚ ⬚
```

© Pearson Education, Inc. 2

Solve & Share

Find 375 + 235. Explain your strategy.

I can ...
use different addition strategies and explain why they work.

© **Content Standards** 2.NBT.B.9, 2.NBT.B.7
Mathematical Practices MP.2, MP.3, MP.4, MP.5

Lauren, Nate, and Josh use different ways to find 257 + 126.

Lauren uses an open number line. She starts at 257 and mentally adds up the hundreds, the tens, and the ones.

Lauren's Number Line

+100   +10 +10 +3 +3

257   357   367   377 | 383
                              380

Nate draws place-value blocks. He regroups 10 ones as 1 ten.

Nate's Place-Value Blocks

| Hundreds | Tens | Ones |

257 + 126 = 383

Josh uses place value to write the addends in a column. He regroups 10 ones as 1 ten.

Josh's Addition

```
  1
  257
+ 126
-----
  383
```

Why does each of these strategies work?

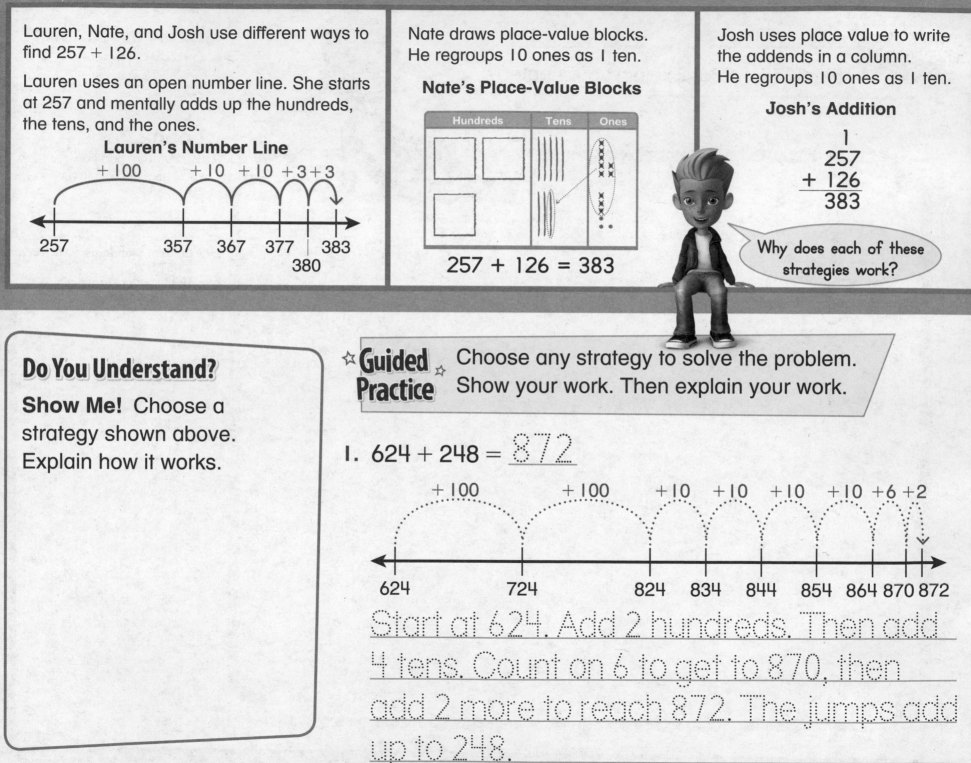

Do You Understand?

Show Me! Choose a strategy shown above. Explain how it works.

☆ **Guided Practice** ☆ Choose any strategy to solve the problem. Show your work. Then explain your work.

1. 624 + 248 = _872_

+100   +100   +10 +10 +10 +10 +6 +2

624   724   824 834 844 854 864 870 872

Start at 624. Add 2 hundreds. Then add 4 tens. Count on 6 to get to 870, then add 2 more to reach 872. The jumps add up to 248.

© Pearson Education, Inc. 2

Topic 10 | Lesson 6

Tools   Assessment

Independent Practice

Choose any strategy to solve each addition problem.
Show your work. Then explain.

2. 212 + 487 = _____

3. 874 + 109 = _____

_____

_____

_____

_____

4. 419 + 532 = _____

5. 650 + 270 = _____

How many different ways can you use?

_____

_____

Math Practices and Problem Solving

Solve each problem any way you choose. Show your work.

6. **© MP.2 Reasoning** Lee School needs 407 folders for its students. Jefferson School needs 321 folders for its students. How many folders do both schools need?

_____ folders

7. **© MP.2 Reasoning** There are 229 people at the football game. 108 more people arrive at the game. How many people are at the football game now?

_____ people

8. **Higher Order Thinking** Tommy found $125 + 598$. Since 598 is close to 600, he added $125 + 600 = 725$. Then he subtracted 2 to get 723.

Why did Tommy subtract 2? Explain.

_____

_____

_____

_____

_____

9. **© Assessment** There are 192 ants on an ant farm. 397 more ants join the ant farm. How many ants are on the ant farm now?

Use the number line to solve. Explain.

⟵————————————————⟶

_____

_____

_____

_____

© Pearson Education, Inc. 2

Name _____

Another Look! Find 219 + 468.

One Way

You can use mental math and an open number linc to keep track of your thinking.
You can add numbers in any order.
You can start with 468 and add 219.

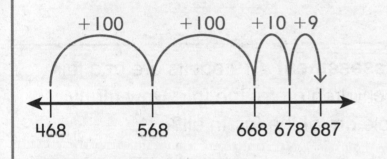

+100   +100   +10 +9

468   568   668 678 687

Another Way

You can also use paper and pencil to find the sum. Regroup if you need to.

$$\begin{array}{r} 1 \\ 219 \\ + 468 \\ \hline 687 \end{array}$$

To add 9, think add 10. Then subtract 1.

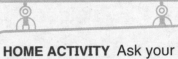

HOME ACTIVITY Ask your child to explain how to solve 429 + 378.

Choose any strategy to solve the addition problem. Show your work. Then explain your work.

1. 192 + 587 = _____

2. 269 + 658 = _____

© **MP.2 Reasoning** Choose any strategy to solve the addition problem. Show your work. Then explain your work.

3. $635 + 284 =$ _____

_____

_____

4. $701 + 103 =$ _____

_____

_____

5. Higher Order Thinking Explain TWO different ways to find $562 + 399$.

One Way

Another Way

6. © **Assessment** 519 adults are at a fair. 369 children are at the fair. How many people are at the fair in all?

Use the number line to solve. Explain.

_____

_____

_____

Name _____

Solve & Share

Solve the problems in Group 1.
Then, solve the problems in Group 2.

Tell how the problems in Group 1 are alike.
Tell how the problems In Group 2 are alike.

I can ...
think about and check my work as I solve a problem.

© **Mathematical Practices** MP.8
Also MP.1, MP.2, MP.3, MP.4
Content Standards 2.NBT.B.7, 2.NBT.B.9

Group 1		**Group 2**	

$$23 \atop +14$$ $$525 \atop +261$$ $$28 \atop +27$$ $$337 \atop +124$$

Thinking Habits

What can I use from one problem to help with another problem?

Are there things that repeat?

When you use this way to add, you need to use repeated reasoning.

$$\begin{array}{r} 235 \\ + 489 \\ \hline \end{array}$$

How can I use repeated reasoning?

I can use what I know, look for things that repeat, and check my work as I add each place.

Add each place from right to left.

Decide if you need to regroup to make a ten or a hundred.

$$\begin{array}{r} 11 \\ 235 \\ + 489 \\ \hline 724 \end{array}$$

Do You Understand?

Show Me! What is $5 + 9$? How is it shown in the problem $235 + 489$?

Hundreds	Tens	Ones
☐	☐	
2	3	5
+ 4	8	9

☆ Guided Practice ☆

Use repeated reasoning to solve each problem. Circle any problem where you regrouped to make a ten or a hundred.

1.
$$\begin{array}{r} 1 \\ 157 \\ + 229 \\ \hline 386 \end{array}$$

2.
$$\begin{array}{r} 214 \\ + 331 \\ \hline \end{array}$$

3.
$$\begin{array}{r} 544 \\ + 265 \\ \hline \end{array}$$

4.
$$\begin{array}{r} 651 \\ + 232 \\ \hline \end{array}$$

5.
$$\begin{array}{r} 455 \\ + 223 \\ \hline \end{array}$$

6.
$$\begin{array}{r} 738 \\ + 162 \\ \hline \end{array}$$

Tools   Assessment

Independent Practice ☆ Solve each problem.

7. Write a problem where you need to regroup to make a ten or a hundred. Each addend must be three digits. Solve your problem. Then explain why you needed to regroup.

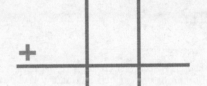

_____

_____

_____

_____

8. Write a problem where you do not need to regroup to make a ten or a hundred. Each addend must be three digits. Solve your problem. Then explain why you don't need to regroup.

_____

_____

_____

_____

Math Practices and Problem Solving

Tickets Sold

The table shows how many tickets were sold at a theater.

How many tickets were sold on Thursday and Saturday?

TICKETS

Tickets Sold	
Thursday	198
Friday	245
Saturday	367

25145843

25145843

9. **MP.1 Make Sense** Which numbers and operation can you use to solve the problem?

_____

_____

10. **MP.4 Model** Write an equation that shows the problem you need to solve.

_____ ◯ _____ = _____

11. **MP.8 Generalize** Use what you know about adding 3-digit numbers to solve the problem. Explain what you did.

_____

_____

_____

_____

Help   Tools   Games

Another Look!

When you add problems like this, you use repeated reasoning.

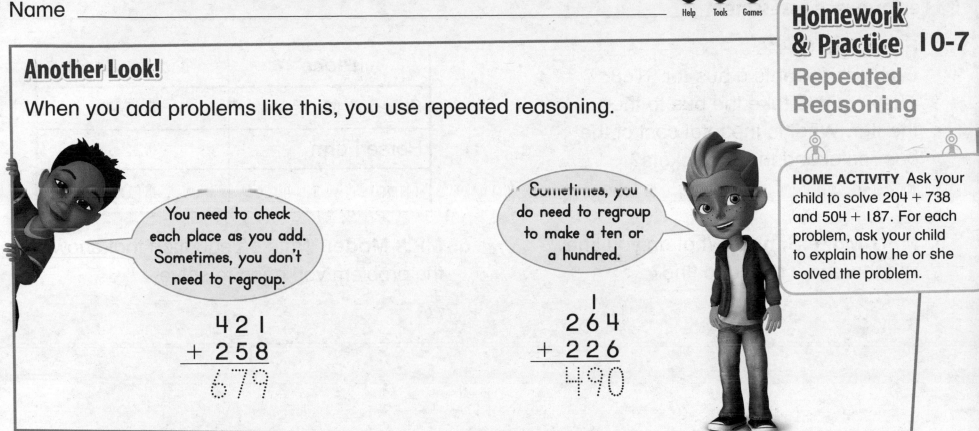

You need to check each place as you add. Sometimes, you don't need to regroup.

$$\begin{array}{r} 421 \\ +\ 258 \\ \hline 679 \end{array}$$

Sometimes, you do need to regroup to make a ten or a hundred.

$$\begin{array}{r} {\scriptstyle 1} \\ 264 \\ +\ 226 \\ \hline 490 \end{array}$$

HOME ACTIVITY Ask your child to solve 204 + 738 and 504 + 187. For each problem, ask your child to explain how he or she solved the problem.

Use repeated reasoning to solve each problem. Circle any problem where you regrouped to make a ten or a hundred.

1.
$$\begin{array}{r} 242 \\ +139 \\ \hline \end{array}$$

2.
$$\begin{array}{r} 432 \\ +257 \\ \hline \end{array}$$

3.
$$\begin{array}{r} 192 \\ +406 \\ \hline \end{array}$$

4.
$$\begin{array}{r} 371 \\ +240 \\ \hline \end{array}$$

Field Trip Costs

Don's class rents a bus for $168. They want to take the bus to the theater. What is the total cost of the bus rental and theater tickets?

Place	Ticket Cost
Science Museum	$158
Horse Farm	$225
Theater	$137

5. **MP.1 Make Sense** What do you know? What are you asked to find?

_____

_____

_____

_____

6. **MP.4 Model** Write an equation that shows the problem you need to solve.

7. **MP.8 Generalize** Use what you know about adding 3-digit numbers to solve the problem. Explain what you did.

_____

_____

_____

_____

Name _____

Point & Tally

Find a partner. Get paper and a pencil. Each partner chooses a different color: light blue or dark blue.

Partner 1 and Partner 2 each point to a black number at the same time. Both partners subtract Partner 2's number from Partner 1's number.

If the answer is on your color, you get a tally mark. Work until one partner gets seven tally marks.

I can ...
subtract within 100.

© Content Standard 2.NBT.B.5

Partner 1							Partner 2
59	53	19	43	62	37	30	45
78	48	65	81	32	51	76	27
92	14	71	58	66	48	25	16
82	44	37	55	47	33	67	11
64							34

Tally Marks for Partner 1	Tally Marks for Partner 2

A-Z Glossary

Word List
- addend
- break apart
- digits
- hundreds
- mental math
- open number line
- partial sum
- sum

Understand Vocabulary

Choose a term from the Word List to complete each sentence.

1. When adding $193 + 564$, the sum of $90 + 60$ is called a

   _____.

2. In $709 + 187$, 709 is an _____.

3. You can use an _____ to count on.

---

4. In 841, there are

   _____ hundreds.

5. Give the value of each digit in 610.

   _____

6. Use mental math to find $198 + 362$.

   _____

Use Vocabulary in Writing

7. Use words to tell how to find $249 + 201$. Use terms from the Word List.

   _____

   _____

   _____

   _____

Name _____

Set A

You can use mental math to add 10 or 100 to a number.

$362 + 10 = ?$
The tens digit goes up by 1.
$362 + 10 = 372$

$362 + 100 = ?$
The hundreds digit goes up by 1.
$362 + 100 = 462$

Add using mental math.

1. $600 + 10 =$ _____
   $600 + 100 =$ _____

2. $543 + 10 =$ _____
   $543 + 100 =$ _____

3. $799 + 10 =$ _____
   $799 + 100 =$ _____

Set B

You can use an open number line to add. Find $327 + 126$.

First, place 327 on the line.

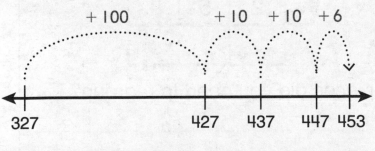

Count on by 100s, 10s, and 6 more on the line.

So, $327 + 126 =$ 453.

Use an open number line to find each sum.

4. $594 + 132 =$ _____

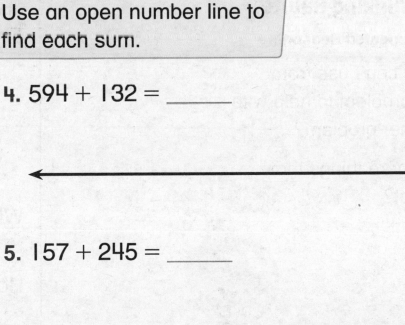

5. $157 + 245 =$ _____

You can draw place-value blocks to show addition. Find 163 + 144.

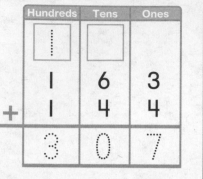

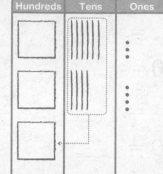

Hundreds	Tens	Ones
1	6	3
+ 1	4	4
3	0	7

Add. Regroup and draw models if needed.

6.

Hundreds	Tens	Ones
4	0	8
+ 3	2	6

7.

Hundreds	Tens	Ones
2	2	5
+ 3	6	1

Thinking Habits

Repeated Reasoning

What can I use from one problem to help with another problem?

Are there things that repeat?

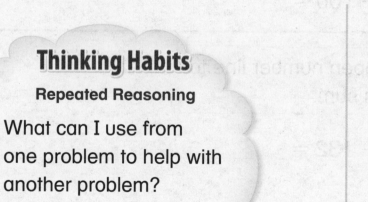

Solve the problem. Use repeated reasoning.

8. Find the sum.

Hundreds	Tens	Ones
5	6	8
+ 2	5	4

Which places did you need to regroup?

_____

How does regrouping work?

_____

© Pearson Education, Inc. 2

Name _____

1. Emily has 100 sun stickers. She has 382 star stickers and 10 moon stickers. How many sun and star stickers does Emily have?

Ⓐ 492   Ⓒ 393

Ⓑ 482   Ⓓ 392

2. Tyrone collects baseball cards. He gives 138 cards to his friend. Now he has 428 cards. How many baseball cards did Tyrone have before he gave some away?

Ⓐ 290   Ⓒ 556

Ⓑ 550   Ⓓ 566

---

3. Use the open number line to solve the problem. Write the missing numbers in the boxes.

421 + 250 = ?

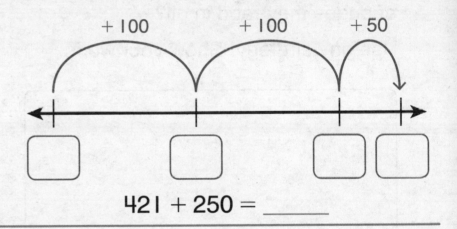

421 + 250 = _____

---

4. Which is the same amount as 528 + 167? Choose all that apply.

☐ 500 + 80 + 15   ☐ 500 + 180 + 15   ☐ 600 + 90 + 5   ☐ 600 + 80 + 15

---

5. Is the sum equal to 488? Choose Yes or No.

478 + 10 = ?   388 + 100 = ?   248 + 240 = ?   188 + 300 = ?

○ Yes ○ No   ○ Yes ○ No   ○ Yes ○ No   ○ Yes ○ No

6. Rich has 335 pennies.
Beth has 58 more pennies than Rich.
How many pennies do they have in all?

Ⓐ 277

Ⓑ 393

Ⓒ 628

Ⓓ 728

7. Use the numbers on the cards.
Write the missing digits.

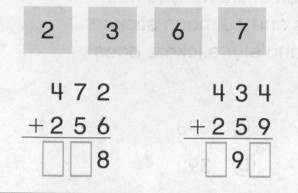

```
  4 7 2          4 3 4
+ 2 5 6        + 2 5 9
─────          ─────
□ □ 8          □ 9 □
```

8. Molly reads 184 pages. Pat reads 294 pages. What is the total number of pages they read in all?

Use any strategy. Show your work.

_____ pages

9. On Saturday, 449 people visit the zoo.
On Sunday, 423 people visit the zoo.
How many people visit the zoo in all?

Use the open number line to solve.
Explain your work.

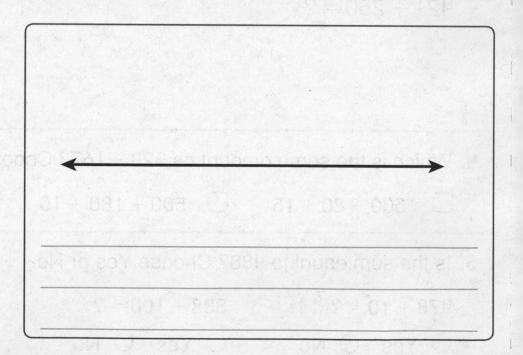

Name _____

Recycling Race

Westbrook School is having a recycling contest. The table shows the number of cans each grade collected in February.

Cans Collected in February	
First grade	264
Second grade	302
Third grade	392
Fourth grade	425

1. How many cans did the first-grade students and the second-grade students collect in all?
Use the open number line to solve.

_____ cans

2. Bruce used partial sums to find how many cans the third-grade students and fourth-grade students collected in all.

@ Performance Assessment

$$
\begin{array}{r}
392 \\
+ 425 \\
\end{array}
$$

Hundreds: 700
Tens: 11
Ones: + 7
718

Do you agree with his answer?
Circle **yes** or **no**.

Explain your answer.

_____
_____
_____
_____
_____

3. Which two grades collected a total of 689 cans? Choose any strategy to solve the problem. Show your work. Explain which strategy you used.

The _____ grade and the _____ grade collected a total of 689 cans.

Here are some addition strategies you have learned.

Addition Strategies

Open Number Line   Partial Sums
Compensation   Place-value Blocks
Mental Math   Regrouping
Break apart numbers

4. The second-grade students collected 432 cans in March. They collected 198 cans in April. Tom and Bill each add to find how many cans the class collected in all. One of them checks his work and finds the correct sum.

Tom's Way	Bill's Way
$\begin{array}{r} 11 \\ 432 \\ +\ 198 \\ \hline 630 \end{array}$	$\begin{array}{r} 432 \\ +\ 198 \\ \hline 520 \end{array}$

Who added correctly? Explain.

_____

_____

Who answered incorrectly? What did he do wrong?

_____

_____

_____

© Pearson Education, Inc. 2

Topic 10 | Performance Assessment

Subtract Within 1,000 Using Models and Strategies

Essential Question: What are strategies for subtracting numbers to 1,000?

Bees help move pollen from one flower to another!

Moving the pollen helps plants grow fruit and vegetables.

Wow! Let's do this project and learn more.

Math and Science Project: Making Models

Find Out Use a paintbrush as a model of a bee's leg. Dip the brush in a bowl of sugar. Then dip the brush in a bowl of pepper. Take turns. What happens to the sugar? What happens to the pepper?

Journal: Make a Book Show what you learn in a book. In your book, also:

• Tell how bees help move pollen between plants.

• Show how to use a model to help subtract three-digit numbers.

Name _____

Review What You Know

Vocabulary

1. Circle each number that is **less than** 607.

598

608

706

2. Circle each number that is **greater than** 299.

352

300

298

3. Circle the group of numbers that **decrease** by 100 from left to right.

650, 550, 450, 350

320, 420, 520, 620

570, 560, 550, 540

Subtraction Facts

4. Write each difference.

$$14 \quad\quad 11 \quad\quad 16$$
$$-7 \quad\quad -4 \quad\quad -9$$

Think of addition facts to help.

Regrouping

5. Use regrouping to find the difference. Be ready to explain your work.

$$54$$
$$-29$$

Math Story

6. Ben has 64 comic books. He gives 36 comic books to friends. How many comic books does Ben have left?

_____ comic books

Solve & Share

There are 456 ears of corn growing in a field. How many ears will be left if 10 ears are harvested? How many ears will be left if 100 ears are harvested?

How can you use mental math to find your answers?

I can ...
subtract 10 or 100 mentally using what I know about place value.

© **Content Standards** 2.NBT.B.8, 2.NBT.B.9
Mathematical Practices MP.1, MP.2, MP.4, MP.7

456 − 10 = _____

456 − 100 = _____

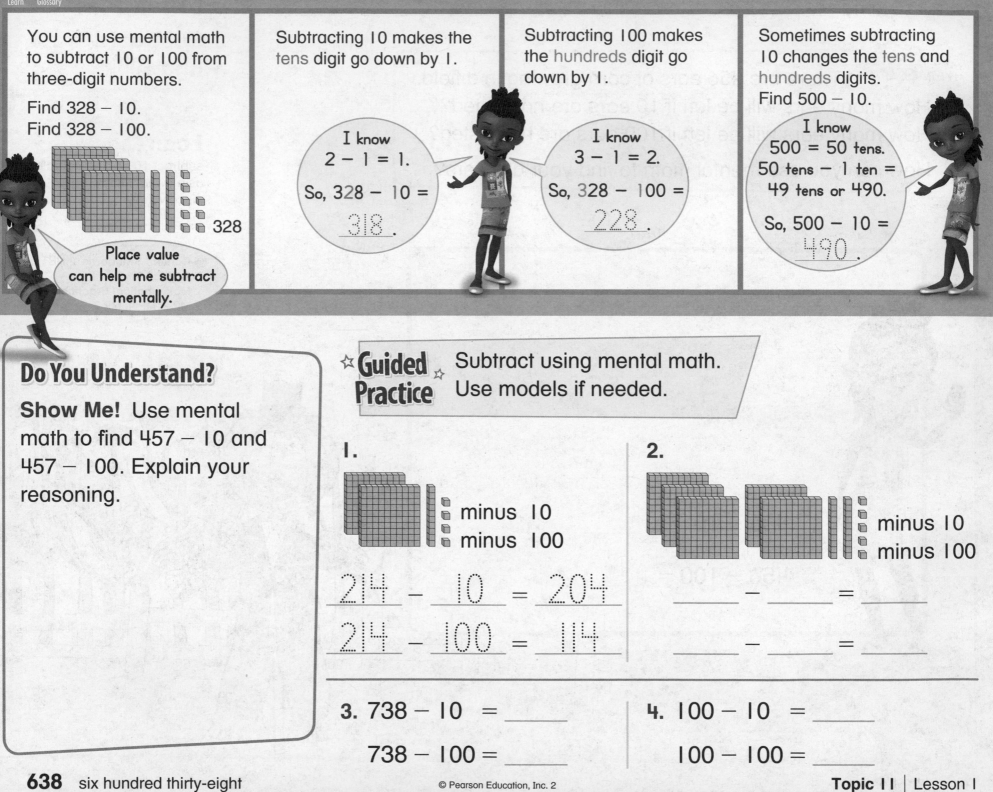

You can use mental math to subtract 10 or 100 from three-digit numbers.

Find 328 − 10.
Find 328 − 100.

Place value can help me subtract mentally.

328

Subtracting 10 makes the tens digit go down by 1.

I know
2 − 1 = 1.
So, 328 − 10 = 318.

Subtracting 100 makes the hundreds digit go down by 1.

I know
3 − 1 = 2.
So, 328 − 100 = 228.

Sometimes subtracting 10 changes the tens and hundreds digits.
Find 500 − 10.

I know
500 = 50 tens.
50 tens − 1 ten = 49 tens or 490.

So, 500 − 10 = 490.

Do You Understand?

Show Me! Use mental math to find 457 − 10 and 457 − 100. Explain your reasoning.

☆ Guided Practice ☆

Subtract using mental math. Use models if needed.

1.

minus 10
minus 100

214 − 10 = 204

214 − 100 = 114

2.

minus 10
minus 100

____ − ____ = ____

____ − ____ = ____

3. 738 − 10 = _____

738 − 100 = _____

4. 100 − 10 = _____

100 − 100 = _____

© Pearson Education, Inc. 2

Independent Practice ☆ Subtract using mental math. Use models if needed.

5. 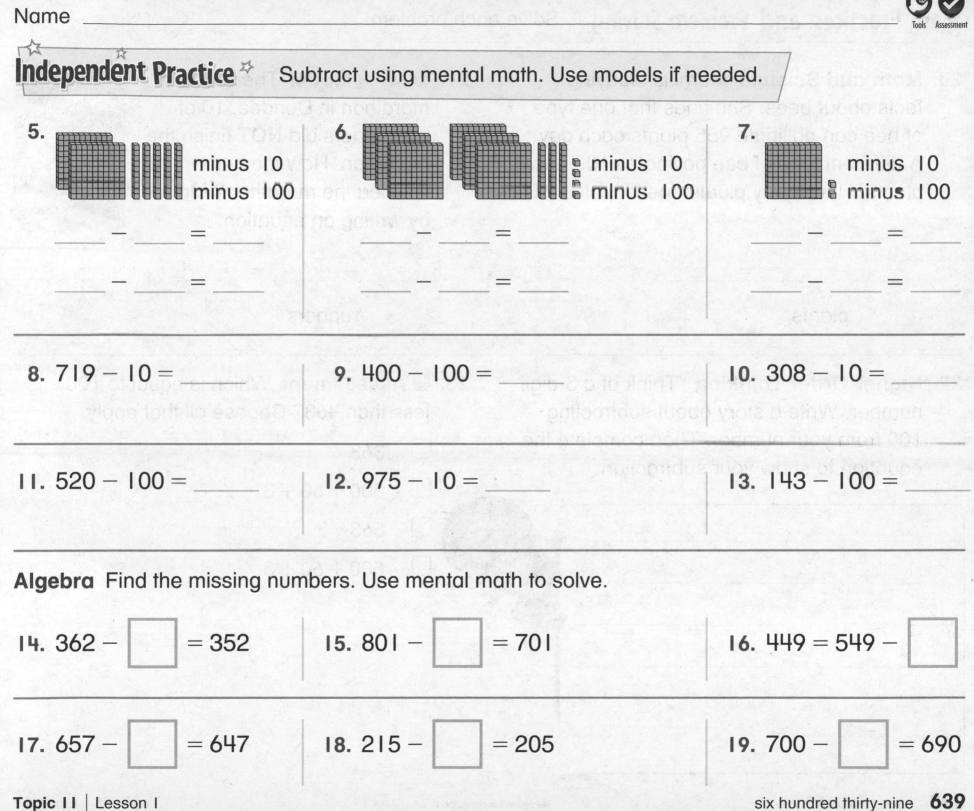 minus 10
minus 100

____ – ____ = ____

____ – ____ = ____

6. minus 10
minus 100

____ – ____ = ____

____ – ____ = ____

7. minus 10
minus 100

____ – ____ = ____

____ – ____ = ____

8. 719 – 10 = _____

9. 400 – 100 = _____

10. 308 – 10 = _____

11. 520 – 100 = _____

12. 975 – 10 = _____

13. 143 – 100 = _____

Algebra Find the missing numbers. Use mental math to solve.

14. 362 – ☐ = 352

15. 801 – ☐ = 701

16. 449 = 549 – ☐

17. 657 – ☐ = 647

18. 215 – ☐ = 205

19. 700 – ☐ = 690

20. Math and Science Marni is studying facts about bees. She finds that one type of bee can pollinate 955 plants each day. A different type of bee pollinates 100 fewer plants. How many plants does it pollinate?

_____ − _____ = _____

_____ plants

21. © MP.4 Model There was a marathon in Dundee. 10 of the runners did **NOT** finish the marathon. How many runners finished the marathon? Model by writing an equation.

_____ − _____ = _____

_____ runners

22. Higher Order Thinking Think of a 3-digit number. Write a story about subtracting 100 from your number. Then complete the equation to show your subtraction.

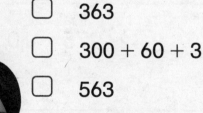

_____

_____

_____

_____

_____ − _____ = _____

23. © Assessment Which is equal to 100 less than 463? Choose all that apply.

☐ 363

☐ 300 + 60 + 3

☐ 563

☐ 500 + 60 + 3

© Pearson Education, Inc. 2

Another Look! Use mental math to subtract 10 or 100 from 3-digit numbers.
Find 278 − 10 and 278 − 100.

minus 10
minus 100

> Place value can help you subtract 10 or 100 mentally.

The tens digit goes down by 1 when you subtract 278 − 10.

$278 - 10 = 2\underline{6}8$

The hundreds digit goes down by 1 when you subtract 278 − 100.

$278 - 100 = \underline{1}78$

HOME ACTIVITY Choose a number between 300 and 400. Ask your child to subtract 10 from the number and tell you the difference. Repeat with subtracting 100 from the same number.

Subtract using mental math. Use models if needed.

1.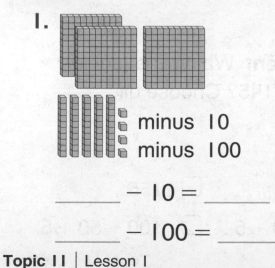
minus 10
minus 100

_____ − 10 = _____

_____ − 100 = _____

2.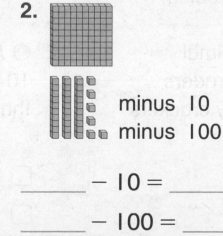
minus 10
minus 100

_____ − 10 = _____

_____ − 100 = _____

3.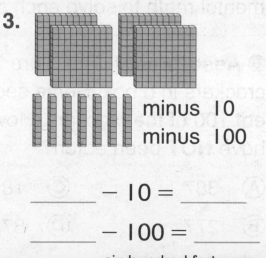
minus 10
minus 100

_____ − 10 = _____

_____ − 100 = _____

4. ☐69 − 100 = 469

5. ☐00 − 10 = 790

6. 402 − 10 = 3☐2

A-Z Vocabulary Use mental math. Write the missing digit. Then complete the sentence with **greater than** or **less than**.

7. 271 − 100 = 1☐1

171 is 100 _____ 271.

8. 475 − 100 = ☐75

475 is 100 _____ 375.

9. 612 − ☐0 = 602

602 is ten _____ 612.

---

10. **Higher Order Thinking** Adam is subtracting 708 − 10 mentally. He thinks the tens digit and the hundreds digit will change. He gets 698 for his answer. Is Adam's thinking correct? Explain.

_____

_____

_____

_____

Use mental math to solve each story problem.

11. © **Assessment** There are 287 animal crackers in a box. Some second graders eat 100 of the crackers. How many crackers have **NOT** been eaten?

Ⓐ 387

Ⓒ 187

Ⓑ 277

Ⓓ 87

12. © **Assessment** Which is equal to 10 less than 145? Choose all that apply.

☐ 135

☐ 155

☐ 100 + 30 + 5

☐ 100 + 50 + 5

Solve & Share

Marcus had 306 stickers. He gave 211 stickers to Juan. How many stickers does Marcus have left?

Use the open number line to solve.

Lesson 11-2
Count Back to Subtract on an Open Number Line

I can ...
use an open number line to count back to subtract 3-digit numbers.

Ⓒ **Content Standards** 2.NBT.B.7, 2.NBT.B.9
Mathematical Practices MP.4, MP.5, MP.7

———— − ———— = ————

Find 580 − 232. Use an open number line.

One Way

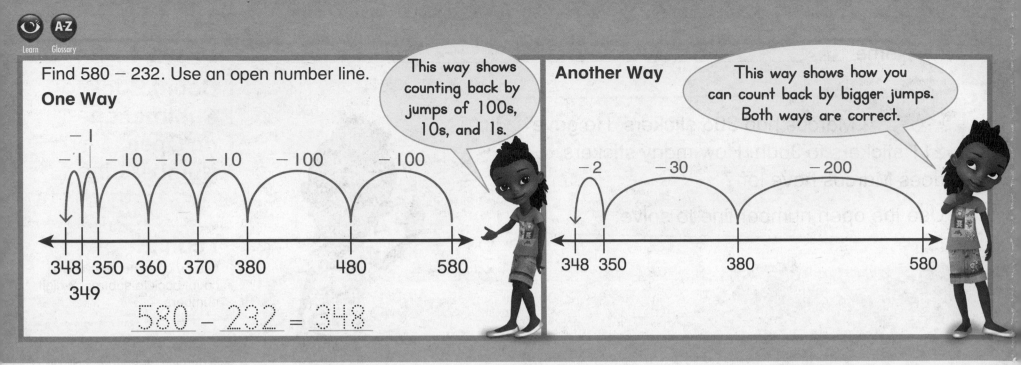

This way shows counting back by jumps of 100s, 10s, and 1s.

Another Way

This way shows how you can count back by bigger jumps. Both ways are correct.

$$580 - 232 = 348$$

Do You Understand?

Show Me! How can an open number line help you keep track as you count back?

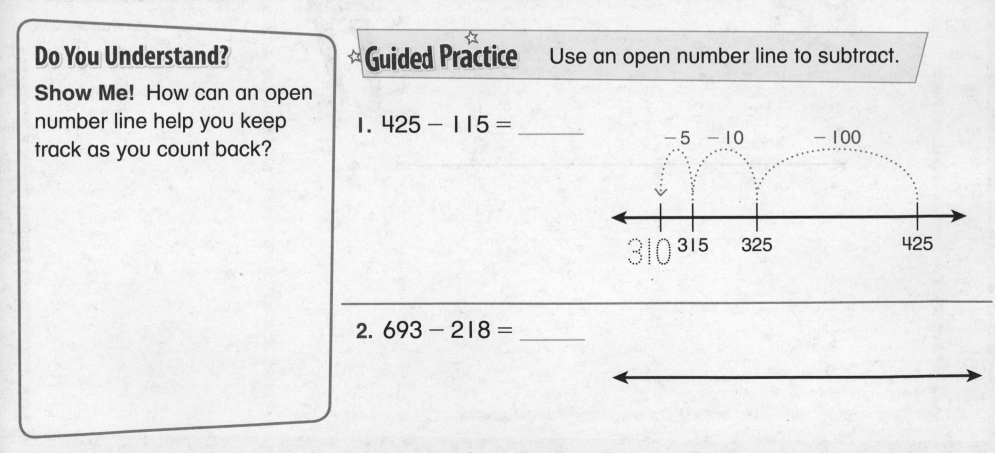

⭐ **Guided Practice**   Use an open number line to subtract.

1. $425 - 115 = \underline{\hphantom{000}}$

2. $693 - 218 = \underline{\hphantom{000}}$

© Pearson Education, Inc. 2

Name _____

Independent Practice ☆ Use an open number line to find each difference.

3. 451 − 132 = _____

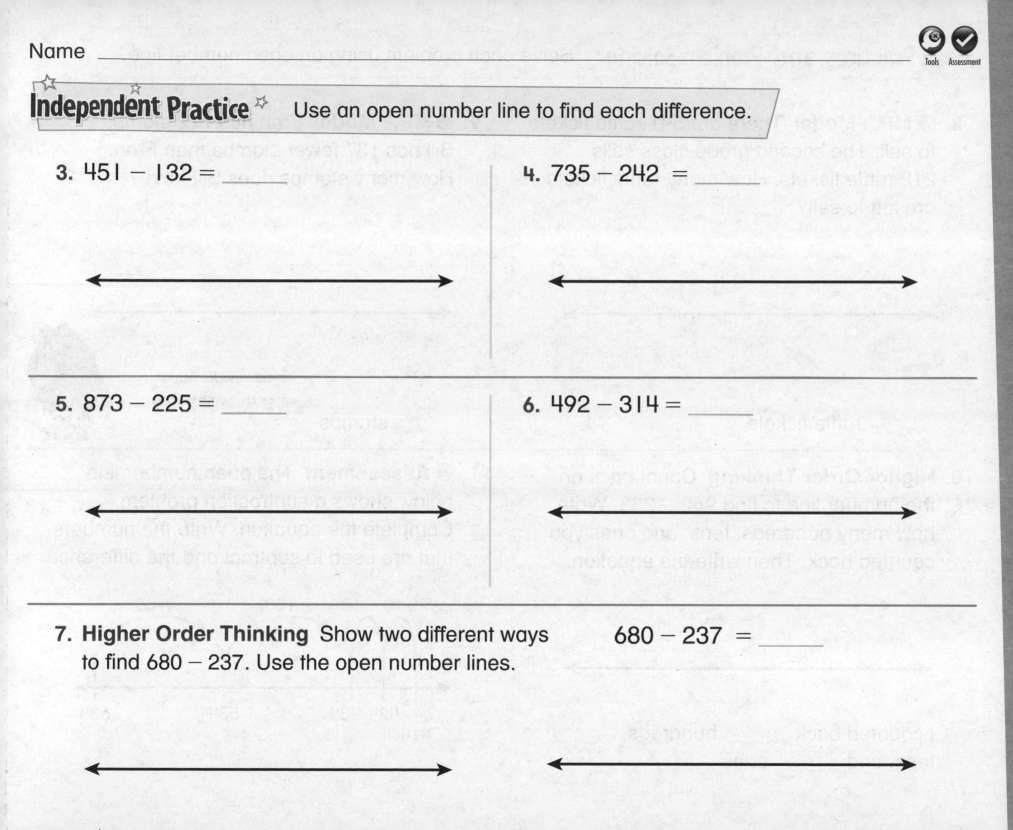

4. 735 − 242 = _____

5. 873 − 225 = _____

6. 492 − 314 = _____

7. **Higher Order Thinking** Show two different ways to find 680 − 237. Use the open number lines.

680 − 237 = _____

8. © **MP.4 Model** There are 541 raffle tickets to sell. The second grade class sells 212 raffle tickets. How many raffle tickets are left to sell?

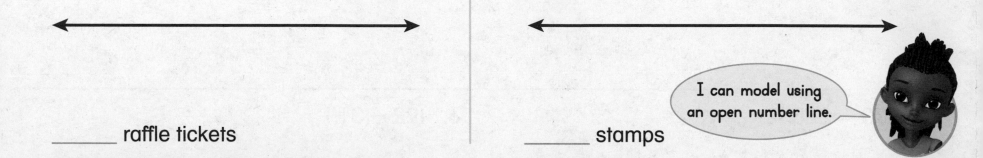

_____ raffle tickets

9. © **MP.4 Model** Fran has 712 stamps. Bill has 137 fewer stamps than Fran. How many stamps does Bill have?

_____ stamps

I can model using an open number line.

10. **Higher Order Thinking** Count back on the number line to find 962 − 233. Write how many hundreds, tens, and ones you counted back. Then write the equation.

I counted back _____ hundreds, _____ tens, and _____ ones.

_____ ◯ _____ = _____

11. © **Assessment** The open number line below shows a subtraction problem. Complete the equation. Write the numbers that are used to subtract and the difference.

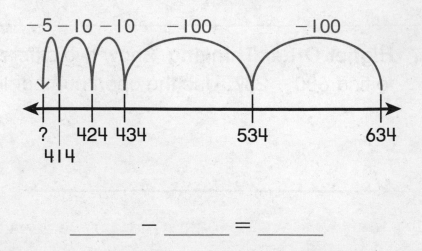

−5 −10 −10   −100   −100

? | 424 434   534   634
414

_____ − _____ = _____

© Pearson Education, Inc. 2

Name _____

Another Look! Find 917 − 322.

Here is one way.

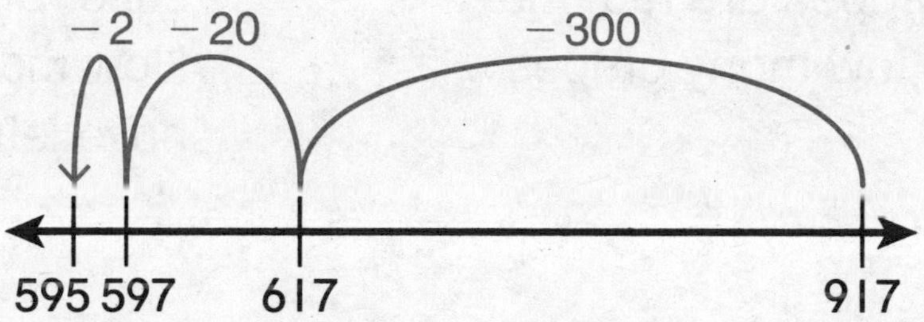

I can count back by 100s, 10s, and 1s or make bigger jumps to find 917 − 322.

-2 -20 -300

595 597   617   917

So, 917 − 322 = 595

HOME ACTIVITY Tell your child to find 445 − 152 using an open number line.

Use an open number line to find each difference.

1. 925 − 230 = _____

2. 384 − 126 = _____

Solve each problem using an open number line.

3. **© MP.4 Model** 464 grapes are in a basket. 126 of the grapes are red and the rest are green. How many grapes are green?

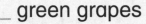

_____ green grapes

4. **© MP.4 Model** Gabby has 592 bottle caps. She gives 215 bottle caps to Leroy. How many bottle caps does Gabby have left?

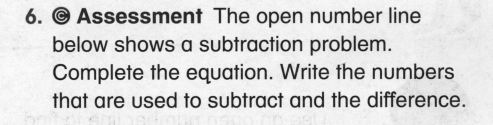

_____ bottle caps

5. **Higher Order Thinking** Write a math story for 348 − 144. Draw an open number line to solve the problem.

_____

_____

_____

348 − 144 = _____

6. **© Assessment** The open number line below shows a subtraction problem. Complete the equation. Write the numbers that are used to subtract and the difference.

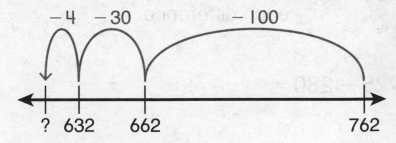

_____ − _____ = _____

© Pearson Education, Inc. 2

Name _____

Solve

Lesson 11-3
Add Up to
Subtract on
an Open
Number Line

Solve & Share

There are 224 girls and some boys in a parade. There are 471 children in the parade. How many boys are in the parade?

Use the open number line to solve the problem. Show your work.

I can ...
use an open number line to add up to subtract 3-digit numbers.

© **Content Standards** 2.NBT.B.7, 2.NBT.B.9
Mathematical Practices MP.2, MP.4, MP.6, MP.7, MP.8

←————————————————————————→

_____ – _____ = _____

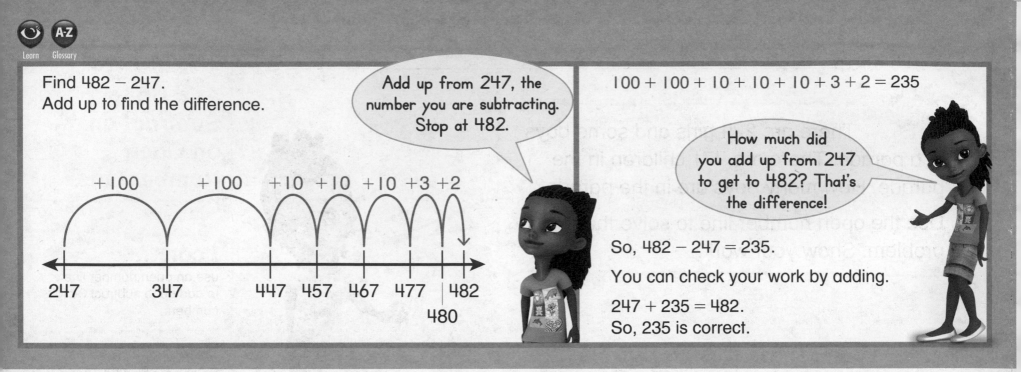

Find 482 − 247.
Add up to find the difference.

Add up from 247, the number you are subtracting. Stop at 482.

+100   +100   +10 +10 +10 +3 +2

247   347   447   457   467   477 | 482
                                                              480

$100 + 100 + 10 + 10 + 10 + 3 + 2 = 235$

How much did you add up from 247 to get to 482? That's the difference!

So, $482 − 247 = 235$.

You can check your work by adding.

$247 + 235 = 482$.
So, 235 is correct.

Do You Understand?

Show Me! What is another way you could add up to find 482 − 247?

☆ **Guided Practice**   Add up to subtract. Check your work.

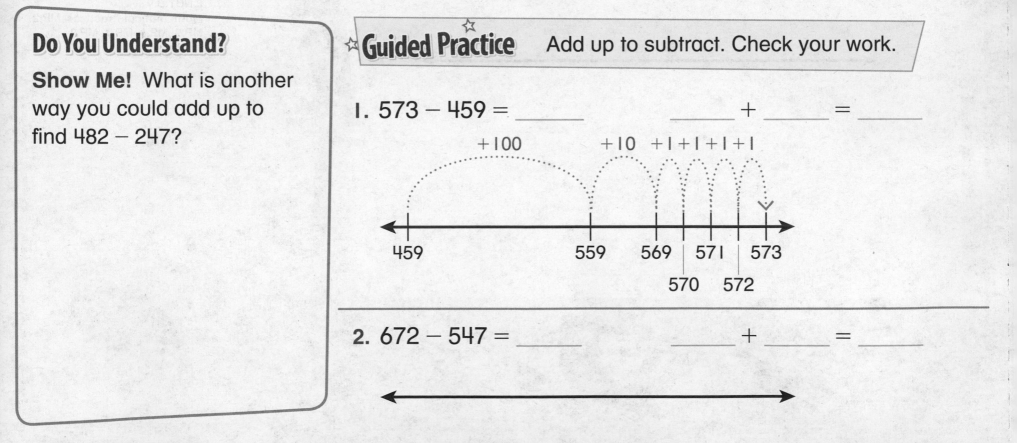

1. 573 − 459 = _____   _____ + _____ = _____

+100   +10 +1+1+1+1

459   559   569 | 571 | 573
                                            570   572

2. 672 − 547 = _____   _____ + _____ = _____

Independent Practice Add up on the open number line to find each difference. Then add to check your work.

3. 530 − 318 = _____

_____ + _____ = _____

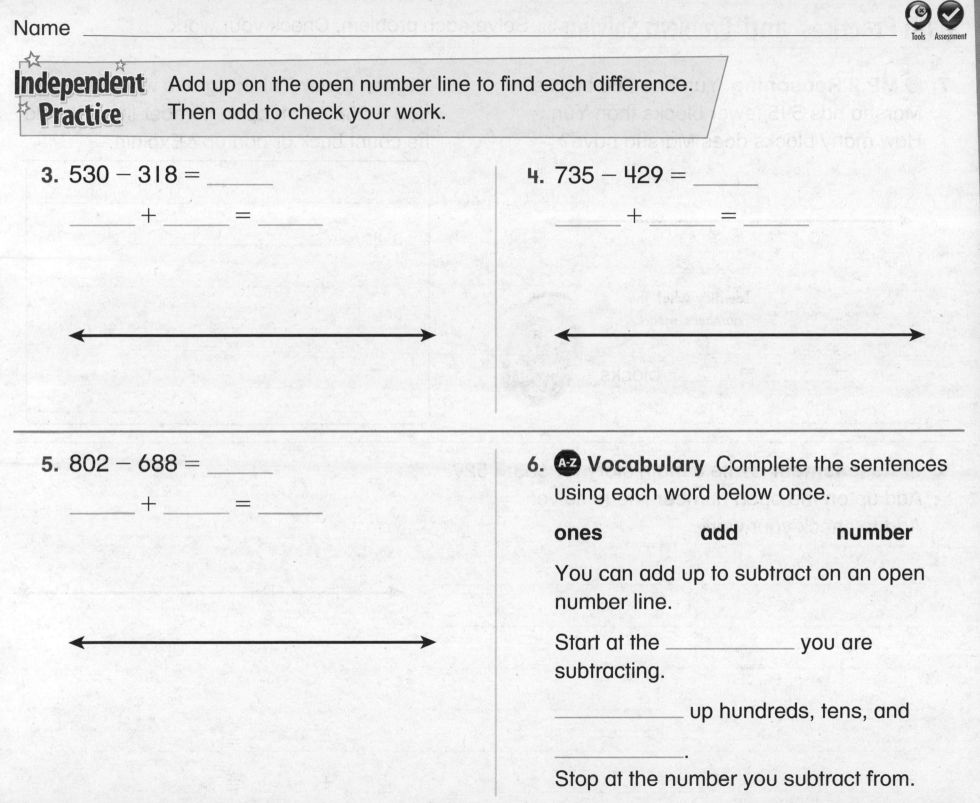

4. 735 − 429 = _____

_____ + _____ = _____

5. 802 − 688 = _____

_____ + _____ = _____

6. **A-Z Vocabulary** Complete the sentences using each word below once.

ones   **add**   **number**

You can add up to subtract on an open number line.

Start at the _____ you are subtracting.

_____ up hundreds, tens, and

_____.

Stop at the number you subtract from.

7. © MP.2 Reasoning Yun has 780 blocks. Marsha has 545 fewer blocks than Yun. How many blocks does Marsha have?

Identify what the numbers mean.

_____ − _____ = _____ blocks

_____ + _____ = _____

8. Higher Order Thinking Vic wants to find 463 − 258 on an open number line. Should he count back or add up? Explain.

9. © Assessment Write a math story for 653 − 529. Add up on the open number line to solve. Add to check your work.

_____ − _____ = _____

_____ + _____ = _____

Name _____

Another Look! Find 664 − 450.

Here is one way.

+100   +100   +10   +4

← 450 ____ 550 ____ 650 ____ 660 664 →

Add hundreds, tens, and ones. 100 + 100 + 10 + 4 = 214

I can add up to subtract!
So, 664 − 450 = 214.

Check: 214 + 450 = 664

HOME ACTIVITY Have your child add up to subtract 873 − 659 on an open number line. Then have your child check the answer using addition.

Add up on the open number line to find each difference.
Then add to check your work.

1. 994 − 770 = _____

____ + ____ = ____

←_____→

2. 831 − 716 = _____

____ + ____ = ____

←_____→

Solve each problem. Check your work.

3. © **MP.2 Reasoning** April has 365 stickers. She gives 238 stickers to Gwen. How many stickers does April have left?

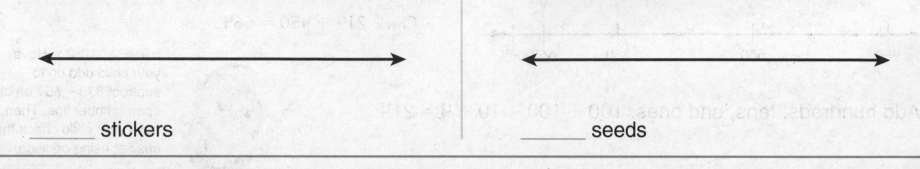

_____ stickers

4. **Math and Science** A group of birds had 362 seeds. Some seeds fell to the ground. Now the birds have 237 seeds. How many seeds fell?

_____ seeds

5. **Higher Order Thinking** Ricky added up on the number line and found $535 - 315 = 210$. Is his work correct? Explain.

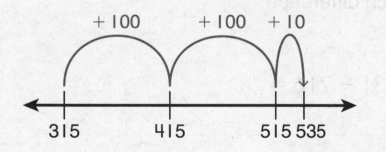

6. © **Assessment** Show one way to add up on the open number line to find $560 - 340$. Write the difference. Then explain your work.

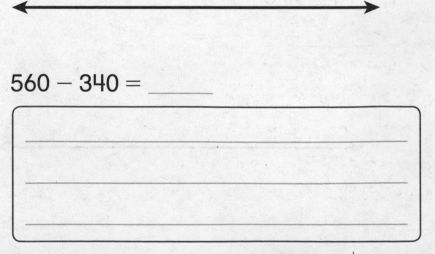

$560 - 340 =$ _____

© Pearson Education, Inc. 2

Topic 11 | Lesson 3

Solve & Share

Ami and Jorge enter their pumpkins in the Giant Pumpkin Contest. Ami's pumpkin weighs 335 pounds. Jorge's pumpkin weighs 302 pounds. How many more pounds does Ami's pumpkin weigh?

Show how you can use mental math to solve.

Solve

Lesson 11-4
Subtract Using Mental Math

I can ...
use mental math to subtract.

© Content Standards 2.NBT.B.7, 2.NBT.B.9
Mathematical Practices MP.1, MP.2, MP.3, MP.7

_____ – _____ = _____

_____ more pounds

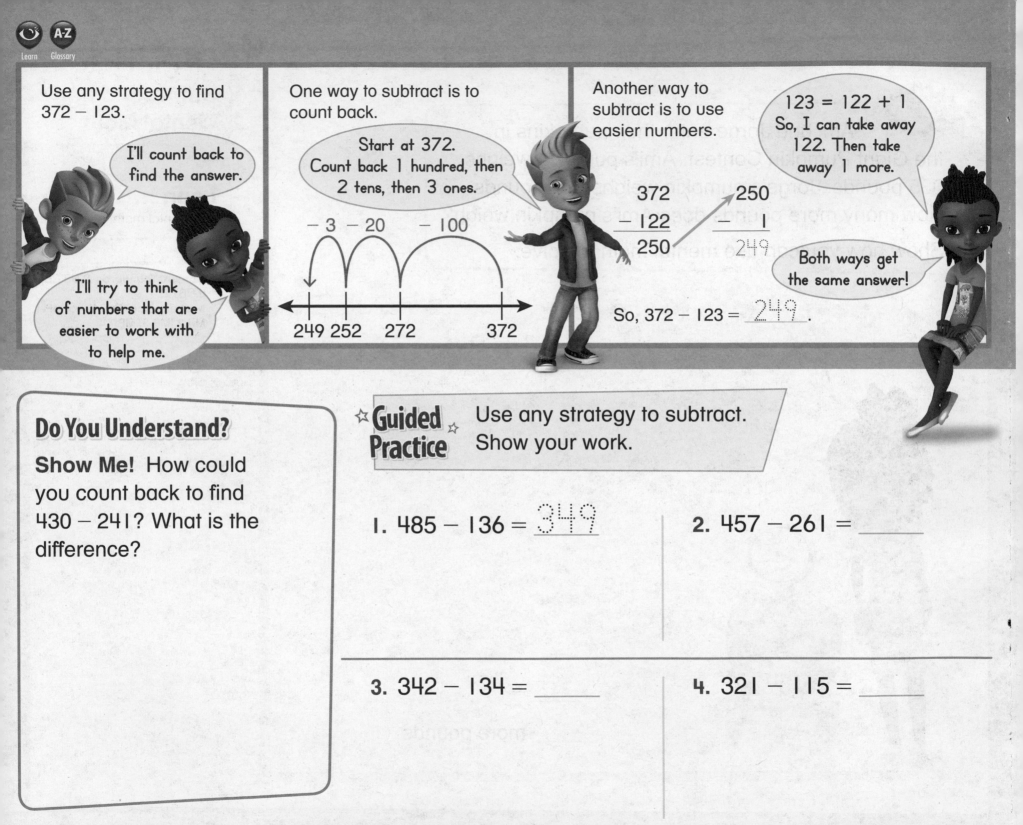

Use any strategy to find 372 − 123.

I'll count back to find the answer.

I'll try to think of numbers that are easier to work with to help me.

One way to subtract is to count back.

Start at 372. Count back 1 hundred, then 2 tens, then 3 ones.

− 3 − 20 − 100

249 252 272   372

Another way to subtract is to use easier numbers.

123 = 122 + 1
So, I can take away 122. Then take away 1 more.

372   250
− 122   − 1
250   249

Both ways get the same answer!

So, 372 − 123 = 249.

Do You Understand?

Show Me! How could you count back to find 430 − 241? What is the difference?

☆ Guided Practice ☆

Use any strategy to subtract. Show your work.

1. 485 − 136 = 349

2. 457 − 261 = _____

3. 342 − 134 = _____

4. 321 − 115 = _____

Name _____

Independent Practice ✧ Use any strategy to subtract. Show your work.

5. 598 − 319 = _____

6. 794 − 452 = _____

7. 871 − 355 = _____

8. 649 − 525 = _____

9. 463 − 244 = _____

10. 304 − 198 = _____

11. Number Sense Leo says that the difference of
526 − 217 is greater than 200.
Is what Leo says reasonable? Why or why not?

Sometimes it can help
to use numbers that are close
but easier to subtract.

_____

_____

_____

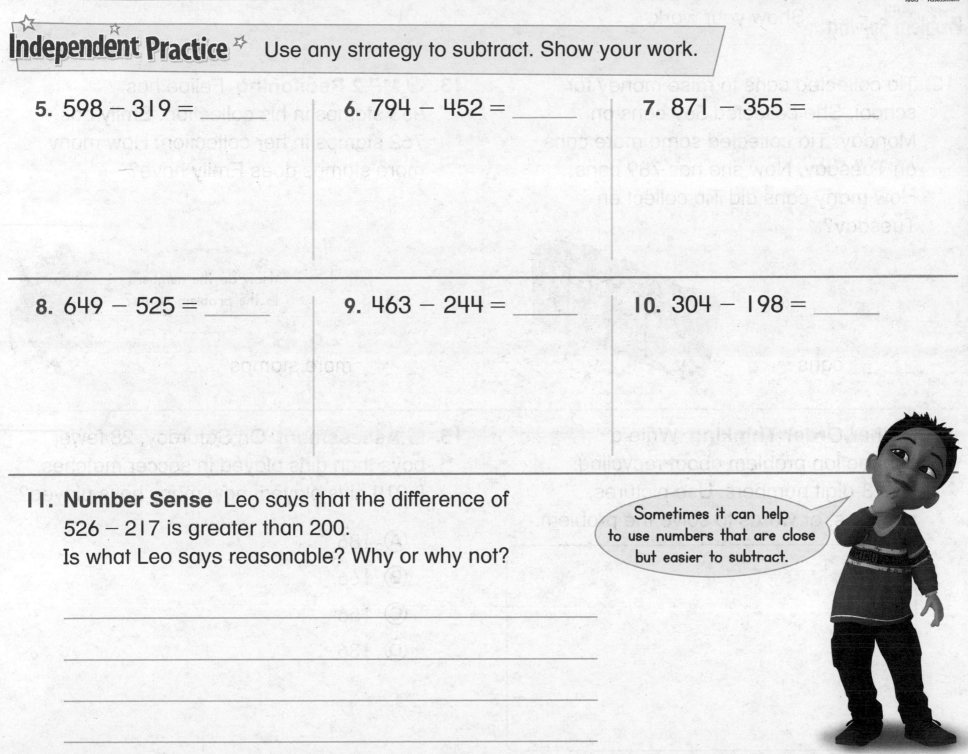

Use any strategy to solve each problem. Show your work.

12. Tia collected cans to raise money for school. She collected 569 cans on Monday. Tia collected some more cans on Tuesday. Now she has 789 cans. How many cans did Tia collect on Tuesday?

_____ cans

13. © **MP.2 Reasoning** Felipe has 453 stamps in his collection. Emily has 762 stamps in her collection. How many more stamps does Emily have?

How do the numbers in the problem relate?

_____ more stamps

14. **Higher Order Thinking** Write a subtraction problem about recycling. Use 3-digit numbers. Use pictures, numbers, or words to solve the problem.

15. © **Assessment** On Saturday, 28 fewer boys than girls played in soccer matches. If 214 girls played, how many boys played?

Ⓐ 186

Ⓑ 166

Ⓒ 156

Ⓓ 136

© Pearson Education, Inc. 2

Name _____

Another Look! Find 361 − 142.

One Way
Start at 361 and count back 142.

Remember, 142 is
1 hundred, 4 tens, and 2 ones.

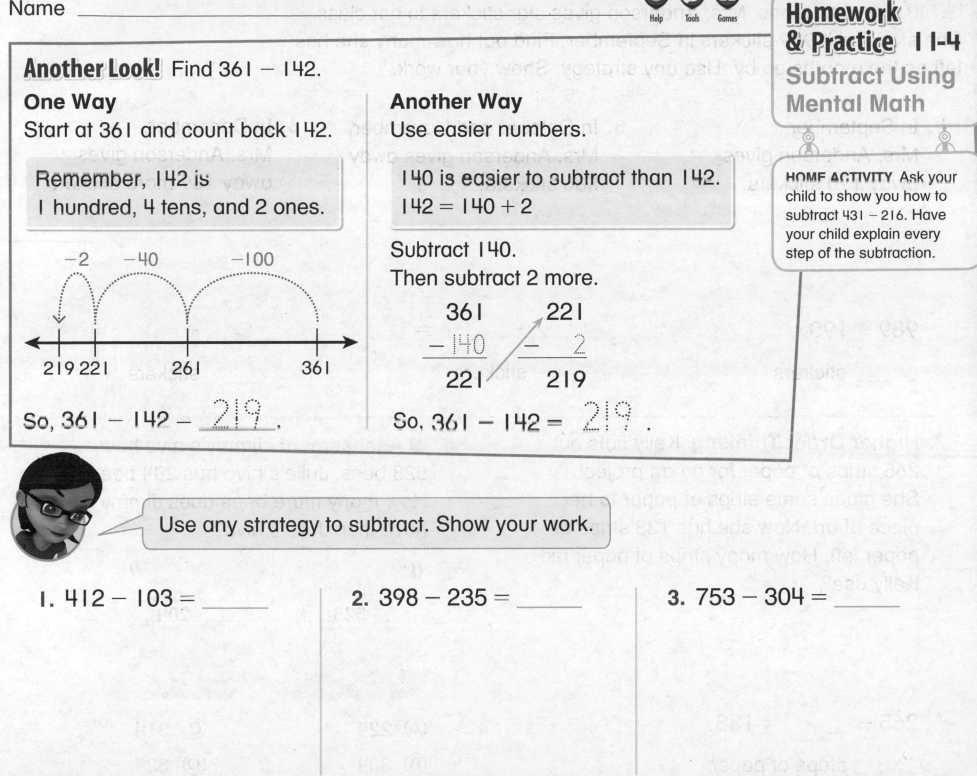

−2   −40   −100

219 221   261   361

So, 361 − 142 = __219__.

Another Way
Use easier numbers.

140 is easier to subtract than 142.
142 = 140 + 2

Subtract 140.
Then subtract 2 more.

361   221
− 140   − 2
221   219

So, 361 − 142 = __219__.

HOME ACTIVITY Ask your child to show you how to subtract 431 − 216. Have your child explain every step of the subtraction.

Use any strategy to subtract. Show your work.

1. 412 − 103 = _____

2. 398 − 235 = _____

3. 753 − 304 = _____

© **MP.I Make Sense** Mrs. Anderson gives star stickers to her class. She starts with 989 stickers in September. Find out how many she has left as the months go by. Use any strategy. Show your work.

4. In September, Mrs. Anderson gives away 190 stickers.

989 − 190 = _____

_____ stickers

5. In October and November, Mrs. Anderson gives away 586 stickers.

_____ − _____ = _____

_____ stickers

6. In December, Mrs. Anderson gives away 109 more stickers.

_____ − _____ = _____

_____ stickers

---

7. Higher Order Thinking Kelly cuts out 265 strips of paper for an art project. She glues some strips of paper to her piece of art. Now she has 138 strips of paper left. How many strips of paper did Kelly use?

265 − _____ = 138

_____ strips of paper

8. © **Assessment** Jimmy's hive has 528 bees. Julie's hive has 204 bees. How many more bees does Jimmy's hive have than Julie's hive?

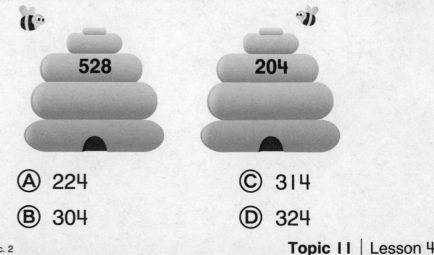

Ⓐ 224   Ⓒ 314

Ⓑ 304   Ⓓ 324

© Pearson Education, Inc. 2

Solve & Share

427 people are at the beach. 182 people are swimming. How many people are **NOT** swimming?

Use place-value blocks to help. Draw your blocks below and solve.

I can ...
use models to subtract 3-digit numbers.

© **Content Standards** 2.NBT.B.7, 2.NBT.B.9
Mathematical Practices MP.1, MP.4, MP. 5, MP.8

Hundreds	Tens	Ones		Hundreds	Tens	Ones

Use models to find 328 − 133. First, subtract the ones.

Hundreds	Tens	Ones
		•••
		✕✕✕

Hundreds	Tens	Ones
3	2	8
− 1	3	3
		5

Regroup 1 hundred as 10 tens.

Hundreds	Tens	Ones
		••••

Hundreds	Tens	Ones
2	12	
3̷	2̷	8
− 1	3	3
		5

Subtract the tens and the hundreds.

Hundreds	Tens	Ones
✕		••••

Hundreds	Tens	Ones
2	12	
3̷	2̷	8
− 1	3	3
1	9	5

So, 328 − 133 = 195.

Do You Understand?

Show Me! Explain why regrouping works in the problem above.

☆ Guided Practice ☆

Subtract. Draw place-value blocks to show your work. Regroup if needed.

1.
Hundreds	Tens	Ones
2	12	
3̷	2̷	6
− 1	4	3
1	8	3

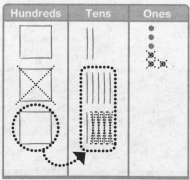

2.
Hundreds	Tens	Ones
3	6	3
− 1	2	7

Hundreds	Tens	Ones

3.
Hundreds	Tens	Ones
5	4	6
− 2	7	1

Hundreds	Tens	Ones

© Pearson Education, Inc. 2

Independent Practice

Subtract. Draw place-value blocks to show your work. Regroup if needed.

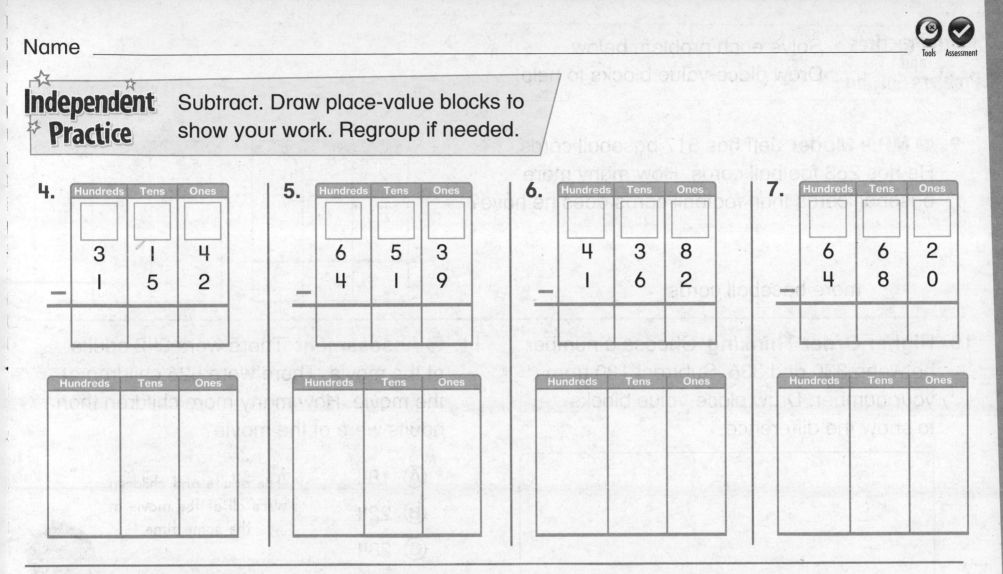

4.

Hundreds	Tens	Ones
□	□	□
3	1	4
− 1	5	2

Hundreds	Tens	Ones

5.

Hundreds	Tens	Ones
□	□	□
6	5	3
− 4	1	9

Hundreds	Tens	Ones

6.

Hundreds	Tens	Ones
□	□	□
4	3	8
− 1	6	2

Hundreds	Tens	Ones

7.

Hundreds	Tens	Ones
□	□	□
6	6	2
− 4	8	0

Hundreds	Tens	Ones

8. Higher Order Thinking Find the missing numbers. Explain your steps for solving.

Hundreds	Tens	Ones
□	□	□
8	5	4
− 2	9	
		2

Hundreds	Tens	Ones

_____

_____

_____

_____

Solve each problem below.
Draw place-value blocks to help.

9. © **MP.4 Model** Jeff has 517 baseball cards. He has 263 football cards. How many more baseball cards than football cards does he have?

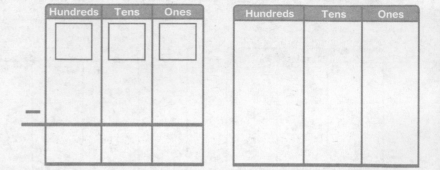

_____ more baseball cards

---

10. **Higher Order Thinking** Choose a number between 330 and 336. Subtract 180 from your number. Draw place-value blocks to show the difference.

11. © **Assessment** There were 342 adults at the movie. There were 526 children at the movie. How many more children than adults were at the movie?

Ⓐ 184
Ⓑ 224
Ⓒ 284
Ⓓ 868

The adults and children were all at the movie at the same time.

© Pearson Education, Inc. 2

Topic 11 | Lesson 5

Help   Tools   Games

Another Look! You can follow these steps to subtract three-digit numbers.

Find 327 − 164.

Step 1: Subtract the ones. Regroup if needed.

Step 2: Subtract the tens. Regroup if needed.

Step 3: Subtract the hundreds.

HOME ACTIVITY Have your child draw place-value blocks to model and find 583 − 274.

Think: Regroup 1 hundred for 10 tens. Draw place-value blocks to help.

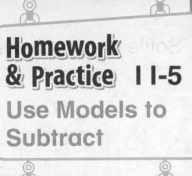

Hundreds	Tens	Ones
2	12	
3̸	2̸	7
1	6	4
1	6	3

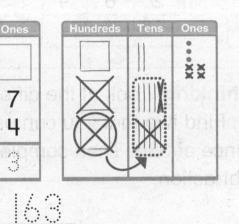

327 − 164 = 163

Subtract to find each difference. Draw place-value blocks to help.

1.

Hundreds	Tens	Ones
4	14	
5̸	4̸	9
2	9	5
2	5	4

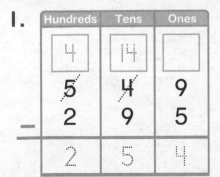

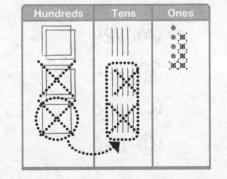

2.

Hundreds	Tens	Ones
8	3	5
5	1	6

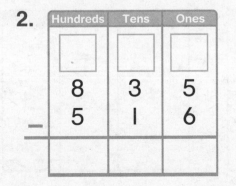

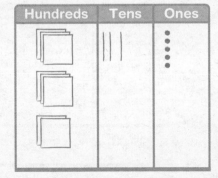

Solve the problems below. Remember to regroup when you need to.

3. © **MP.8 Generalize** Subtract. Then circle the problems where you regrouped to solve.

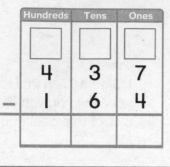 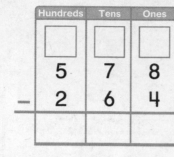 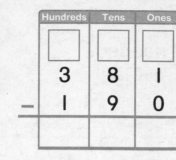 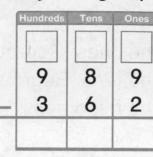 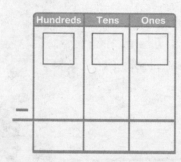

Hundreds	Tens	Ones
4	3	7
− 1	6	4

Hundreds	Tens	Ones
5	7	8
− 2	6	4

Hundreds	Tens	Ones
3	8	1
− 1	9	0

Hundreds	Tens	Ones
9	8	9
− 3	6	2

Hundreds	Tens	Ones
6	2	3
− 3	7	1

4. **Higher Order Thinking** Look at the differences in the problems above. Find two that you can use to subtract and get a difference of 354. Then complete the workmat to show your subtraction.

Hundreds	Tens	Ones
−		

5. © **Assessment** A farm has 319 animals. 136 of the animals are pigs. How many animals are **NOT** pigs?

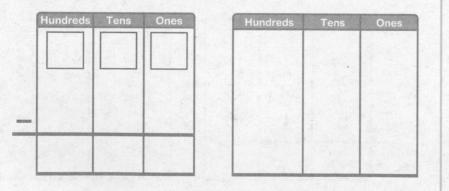 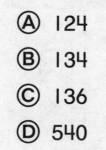

Hundreds	Tens	Ones
−		

Hundreds	Tens	Ones

_____ animals are **NOT** pigs.

6. © **Assessment** An office building is 332 feet tall. An apartment building is 208 feet tall. How many feet taller is the office building?

Ⓐ 124

Ⓑ 134

Ⓒ 136

Ⓓ 540

Name _____

Solve & Share

Find 532 − 215. Use any strategy. Then explain why your strategy works.

Explain Subtraction Strategies

I can ...
explain why subtraction strategies work using models, place value, and mental math.

© **Content Standards** 2.NBT.B.7, 2.NBT.B.9
Mathematical Practices MP.2, MP.3, MP.4

_____

_____

Find 437 − 245. Use any strategy.

One way Draw place-value blocks to show 437. Regroup 1 hundred as 10 tens. Then subtract.

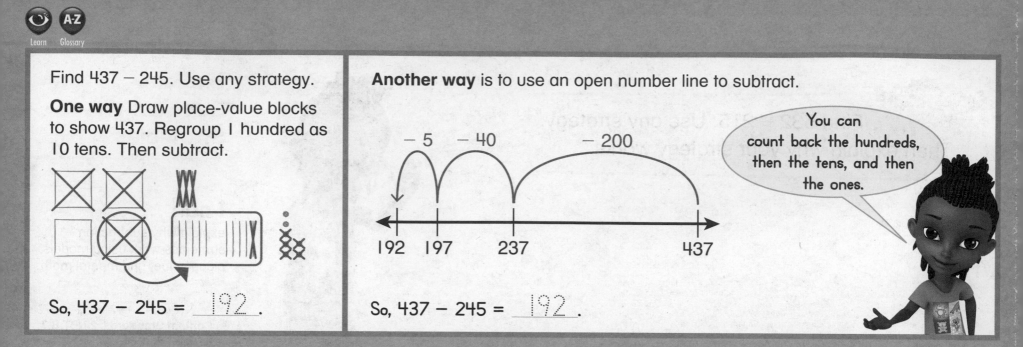

So, 437 − 245 = _192_ .

Another way is to use an open number line to subtract.

−5   −40   −200

192 197   237   437

So, 437 − 245 = _192_ .

> You can count back the hundreds, then the tens, and then the ones.

Do You Understand?

Show Me! Do you think both of these strategies are good for finding 437 − 245? Explain.

☆ **Guided Practice** ☆ Subtract any way you choose. Show your work. Then explain why the strategy works.

1. 345 − 116 = _229_

© Pearson Education, Inc. 2

Topic 11 | Lesson 6

Independent Practice   Choose any strategy to solve each subtraction problem. Show your work. Then explain why the stategy works.

2. 312 − 179 = _____

_____

_____

_____

3. 464 − 155 = _____

_____

_____

_____

4. 612 − 478 = _____

_____

_____

_____

5. **Number Sense** Use place value to find 748 − 319. Complete the equations.

319 = 300 + _____ + 9

Hundreds: 748 − _____ = _____

Tens: _____ − 10 = _____

Ones: _____ − _____ = _____

6. © MP.3 Explain Ava wants to use mental math to find $352 - 149$. Show how she could find the difference. Is this a good strategy for Eva to use? Explain why or why not.

7. Higher Order Thinking Kristin found $562 - 399 = 163$ using an open number line. She added up to subtract. First she added 1, then 100, and then 62.

Draw Kristin's number line. Do you think Kristin's strategy was helpful? Explain.

8. © Assessment Jeff counted back on this open number line to find $812 - 125$.

Use the numbers on the cards to find the missing numbers in the open number line. Write the missing numbers.

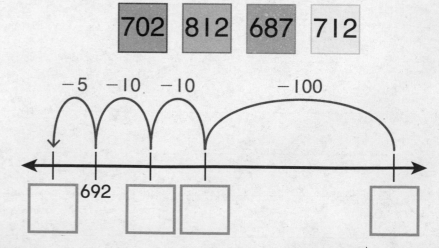

702 812 687 712

692

© Pearson Education, Inc. 2

Name _____

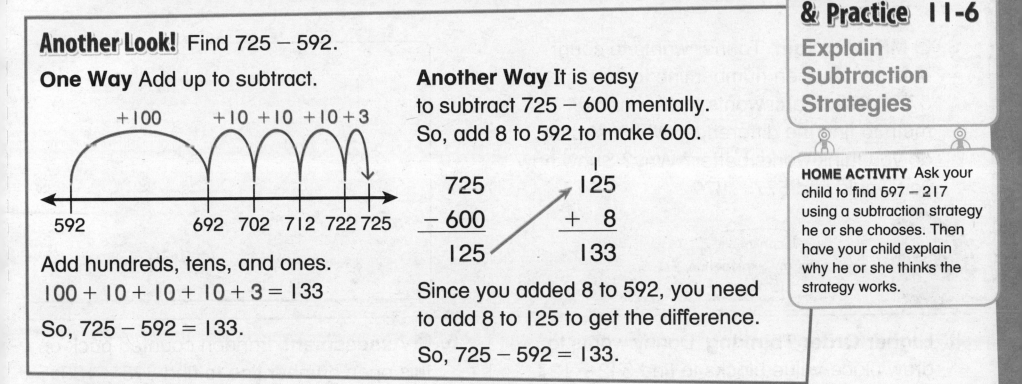

Another Look! Find 725 − 592.

One Way Add up to subtract.

+100   +10 +10 +10 +3

592   692 702 712 722 725

Add hundreds, tens, and ones.

100 + 10 + 10 + 10 + 3 = 133

So, 725 − 592 = 133.

Another Way It is easy
to subtract 725 − 600 mentally.
So, add 8 to 592 to make 600.

$$725 - 600 = 125$$

$$125 + 8 = 133$$

Since you added 8 to 592, you need
to add 8 to 125 to get the difference.

So, 725 − 592 = 133.

HOME ACTIVITY Ask your child to find 597 − 217 using a subtraction strategy he or she chooses. Then have your child explain why he or she thinks the strategy works.

Choose any strategy to solve each subtraction problem.
Show your work. Then explain why the strategy works.

1. 926 − 407 = _____

2. 532 − 241 = _____

Solve each problem.

3. **© MP.3 Explain** Tanner wants to count back on an open number line to find 577 − 479. Marci wants to use mental math to find the difference. Which strategy do you think works better? Why? Show how you would find 577 − 479.

I can make sure my explanation is clear.

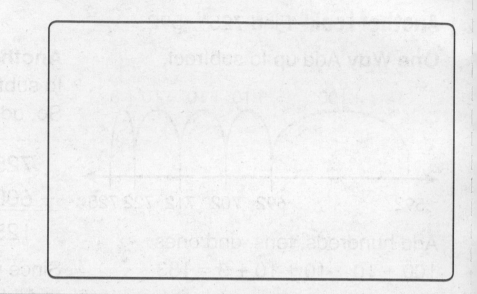

4. **Higher Order Thinking** Danny wants to draw place-value blocks to find 342 − 127. Draw the blocks he would use. Explain why this strategy works.

5. **© Assessment** Landon counted back on this open number line to find 898 − 133.

Use the numbers on the cards to find the missing numbers in the open number line. Write the missing numbers.

778 898 765 798

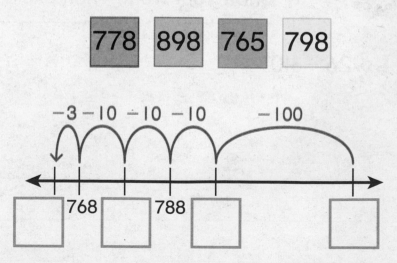

768   788

© Pearson Education, Inc. 2
Topic 11 | Lesson 6

Solve & Share

Jody wants to bake 350 muffins. She bakes one batch of 160 muffins and one batch of 145 muffins. How many more muffins does Jody need to bake?

Solve any way you choose. Show your work.

Lesson 11-7
Make Sense and Persevere

I can ...
solve problems that take more than one step.

Ⓒ Mathematical Practices
MP.1 Also MP.2, MP.3, MP.8
Content Standards 2.NBT.B.7, 2.NBT.B.9

Thinking Habits
What do I know?

What do I need to find?

How can I check that my solution makes sense?

Grade 2 wants to sell 10 more tickets to the school play than Grade 1.

Grade 1 sold 476 tickets. Grade 2 sold 439 tickets.

How many more tickets does Grade 2 have to sell to reach their goal?

How can I make sense of the problem?

I can see what I know. I can find hidden questions. I can choose a strategy to solve the problem.

An easy first step is to answer the hidden question.

What is the Grade 2 goal?

Grade 2 Goal
476 + 10 = 486 tickets

Now I can subtract the number of tickets Grade 2 sold from their goal.

$$\begin{array}{r} 7\ 16 \\ 4\ 8\ 6 \\ -\ 4\ 3\ 9 \\ \hline 4\ 7 \end{array}$$

Grade 2 needs to sell 47 more tickets to reach their goal.

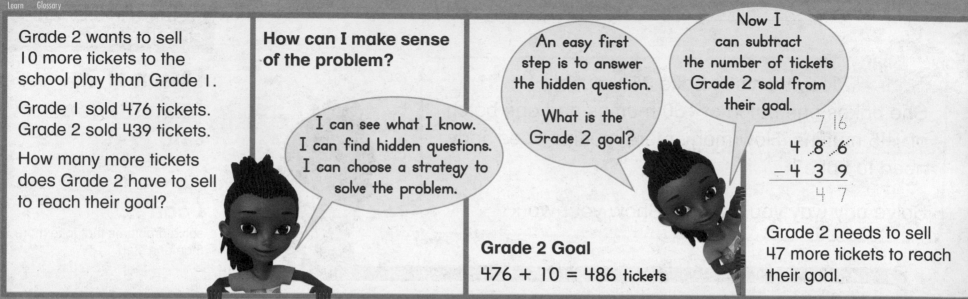

Do You Understand?

Show Me! What questions can you ask yourself when you get stuck? Be ready to explain how questions can help.

☆ **Guided Practice** ☆ Solve the problem. Remember to ask yourself questions to help. Show your work.

1. Kim had 455 shells. First, she gives 134 of the shells to a friend. Then she finds 54 more shells. How many shells does Kim have now?

What will you find first? Which operation will you use?

© Pearson Education, Inc. 2

Topic 11 | Lesson 7

☆ **Independent Practice** ☆   Use the table to solve each problem. Show your work.

Weights of Wild Animals (in pounds)				
Animal	Arctic Wolf	Black Bear	Grizzly Bear	Mule Deer	Polar Bear
Weight	176	270	990	198	945

2. How much heavier is a grizzly bear than an arctic wolf and a black bear together?

3. How much less does a black bear weigh than the weight of 2 mule deer?

4. How much more does a polar bear weigh than an arctic wolf, a black bear, and a mule deer together?

You know how to add three 2-digit numbers.

How can that help you add three 3-digit numbers?

Math Practices and Problem Solving

© **Performance Assessment** _____

Big Truck

The picture at the right shows the height of a truck and the height of a smokestack on top of the truck. The height of a bridge is 144 inches.

Use the information at the right.
Can the truck travel under the bridge?

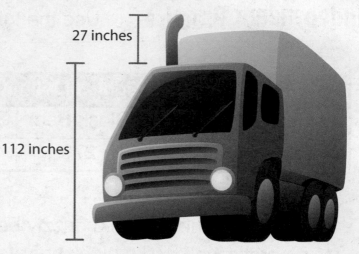

27 inches

112 inches

5. **MP.1 Make Sense** What do you know? What are you trying to find?

_____

_____

_____

_____

6. **MP.1 Make Sense** What hidden question do you need to answer first? Find the answer to the hidden question.

7. **MP.3 Explain** Can the truck travel under the bridge? Show your work. Why does your solution make sense?

© Pearson Education, Inc. 2

Name _____

Another Look! You need to use more than one step to solve some problems.

Read the problem. Complete the steps to solve.

Carl has 254 baseball cards.
He gives 145 cards to John and 56 to Amy.
How many cards does Carl have left?

Step 1 Add to find the number of cards Carl gives to John and Amy.

$$\underline{145} + \underline{56} = \underline{201}$$

Step 2 Subtract the number of cards Carl gives away from tho number of cards he has.

$$\underline{254} - \underline{201} = \underline{53} \qquad \underline{53} \text{ cards left}$$

Think: Is there a hidden question to answer first?

Think: Does my answer make sense?

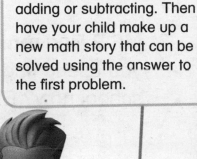

HOME ACTIVITY Ask your child to make up a math story that can be solved by adding or subtracting. Then have your child make up a new math story that can be solved using the answer to the first problem.

Solve the problem. Show your work.
Be ready to explain why your answer makes sense.

1. Mr. Wu buys a box of 300 nails. He uses 156 nails to build a deck. He uses 98 nails to build stairs. How many nails are left?

A School of Fish

Some fish travel in large groups called schools. Swimming in schools helps keep fish safe.

375 fish are swimming in a school. First, 47 fish swim away. Then 116 more fish join the school. How many fish are in the school now?

2. **MP.2 Reasoning** Which operations will you use to find how many fish are in the school now? Explain.

_____

_____

_____

3. **MP.8 Generalize** Are there now more or less than 375 fish in the school? Explain how you know.

_____

_____

_____

4. **MP.1 Make Sense** How many fish are in the school now? Show your work.

Follow the Path

Color a path from **Start** to **Finish**. Follow the sums and differences that are even numbers. You can only move up, down, right, or left.

I can ...
add and subtract within 20.

Content Standard 2.OA.B.2

Start								
6 + 6	10 + 8	16 − 8	9 − 0	14 − 4	6 − 2	10 + 10	8 − 3	2 + 7
5 + 4	9 − 4	11 − 9	10 + 5	13 − 5	2 − 1	7 + 9	10 − 9	10 + 9
15 − 8	3 + 10	5 + 1	9 + 8	6 + 8	12 − 5	7 + 7	16 − 9	13 − 8
12 − 9	14 − 7	14 − 6	16 − 7	9 + 9	5 + 6	8 − 6	2 + 5	4 + 7
8 + 9	9 + 6	7 + 5	12 − 8	1 + 7	18 − 9	6 − 0	17 − 9	15 − 7

Finish

Understand Vocabulary
Draw a line from each term to its example.

1. hundreds

2. bar diagram

3. regroup

63 = 5 tens and 13 ones

<u>8</u>23

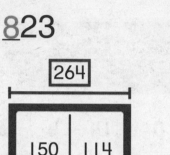

Word List
- bar diagram
- difference
- hundreds
- mental math
- open number line
- regroup

4. This open number line is incomplete. It needs to show counting back to find 538 − 115. Write in the missing numbers and labels.

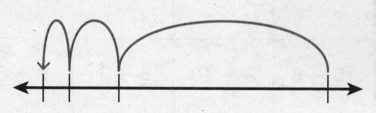

Use Vocabulary in Writing
5. Find 205 − 121. Use terms from the Word List to explain your work.

```
  2 0 5
− 1 2 1
```

© Pearson Education, Inc. 2

Name _____

Set A

You can subtract 10 or 100 mentally.

$549 - 10 = ?$

The tens digit goes down by 1.

$549 - 10 = 539$

$549 - 100 = ?$

The hundreds digit goes down by 1.

$549 - 100 = 449$

Subtract using mental math.

1. $426 - 10 =$ _____

    $426 - 100 =$ _____

2. $287 - 10 =$ _____

    $287 - 100 =$ _____

3. $800 - 10 =$ _____

    $800 - 100 =$ _____

Set B

Find $673 - 458$. Start at 458 on an open number line. Add up to 673.

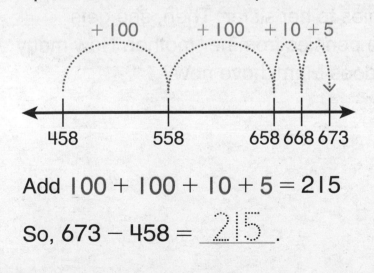

Add $100 + 100 + 10 + 5 = 215$

So, $673 - 458 = 215$.

Use an open number line to subtract.

4. $449 - 217 =$ _____

5. $903 - 678 =$ _____

You can draw place-value blocks to show subtraction. Find 327 − 219.

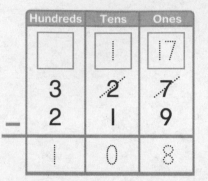

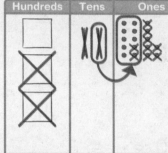

Hundreds	Tens	Ones
	1	17
3	2̸	7̸
− 2	1	9
1	0	8

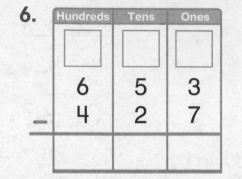

Subtract. Draw models and regroup if needed.

6.

Hundreds	Tens	Ones
6	5	3
− 4	2	7

Hundreds	Tens	Ones

Set D

Thinking Habits

Persevere

What do I know?

What do I need to find?

How can I check that my solution makes sense?

Solve the problem.
Ask yourself questions to help.

7. Marni has 354 pennies. First, she gives 149 pennies to her sister. Then, she gets 210 more pennies from her mother. How many pennies does Marni have now?

Topic 11 | Reteaching

Name _____

1. Which equals 100 less than 763?
Choose all that apply.

☐ 663

☐ 600 + 60 + 3

☐ 863

☐ 800 + 60 + 3

2. The open number line below
shows subtraction.

© Assessment

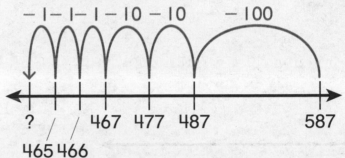

Complete the equation. Write the
numbers being subtracted and the
difference.

_____ − _____ = _____

3. Is the difference equal to 462?
Choose Yes or No. Use different
strategies to subtract.

998 − 536 = ?   ○ Yes   ○ No

842 − 380 = ?   ○ Yes   ○ No

687 − 125 = ?   ○ Yes   ○ No

924 − 462 = ?   ○ Yes   ○ No

4. There are 537 boys and 438 girls at the
concert. How many more boys than girls
are at the concert?

Ⓐ 89

Ⓑ 99

Ⓒ 101

Ⓓ 109

5. Show how to add up on an open number line to find 740 − 490. Then write the difference below.

←————————————————→

740 − 490 = _____

6. Look at your work in Item 5. Why can you use adding up on an open number line to find 740 − 490? Choose all that apply.

☐ You can always add up to subtract on an open number line.

☐ You can't always add up to subtract on an open number line.

☐ An open number line helps you break apart numbers to subtract.

☐ An open number line should be used for any type of problem.

7. Use the numbers on the cards to find the missing numbers in the subtraction problem. Use the place-value models to help. Write the missing numbers.

| 7 | 6 | 1 | 2 |

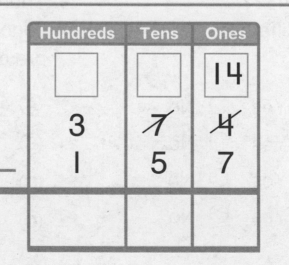

Hundreds	Tens	Ones
		14
3	7̶	4̶
1	5	7

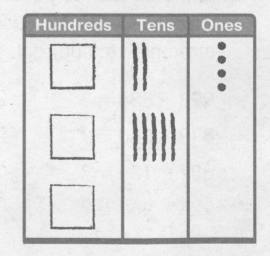

Hundreds	Tens	Ones

© Pearson Education, Inc. 2

Topic 11 | Assessment

Name _____

Bead It!

The chart shows the number of beads sold at Betty's craft store for 4 weeks.

Number of Beads Sold	
Week 1	400
Week 2	536
Week 3	675
Week 4	289

1. How many more beads did Betty sell in Week 2 than in Week 1? Use mental math to solve. Write the missing numbers in the equation.

_____ − _____ = _____

_____ more beads

2. 458 glass beads were sold in Week 3. The other beads sold in Week 3 were plastic. How many plastic beads were sold in Week 3?

Ⓒ **Performance Assessment**

Use the open number line to solve.

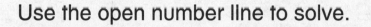

_____ − _____ = _____

Explain how you solved the problem. Tell how you know your answer is correct.

3. Dex buys 243 beads at Betty's store. He uses 118 of them to make a bracelet. How many beads does Dex have left?

Solve the problem. Show your work. Explain which strategy you used.

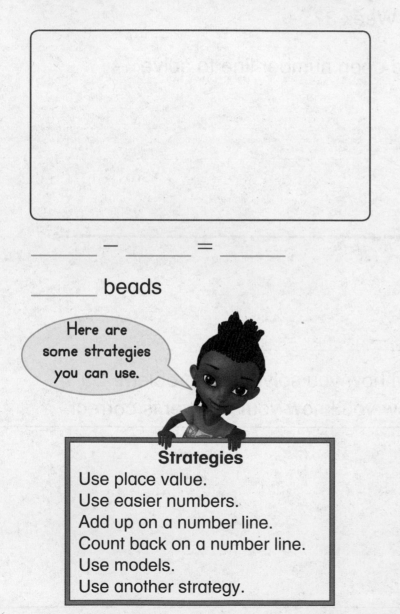

_____ – _____ = _____

_____ beads

Here are some strategies you can use.

Strategies
Use place value.
Use easier numbers.
Add up on a number line.
Count back on a number line.
Use models.
Use another strategy.

4. Ginny buys 958 beads. 245 beads are blue. 309 beads are orange. 153 beads are white. The rest are red. How many red beads does Ginny buy?

Part A
What is the hidden question in the problem?

_____

_____

Part B
Solve the problem. Show your work. Explain which strategy you used.

_____ red beads

© Pearson Education, Inc. 2

TOPIC 12 Measuring Length

Essential Question: What are ways to measure length?

Digital Resources

Solve Learn Glossary

Tools Assessment Help Games

Look how tall sunflowers grow!

Sunlight and water help plants grow.

Wow! Let's do this project and learn more.

Math and Science Project: Growing and Measuring

Find Out Grow bean plants. Give them numbers. Put some in sunlight. Put some in a dark place. Water some of the plants. Do not water some of the plants. See how the plants in each group grow.

Journal: Make a Book Show what you learn in a book. In your book, also:

- Tell if plants need sunlight and water to grow.
- Find plants to measure. Draw pictures of the plants. Tell how tall each plant is.

Name _____

Review What You Know

1. Draw a line to show the **length** of the bat.

2. School is getting out. Circle **a.m.** or **p.m.**

a.m.

p.m.

3. Draw clock hands to show **quarter past** 10.

Estimating and Measuring Length

4. Use snap cubes.

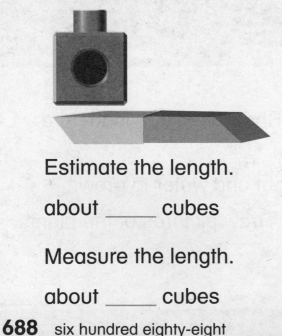

Estimate the length.

about _____ cubes

Measure the length.

about _____ cubes

5.

Estimate the length.

about _____ cubes

Measure the length.

about _____ cubes

Skip Counting

6. Write the missing numbers.

5, 10, _____, 20, _____

210, 220, _____, 240

400, _____, 600, 700

Look for a pattern.

© Pearson Education, Inc. 2

My Word Cards

Study the words on the front of the card.
Complete the activity on the back.

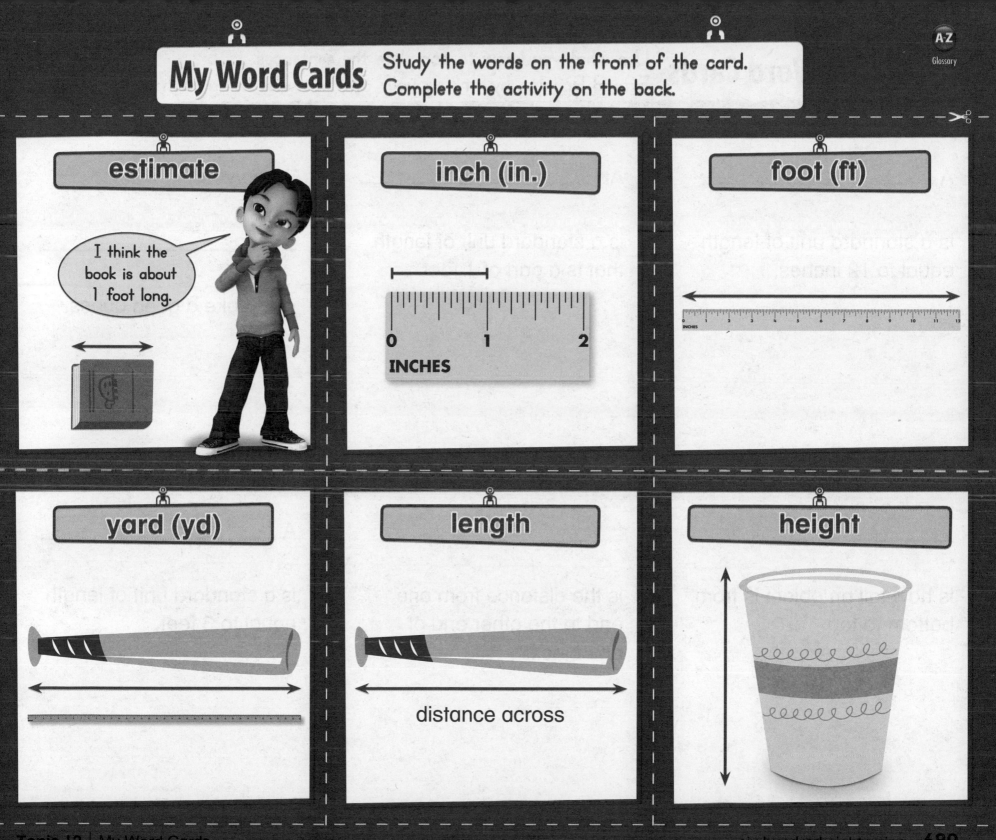

estimate

I think the book is about 1 foot long.

inch (in.)

0   1   2
INCHES

foot (ft)

yard (yd)

length

distance across

height

Use what you know to complete the sentences.
Extend learning by writing your own sentence using each word.

A _____

is a standard unit of length
equal to 12 inches.

An _____

is a standard unit of length
that is a part of 1 foot.

When you

_____,

you make a good guess.

_____

is how tall an object is from
bottom to top.

_____

is the distance from one
end to the other end of
an object.

A _____

is a standard unit of length
equal to 3 feet.

© Pearson Education, Inc. 2

My Word Cards

Study the words on the front of the card.
Complete the activity on the back.

A-Z
Glossary

nearest inch

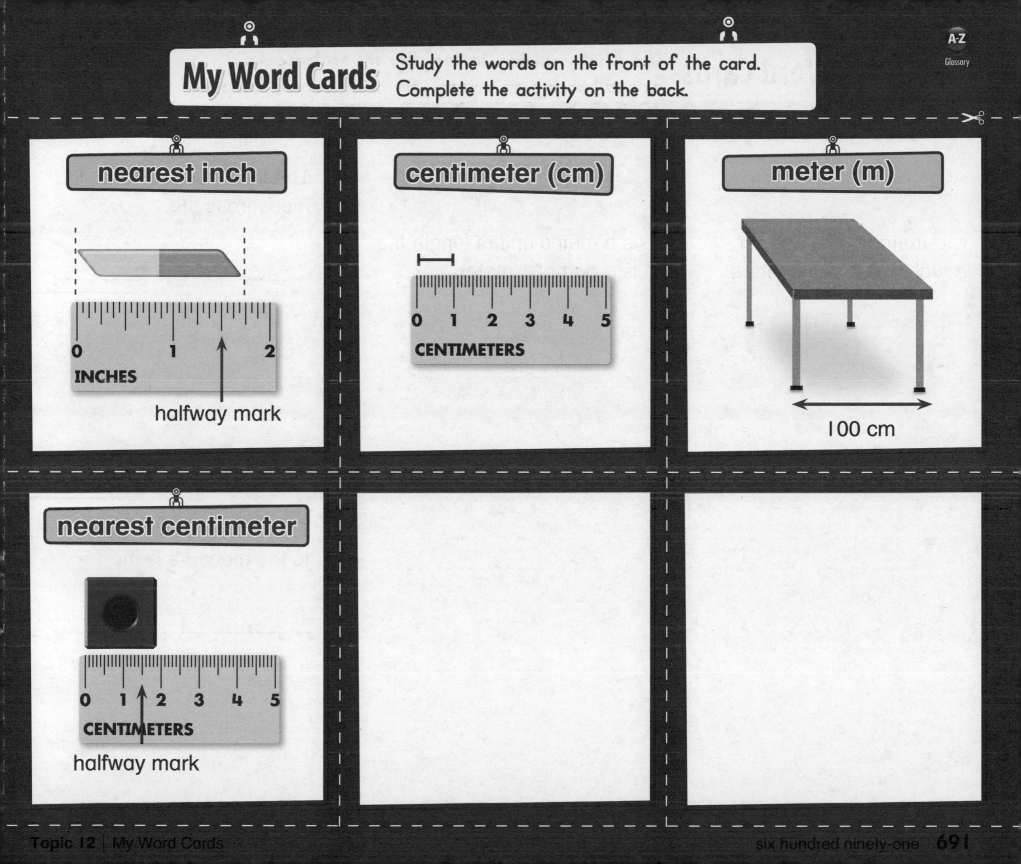

INCHES

halfway mark

centimeter (cm)

CENTIMETERS

meter (m)

100 cm

nearest centimeter

CENTIMETERS

halfway mark

A _____

is a metric unit of length
equal to 100 centimeters.

A _____

is a metric unit of length that
is a part of 1 meter.

The inch closest to the
measure is the

_____.

The closest centimeter
to the measure is the

_____.

© Pearson Education, Inc. 2

Solve & Share

Your thumb is about 1 inch long. Use your thumb to find three objects that are each about 1 inch long. Draw the objects.

From your elbow to your fingers is about 1 foot long. Use this part of your arm to find three objects that are each about 1 foot long. Draw the objects.

I can ...
estimate the length of an object by relating the length of the object to a measurement I know.

© **Content Standard** 2.MD.A.3
Mathematical Practices MP.2, MP.5, MP.6

about 1 inch	about 1 foot

You can use the length of objects you know to **estimate** the length of other objects.

Some small paper clips are 1 inch (1 in.) long.

Use a small paperclip to estimate how long the eraser is.

The eraser is about 2 paper clips long. So, it is about 2 inches long.

You can estimate with objects that are about 1 foot (ft) and 1 yard (yd) in length, too.

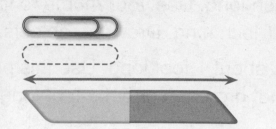

Do You Understand?

Show Me! Is your height closer to 4 feet or 4 yards? How do you know?

☆ Guided Practice ☆

Write the name and length of an object whose length you know. Then use that object to help you estimate the length of the object shown.

Object	Object Whose Length I Know	Estimate
1.	My paper clip is _1 inch_ long.	My pencil is about _____ long.
2.	My _book_ is _____ long.	My desk is about _____ long.

© Pearson Education, Inc. 2
Topic 12 | Lesson 1

Name _____

Independent Practice

Write the name and length of an object whose length you know.
Then use that object to help you estimate the length of the object shown.

Object	Object Whose Length I Know	Estimate
3.	My _____ is _____ long.	My hand is about _____ long.
4.	My _____ is _____ long.	My chair is about _____ high.

5. **Higher Order Thinking** Would you estimate the distance from your classroom to the principal's office in inches, feet or yards? Explain.

A giant step is about a yard.

_____

_____

_____

_____

6. **A-Z Vocabulary** Complete the sentence using one of the words below.

exact   estimated   inch

An _____ measurement is a good guess.

7. © **MP.2 Reasoning** Joy and Kyle estimate the height of their classroom. Joy estimates the height to be 10 feet. Kyle estimates the height to be 10 yards. Who has the better estimate? Explain.

_____

_____

_____

_____

8. **Higher Order Thinking** A city wants to build a bridge over a river. Should they plan out an exact length of the bridge or is an estimated length good enough? Explain.

_____

_____

_____

9. © **Assessment** Draw a line from each estimate to a matching object.

| About 1 inch | About 1 foot | About 3 feet |

Name _____

Another Look!

A small paper clip is about 1 inch long.

about 1 inch

A tablet computer is about 1 foot long. There are 12 inches in 1 foot.

about 1 foot

A scarf is about 1 yard long. There are 3 feet in 1 yard.

about 1 yard

HOME ACTIVITY Have your child identify three objects that are about 1 inch, 1 foot, and 1 yard in length or height.

About how long or tall is each object? Circle the answer.

1.
about 1 inch
about 1 foot
about 1 yard

2.
about 1 inch
about 1 foot
about 1 yard

3.
about 1 inch
about 1 foot
about 1 yard

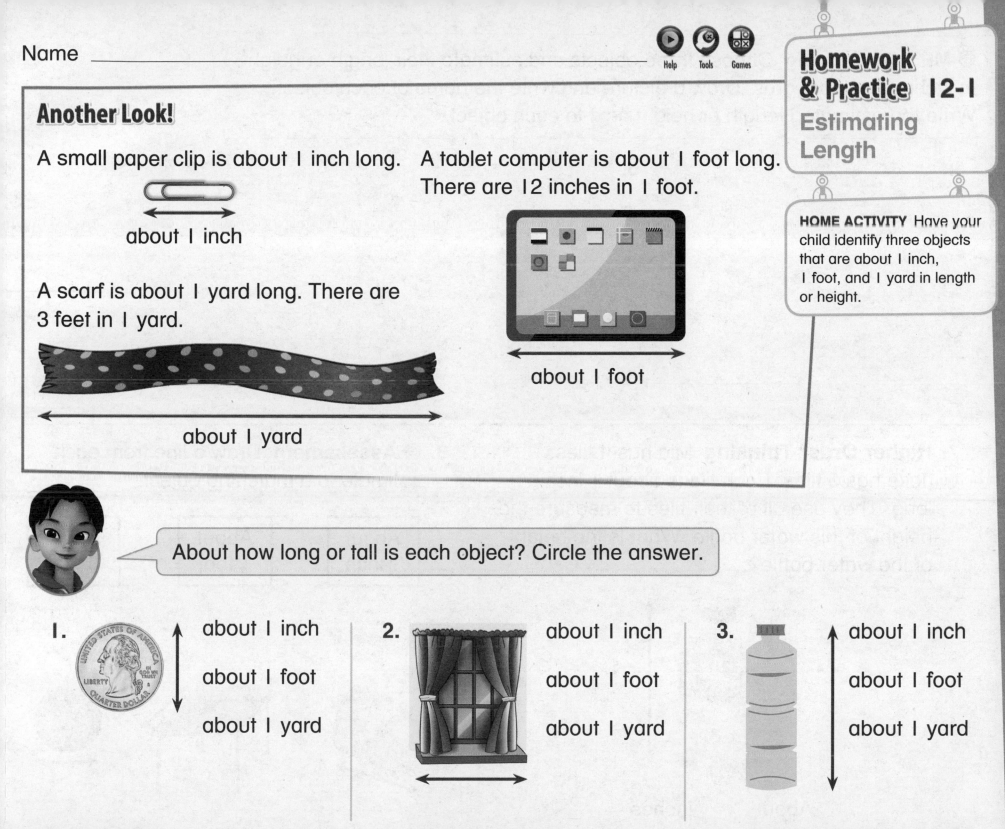

© MP.2 Reasoning Choose three objects and estimate their length or height in inches, feet, or yards. Draw a picture and write the name of each object. Write the estimated length or height next to each object.

4.

5.

6.

---

7. Higher Order Thinking Mia has 4 tiles. Jake has 5 tiles. Each tile is about 1 inch long. They use all of their tiles to measure the height of this water bottle. What is the height of the water bottle?

About _____ inches

8. © Assessment Draw a line from each estimate to a matching object.

About 1 inch	About 1 foot	About 3 feet

© Pearson Education, Inc. 2

Topic 12 | Lesson 1

Solve

Solve & Share

The orange square is 1 inch long. How can you use 1 inch squares to find the length of the line in inches? Measure the line and explain.

I can ...
estimate measures and use a ruler to measure length and height to the nearest inch.

© **Content Standards** 2.MD.A.3, 2.MD.A.1
Mathematical Practices MP.1, MP.3, MP.5, MP.6

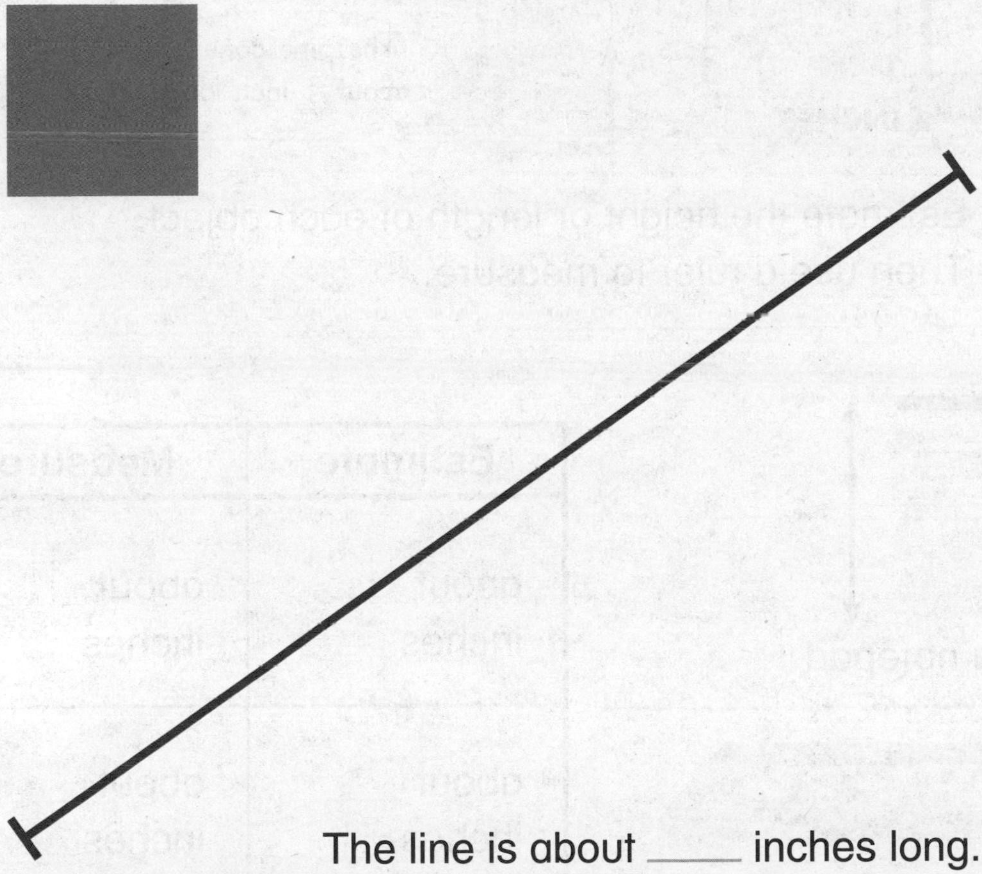

The line is about _____ inches long.

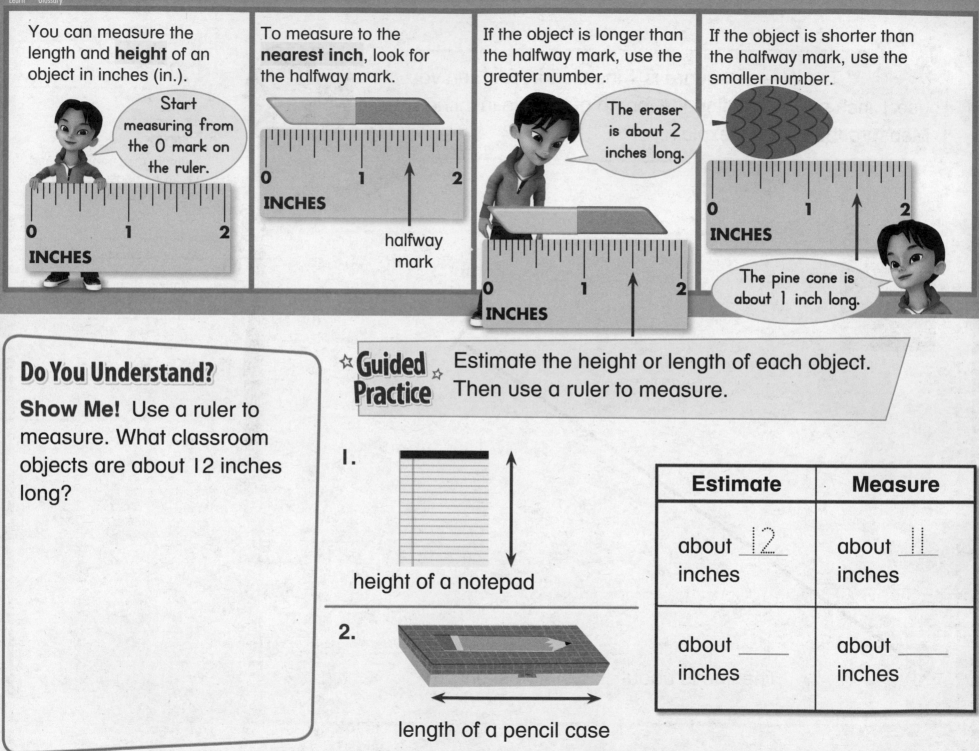

You can measure the length and **height** of an object in inches (in.).

Start measuring from the 0 mark on the ruler.

0 1 2
INCHES

To measure to the **nearest inch**, look for the halfway mark.

0 1 2
INCHES

halfway mark

If the object is longer than the halfway mark, use the greater number.

The eraser is about 2 inches long.

0 1 2
INCHES

If the object is shorter than the halfway mark, use the smaller number.

0 1 2
INCHES

The pine cone is about 1 inch long.

Do You Understand?

Show Me! Use a ruler to measure. What classroom objects are about 12 inches long?

☆ **Guided Practice** ☆ Estimate the height or length of each object. Then use a ruler to measure.

1. height of a notepad

2. length of a pencil case

Estimate	Measure
about 12 inches	about 11 inches
about ___ inches	about ___ inches

© Pearson Education, Inc. 2

Tools Assessment

Independent Practice

Estimate the height or length of each object.
Then use a ruler to measure.

3.

length of a
book bag

Estimate	Measure
about ____ inches	about ____ inches
about ____ inches	about ____ inches

5.

height of
a cup

Estimate	Measure
about ____ inches	about ____ inches
about ____ inches	about ____ inches

4.

length of a
paintbrush

6.

length of a
crayon box

Higher Order Thinking Think about how to use a ruler to solve each problem.

7. Jason measures an object. The object
is just shorter than the halfway mark
between 8 and 9 on his inch ruler.
How long is the object?

about _____ inches

8. Gina measures an object. The object
is just longer than the halfway mark
between 9 and 10 on her inch ruler.
How long is the object?

about _____ inches

9. © MP.3 Explain
Pam says that each cherry is about 1 inch wide. Is she correct? Explain.

_____

_____

10. A-Z Vocabulary Find an object in the classroom that measures about 6 inches. Write a sentence to describe the object. Use these words.

estimate   inches

_____

_____

_____

_____

11. Higher Order Thinking Explain how to use an inch ruler to measure the length of an object.

_____

_____

_____

_____

12. © Assessment Use a ruler. About how many inches long are the two stamps together?

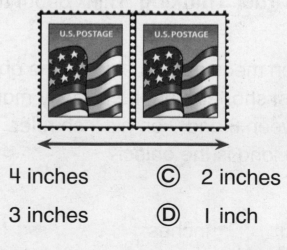

Ⓐ 4 inches   Ⓒ 2 inches

Ⓑ 3 inches   Ⓓ 1 inch

     Topic 12 | Lesson 2

Name _____

Another Look! You can use a ruler to measure inches.

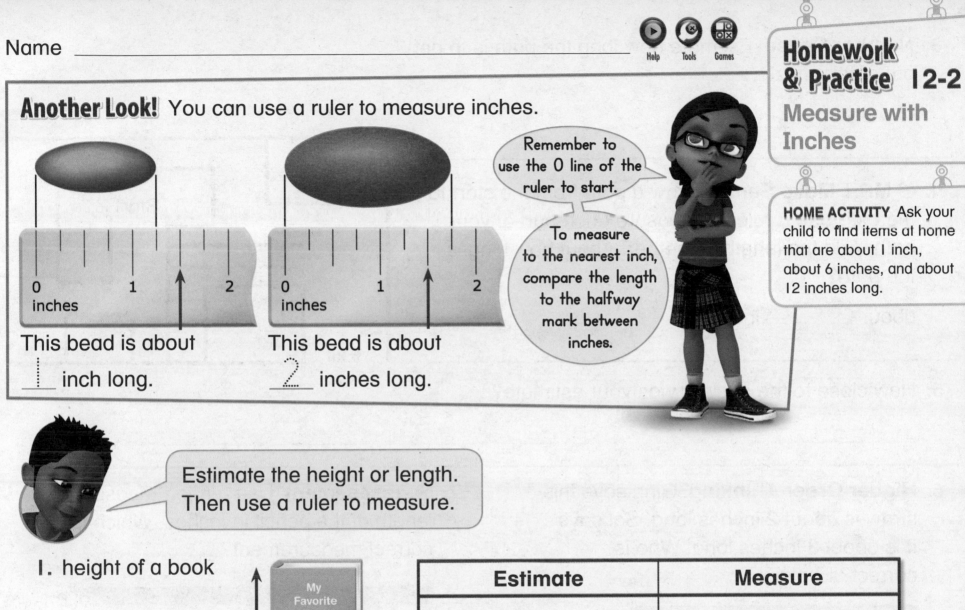

This bead is about
__1__ inch long.

This bead is about
__2__ inches long.

Remember to use the 0 line of the ruler to start.

To measure to the nearest inch, compare the length to the halfway mark between inches.

HOME ACTIVITY Ask your child to find items at home that are about 1 inch, about 6 inches, and about 12 inches long.

Estimate the height or length. Then use a ruler to measure.

1. height of a book

My Favorite Book

2. length of a pencil

Estimate	Measure
about ___ inches	about ___ inches
about ___ inches	about ___ inches

3. **Number Sense** Estimate how long the path is to get out of this maze.

about _____ inches

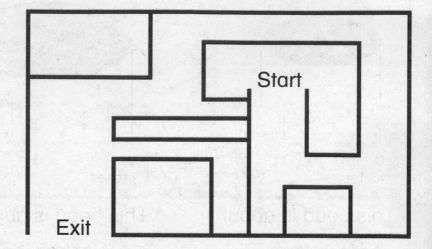

4. **© MP.I Make Sense** Draw a path from the start to the exit. Use a ruler to measure each part of your path. Add the lengths together. About how long is the path?

about _____ inches

5. How close to the answer was your estimate?

_____

6. **Higher Order Thinking** Gina says this straw is about 2 inches long. Sal says it is about 3 inches long. Who is correct? Explain.

_____

_____

_____

7. **© Assessment** Use a ruler. Measure the length of the pencil in inches. Which is the correct measurement?

Ⓐ about 2 inches

Ⓑ about 3 inches

Ⓒ about 4 inches

Ⓓ about 5 inches

© Pearson Education, Inc. 2

Name _____

Solve & Share

Which objects in the classroom are about I inch, about I foot, and about I yard long? Show these objects below.

I can ...
estimate measures and use tools to measure the length and height of objects to the nearest inch, foot, and yard.

© **Content Standards** 2.MD.A.1, 2.MD.A.3
Mathematical Practices MP.2, MP.5, MP.6, MP.8

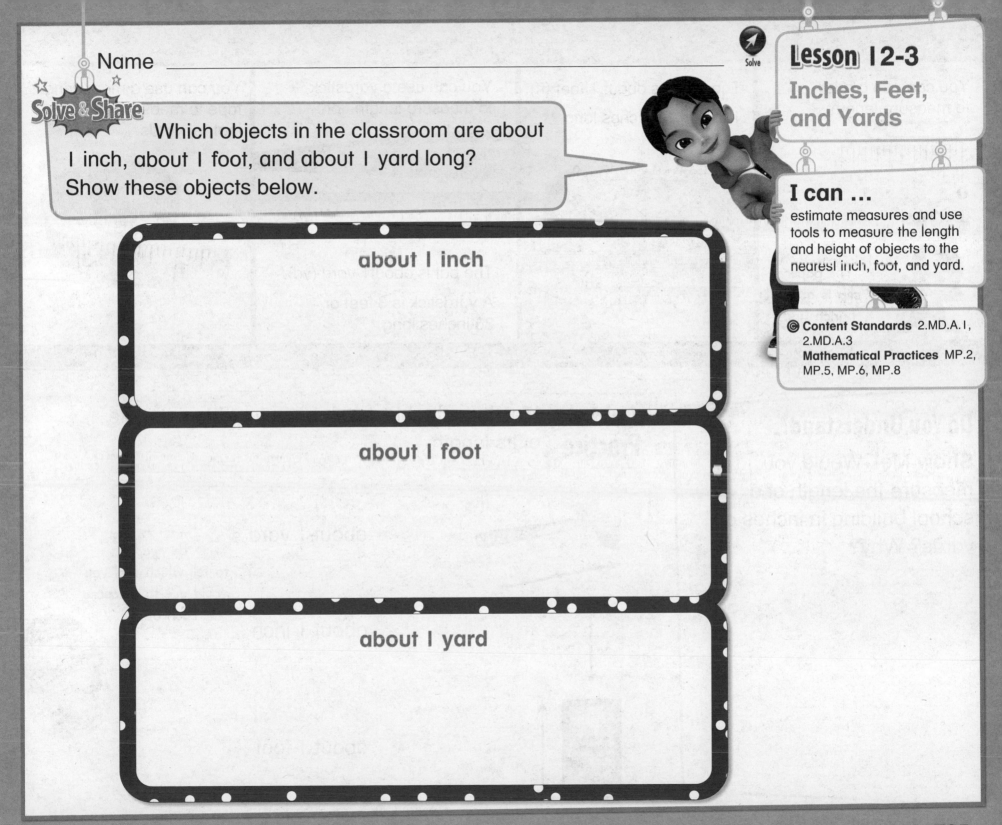

about I inch

about I foot

about I yard

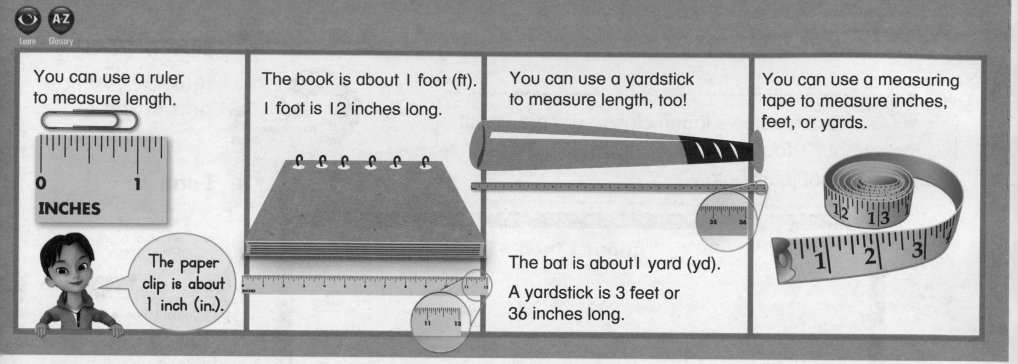

You can use a ruler to measure length.

INCHES
0   1

The paper clip is about 1 inch (in.).

The book is about 1 foot (ft).

1 foot is 12 inches long.

You can use a yardstick to measure length, too!

The bat is about 1 yard (yd).

A yardstick is 3 feet or 36 inches long.

You can use a measuring tape to measure inches, feet, or yards.

Do You Understand?

Show Me! Would you measure the length of a school building in inches or yards? Why?

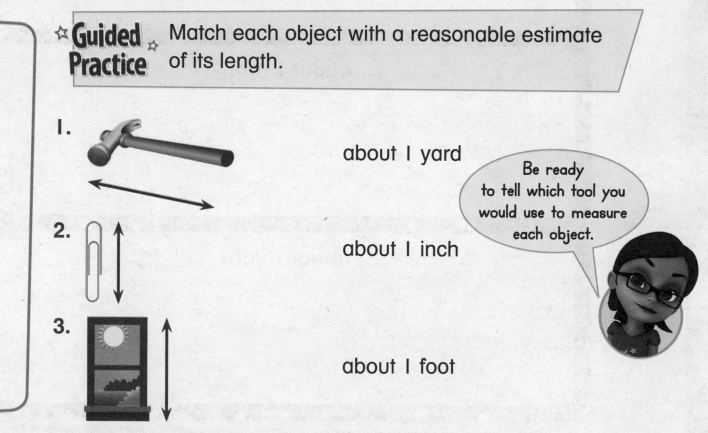

☆ **Guided Practice** ☆ Match each object with a reasonable estimate of its length.

1.

about 1 yard

Be ready to tell which tool you would use to measure each object.

2.

about 1 inch

3.

about 1 foot

Topic 12 | Lesson 3

Tools Assessment

Independent Practice Estimate the length of each object. Choose a ruler, yardstick, or measuring tape to measure. Write the tool you used.

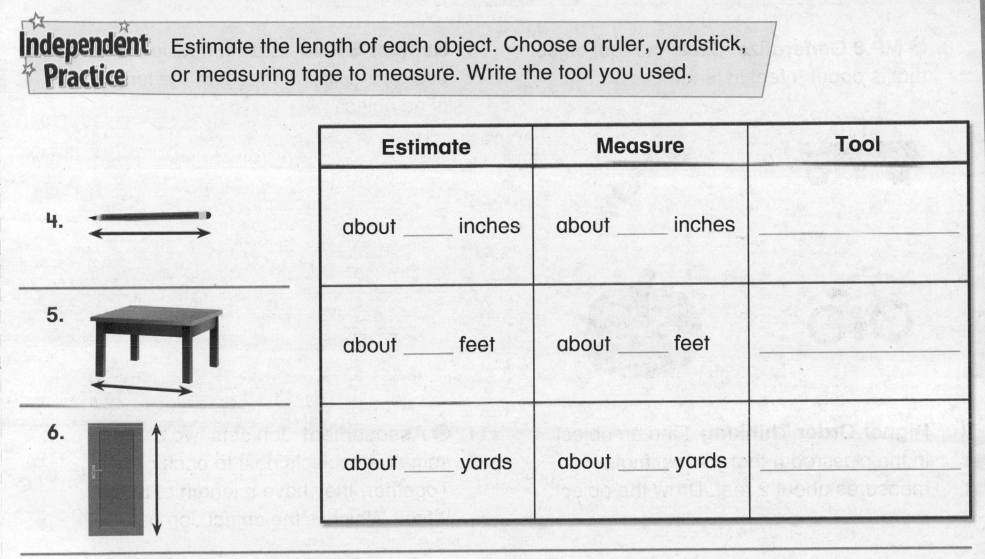

	Estimate	Measure	Tool
4.	about ____ inches	about ____ inches	_____
5.	about ____ feet	about ____ feet	_____
6.	about ____ yards	about ____ yards	_____

7. **Higher Order Thinking** Explain how you could use a foot ruler to measure the length of a room in feet.

_____

_____

_____

_____

8. © MP.8 Generalize Circle the real object that is about 4 feet in length.

9. Number Sense Explain how to use a yardstick to measure the length of an object.

_____

_____

_____

_____

_____

_____

10. Higher Order Thinking Find an object in the classroom that you estimate measures about 2 feet. Draw the object.

What tool would you use to measure it? Explain why you chose the tool you did.

_____

11. © Assessment Jon sets two of the same real objects next to each other. Together, they have a length of about 4 feet. Which is the object Jon uses?

Ⓐ   Ⓒ

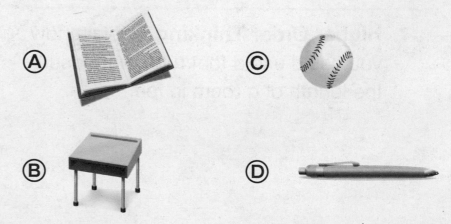

Ⓑ   Ⓓ

Name _____

Another Look! You can use a yardstick to measure objects to the nearest foot.

Remember, I foot is 12 inches long.
So 2 feet are 24 inches long.
I yard is 36 inches long
or 3 feet long.

Think: Is the string closer to 2 feet long or closer to 3 feet long?

HOME ACTIVITY Have your child identify three objects at home that are about I inch, I foot, and I yard in length.

0	12	24	36

This string is about
_2_ feet long.

0	12	24	36

This string is about
_3_ feet long.

Estimate the height or length of each object.
Then measure.

I. the height of the doorway

Estimate: about _____ feet

Measure: about _____ feet

2. the height of a chair

Estimate: about _____ feet

Measure: about _____ feet

3. the width of a window

Estimate: about _____ feet

Measure: about _____ feet

4. © MP.2 Reasoning Draw a picture of and name objects that have these lengths.

more than 6 inches but less than 1 foot

more than 1 foot but less than 2 feet

more than 2 feet but less than 1 yard

5. Math and Science Jay planted sunflowers in a sunny spot. He gave them water and watched them grow to be taller than he is. He measured the heights of the plants when they were full-grown. Were they 8 inches or 8 feet tall? Explain.

_____

_____

_____

_____

6. Higher Order Thinking Which tool would you choose to measure the number of inches around your waist? Explain.

_____

_____

_____

7. © Assessment Use a ruler. About how long is the crayon?

Ⓐ about 1 inch

Ⓑ about 2 inches

Ⓒ about 4 inches

Ⓓ about 6 inches

Name _____

Solve & Share

Choose an object. Measure your object in feet. Then measure it in inches.

Do you need more feet or more inches to measure your object? Why?

I can ...
estimate and measure the length and height of objects in inches, feet, and yards.

© **Content Standards** 2.MD.A.2, 2.MD.A.1
Mathematical Practices MP.2, MP.3, MP.5, MP.6, MP.8

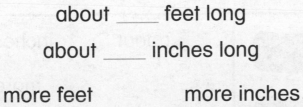

about ____ feet long

about ____ inches long

more feet   more inches

Do You Understand?

Show Me! Would you use a ruler, a yardstick, or measuring tape to measure the height of a door? Why?

☆ **Guided Practice** ☆ Measure each object using different units. Circle the unit you use more of to measure each object.

1. about _____ feet   about _____ yards

more feet

more yards

2. about _____ inches   about _____ feet

more inches

more feet

Tools Assessment

Independent Practice

Measure each object using different units.
Circle the unit you use fewer of to measure each object.

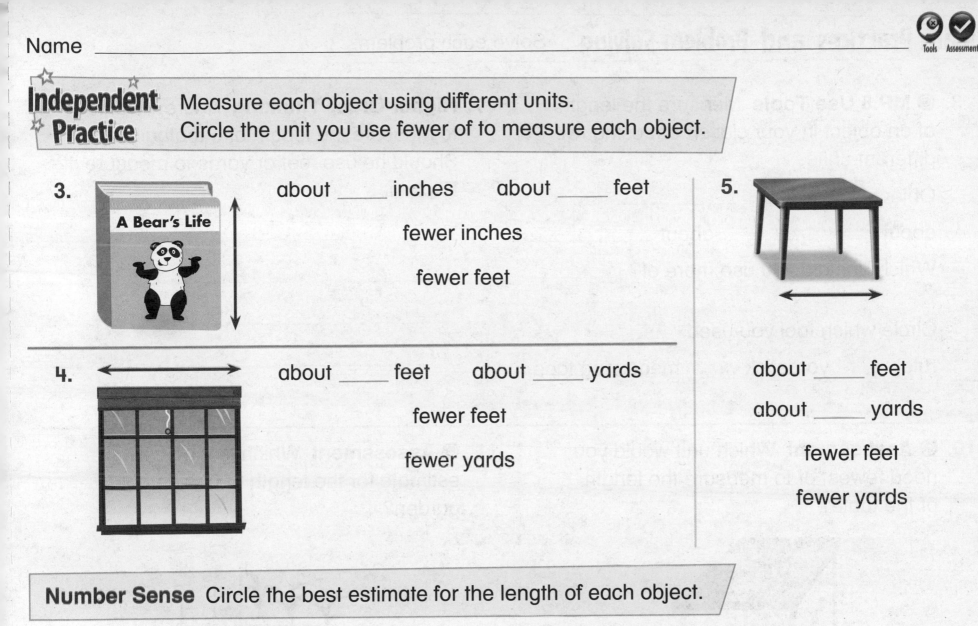

3. A Bear's Life

about ____ inches   about ____ feet

fewer inches

fewer feet

5.

about ____ feet

about ____ yards

fewer feet

fewer yards

4.

about ____ feet   about ____ yards

fewer feet

fewer yards

Number Sense Circle the best estimate for the length of each object.

6. About how long is a key?

2 inches   2 feet   2 yards

Which tool would you use to measure the length of a key?

_____

7. About how long is a suitcase?

2 inches   2 feet   2 yards

Which tool would you use to measure the length of a suitcase?

_____

8. © **MP.5 Use Tools** Measure the length of an object in your classroom using two different units.

Object: _____

about _____   about _____

Which unit did you use more of? _____

Circle which tool you used.

ruler   yardstick   measuring tape

9. **Higher Order Thinking** Andrew wants to measure the length of a football field. Should he use feet or yards to measure it? Explain.

_____

_____

_____

_____

10. © **Assessment** Which unit would you need fewest of to measure the length of the table?

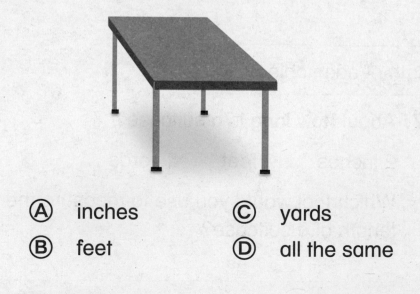

Ⓐ   inches   Ⓒ   yards

Ⓑ   feet   Ⓓ   all the same

11. © **Assessment** Which is the best estimate for the length of a vegetable garden?

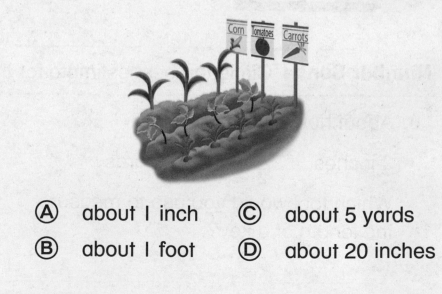

Ⓐ   about 1 inch   Ⓒ   about 5 yards

Ⓑ   about 1 foot   Ⓓ   about 20 inches

Name _____

Help Tools Games

Homework
& Practice 12-4
Measure Length
Using Different
Customary Units

Another Look! You can measure using different units.

Derrick measured the gift box in inches and in feet.

The gift box is about

⎪⎪ inches long.

The gift box is about

⎪ foot long.

It takes more inches than feet to measure the gift box
because an inch is a smaller unit.

If you use smaller units, you need to use more units.

HOME ACTIVITY Have
your child use a foot ruler
to measure objects in both
inches and in feet. Then ask
your child if he or she used
more inches or more feet to
measure each object.

Measure each object using different units.
Circle the unit you need more of to measure each object.

1.   about _____ feet   about _____ yards

                 more feet

                 more yards

2.   about _____ inches   about _____ feet

                 more inches

                 more feet

3. **© MP.3 Explain** Trina says that her dollhouse is about 8 yards tall. Is Trina's estimate a good estimate? Explain.

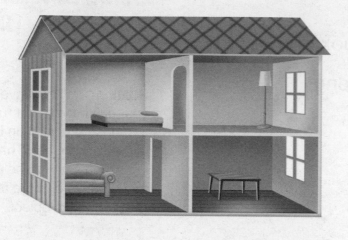

_____

_____

_____

4. **Higher Order Thinking** Sarah wants to measure the length of her math book. Should she use inches, feet, or yards? Explain.

_____

_____

_____

5. **© Assessment** Which unit would you need the most of to measure the height of the umbrella?

Ⓐ inches

Ⓑ feet

Ⓒ yards

Ⓓ all the same

6. **© Assessment** Which is the best estimate for the length of a pen?

Ⓐ about 10 inches

Ⓑ about 6 inches

Ⓒ about 5 feet

Ⓓ about 10 yards

© Pearson Education, Inc. 2

Name _____

Solve & Share

The green cube is 1 centimeter long. How can you use 1 centimeter cubes to find the length of the line in centimeters? Measure the lino and explain.

I can ...
estimate measures and use a ruler to measure length and height to the nearest centimeter.

Ⓒ **Content Standards** 2.MD.A.3, 2.MD.A.1
Mathematical Practices MP.2, MP.3, MP.5, MP.6, MP.7

The line is _____ centimeters long.

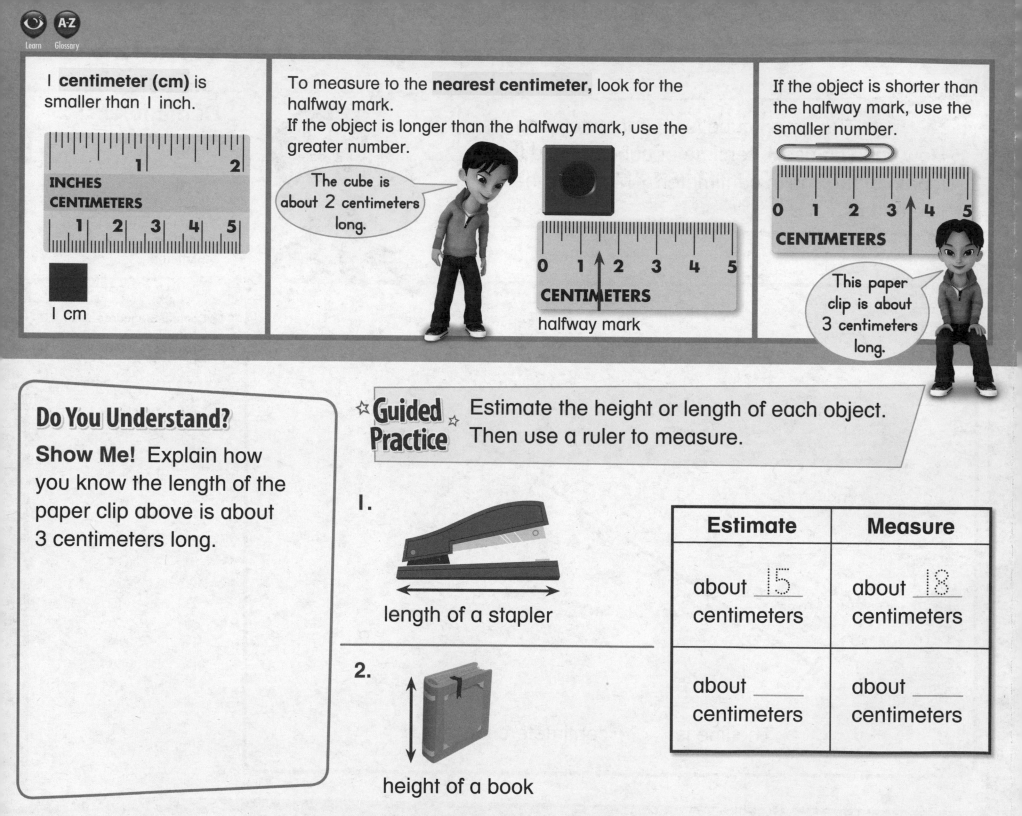

Learn A-Z Glossary

1 **centimeter (cm)** is smaller than 1 inch.

INCHES
CENTIMETERS

1 cm

To measure to the **nearest centimeter,** look for the halfway mark.
If the object is longer than the halfway mark, use the greater number.

The cube is about 2 centimeters long.

CENTIMETERS

halfway mark

If the object is shorter than the halfway mark, use the smaller number.

CENTIMETERS

This paper clip is about 3 centimeters long.

Do You Understand?

Show Me! Explain how you know the length of the paper clip above is about 3 centimeters long.

☆Guided☆ Practice

Estimate the height or length of each object. Then use a ruler to measure.

1.

length of a stapler

2.

height of a book

Estimate	Measure
about 15 centimeters	about 18 centimeters
about ___ centimeters	about ___ centimeters

© Pearson Education, Inc. 2

Independent Practice   Estimate the width, height, or length of each real object. Then use a ruler to measure.

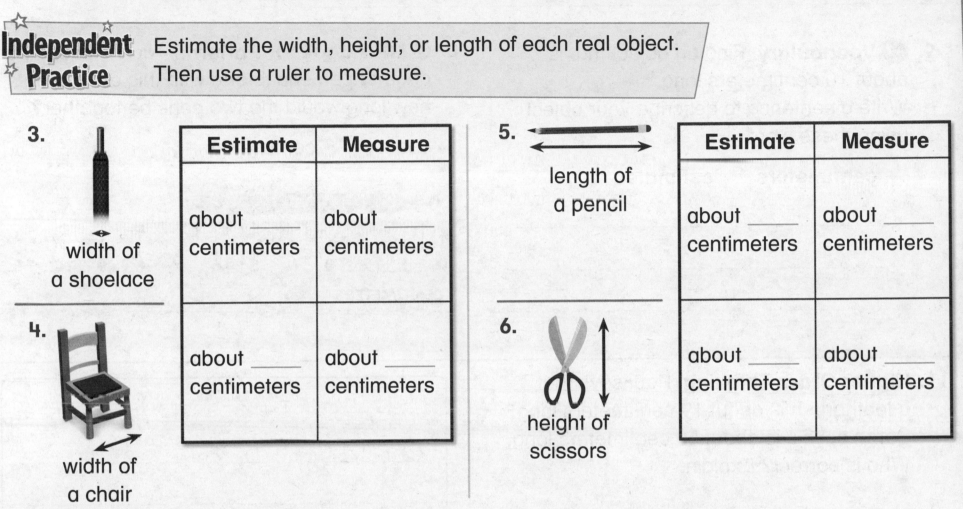

3.

width of a shoelace

Estimate	Measure
about _____ centimeters	about _____ centimeters
about _____ centimeters	about _____ centimeters

4.

width of a chair

5.

length of a pencil

Estimate	Measure
about _____ centimeters	about _____ centimeters
about _____ centimeters	about _____ centimeters

6.

height of scissors

Higher Order Thinking Explain whether each estimate is reasonable or not.

7. Josh estimated that the length of his reading book is about 6 centimeters.

_____

_____

8. Shae estimated that the height of her desk is about 10 centimeters.

_____

_____

9. **A-Z Vocabulary** Find an object that is about 10 centimeters long.
Write a sentence to describe your object using these words.

centimeters   **estimate**

_____

_____

10. © **MP.7 Look for Patterns** Nick wants to put another pen end to end with this one. About how long would the two pens be together?

about _____ centimeters

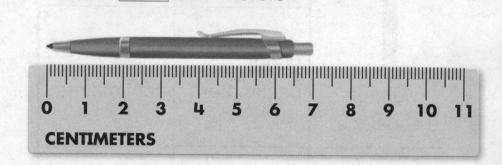

11. **Higher Order Thinking** Paul says that a toothbrush is about 19 centimeters long. Sarah says it is about 50 centimeters long. Who is correct? Explain.

_____

_____

_____

12. © **Assessment** Mary measures the length of her eraser to the nearest centimeter. What is the length of her eraser to the nearest centimeter?

_____ centimeters

© Pearson Education, Inc. 2

Topic 12 | Lesson 5

Name _____

Another Look! You can use a ruler to measure centimeters.

To measure to the nearest centimeter, look at the halfway mark between centimeters. If the object is longer, use the greater number. If the object is shorter, use the smaller number.

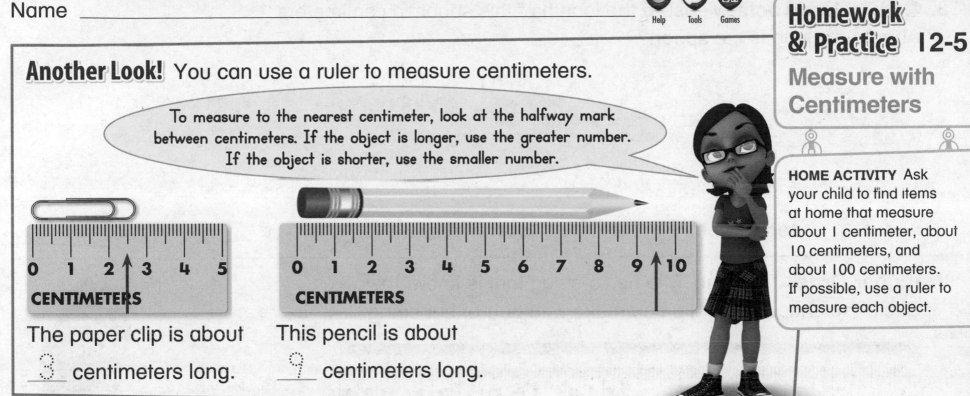

CENTIMETERS

CENTIMETERS

The paper clip is about _3_ centimeters long.

This pencil is about _9_ centimeters long.

HOME ACTIVITY Ask your child to find items at home that measure about 1 centimeter, about 10 centimeters, and about 100 centimeters. If possible, use a ruler to measure each object.

Estimate the height or length. Then use a ruler to measure.

1. length of a tape dispenser

2. height of a book

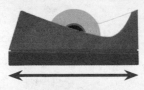

Estimate	Measure
about ____ centimeters	about ____ centimeters
about ____ centimeters	about ____ centimeters

Topic 12 | Lesson 5

Digital Resources at PearsonRealize.com

seven hundred twenty-one **721**

3. © **MP.5 Use Tools** Measure the length of this spoon in centimeters. About how long is the spoon?

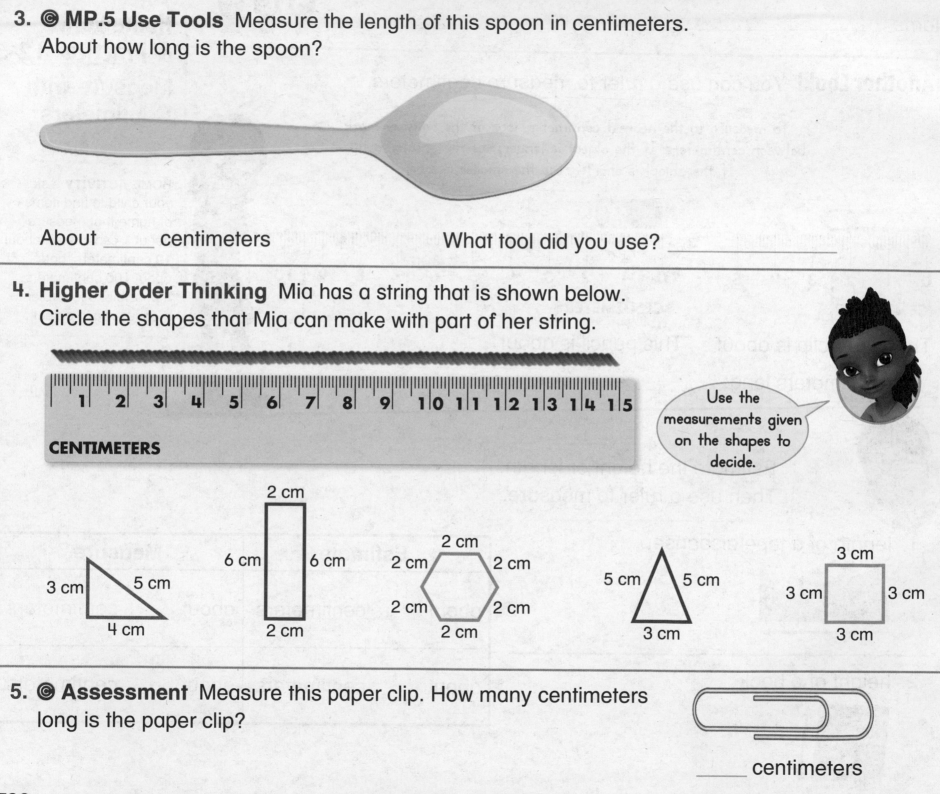

About _____ centimeters   What tool did you use? _____

4. **Higher Order Thinking** Mia has a string that is shown below. Circle the shapes that Mia can make with part of her string.

Use the measurements given on the shapes to decide.

CENTIMETERS
1 2 3 4 5 6 7 8 9 10 11 12 13 14 15

3 cm 5 cm
4 cm

2 cm
6 cm 6 cm
2 cm

2 cm
2 cm 2 cm
2 cm 2 cm
2 cm

5 cm 5 cm
3 cm

3 cm
3 cm 3 cm
3 cm

5. © **Assessment** Measure this paper clip. How many centimeters long is the paper clip?

_____ centimeters

© Pearson Education, Inc. 2   **Topic 12** | Lesson 5

Name _____

Solve & Share

Which objects in the classroom are about 3 centimeters long?
Which objects are about 1 meter long?
Show these objects below.

I can ...
estimate measures and use a ruler, meter stick, or tape measure to measure length and height to the nearest centimeter or meter.

© **Content Standards** 2.MD.A.1, 2.MD.A.3
Mathematical Practices MP.2, MP.3, MP.5, MP.6, MP.8

about 3 centimeters

about 1 meter

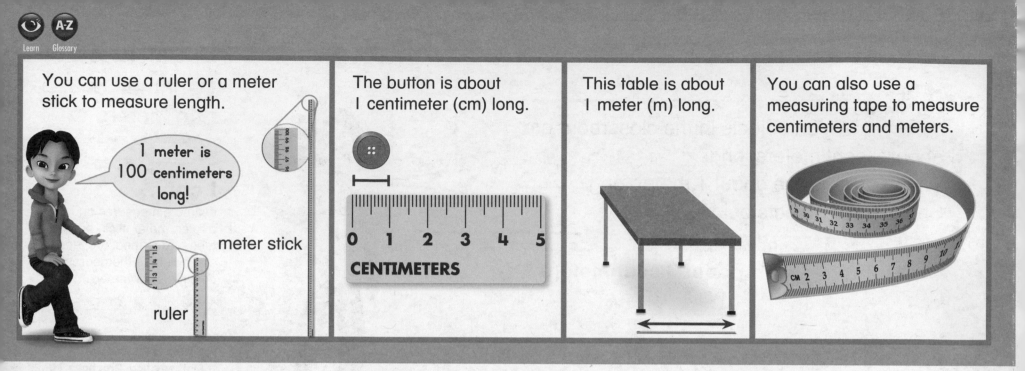

You can use a ruler or a meter stick to measure length.

1 meter is 100 centimeters long!

meter stick

ruler

The button is about 1 centimeter (cm) long.

0 1 2 3 4 5

CENTIMETERS

This table is about 1 meter (m) long.

You can also use a measuring tape to measure centimeters and meters.

Do You Understand?

Show Me! Would you measure the length of a house in centimeters or meters? Why?

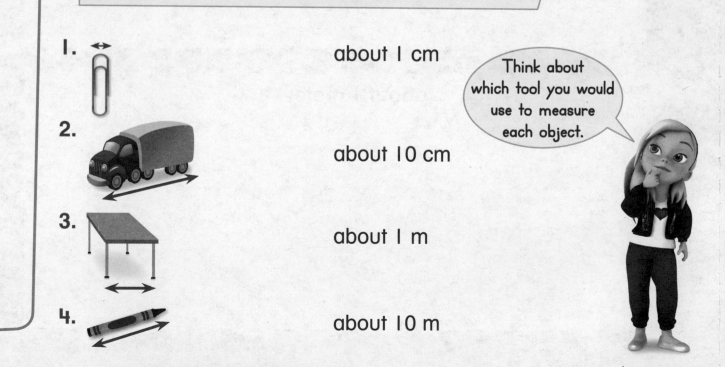

☆ **Guided Practice** ☆ Match each object with a reasonable estimate of its length.

1.   about 1 cm

2.   about 10 cm

3.   about 1 m

4.   about 10 m

Think about which tool you would use to measure each object.

Independent Practice

Estimate the length or height of each real object shown.
Then choose a tool and measure. Write the tool you used.

	Estimate	Measure	Tool
5.	about _____ cm	about _____ cm	_____
6.	about _____ m	about _____ m	_____
7.	about _____ cm	about _____ cm	_____
8.	about _____ m	about _____ m	_____

9. Tom uses a meter stick to measure the length of a fence. He moves the meter stick 5 times to measure from one end to the other end. How long is the fence?

_____ meters

10. **Higher Order Thinking** Debbie says that her doll is about 30 meters long. Do you think this is a good estimate? Why or why not?

_____

_____

11. © **MP.6 Be Precise** Choose an object to measure. Use metric units. Draw the object and write your measurements.

Remember to include the units.

12. Circle the real object that would be about 2 meters long.

13. **Higher Order Thinking** Each side of a place-value cube is 1 centimeter long. Use a place value cube to draw a 5 centimeter ruler.

14. © **Assessment** Measure each line. Which lines are at least 6 centimeters long? Choose all that apply.

Name _____

Another Look! You can use a meter stick to measure length in meters.

Step 1: Line up a meter stick with one end of an object.

Step 2: Mark the spot where the other end of the meter stick sits on the object.

Step 3: Then move the meter stick so the 0 end starts where you marked.

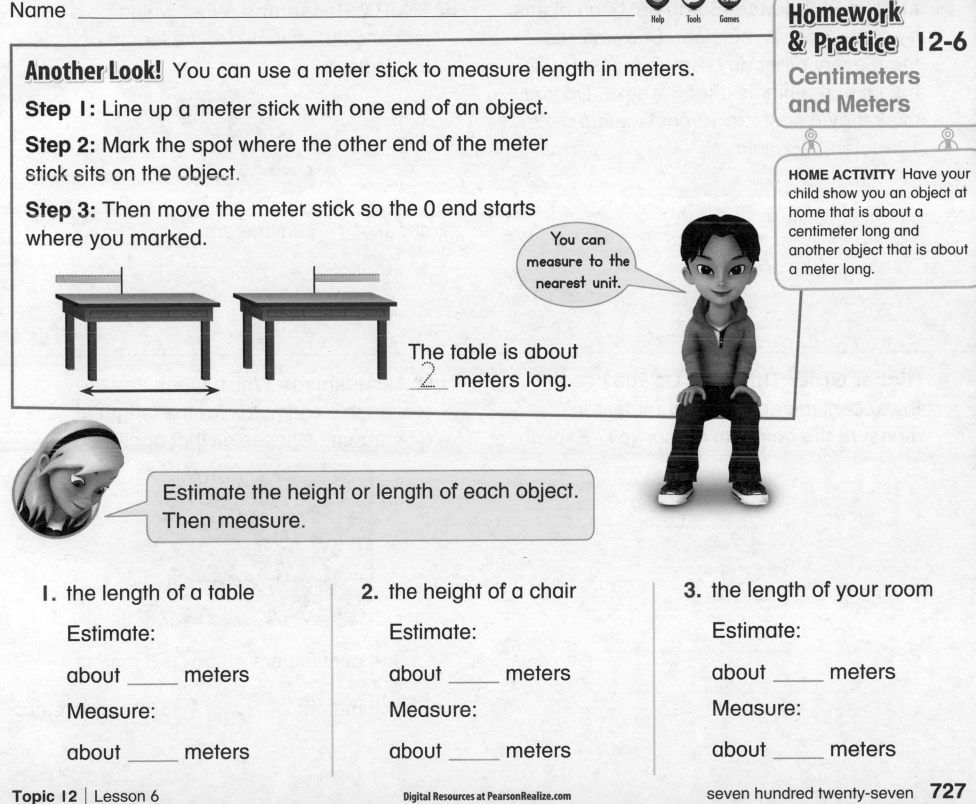

You can measure to the nearest unit.

The table is about ___2___ meters long.

HOME ACTIVITY Have your child show you an object at home that is about a centimeter long and another object that is about a meter long.

Estimate the height or length of each object. Then measure.

1. the length of a table

Estimate:

about _____ meters

Measure:

about _____ meters

2. the height of a chair

Estimate:

about _____ meters

Measure:

about _____ meters

3. the length of your room

Estimate:

about _____ meters

Measure:

about _____ meters

Digital Resources at PearsonRealize.com

4. Math and Science Sarah put bean plants by a window with sunlight. She watered them every other day. Sarah measured the height of the plants after 3 weeks. Do you think they measured 12 centimeters or 12 meters? Explain.

_____

_____

_____

5. © MP.2 Reasoning What would be a reasonable estimate for the length of a calculator?

about _____ centimeters

6. Higher Order Thinking Do you need fewer centimeters or fewer meters to measure the height of a doorway? Explain.

_____

_____

_____

_____

7. © Assessment Which measures are reasonable estimates for the length of a bedroom? Choose all that apply.

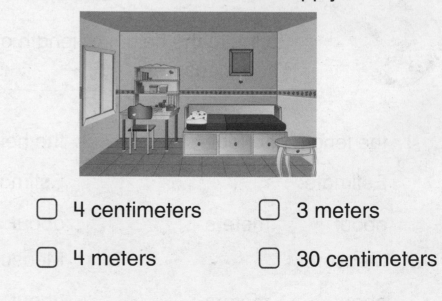

◻ 4 centimeters   ◻ 3 meters

◻ 4 meters   ◻ 30 centimeters

© Pearson Education, Inc. 2

Solve & Share

Measure this pencil in inches. Then measure it again in centimeters. Which measurement has more units?

Lesson 12-7

Measure Length Using Different Metric Units

I can ...
measure the length and height of objects using different metric units.

© **Content Standards** 2.MD.A.2, 2.MD.A.1
Mathematical Practices MP.1, MP.2, MP.3, MP.5, MP.6

about _____ inches   about _____ centimeters

Which has more units? _____

You can use different units to measure the lengths of objects. Would you use more centimeters or more meters to measure the desk?

Measure the length using centimeters.

It is about 91 centimeters long!

89 90 91 92 93

Measure the length using meters.

It is about 1 meter long!

I used more centimeters than meters because a centimeter is a much smaller unit than a meter.

Do You Understand?

Show Me! Would it take more centimeters or more meters to measure the height of a wall? Why?

☆ **Guided Practice** ☆   Measure each object using different units. Circle the unit you need more of to measure each object.

1.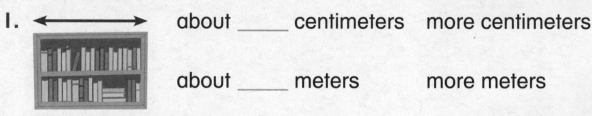

about _____ centimeters   more centimeters

about _____ meters   more meters

2.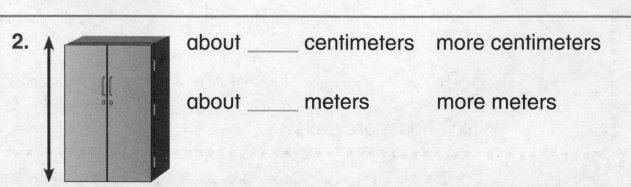

about _____ centimeters   more centimeters

about _____ meters   more meters

Independent Practice Measure each object using different units.
Circle the unit you need fewer of to measure each object.

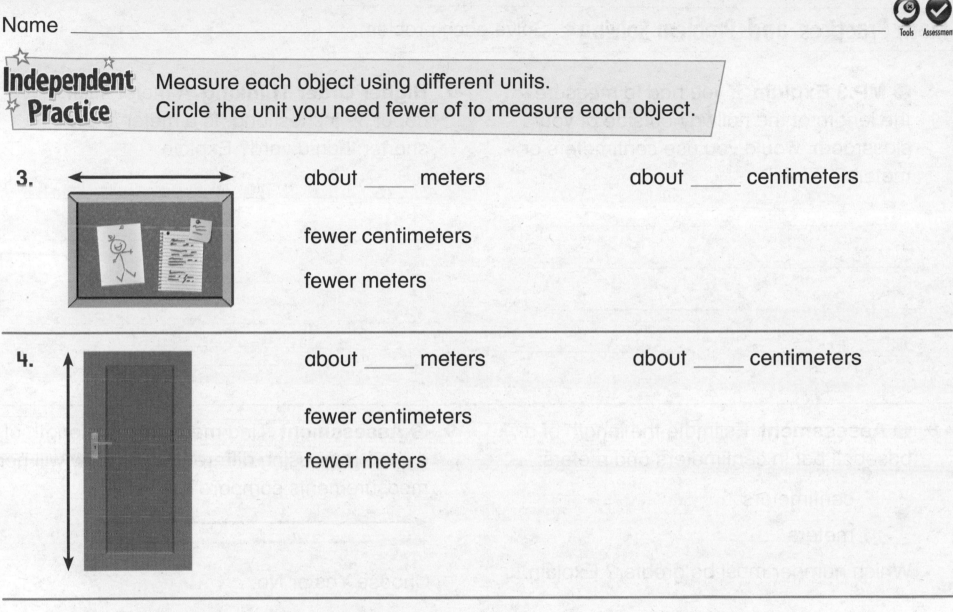

3.

about _____ meters   about _____ centimeters

fewer centimeters

fewer meters

4.

about _____ meters   about _____ centimeters

fewer centimeters

fewer meters

5. **Higher Order Thinking** Jay measured the height of his bedroom in both centimeters and meters. Did he use fewer centimeters or fewer meters? Explain.

_____

_____

_____

_____

6. © **MP.3 Explain** If you had to measure the length of the hallway outside of your classroom, would you use centimeters or meters? Explain.

_____

_____

_____

7. **Higher Order Thinking** A meter stick is about 39 inches long. Is a meter longer or shorter than a yard? Explain.

_____

_____

_____

_____

8. © **Assessment** Estimate the length of a baseball bat in centimeters and meters.

_____ centimeters

_____ meters

Which number must be greater? Explain.

_____

_____

_____

_____

9. © **Assessment** Tina measures the length of a jump rope using different units. How will her measurements compare?

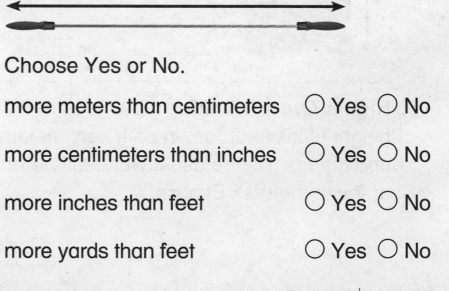

Choose Yes or No.

more meters than centimeters ⚪ Yes ⚪ No

more centimeters than inches ⚪ Yes ⚪ No

more inches than feet ⚪ Yes ⚪ No

more yards than feet ⚪ Yes ⚪ No

Name _____

Help   Tools   Games

Homework
& Practice 12-7
Measure Length
Using Different
Metric Units

Another Look! You can measure using different units.

Andy measures the length of the television using both centimeters and meters.

The television is about

_1_ meter long.

The television is about

_88_ centimeters long.

It takes fewer meters than centimeters to measure the television.
If you use larger units, you will use fewer of them.

HOME ACTIVITY Select two objects in your home, such as a table or a window. Ask your child if he or she would use more centimeters or meters to measure each object.

Measure each object using centimeters and meters.
Circle the unit you need fewer of to measure each object.

1.

about _____ centimeters   fewer centimeters

about _____ meters   fewer meters

2.

about _____ centimeters   fewer centimeters

about _____ meters   fewer meters

3. **© MP.1 Make Sense** Circle the objects that are easier to measure using centimeters. Cross out the objects that are easier to measure using meters.

4. **Higher Order Thinking** Shane and Karen want to measure the length of a soccer field.

   Should they use centimeters or meters to measure it? Explain.

   _____

   _____

   _____

Think about the size of one unit.

5. **© Assessment** Carlos measures the length of a couch in centimeters and meters. How will his measurements compare?

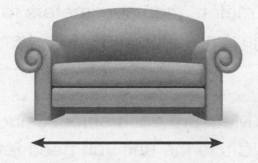

Choose Yes or No.

more centimeters than meters ○ Yes ○ No

fewer centimeters than meters ○ Yes ○ No

fewer meters than centimeters ○ Yes ○ No

the same number of centimeters and meters ○ Yes ○ No

Name _____

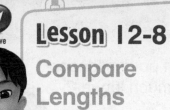

Solve & Share

Circle two paths. Estimate which one is longer. How can you check if your estimate is correct?

I can ...
tell how much longer one object is than another.

© **Content Standards** 2.MD.A.4, 2.MD.B.5
Mathematical Practices MP.2, MP.3, MP.4, MP.5, MP.6

Estimate: The _____ path is longer.

Measure: The _____ path is longer.

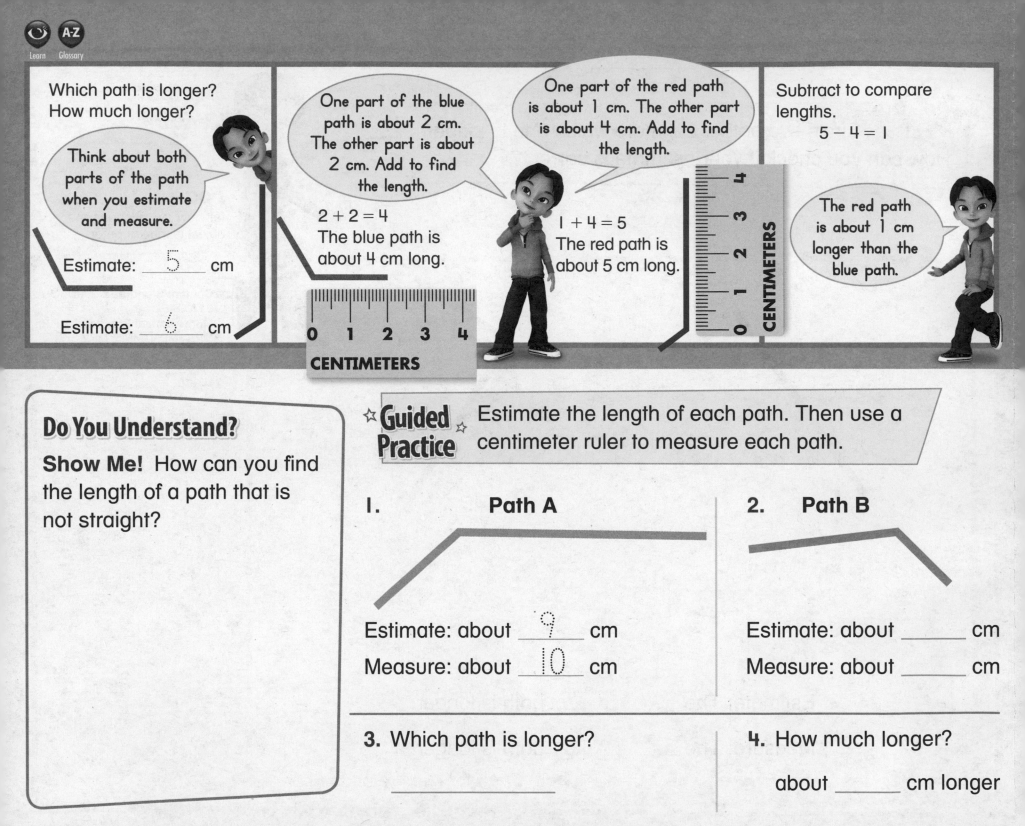

Which path is longer?
How much longer?

Think about both parts of the path when you estimate and measure.

Estimate: ___5___ cm

Estimate: ___6___ cm

One part of the blue path is about 2 cm. The other part is about 2 cm. Add to find the length.

$2 + 2 = 4$
The blue path is about 4 cm long.

CENTIMETERS
0 1 2 3 4

One part of the red path is about 1 cm. The other part is about 4 cm. Add to find the length.

$1 + 4 = 5$
The red path is about 5 cm long.

CENTIMETERS

Subtract to compare lengths.
$5 - 4 = 1$

The red path is about 1 cm longer than the blue path.

Do You Understand?

Show Me! How can you find the length of a path that is not straight?

☆ **Guided Practice** ☆ Estimate the length of each path. Then use a centimeter ruler to measure each path.

1.   **Path A**

Estimate: about ___9___ cm

Measure: about ___10___ cm

2.   **Path B**

Estimate: about _____ cm

Measure: about _____ cm

3. Which path is longer?

_____

4. How much longer?

about _____ cm longer

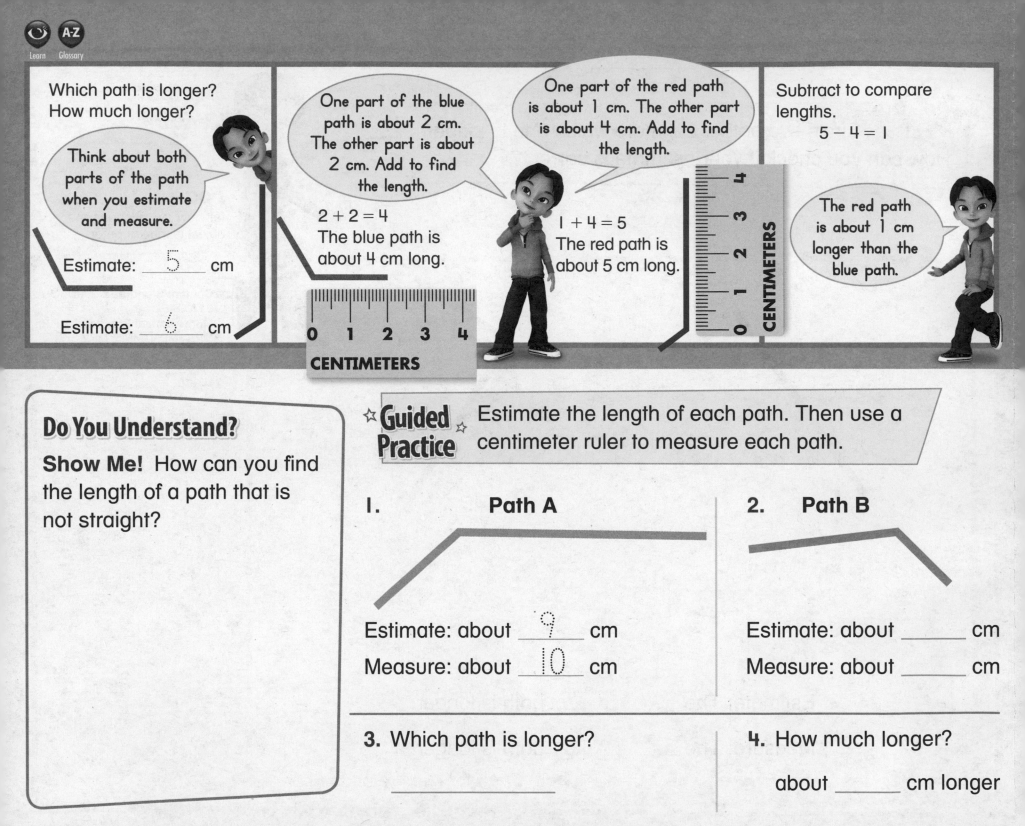

© Pearson Education, Inc. 2

Name _____

Independent Practice

Estimate the length of each path.
Then use a centimeter ruler to measure each path.

5.

Path C

Estimate: about _____ centimeters

Measure: about _____ centimeters

6.

Path D

Estimate: about _____ centimeters

Measure: about _____ centimeters

7. Which path is longer?

_____

8. How much longer?

about _____ centimeters longer

Higher Order Thinking   Think about the length of each object.
Circle the best estimate of its length.

9. a key

about 1 cm   about 6 cm   about 20 cm

Think about objects that are about 1 cm long to help.

10. a pen

about 2 cm   about 4 cm   about 15 cm

Use your estimates to complete:

A pen is about _____ cm longer

than a _____.

11. © **MP.3 Explain** A path has two parts. The total length of the path is 12 cm. If one part is 8 cm, how long is the other part? Explain.

_____ centimeters

12. **Higher Order Thinking** Draw a path with two parts. Measure the length to the nearest centimeter. Write an equation to show the length of your path.

13. **Higher Order Thinking** Beth drew a picture of a bike path. Use tools. Measure the length of the path below. Write the total length.

Beth's Path

about _____ centimeters

14. © **Assessment** Peter measures a path that has a total length of 12 cm. Janna measures a path that has two parts. Each part measures 7 cm.

How much longer is Janna's path than Peter's path? Show your work.

_____

_____

_____

© Pearson Education, Inc. 2

Name _____

Another Look! You can write an equation
to help you find the total length of a path.
What is the total length of Path A?

Path A

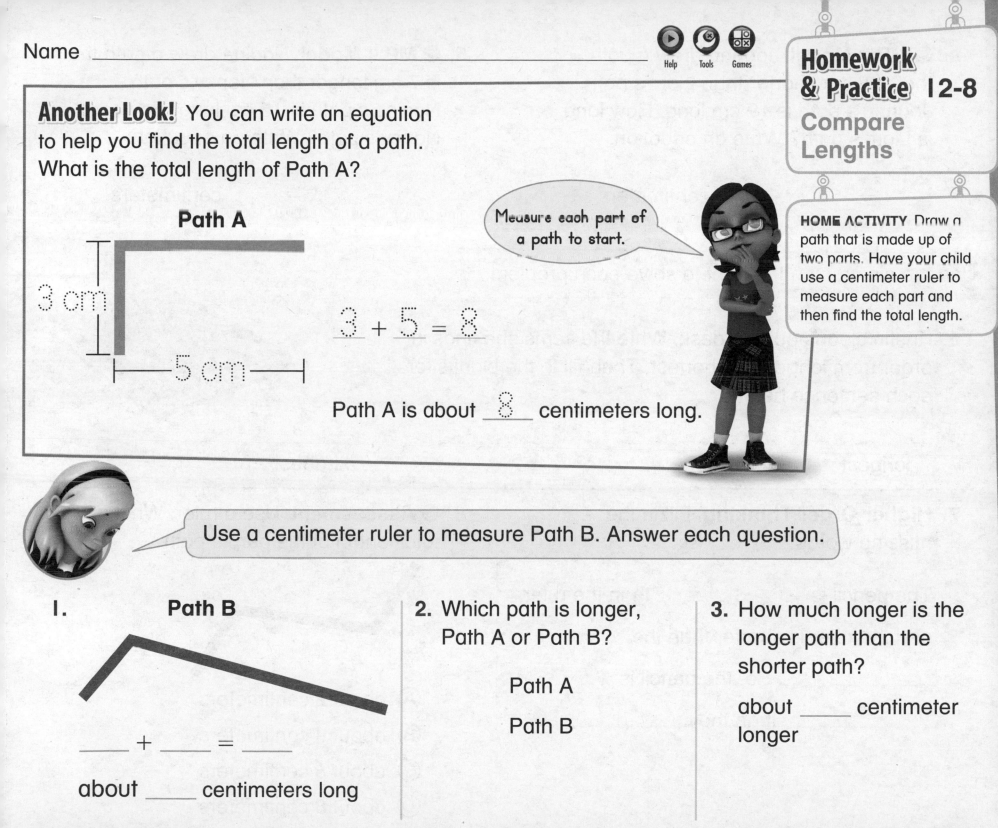

3 cm

5 cm

$\underline{3} + \underline{5} = \underline{8}$

Path A is about __8__ centimeters long.

Measure each part of
a path to start.

HOME ACTIVITY Draw a
path that is made up of
two parts. Have your child
use a centimeter ruler to
measure each part and
then find the total length.

Use a centimeter ruler to measure Path B. Answer each question.

1.   **Path B**

____ + ____ = ____

about ____ centimeters long

2. Which path is longer,
   Path A or Path B?

   Path A

   Path B

3. How much longer is the
   longer path than the
   shorter path?

   about ____ centimeter
   longer

4. © MP.4 Model Joanna drew a path that is 8 cm shorter than Liam's path. Joanna's path is 19 cm long. How long is Liam's path? Write an equation.

_____ + _____ = _____ centimeters

5. © MP.4 Model Nadine drew a path that is 7 cm longer than Nancy's path. Nadine's path is 15 cm long. How long is Nancy's path? Write an equation.

_____ − _____ = _____ centimeters

Use the pictures on the right to solve each problem.

6. Kristin cleans out her desk. Write the items she finds in order from longest to shortest. Then fill in the blanks for each sentence below.

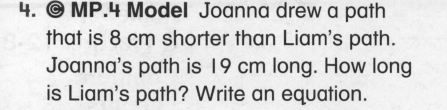

_____   _____   _____   _____

longest   shortest

7. Higher Order Thinking Fill in the missing words.

The pencil is _____ than the ruler,

and the ruler is shorter than the

_____. So, the pencil is

_____ than the _____.

8. © Assessment Use a ruler. What is the total length of the purple path?

Ⓐ about 2 centimeters

Ⓑ about 4 centimeters

Ⓒ about 6 centimeters

Ⓓ about 8 centimeters

© Pearson Education, Inc. 2

Solve & Share

Zeke measures the snake and says it is about 4 inches long. Jay says it is about 5 inches long.

Who measures the snake more precisely? Measure and explain.

I can ...
choose tools, units, and methods that help me be precise when I measure.

© **Mathematical Practices**
MP.6 Also MP.1, MP.2, MP.3, MP.5
Content Standards 2.MD.A.1, 2.MD.A.3

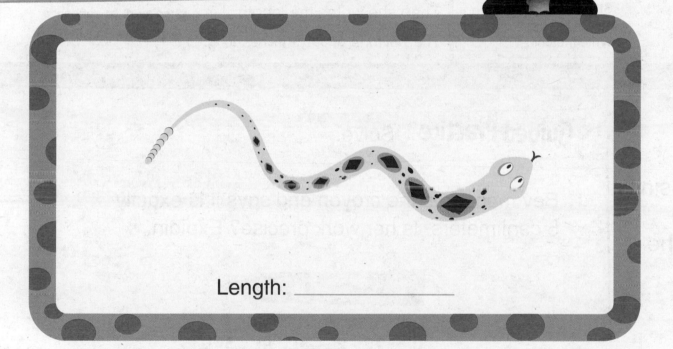

Length: _____

Thinking Habits
Which unit of measure will I use?

Is my work precise?

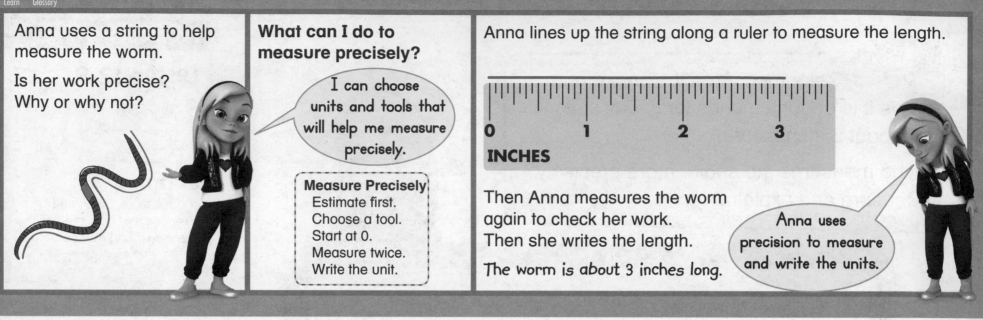

Anna uses a string to help measure the worm.

Is her work precise? Why or why not?

What can I do to measure precisely?

I can choose units and tools that will help me measure precisely.

Measure Precisely
Estimate first.
Choose a tool.
Start at 0.
Measure twice.
Write the unit.

Anna lines up the string along a ruler to measure the length.

Then Anna measures the worm again to check her work. Then she writes the length.

The worm is about 3 inches long.

Anna uses precision to measure and write the units.

Do You Understand?

Show Me! How does using a string help Anna use precision to measure the worm?

☆ Guided Practice   Solve.

1. Bev measures the crayon and says it is exactly 5 centimeters. Is her work precise? Explain.

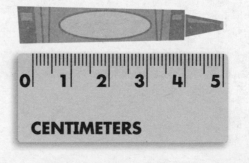

CENTIMETERS

_____

_____

Independent Practice ☆ Solve each problem.

2. Traci measures the length of her pencil.
   She uses a centimeter ruler.
   Traci writes 17 for the length.
   Is her answer precise? Explain.

3. Steve uses centimeter cubes. He says
   the pencil is 9 centimeters long. Is his
   work precise? Explain.

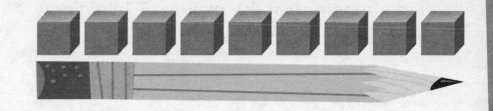

4. Use a centimeter ruler to measure the pencil yourself.
   How long is the pencil? Explain what you did to make sure
   your work is precise.

Math Practices and Problem Solving

© Performance Assessment

Shoestring

Katie lost a shoestring.
The shoestring has the same length as the
shoestring at the right.
What is the length of the shoestring Katie lost?

5. **MP.1 Make Sense** Estimate the length of
the shoestring in the picture. Explain how
your estimate helps you measure.

_____

_____

_____

6. **MP.5 Use Tools** What tools can you use
to measure the shoestring? Explain.

_____

_____

_____

_____

7. **MP.6 Be Precise** Measure the shoestring.
Tell why your work is precise.

_____

_____

Name _____

Another Look! Amy uses a button to measure the length of a glue stick. She knows one button is 1 centimeter. She finds that the glue stick is 5 cm.

Amy used a ruler to check her work. She started at the 0 mark.

First time: 5 cm   **Second time: 5 cm**

Amy got the same answer both times. So, she knows her work is precise! It helps to measure twice!

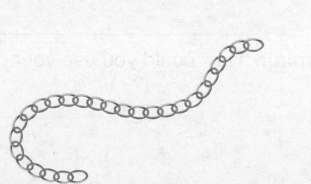

HOME ACTIVITY Have your child measure the length of a household item. Have your child choose the unit to use. Ask your child to explain how he or she knows the measurement is precise.

Solve the problem. You can use string or buttons to help.

1. Find the length of the chain at the right.
Estimate and use tools to measure.

Estimate: _____

Actual measurement: _____

© Performance Assessment

Distance Around Your Shoe

Shoes have different sizes and shapes.
The picture shows the bottom of a shoe.
What is the total distance around the bottom
of one of your shoes?

2. **MP.2 Reasoning** What units of measure
will you use? Explain.

_____

_____

_____

_____

_____

3. **MP.6 Be Precise** What is the distance
around one of your shoes? Explain how
you found it.

_____

_____

_____

_____

_____

_____

4. **MP.3 Explain** How could you use your other shoe to check your work?

_____

_____

_____

Find a Match

Find a partner. Point to a clue. Read the clue.

Look below the clues to find a match. Write the clue letter in the box next to the match.

Find a match for every clue.

I can ...
add and subtract within 100.

© Content Standard 2.NBT.B.5

Clues

A The sum is between 47 and 53.

B The difference equals 56 − 20.

C The sum equals 100.

D The difference equals 79 − 27.

E The difference is between 25 and 35.

F The sum equals 41 + 56.

G The difference is less than 20.

H The sum equals 26 + 19.

81 − 29	60 − 24

34 + 11	23 + 27

63 − 34	32 + 65

56 + 44	47 − 31

Word List
- centimeter (cm)
- estimate
- foot (ft)
- height
- inch (in.)
- length
- meter (m)
- nearest centimeter
- nearest inch
- yard (yd)

Understand Vocabulary

1. Circle the unit that has the *greatest* length.

foot   meter   inch

2. Circle the unit that has the *shortest* length.

yard   inch   centimeter

3. Cross out the unit you would **NOT** use to measure the length of a book.

inch   centimeter   yard

4. Cross out the unit you would **NOT** use to measure the height of a house.

inch   foot   meter

Estimate the length of each item.

5. pencil

_____

6. paper clip

_____

7. school desk

_____

Use Vocabulary in Writing

8. Use words to tell how to find the height of a table. Use terms from the Word List.

_____
_____
_____
_____
_____

Name _____

Set A _____

There are 12 inches in 1 foot.
There are 3 feet in 1 yard.
You can use lengths of objects you know to estimate lengths of other objects.

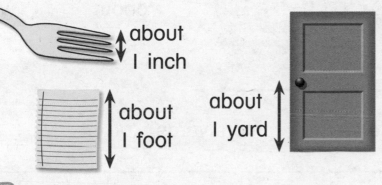

about 1 inch

about 1 foot

about 1 yard

Estimate the lengths of two classroom objects in feet. Name each object and write your estimate.

1. Object: _____

about _____ feet

2. Object: _____

about _____ feet

Set B _____

You can measure the length of an object to the nearest inch.

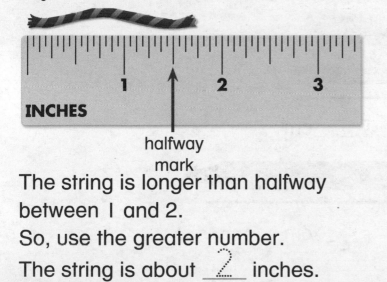

halfway mark

The string is longer than halfway between 1 and 2.
So, use the greater number.
The string is about _2_ inches.

Find objects like the ones shown. Use a ruler to measure their lengths.

3.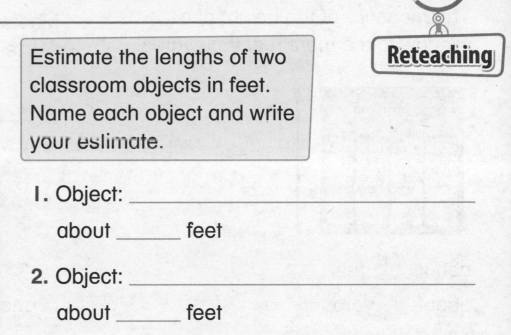

about _____ inches

4.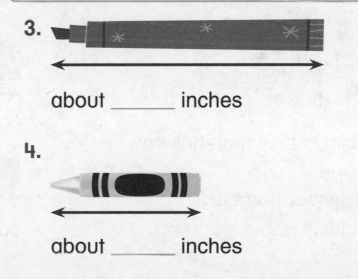

about _____ inches

The measure of the height of a window takes *more* feet than yards.

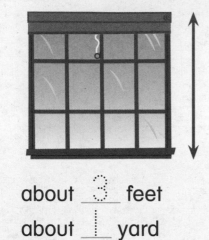

about _3_ feet

about _1_ yard

Measure the object in inches and feet. Circle the unit you needed *more* of.

5.

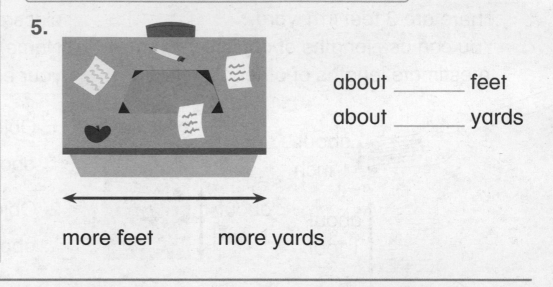

about _____ feet

about _____ yards

more feet   more yards

You can measure the length of an object to the nearest centimeter.

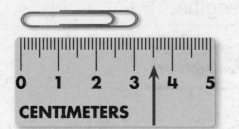

0 1 2 3 4 5

CENTIMETERS

The paper clip is less than halfway between 3 and 4.

So, use the lesser number.

The paper clip is about _3_ cm.

Find objects like the ones shown. Use a ruler to measure their lengths.

6.

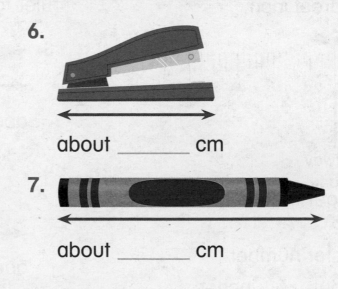

about _____ cm

7.

about _____ cm

Set E

There are 100 centimeters in
1 meter.

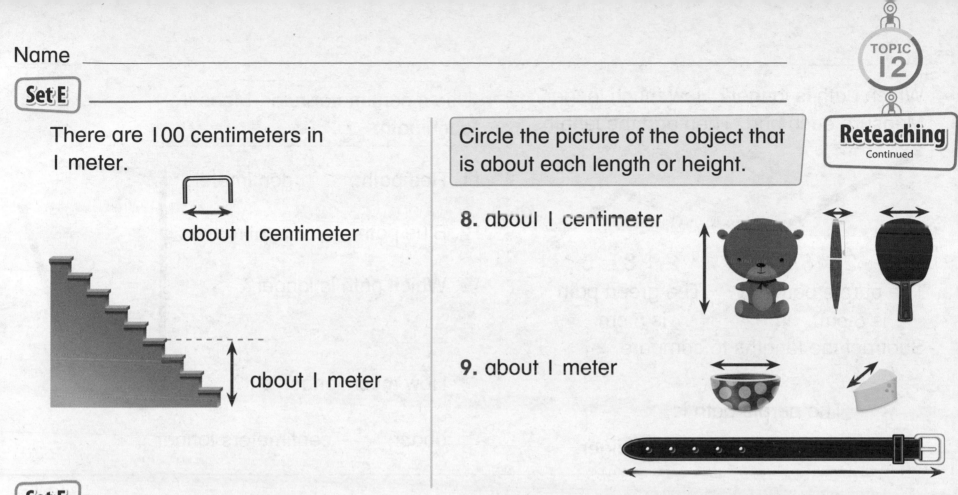

about 1 centimeter

about 1 meter

Circle the picture of the object that
is about each length or height.

8. about 1 centimeter

9. about 1 meter

Set F

The measure of the height of this cart
takes *fewer* meters than centimeters.

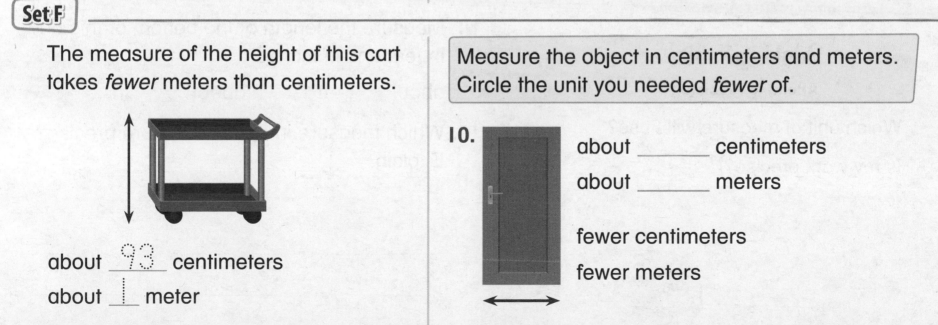

about __93__ centimeters

about __1__ meter

Measure the object in centimeters and meters.
Circle the unit you needed *fewer* of.

10.

about _____ centimeters

about _____ meters

fewer centimeters

fewer meters

Which path is longer? How much longer?
Measure each part. Then add the lengths.

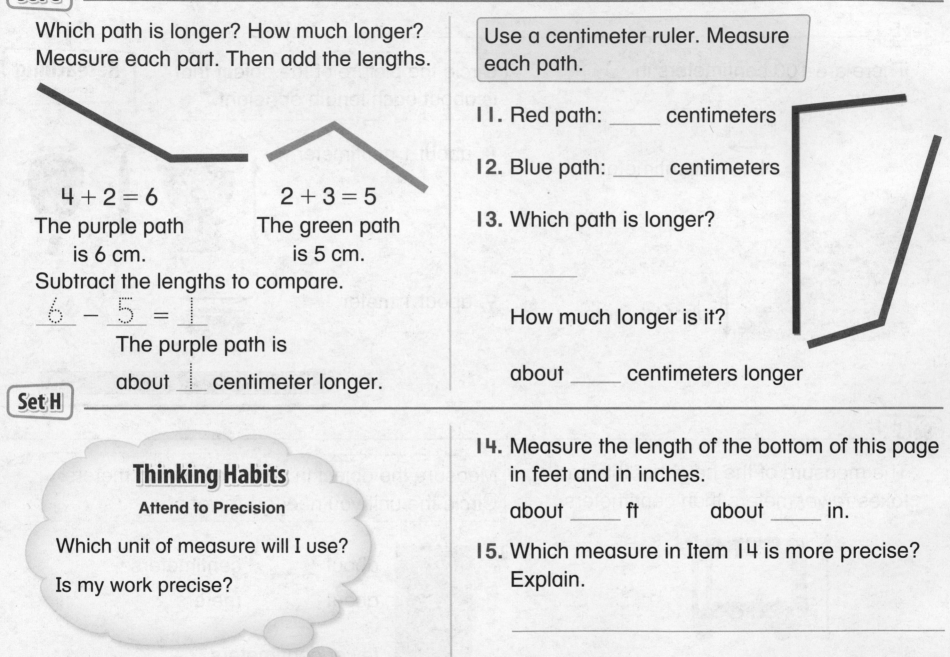

$4 + 2 = 6$

The purple path
is 6 cm.

$2 + 3 = 5$

The green path
is 5 cm.

Subtract the lengths to compare.

$6 - 5 = 1$

The purple path is

about 1 centimeter longer.

Use a centimeter ruler. Measure each path.

11. Red path: _____ centimeters

12. Blue path: _____ centimeters

13. Which path is longer?

_____

How much longer is it?

about _____ centimeters longer

Thinking Habits

Attend to Precision

Which unit of measure will I use?

Is my work precise?

14. Measure the length of the bottom of this page in feet and in inches.

about _____ ft   about _____ in.

15. Which measure in Item 14 is more precise? Explain.

_____

_____

_____

© Pearson Education, Inc. 2

Name _____

1. Estimate. About how tall is the flower?

Ⓐ about 5 cm

Ⓑ about 10 cm

Ⓒ about 15 cm

Ⓓ about 1 meter

I cm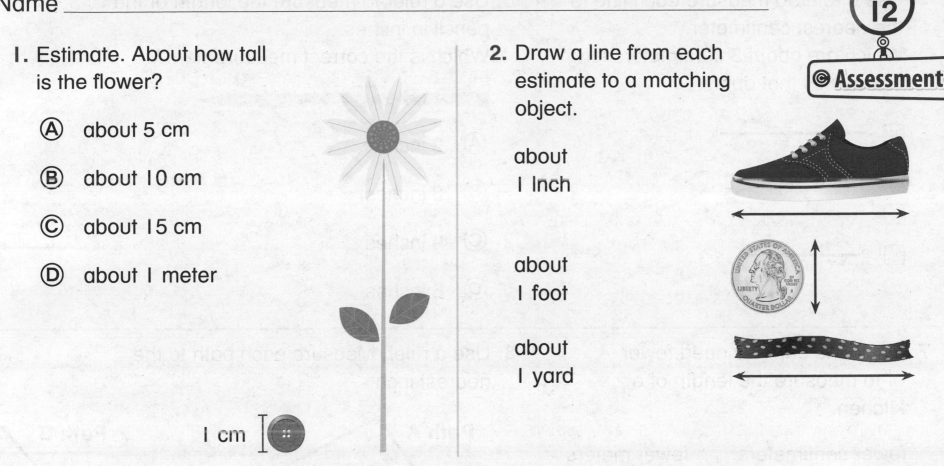

2. Draw a line from each estimate to a matching object.

about 1 Inch

about 1 foot

about 1 yard

3. Which units would you need the fewest of to measure the height of a fence?

Ⓐ inches

Ⓑ feet

Ⓒ yards

Ⓓ all the same

4. Dan measures the width of the window with a yardstick. He says it measures 3. Is his answer precise? Explain.

_____

_____

_____

_____

5. Use a ruler to measure each line to the nearest centimeter.
Which are about 3 centimeters long? Choose all that apply.

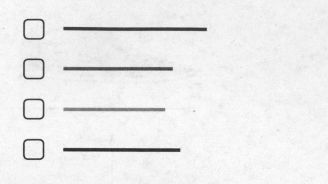

6. Use a ruler to measure the length of the pencil in inches.
Which is the correct measurement?

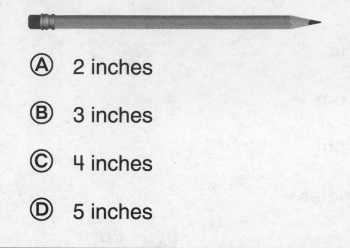

Ⓐ 2 inches

Ⓑ 3 inches

Ⓒ 4 inches

Ⓓ 5 inches

---

7. Circle the unit you need fewer of to measure the length of a kitchen.

fewer centimeters   fewer meters

Circle the unit you need fewer of to measure the length of a table.

fewer feet   fewer yards

8. Use a ruler. Measure each path to the nearest inch.

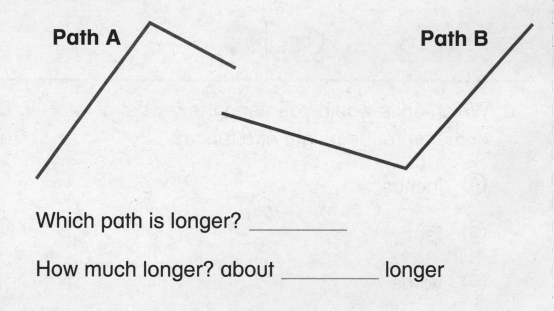

Which path is longer? _____

How much longer? about _____ longer

Name _____

9. Use a ruler. Measure the length of the marker to the nearest centimeter. How long is the marker?

Ⓐ 6 centimeters

Ⓑ 9 centimeters

Ⓒ 12 centimeters

Ⓓ 15 centimeters

10. A path has two parts. The total length of the path is 15 cm. One part of the path is 9 cm long. How long is the other part?

Ⓐ 24 cm

Ⓑ 15 cm

Ⓒ 9 cm

Ⓓ 6 cm

---

11. Use a ruler. Measure each path to the nearest centimeter.

Path A

Path B

Which path is longer? _____

How much longer?

about _____ longer

12. Measure the gray line with tools you need to be precise. Choose all the measurements that are precise.

☐ 4 centimeters

☐ 4 inches

☐ 10

☐ 10 centimeters

13. Juan uses different units to measure a jump rope. Compare the measurements.

Choose Yes or No.

more inches than feet ○ Yes ○ No

fewer inches than feet ○ Yes ○ No

more centimeters than meters ○ Yes ○ No

fewer centimeters than meters ○ Yes ○ No

14. Kendra measures her crayon to the nearest centimeter.
What is the length of her crayon to the nearest centimeter?

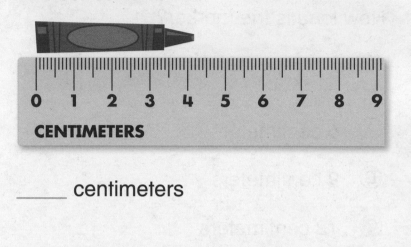

_____ centimeters

15. Kim's softball bat is 1 yard long. She uses 3 bats to measure the length of the classroom whiteboard. About how long is the whiteboard?

3 inches   3 feet   1 yard   3 yards
Ⓐ   Ⓑ   Ⓒ   Ⓓ

16. Kevin measured the length of a car in inches and in feet. Why is the number of feet less than the number of inches?

96 inches or 8 feet

Name _____

Happy Hiking!
The Torres family loves to hike.
They use this map to plan their hiking trip.

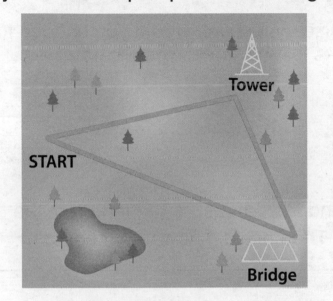

START

Tower

Bridge

1. Use a centimeter ruler.
Find the total length of the triangle
hiking path shown on the map.

about _____ centimeters

Explain how you found the length.

_____

_____

_____

2. Debbie Torres uses a backpack
for hiking.
She wants to measure its length.
She wants to be precise. Should she
use inches, feet, or yards?
Explain your answer.

Length of a backpack

_____

_____

_____

_____

3. Daniel Torres estimates the height of his water bottle. Is his estimate reasonable? Explain.

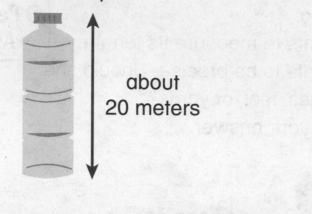

about
20 meters

_____

_____

_____

4. Maria Torres says that it would take more yards than feet to measure the height of the tower. Do you agree? Circle Yes or No. Then explain why.

Yes   No

_____

_____

_____

5. On the hike, the Torres family sees a caterpillar. Use the picture below to answer the questions.

Part A

To be precise, which unit would you choose to measure the length of the caterpillar?

_____

_____

Part B

Estimate and then measure the length of the caterpillar. Then explain how you measured.

Estimate: _____

Measurement: _____

_____

_____

_____

_____

More Addition, Subtraction, and Length

Essential Question: How can you add and subtract lengths?

Digital Resources

Solve   Learn   Glossary

Tools   Assessment   Help   Games

Look at the big waves! Look at the big rock!

Water and land in an area can have different sizes and shapes.

Wow! Let's do this project and learn more.

Math and Science Project: Modeling Land, Water, and Length

Find Out Find and share books and other sources that show the shapes and kinds of land and water in an area. Draw a picture or make a model to show the land or water in an area.

Journal: Make a Book Show what you learn in a book. In your book, also:

• Draw a picture to show the shape of some land or water in your area.

• Make up a math story about lengths. Draw a picture to show how to solve the problem in your story.

Name _____

Review What You Know

1. Circle the measuring unit that is better to **estimate** the **length** of a room.

   meter

   centimeter

2. Circle the number of feet in 1 **yard**.

   2 feet

   3 feet

   4 feet

   12 feet

3. The clock shows the time a math class begins. Circle **a.m.** or **p.m.**

   a.m.

   p.m.

Estimate

4. **Estimate** the length of the eraser in centimeters.

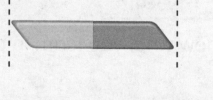

   About _____ centimeters

Compare

5. A sidewalk is 632 yards long. A jogging trail is 640 yards long.

   Use <, >, or = to compare the lengths.

   632 ◯ 640

Rectangles

6. Label the 2 missing lengths of the sides of the rectangle.

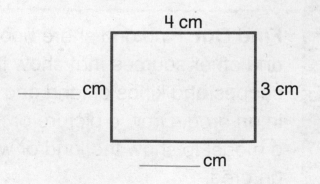

   4 cm

   _____ cm

   3 cm

   _____ cm

Topic 13

Name _____

Solve & Share

What is the total distance around the blue rectangle in centimeters? Show your work. Did you add or subtract?

I can ...
solve problems by adding or subtracting length measurements.

© **Content Standard** 2.MD.B.5
Mathematical Practices MP.2, MP.4, MP.6

_____ ◯ _____ ◯ _____ ◯ _____ = _____

The distance around the blue rectangle is _____ centimeters.

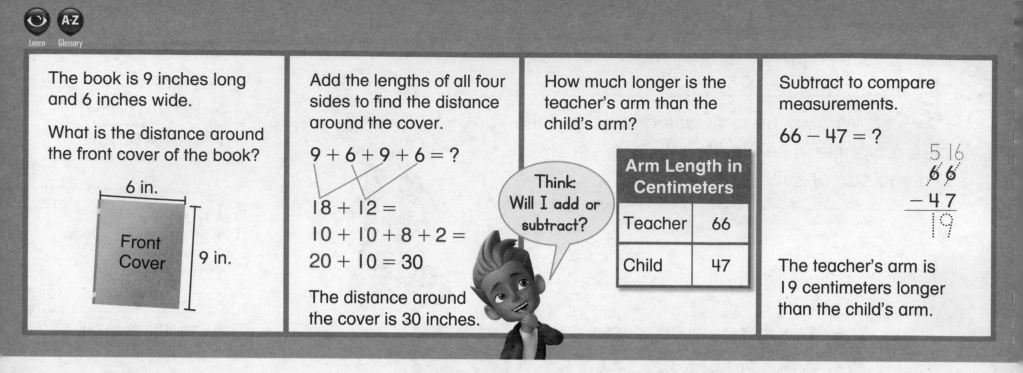

The book is 9 inches long and 6 inches wide.

What is the distance around the front cover of the book?

6 in.

Front Cover

9 in.

Add the lengths of all four sides to find the distance around the cover.

$9 + 6 + 9 + 6 = ?$

$18 + 12 =$

$10 + 10 + 8 + 2 =$

$20 + 10 = 30$

The distance around the cover is 30 inches.

How much longer is the teacher's arm than the child's arm?

Think: Will I add or subtract?

Arm Length in Centimeters	
Teacher	66
Child	47

Subtract to compare measurements.

$66 - 47 = ?$

$$\begin{array}{r} 5\,16 \\ \cancel{6}\,\cancel{6} \\ -\ 4\,7 \\ \hline 1\,9 \end{array}$$

The teacher's arm is 19 centimeters longer than the child's arm.

Do You Understand?

Show Me! Explain how to find the distance around a square park that is 2 miles long on each side.

☆ Guided Practice ☆

Decide if you need to add or subtract. Then write an equation to help solve each problem.

1. What is the distance around the baseball card?

$10 + 7 + 10 + 7 = 34$

Distance around: __34__ cm

10 cm

7 cm

2. What is the distance around the puzzle?

_____

Distance around: _____ in.

15 in.

12 in.

© Pearson Education, Inc. 2

Name _____

Independent Practice

Decide if you need to add or subtract.
Then write an equation to help solve each problem.

3. What is the distance around the door?

_____

Distance around: _____ ft

3 ft

7 ft

4. What is the distance around the cell phone?

_____

Distance around: _____ in.

2 in.

4 in.

5. How much longer is the red scarf than the blue scarf?

_____

_____ in. longer

60 in.

45 in.

6. Algebra What is the length of the shorter side of the rectangle? Complete the equation to solve.

20 + _____ + 20 + _____ = 60

The shorter side is _____ centimeters.

20 cm

?

Decide if you need to add or subtract.
Then write an equation to help solve each problem.

An equation is a model.

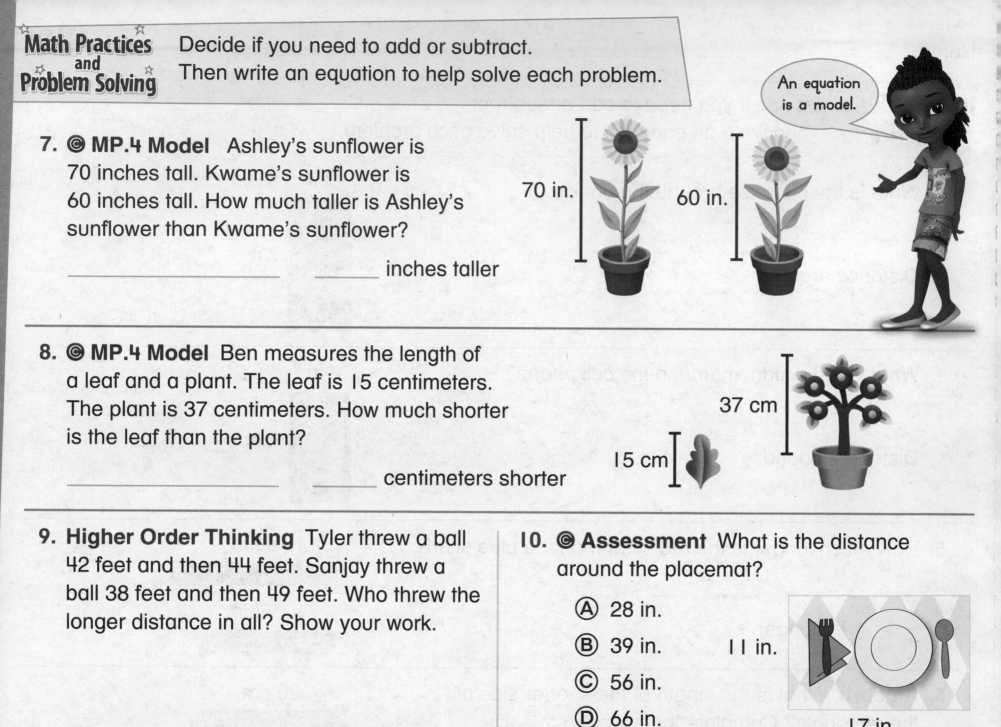

7. © **MP.4 Model**   Ashley's sunflower is 70 inches tall. Kwame's sunflower is 60 inches tall. How much taller is Ashley's sunflower than Kwame's sunflower?

70 in.   60 in.

_____   _____ inches taller

8. © **MP.4 Model** Ben measures the length of a leaf and a plant. The leaf is 15 centimeters. The plant is 37 centimeters. How much shorter is the leaf than the plant?

37 cm

15 cm

_____   _____ centimeters shorter

9. **Higher Order Thinking** Tyler threw a ball 42 feet and then 44 feet. Sanjay threw a ball 38 feet and then 49 feet. Who threw the longer distance in all? Show your work.

10. © **Assessment** What is the distance around the placemat?

Ⓐ 28 in.

Ⓑ 39 in.   11 in.

Ⓒ 56 in.

Ⓓ 66 in.   17 in.

© Pearson Education, Inc. 2

Topic 13 | Lesson 1

Help   Tools   Games

Another Look!

You can use addition or subtraction to solve problems with measurements. How much longer is the snake than the worm?

Subtract to compare.

18 in.

6 in.

$\underline{18} - \underline{6} = \underline{12}$

The snake is __12 inches__ longer than the worm.

HOME ACTIVITY Ask your child to find a rectangular object (*a book, piece of paper, tile, etc.*). Have your child measure each side in inches and write an equation to find the distance around the object.

Decide if you need to add or subtract.
Then write an equation to help solve each problem.

1. How much shorter is the feather than the ribbon?

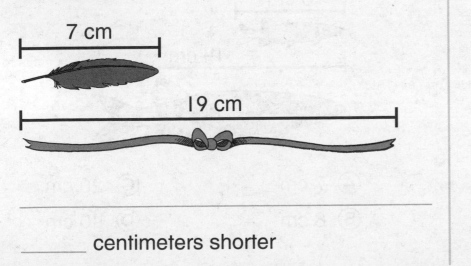

7 cm

19 cm

_____

_____ centimeters shorter

2. What is the distance around the rug?

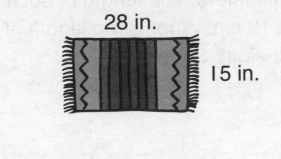

28 in.

15 in.

_____

_____ inches

Decide if you need to add or subtract.
Then write an equation to help solve each problem.

3. © **MP.4 Model** What is the distance
around the front cover of the game box?

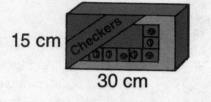

15 cm

30 cm

_____

The distance around the game

box is _____.

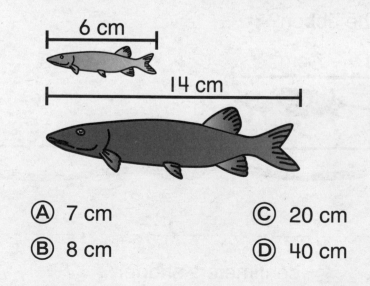

You can model a
problem with an equation.
Include the units in
your answer.

4. **Higher Order Thinking** The distance
around Tim's rectangular book is
48 centimeters. The length of each longer
side is 14 cm. What is the length of each
shorter side? Show your work.

_____

_____

Each shorter side of the book is

_____ long.

5. © **Assessment** How much longer is the
green fish than the blue fish?

6 cm

14 cm

(A) 7 cm   (C) 20 cm

(B) 8 cm   (D) 40 cm

© Pearson Education, Inc. 2

Topic 13 | Lesson 1

Name _____

☆ Solve & Share

Julie and Steve each cut a piece of yarn.
The total length of both pieces is 12 cm.

Use centimeter cubes to measure each piece of yarn.
Circle Julie and Steve's pieces. Then explain your thinking.

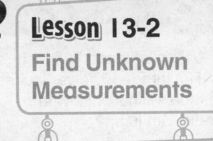

I can ...
add or subtract to solve problems about measurements.

© **Content Standards** 2.MD.B.5, 2.OA.A.1
Mathematical Practices MP.1, MP.2, MP.3, MP.4

_____

_____

_____

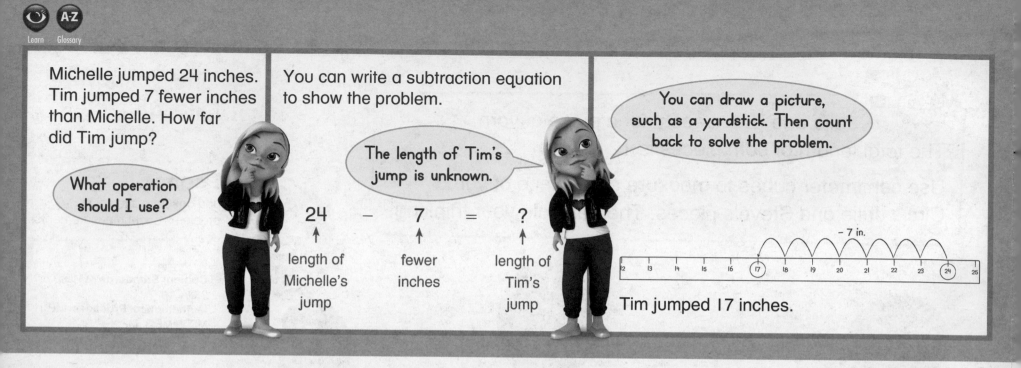

Michelle jumped 24 inches. Tim jumped 7 fewer inches than Michelle. How far did Tim jump?

What operation should I use?

You can write a subtraction equation to show the problem.

The length of Tim's jump is unknown.

24 — 7 = ?

24 ↑ length of Michelle's jump

7 ↑ fewer inches

? ↑ length of Tim's jump

You can draw a picture, such as a yardstick. Then count back to solve the problem.

Tim jumped 17 inches.

Do You Understand?

Show Me! How does drawing a yardstick help you solve the problem above?

☆Guided☆ Practice

Write an equation using a ? for the unknown number. Solve with a picture or another way.

1. A stamp measures 2 centimeters in length. How many centimeters long are two stamps?

2 + 2 = ?

| 1 cm | 1 cm | 1 cm | 1 cm | = 4 cm

_____ cm

2. Stuart's desk is 64 centimeters long. His dresser is 7 centimeters longer than his desk. How long is Stuart's dresser?

_____ _____ cm

© Pearson Education, Inc. 2

Topic 13 | Lesson 2

Independent Practice

Write an equation using a ? for the unknown number.
Solve with a picture or another way.

3. Filipe's pencil box is 24 centimeters long.
Joe's pencil box is 3 centimeters shorter
than Filipe's. How long is Joe's pencil box?

_____   _____ cm

4. Clark threw a red ball and a blue ball. He
threw the red ball 17 feet. He threw the
blue ball 7 feet farther. How far did Clark
throw the blue ball?

_____   _____ ft

5. **Math and Science** Ashlie's map shows
where animals, land, and water are at
a zoo.

The distance around her map is 38 inches.
What is the length of the missing side?

_____

_____ inches

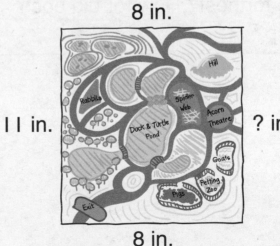

8 in.

11 in.   ? in.

8 in.

6. © **MP.1 Make Sense** A brown puppy is 43 centimeters tall. A spotted puppy is 7 centimeters shorter than the brown puppy. A white puppy is 14 centimeters taller than the brown puppy. How tall is the spotted puppy? Think about what you need to find.

_____ cm

7. **A-Z Vocabulary** Complete the sentences using the terms below.

foot   yard   inch

A paper clip is about 1 _____ long.

My math book is about 1 _____ long.

A baseball bat is about 1 _____ long.

8. **Higher Order Thinking** Jack jumped 15 inches. Tyler jumped 1 inch less than Jack and 2 inches more than Randy. Who jumped the farthest? How far did each person jump?

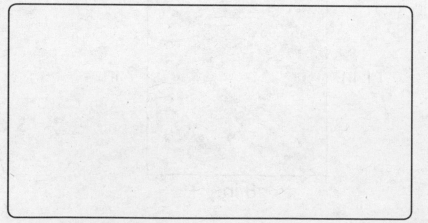

9. © **Assessment** Kim was 48 inches tall in January. She grew 9 inches during the year. How tall is Kim at the end of the year? Write an equation with an unknown and then draw a picture to solve.

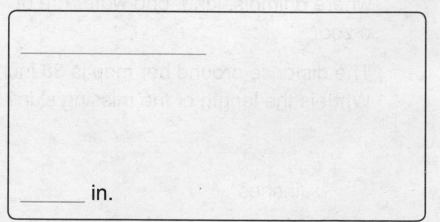

_____ in.

© Pearson Education, Inc. 2

Help   Tools   Games

Another Look!

Lance's boat is 13 meters long.
Cory's boat is 7 meters longer.
How long is Cory's boat?

You can follow these steps to solve word problems.

Step 1 Write an equation to show the problem. $13 + 7 = ?$

Step 2 Draw a picture to help solve.

Step 3 Solve the problem. Cory's boat is 20 meters long.

> You can draw a picture to help.

$+ 2\ m$ $+ 5\ m$

13   15   20

> **HOME ACTIVITY** Have your child draw a picture to solve this problem. *A building is 24 meters tall. The tree next to the building is 5 meters tall. How much shorter is the tree than the building?*

> Write an equation using a ? for the unknown number. Solve with a picture or another way.

1. Suzy's ribbon is 83 centimeters long.
She cuts off 15 centimeters. How long is
Suzy's ribbon now?

_____   _____ cm

Solve each problem.

2. Jackie's shoelaces are 13 inches, 29 inches, and 58 inches long. What is the total length of all of Jackie's shoelaces? Draw a picture and write an equation to solve.

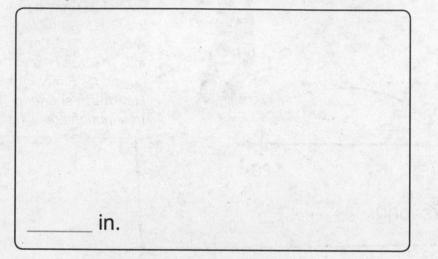

_____ in.

3. © **MP. 2 Reasoning** Mary is 2 inches taller than Bill. Bill is 48 inches tall. How tall is Mary?

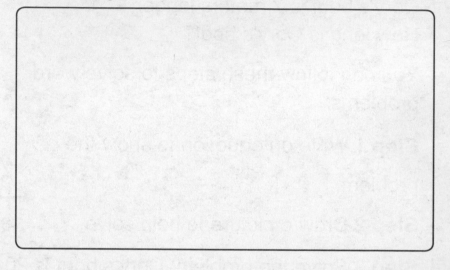

4. Higher Order Thinking Kyle's bedroom is 11 feet long. Garrett's bedroom is 2 feet longer than Kyle's room. Priya's bedroom is 3 feet shorter than Garrett's room. What is the sum of the lengths of Garrett and Priya's bedrooms?

_____ ft

5. © **Assessment** Ryan's desk is 25 inches tall. His floor lamp is 54 inches tall. How many inches taller is Ryan's floor lamp? Write an equation and draw a picture to solve.

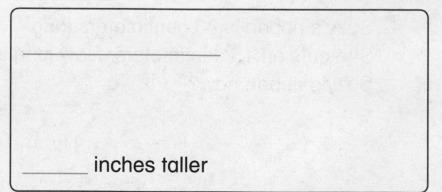

_____ inches taller

Name _____

Solve & Share

Alex has a piece of ribbon that is 45 feet long.
He cuts the ribbon. Now he has 39 feet of ribbon.
How many feet of ribbon did Alex cut off?

Draw a picture and write an equation to solve.
Show your work.

I can ...
add and subtract to solve measurement problems by using drawings and equations.

© **Content Standards** 2.MD.B.5, 2.OA.A.1
Mathematical Practices MP.1, MP.3, MP. 4, MP.6

_____ ◯ _____ = _____

A string is 28 cm.
Alex cuts off a piece.
Now the string is 16 cm.
How long is the piece of
string Alex cut off?

You can write an addition
or subtraction equation.

$$28 - ? = 16$$

length   length   length
at first   cut   now

$$16 + ? = 28$$

length   length   length
now   cut   at first

You can draw a picture for $28 - ? = 16$ or $16 + ? = 28$.

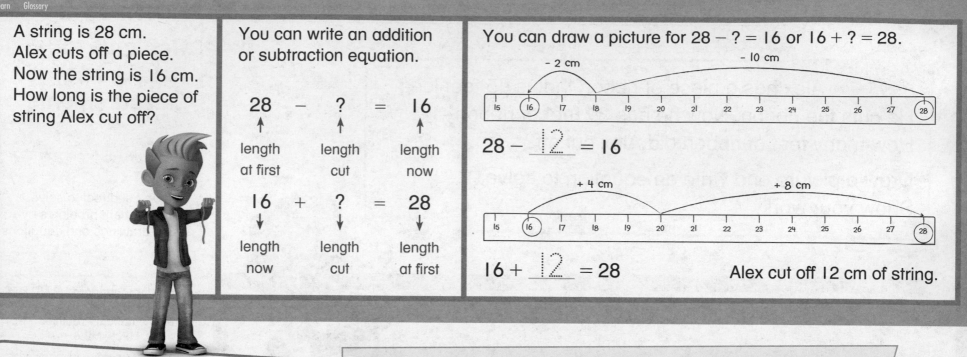

$$28 - \underline{12} = 16$$

$$16 + \underline{12} = 28$$

Alex cut off 12 cm of string.

Do You Understand?

Show Me! How does writing
an equation help you solve
the problem above?

☆ Guided Practice ☆   Write an equation using a ? for the unknown number. Solve with a picture or another way.

1. A plant was 15 inches tall.
   It grew and is now 22 inches
   tall. How many inches did the
   plant grow?

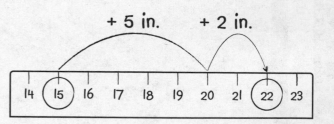

$$15 + ? = 22$$

2. Each bus is 10 meters long.
   Each boat is 7 meters long.
   What is the total length of two
   buses and two boats?

© Pearson Education, Inc. 2

Topic 13 | Lesson 3

Independent Practice

Write an equation using a ? for the unknown number. Solve with a picture or another way.

3. Brent's rope is 49 inches long. He cuts off some of the rope and now it is 37 inches long. How much rope did Brent cut off?

_____   _____

4. Sue ran for some meters and stopped. Then she ran another 22 meters for a total of 61 meters in all. How many meters did she run at first?

_____   _____

5. **Algebra** Solve each equation. Use the chart.

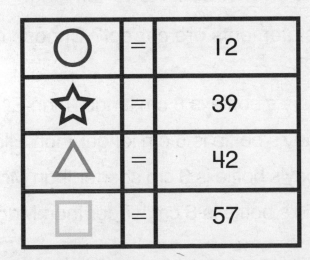

○	=	12
☆	=	39
△	=	42
☐	=	57

○ + ☆ = _____

☐ – ☆ = _____

☆ + △ + ○ = _____

6. © **MP.1 Make Sense** The yellow boat is 15 feet shorter than the green boat. The green boat is 53 feet long. How long is the yellow boat? Think about what you are trying to find.

Write an equation to solve. Show your work.

_____ ft

7. 🅐🅩 **Vocabulary** Steve measured the length of his desk. It measured 2 units.

Circle the unit Steve used.

meter   **foot**   **centimeter**   **inch**

Lori measured the length of her cat. It measured 45 units.

Circle the unit Lori used.

centimeter   **yard**   **inch**   **foot**

8. **Higher Order Thinking** Lucy's ribbon is 1 foot long. Kathleen's ribbon is 15 inches long. Whose ribbon is longer and by how many inches? Explain your thinking.

_____

_____

_____

9. © **Assessment** Mary's water bottle is 25 cm long. Joey's water bottle is 22 cm long. Ella's water bottle is 17 cm long.

Which statements are correct? Choose all that apply.

☐ Mary's bottle is 8 cm longer than Ella's.

☐ Joey's bottle is 6 cm longer than Ella's.

☐ Joey's bottle is 3 cm shorter than Mary's.

☐ Ella's bottle is 8 cm longer than Mary's.

Another Look!

Kelsey is 59 inches tall.

She grows and is now 73 inches tall.

How many inches did Kelsey grow?

Show the problem with an equation: $59 + ? = 73$.

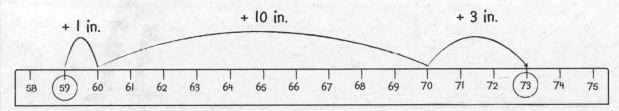

+ 1 in.   + 10 in.   + 3 in.

| 58 | 59 | 60 | 61 | 62 | 63 | 64 | 65 | 66 | 67 | 68 | 69 | 70 | 71 | 72 | 73 | 74 | 75 |

Kelsey grew 14 inches.

> You can draw a picture of a tape measure to solve the problem.

HOME ACTIVITY Have your child draw a picture and write an equation to solve this problem. *Paul has 45 feet of string. Sal cuts some string off. Now Paul has 38 feet of string. How many feet of string did Sal cut off?*

> Write an equation using a ? for the unknown number.
> Solve with a picture or another way.

1. Brigit has a piece of rope. She ties 18 more meters of rope to her rope. Now the rope is 27 meters long. How long was the rope to begin with?

_____   _____

Solve each problem.

2. © MP.3 **Explain** Elizabeth ran 36 meters.
Haruki ran 8 fewer meters than Elizabeth.
Delilah ran 3 fewer meters than Haruki.
How many meters did Delilah run?
Explain your thinking.

_____

_____

_____

3. **Higher Order Thinking** The lengths of the pencils are given at the right.

Write and solve a two-step problem about the pencils.

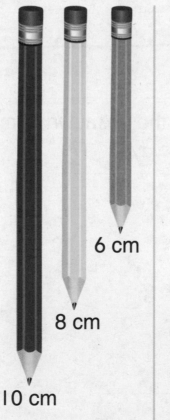

6 cm

8 cm

10 cm

_____

_____

_____

_____

4. © **Assessment** A hammer is 1 foot long.
A car is 15 feet long. A shovel is 4 feet long.

Which statements are correct? Choose all that apply.

☐ The car is 9 ft longer than the hammer.

☐ The hammer is 14 ft shorter than the car.

☐ The shovel is 3 ft longer than the hammer.

☐ The car is 11 feet longer than the shovel.

© Pearson Education, Inc. 2 **Topic 13** | Lesson 3

Name _____

Solve & Share

Amelia walks 18 blocks on Monday and 5 blocks on Tuesday. How many blocks does she walk in all?

Use the number line to show how many blocks Amelia walks. Then write an equation to show your work.

I can ...
add and subtract on a number line.

© **Content Standard** 2.MD.B.6
Mathematical Practices MP.2, MP.3, MP.4, MP.5, MP.7

0   5   10   15   20   25   30

____ ◯ ____ = ____

Amelia walks 17 blocks before dinner. She walks 8 blocks after dinner. How many blocks does she walk in all?

You can use a number line to add lengths.
First, show the 17 blocks Amelia walks before dinner.
Then, add the 8 blocks she walks after dinner.

Start at 0.

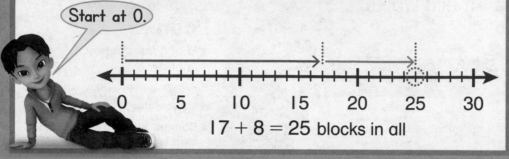

$17 + 8 = 25$ blocks in all

Amelia buys 17 feet of rope. She cuts off 8 feet of rope to make a jump rope. How many feet of rope does she have left?

You can also use a number line to subtract lengths.
First, show the 17 feet of rope.
Then, subtract the 8 feet of rope she cuts off.

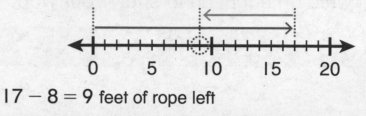

$17 - 8 = 9$ feet of rope left

Do You Understand?

Show Me! Explain how to add 14 inches and 11 inches using a number line.

1. $21 + 7 = \underline{28}$

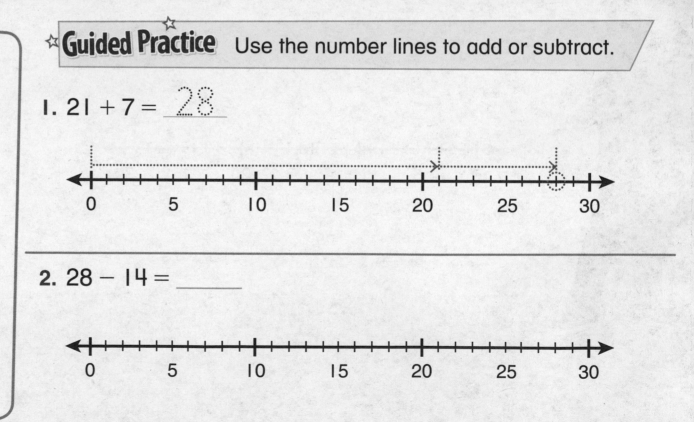

2. $28 - 14 = \underline{\hspace{1cm}}$

Tools   Assessment

Independent Practice ☆ Use the number lines to add or subtract.

3. 80 − 35 = _____

0 5 10 15 20 25 30 35 40 45 50 55 60 65 70 75 80 85 90 95 100

4. 19 + 63 = _____

0 5 10 15 20 25 30 35 40 45 50 55 60 65 70 75 80 85 90 95 100

5. Higher Order Thinking Use the number line to show 15 inches plus 0 inches. Explain your thinking.

0   5   10   15   20   25   30

6. Number Sense Show each number below as a length from 0 on the number line. Draw four separate arrows.

| 9 | 14 | 24 | 28 |

0   5   10   15   20   25   30

7. **© MP.5 Use Tools** A football team gains 15 yards on its first play. The team gains 12 yards on its second play. How many yards does the team gain in two plays?

8. **© MP.5 Use Tools** Mia buys 25 feet of board. She uses 16 feet of board for a sandbox. How many feet of board does she have left?

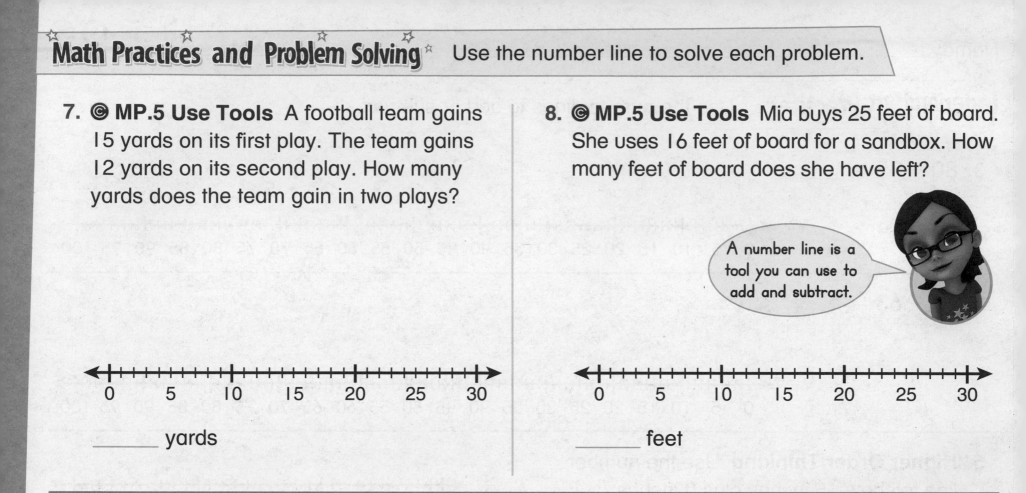

A number line is a tool you can use to add and subtract.

_____ yards

_____ feet

9. **Higher Order Thinking** The runners on the track team ran 12 miles on Monday. On Tuesday, they ran 6 more miles than they ran on Monday. How many miles did they run in all on both days?

10. **© Assessment** Deb has two pencils. One pencil is 9 cm long and the other pencil is 13 cm long. What is the total length of both pencils?

Use the number line to show your work.

_____ miles

_____ centimeters

Name _____

Another Look!

$10 + 19 = ?$

Start at 0. Draw an arrow to show the first length.

Then draw a second arrow that points right to add or left to subtract.

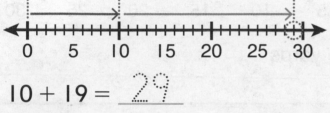

$0 \quad 5 \quad 10 \quad 15 \quad 20 \quad 25 \quad 30$

$10 + 19 = \underline{29}$

$19 - 13 = ?$

You can add or subtract on a number line.

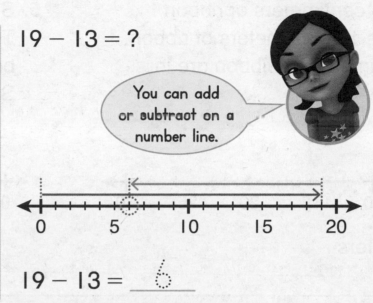

$0 \quad 5 \quad 10 \quad 15 \quad 20$

$19 - 13 = \underline{6}$

HOME ACTIVITY Measure the length of a fork and a spoon in centimeters. Then draw a number line to show how you would find the total length of the two objects.

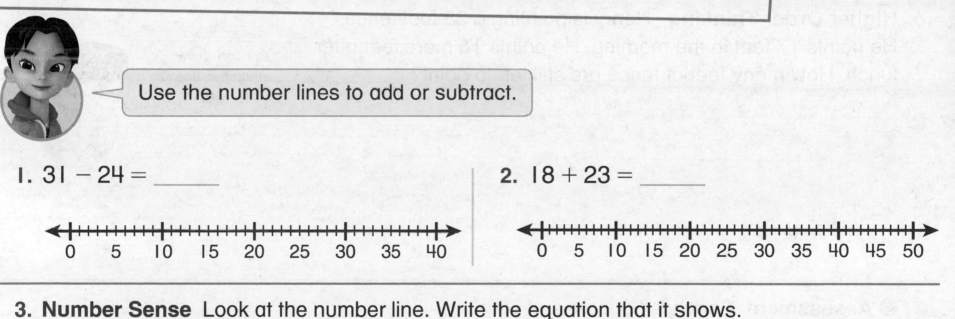

Use the number lines to add or subtract.

1. $31 - 24 = $ _____

$0 \quad 5 \quad 10 \quad 15 \quad 20 \quad 25 \quad 30 \quad 35 \quad 40$

2. $18 + 23 = $ _____

$0 \quad 5 \quad 10 \quad 15 \quad 20 \quad 25 \quad 30 \quad 35 \quad 40 \quad 45 \quad 50$

3. **Number Sense** Look at the number line. Write the equation that it shows.

$0 \quad 5 \quad 10 \quad 15 \quad 20 \quad 25 \quad 30 \quad 35 \quad 40 \quad 45 \quad 50$

_____ ◯ _____ = _____

4. One box has 15 centimeters of ribbon.
Another box has 14 centimeters of ribbon.
How many centimeters of ribbon are in
both boxes?

_____ centimeters

5. Susan kicks a ball 26 yards to Joe.
Then, Joe kicks the ball 18 yards straight
back to Susan. How far is the ball from
Susan now?

_____ yards

6. **Higher Order Thinking** Henry is painting a 38 foot fence.
He paints 17 feet in the morning. He paints 16 more feet after
lunch. How many feet of fence are still left to paint?

You can draw
a number line
to help.

_____ feet

7. © **Assessment** Sam has 38 inches of yarn.
He gives 23 inches of yarn to Lars.
How many inches of yarn does Sam have now?
Show your work on the number line.

_____ inches

     Topic 13 | Lesson 4

Name _____

Solve & Share

Choose a tool to solve each part of the problem.
Be ready to explain which tools you used and why.

Which line is longer? How much longer?
Draw a line that is that length.

Solve

Math Practices and Problem Solving

Lesson 13-5
Use Appropriate Tools

I can ...
choose the best tool to use to solve problems.

© **Mathematical Practices**
MP.5 Also MP.1, MP.3, MP.4, MP.6, MP.8
Content Standards 2.MD.B.5, 2.MD.B.6, 2.OA.A.1

Thinking Habits

Which of these tools can I use?

counters   paper and pencil
cubes   place-value blocks
measuring tools   technology
number line

Am I using the tool correctly?

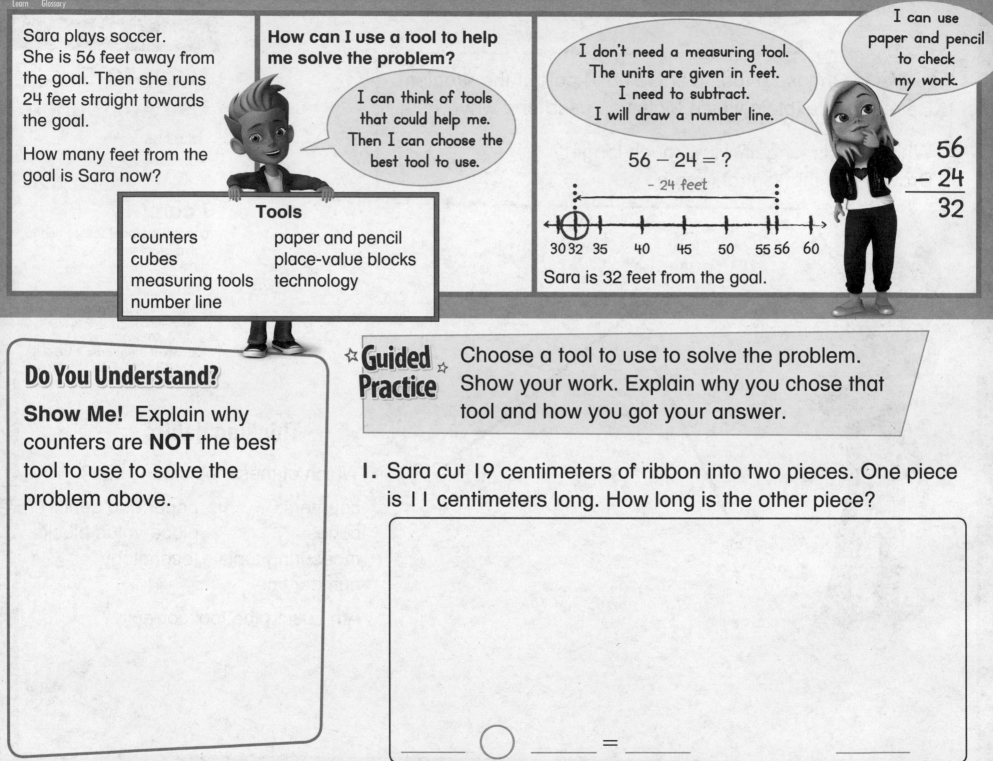

Sara plays soccer. She is 56 feet away from the goal. Then she runs 24 feet straight towards the goal.

How many feet from the goal is Sara now?

How can I use a tool to help me solve the problem?

I can think of tools that could help me. Then I can choose the best tool to use.

Tools

counters   paper and pencil
cubes   place-value blocks
measuring tools   technology
number line

I don't need a measuring tool. The units are given in feet. I need to subtract. I will draw a number line.

I can use paper and pencil to check my work.

$56 - 24 = ?$

$$\begin{array}{r} 56 \\ -24 \\ \hline 32 \end{array}$$

Sara is 32 feet from the goal.

Do You Understand?

Show Me! Explain why counters are **NOT** the best tool to use to solve the problem above.

☆ **Guided Practice** ☆ Choose a tool to use to solve the problem. Show your work. Explain why you chose that tool and how you got your answer.

1. Sara cut 19 centimeters of ribbon into two pieces. One piece is 11 centimeters long. How long is the other piece?

_____ ◯ _____ = _____

Tools   Assessment

Independent Practice ☆   Solve each problem. Show your work.

2. Work with a partner. Measure each other's arm from the shoulder to the tip of the index finger. Measure to the nearest inch. Whose arm is longer and by how much?

Choose a tool to use to solve the problem. Explain why you chose that tool and how you got your answer.

_____ ◯ _____ = _____

_____

3. Marcel jumped 39 centimeters high. Jamal jumped 48 centimeters high. How much higher did Jamal jump than Marcel?

Which tool would you **NOT** use to solve this problem? Explain.

_____ ◯ _____ = _____

_____

Math Practices and Problem Solving

© Performance Assessment

Sailboats

Zak is measuring sailboats at the dock.

Mr. Lee's sailboat is 64 feet long.

Ms. Flint's sailboat is 25 feet shorter than Mr. Lee's boat.

Help Zak find the length of Ms. Flint's boat.

4. **MP.5 Use Tools** Which tool would you **NOT** use to solve this problem? Explain.

_____

_____

_____

5. **MP.6 Be Precise** Will you add or subtract to solve the problem? _____

Write an equation. Use ? for the unknown.

What unit of measure will you use?

_____

6. **MP.3 Explain** What is the length of Ms. Flint's boat? Did you use a tool to solve the problem? Explain.

_____

_____

© Pearson Education, Inc. 2

Name _____

Another Look! What tool would you use to solve this problem?

Valerie drives 21 miles on Monday and 49 miles on Tuesday. How many miles does she drive in all?

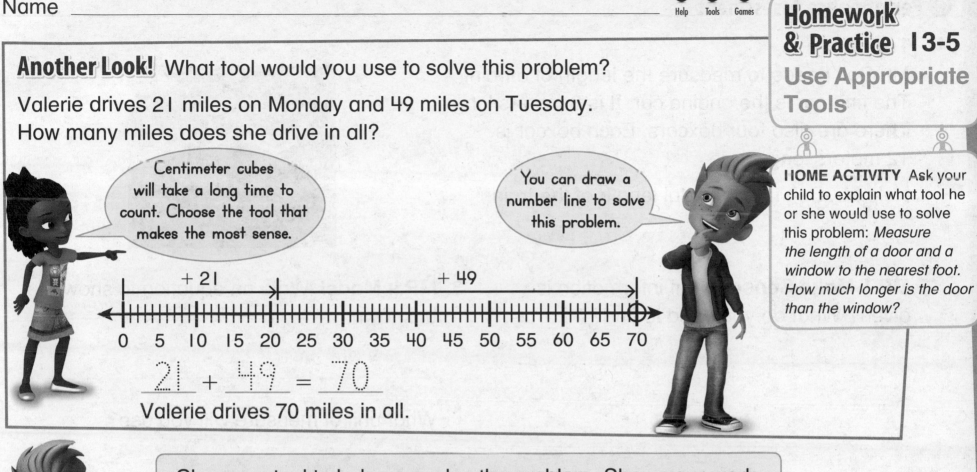

Centimeter cubes will take a long time to count. Choose the tool that makes the most sense.

You can draw a number line to solve this problem.

+ 21   + 49

0 5 10 15 20 25 30 35 40 45 50 55 60 65 70

$\underline{21} + \underline{49} = \underline{70}$

Valerie drives 70 miles in all.

HOME ACTIVITY Ask your child to explain what tool he or she would use to solve this problem: *Measure the length of a door and a window to the nearest foot. How much longer is the door than the window?*

Choose a tool to help you solve the problem. Show your work. Explain why you chose that tool and how you got your answer.

1. Aaron was 38 inches tall when he was 4 years old. Aaron is 8 years old and 47 inches tall. How many inches did Aaron grow?

Trains

Mr. Bolt needs to measure the length of a train.
The first car is the engine car. It is 8 meters long.
There are also four boxcars. Each boxcar is
12 meters long.

Help Mr. Bolt find the total length of the train.

2. **MP.1 Make Sense** What information is given? What do you need to find?

_____

_____

_____

3. **MP.4 Model** Write an equation to show the unknown.

_____

What unit of measure will you use?

_____

4. **MP.5 Use Tools** What is the total length of the train? Choose a tool to solve the problem. Show your work. _____

Follow the Path

Color a path from **Start** to **Finish**. Follow the sums and differences that are odd numbers. You can only move up, down, right, or left.

I can ...
add and subtract within 100.

© Content Standard 2.NBT.B.5

Start								
80 − 23	94 − 73	21 + 22	45 + 36	19 + 24	86 − 53	14 + 15	25 − 17	35 + 49
65 − 21	97 − 35	35 + 23	12 + 20	98 − 12	74 − 48	27 + 48	54 + 46	53 − 31
51 + 21	35 + 52	28 + 43	18 + 31	51 − 38	79 − 24	95 − 30	61 − 29	30 + 24
55 − 27	60 − 17	27 + 39	29 + 49	62 − 28	36 + 56	59 − 31	42 − 26	87 − 45
36 + 16	38 + 25	88 − 53	33 + 18	34 + 49	45 − 32	62 − 23	97 − 38	19 + 74

Finish

A-Z
Glossary

Word List
- centimeter (cm)
- foot (ft)
- height
- inch (in.)
- length
- mental math
- meter (m)
- yard (yd)

Understand Vocabulary

Choose a term from the Word List to complete each sentence.

1. The length of your finger can best be measured

   in centimeters or _____.

2. 100 _____ equals 1 meter.

3. _____ is how tall an object is from bottom to top.

Write T for *true* or F for *false*.

4. _____ 1 yard is 5 feet long.

5. _____ 12 inches is 1 foot long.

6. _____ A centimeter is longer than a meter.

7. _____ You can do mental math in your head.

Use Vocabulary in Writing

8. Tell how to find the total length of two pieces of string. One piece of string is 12 inches long. The other piece is 9 inches long. Use terms from the Word List.

_____

_____

_____

_____

Name _____

Set A

What is the distance around the front of the bookcase?

4 ft

3 ft

Write an equation to help solve.

1. What is the distance around the front of the crayon box?

12 cm

9 cm

Opposite sides have equal measures.

Add the lengths. Write an equation.

$4 + 3 + 4 + 3 = \underline{14}$

Distance around: $\underline{14}$ feet

Distance around: _____ cm

Set B

A kite string is 27 feet long.
Some of the string is cut off.
Now the kite string is 18 feet long.
How many feet of kite string were cut off?

Write an equation and draw a picture.

$27 - ? = 18 \ \text{or} \ 18 + ? = 27$

− 9 ft

| 15 | 16 | 17 | 18 | 19 | 20 | 21 | 22 | 23 | 24 | 25 | 26 | 27 | 28 | 29 | 30 |

$\underline{27} - \underline{9} = \underline{18}$ $\underline{9}$ feet

Write an equation using a symbol, ?, for the unknown number. Then draw a picture to solve.

2. A piece of yarn is 42 inches long. Mia cuts some of it off. It is now 26 inches long. How much yarn did Mia cut off?

_____

Topic 13 | Reteaching

A book measures 10 inches long. Another book measures 13 inches long. What is the total length of both books?

You can show $10 + 13$ on a number line.

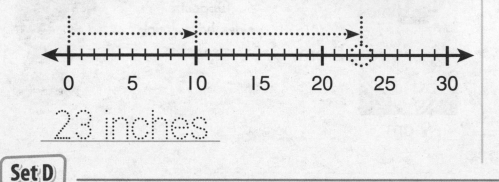

23 inches

Solve the problem using the number line.

3. One room in Jackie's house is 15 feet long. Another room is 9 feet long. What is the total length of both rooms?

_____

Thinking Habits

Use Tools

Which of these tools can I use?

counters   paper and pencil
cubes   place-value blocks
measuring tools technology
number line

Am I using the tool correctly?

Choose a tool to solve the problem.

4. Damon's shoelace is 45 inches long. His shoelace breaks. One piece is 28 inches long. How long is the other piece?

Explain your solution and why you chose the tool you used.

_____ ◯ _____ = _____ _____

© Pearson Education, Inc. 2

Name _____

1. What is the distance around the cover of the notepad?

7 in.

5 in.

Distance around: _____ in.

2. Kate is 48 inches tall. Tom is 2 inches taller than Kate. James is 3 inches shorter than Tom.

How tall is James?

Ⓐ   45 inches   Ⓒ   50 inches

Ⓑ   47 inches   Ⓓ   53 inches

---

3. Alexis has a rope that is 7 feet long. Mariah's rope is 9 feet long. Sam's rope is 3 feet longer than Mariah's rope.

Use the measurements on the cards to complete each sentence.

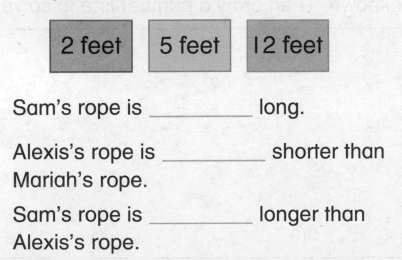

2 feet   5 feet   12 feet

Sam's rope is _____ long.

Alexis's rope is _____ shorter than Mariah's rope.

Sam's rope is _____ longer than Alexis's rope.

4. Joe rides his bike 18 miles. Then he rides 7 more miles.

Use the number line to find how far Joe rides. Then explain your work.

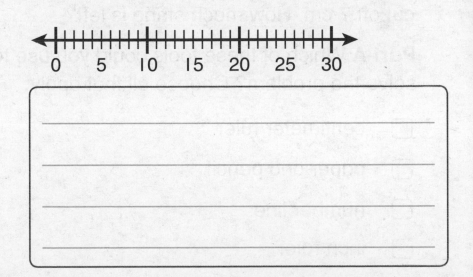

---

5. Pat says that each unknown equals 25 cm. Do you agree? Choose Yes or No.

47 cm + ? = 72 cm   ○ Yes ○ No

? + 39 cm = 54 cm   ○ Yes ○ No

99 cm − 64 cm = ?   ○ Yes ○ No

93 cm − ? = 68 cm   ○ Yes ○ No

6. Grace got a plant that was 34 cm tall. The plant grew and now it is 42 cm tall. How many centimeters did the plant grow?

Ⓐ 8 cm   Ⓒ 42 cm

Ⓑ 12 cm   Ⓓ 76 cm

---

7. Claire rides her bike 26 miles on Saturday and Sunday. She rides 8 miles on Sunday. How many miles does she ride on Saturday?

Write an equation to show the unknown.
Then use the number line to solve the problem.

_____ ◯ _____ = _____

_____ miles

0   5   10   15   20   25   30

---

8. Chris had a string that is 18 cm long. He cut off 7 cm. How much string is left?

Part A Which of these tools could you use to solve the problem? Choose all that apply.

☐ centimeter ruler

☐ paper and pencil

☐ number line

☐ inch ruler

Part B Write an equation to show the unknown. Then draw a number line to solve.

_____ ◯ _____ = _____

_____ cm

Topic 13 | Assessment

Name _____

Fishing Fun

Jim and his family go on a fishing trip. They use a boat and fishing gear to help them catch fish.

1. Jim takes this fishing box with him. What is the distance around the front of the fishing box? Write an equation to help solve the problem.

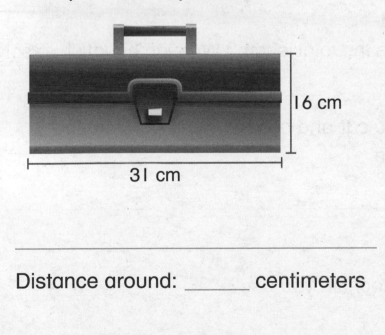

16 cm

31 cm

Distance around: _____ centimeters

2. Jim's fishing pole is 38 inches long. His dad's fishing pole is 96 inches long. How much shorter is Jim's pole than his dad's pole?

Part A Write a subtraction equation that shows the problem.

_____

Part B Solve the problem.

_____ inches shorter

3. Jim catches a fish 49 yards away from the shore. Later, he helps row the boat closer to the shore. Now he is 27 yards away from the shore. How many yards closer to shore is Jim now than when he caught the fish?

Part A Write an addition equation that shows the problem.

_____

Part B Solve the problem.

_____ yards

4. Jim catches a silver fish that is 12 inches long. His sister catches a green fish that is 27 inches long.

What is the total length of both fish? Use the number line to solve.

```
◄─┼┼┼┼┼┼┼┼┼┼┼┼┼┼┼┼┼┼┼┼┼┼┼┼┼┼┼┼┼┼┼┼┼┼┼┼┼┼┼─►
  0    5   10   15   20   25   30   35   40
```

_____ inches

---

5. Jim has 27 yards of fishing line. He gives 12 yards of line to a friend. How many yards of line does Jim have left?

```
◄─┼┼┼┼┼┼┼┼┼┼┼┼┼┼┼┼┼┼┼┼┼┼┼┼┼┼┼┼┼┼┼─►
  0    5   10   15   20   25   30
```

_____ yards

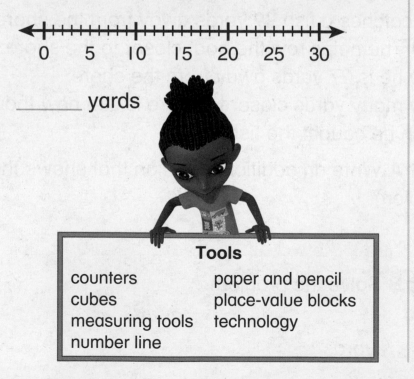

Tools

counters	paper and pencil
cubes	place-value blocks
measuring tools	technology
number line	

6. Jim's family meets a man with a big boat. A parking spot at the dock is 32 feet long. Will the man's car and boat fit in the parking spot?

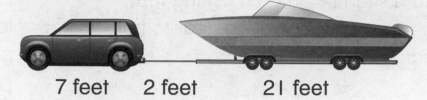

7 feet   2 feet   21 feet

Part A
What do you need to find? _____

_____

_____

Part B
What is the total length? Write an equation to solve.

_____   _____

Will the car and boat fit in the parking spot? Explain.

_____

_____

What tool did you use? _____

© Pearson Education, Inc. 2

Topic 13 | Performance Assessment

Graphs and Data

Essential Question: How can line plots, bar graphs, and picture graphs be used to show data and answer questions?

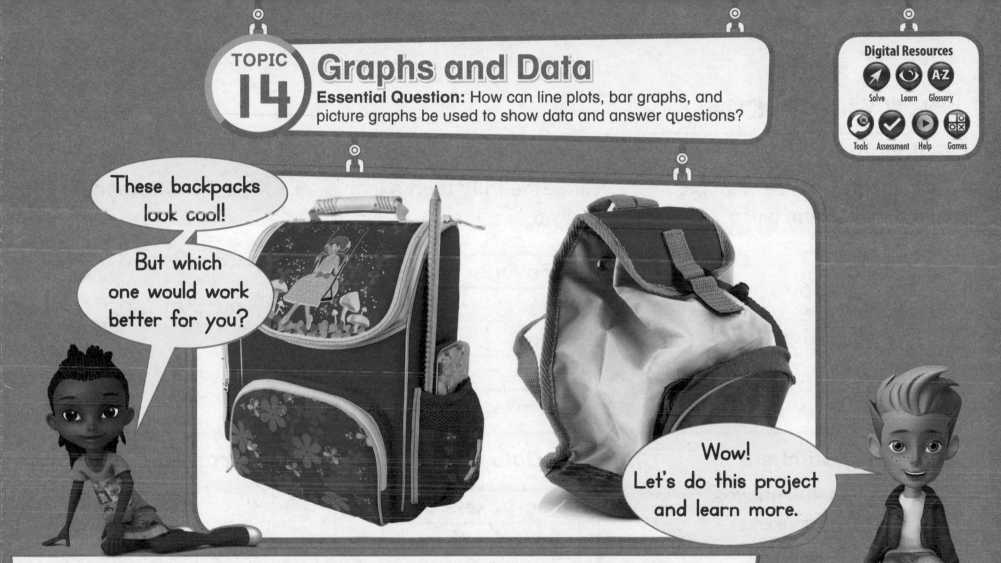

These backpacks look cool!

But which one would work better for you?

Wow! Let's do this project and learn more.

Math and Science Project: Comparing Objects and Data

Find Out Work with a partner.
Compare two backpacks.
Which one holds more?
Which one has more parts?
Which one is easier to put on?
Think of other ways to compare.

Journal: Make a Book Show what you learn in a book. In your book, also:

- Tell one good thing and one bad thing about each backpack.

- Draw line plots, picture graphs, and bar graphs to show and compare data.

Name _____

Review What You Know

Vocabulary

1. Circle the number that has a 6 in the **tens** place.

406

651

160

2. Circle the **tally marks** that show 6.

Favorite Toy	
Car	ⵉ⵿⵿ II
Blocks	IIII
Doll	ⵉ⵿⵿ I

3. Circle the **difference**.

$$22 - 9 = 13$$

$$34 + 61 = 95$$

Comparing Numbers

4. A zoo has 405 snakes. It has 375 monkeys. Compare the number of snakes to the number of monkeys.

Write > or <.

405 ◯ 375

Interpret Data

5.

Picnic Tickets Sold	
Jean	16
Paulo	18
Fatima	12

Who sold the most picnic tickets?

_____

Addition and Subtraction

6. Byron scores 24 points in a game. Ava scores 16 points in the same game. How many more points does Byron score than Ava?

_____ more points

My Word Cards

Study the words on the front of the card. Complete the activity on the back.

A-Z Glossary

data

Favorite Fruit	
Apple	7
Peach	4
Orange	5

line plot

Lengths of Shells

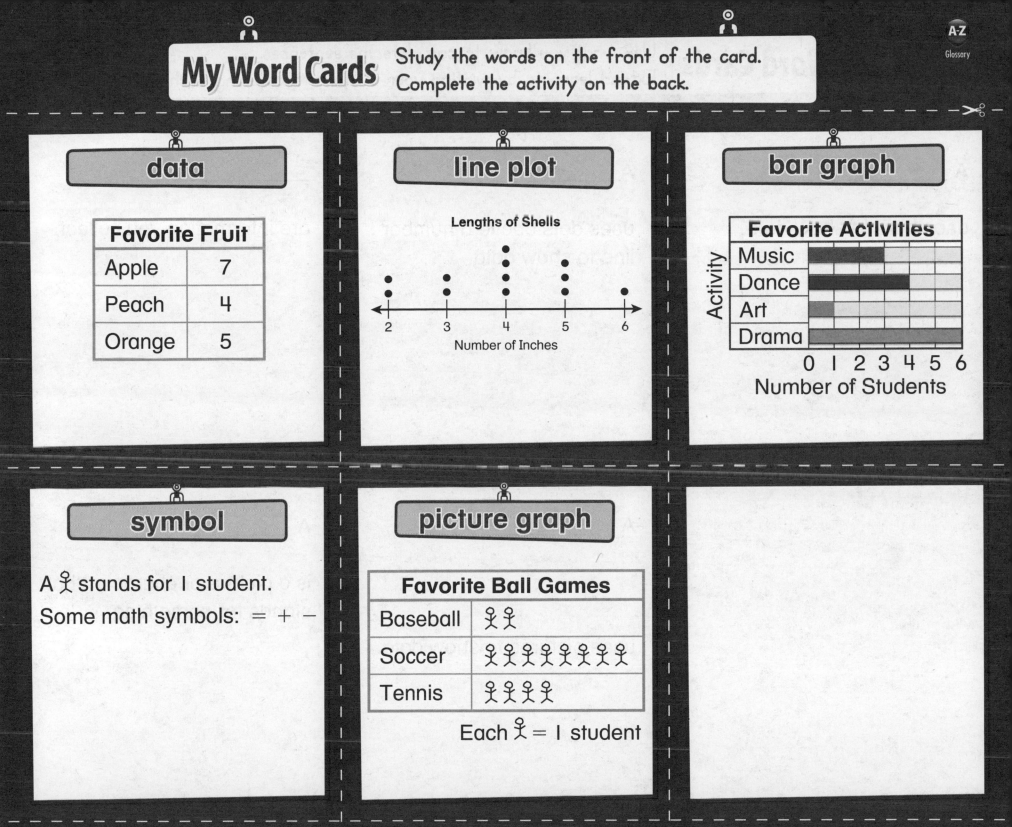

Number of Inches

bar graph

Favorite Activities

Activity: Music, Dance, Art, Drama

0 1 2 3 4 5 6
Number of Students

symbol

A 𝄞 stands for 1 student.
Some math symbols: = + −

picture graph

Favorite Ball Games	
Baseball	𝄞 𝄞
Soccer	𝄞 𝄞 𝄞 𝄞 𝄞 𝄞 𝄞
Tennis	𝄞 𝄞 𝄞 𝄞

Each 𝄞 = 1 student

Use what you know to complete the sentences.
Extend learning by writing your own sentence using each word.

A _____

uses bars to show data.

A _____

uses dots above a number line to show data.

_____

are information you collect.

A _____

_____

uses pictures to show data.

A _____

is a picture or character that stands for something.

© Pearson Education, Inc. 2

Name _____

Solve & Share

Find four objects that are each shorter than 9 inches. Measure the length of each object to the nearest inch. Record the measurements in the table.

Then plot the data on the number line.

Which object is longest? Which is shortest?

I can ...
measure the lengths of objects, then make a line plot to organize the data

Content Standards 2.MD.D.9, 2.MD.A.1
Mathematical Practices MP.2, MP.4, MP.5, MP.6

Object	Length in Inches

Lengths of Objects

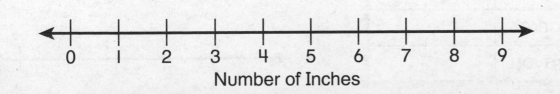

Number of Inches

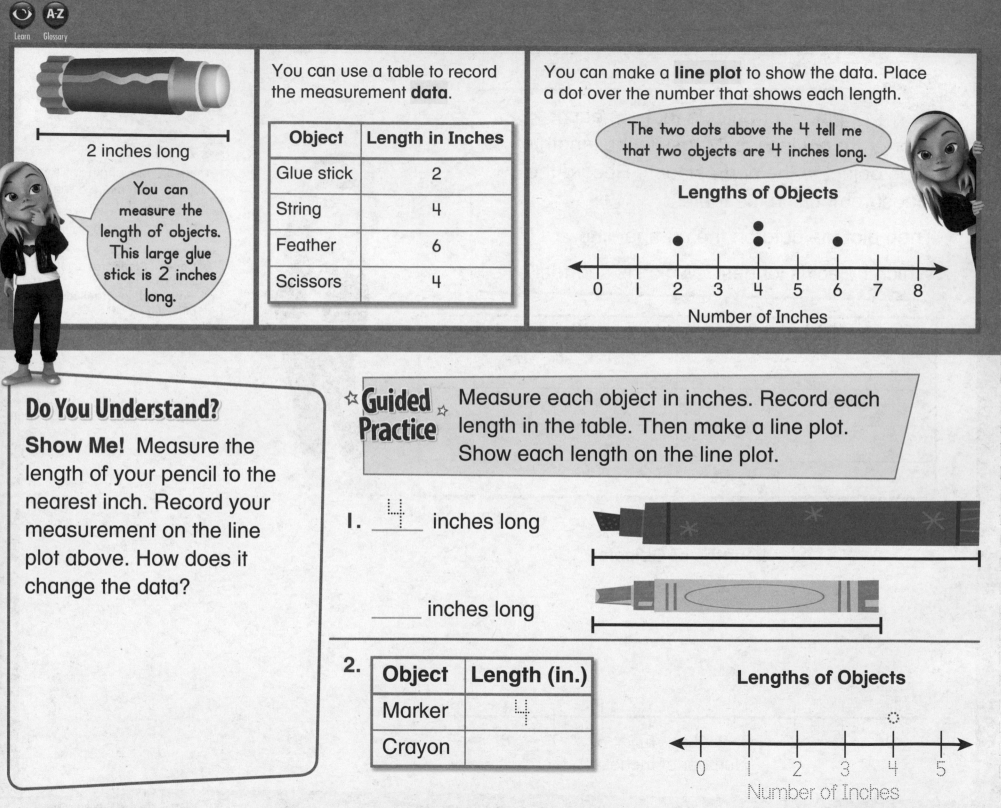

2 inches long

You can measure the length of objects. This large glue stick is 2 inches long.

You can use a table to record the measurement **data**.

Object	Length in Inches
Glue stick	2
String	4
Feather	6
Scissors	4

You can make a **line plot** to show the data. Place a dot over the number that shows each length.

The two dots above the 4 tell me that two objects are 4 inches long.

Lengths of Objects

Number of Inches

Do You Understand?

Show Me! Measure the length of your pencil to the nearest inch. Record your measurement on the line plot above. How does it change the data?

☆ **Guided Practice** ☆ Measure each object in inches. Record each length in the table. Then make a line plot. Show each length on the line plot.

1. __4__ inches long

____ inches long

2.

Object	Length (in.)
Marker	4
Crayon	

Lengths of Objects

Number of Inches

© Pearson Education, Inc. 2

Name _____

Independent Practice

Measure each object in inches. Record each length in the table. Show each length on the line plot.

3. The paintbrush is _____ inches long.

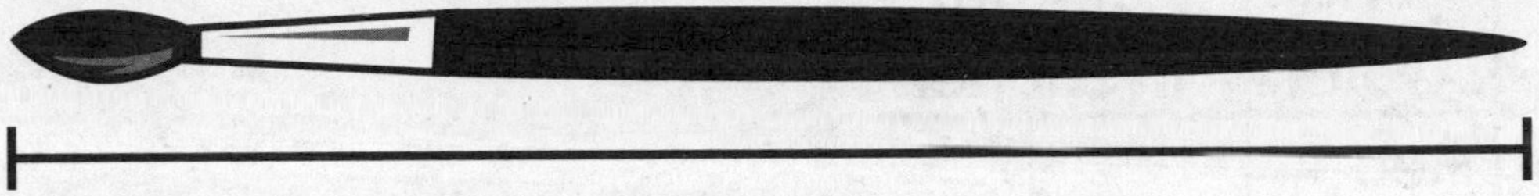

4. The chalk is _____ inches long.

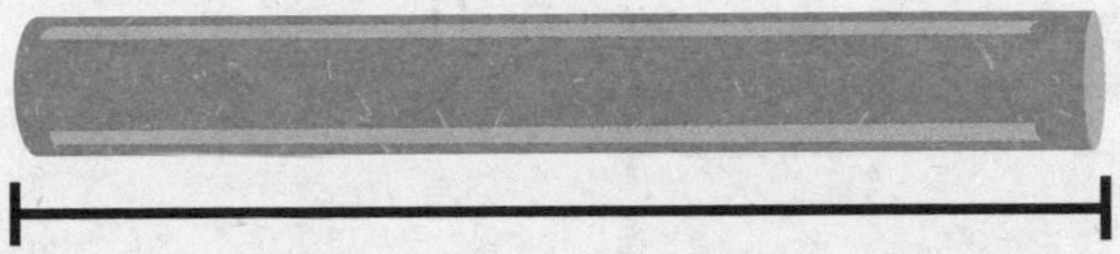

5. The straw is _____ inches long.

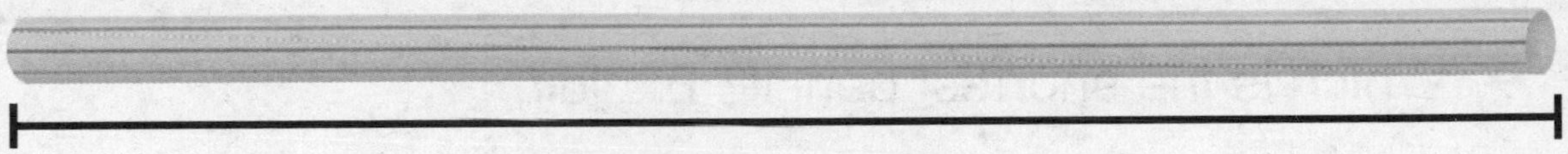

6. The glue stick is _____ inches long.

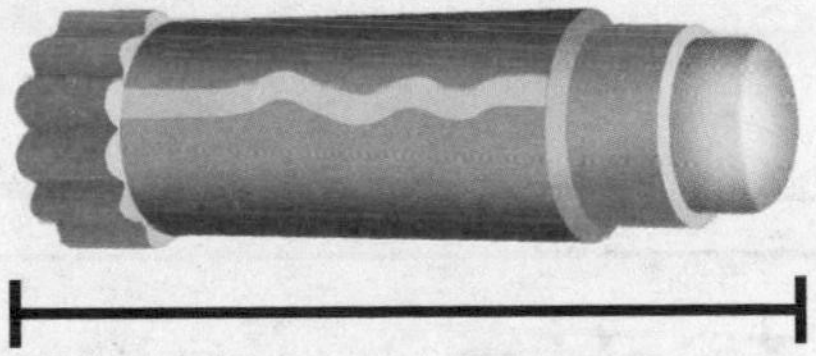

7.

Object	Length in Inches
Paintbrush	
Chalk	
Straw	
Glue Stick	

Lengths of Objects

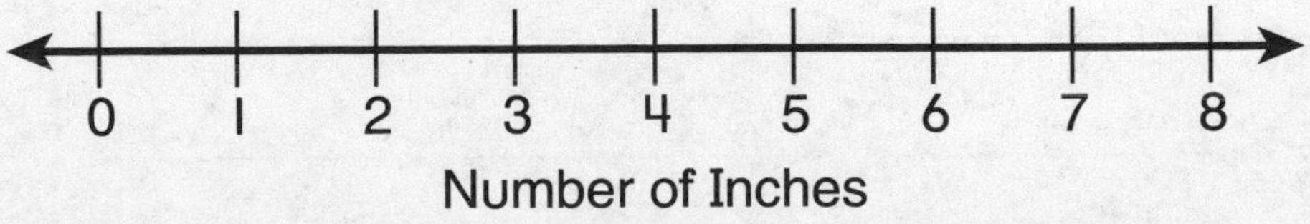

0 1 2 3 4 5 6 7 8

Number of Inches

8. © **MP.4 Model** Sophia measured the length of her colored pencils and made a table. Use the data to make a line plot.

Pencil Color	Length in Inches
Red	4
Blue	3
Green	7
Yellow	9

A line plot can help you make sense of the data.

Lengths of Pencils

0 1 2 3 4 5 6 7 8 9

Number of Inches

9. Which is the shortest pencil? Explain.

10. **Higher Order Thinking** Which two pencils have a total length of 16 inches? Explain.

11. © **Assessment** Measure the length of the purple pencil in inches. Write the length below. Record your measurement on the line plot above in Item 8.

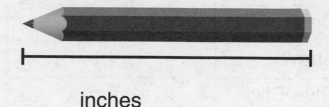

____ inches

Name _____

Another Look! You can make a line plot to show data.

The table shows the lengths of objects in inches.
Use the data from the table to make a line plot.

HOME ACTIVITY Use the line plot to ask your child questions about the data. Encourage your child to explain each answer.

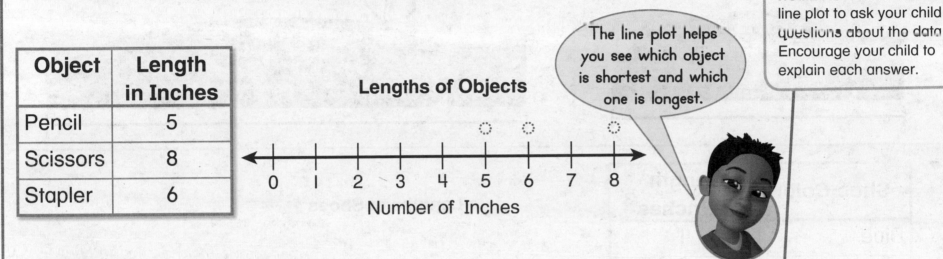

Object	Length in Inches
Pencil	5
Scissors	8
Stapler	6

Lengths of Objects

The line plot helps you see which object is shortest and which one is longest.

0 1 2 3 4 5 6 7 8

Number of Inches

Use the line plot above to answer the questions.

1. Which object is longest? _____

2. Which object is shortest? _____

3. How much shorter is the stapler than the scissors? _____

4. How much longer is the scissors than the pencil? _____

© **MP.6 Be Precise** Measure each shoe in inches. Then record each length in the table. Show each length on the line plot.

5. The green shoe is _____ long.

6. The purple shoe is _____ long.

7.

Shoe Color	Length in Inches
Blue	4
Red	5
Green	
Purple	

Lengths of Shoes

← 0 1 2 3 4 5 6 →

Number of Inches

8. Higher Order Thinking Which three shoes have a total length of 13 inches? Explain.

_____

_____

9. © **Assessment** Measure the length of the yellow shoe in inches. Write the length below. Record your measurement on the line plot above.

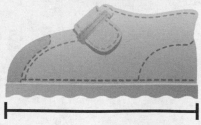

_____

© Pearson Education, Inc. 2

Topic 14 | Lesson 1

Name _____

☆ ☆
Solve & Share

Measure the length of your shoe.
Then use your data and data from your class
to make a line plot.

Tell one thing you learn from the data.

I can ...
measure the lengths of
objects, then make a line plot
to organize the data

© **Content Standards** 2.MD.D.9,
2.MD.A.1
Mathematical Practices MP.2,
MP.4, MP.5, MP.6

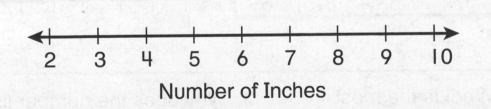

Shoe Lengths

←—+———+———+———+———+———+———+———+———+→
　2　　3　　4　　5　　6　　7　　8　　9　　10
Number of Inches

Some students measure their heights. They record the data in a table. Are there any patterns in the data?

Student Heights in Inches

46	48	47	49
49	47	46	48
48	49	50	47
49	48	49	51

You can make a line plot to look for patterns.

To make a line plot, draw a number line, and write a title and labels to fit your data.

Students' Heights

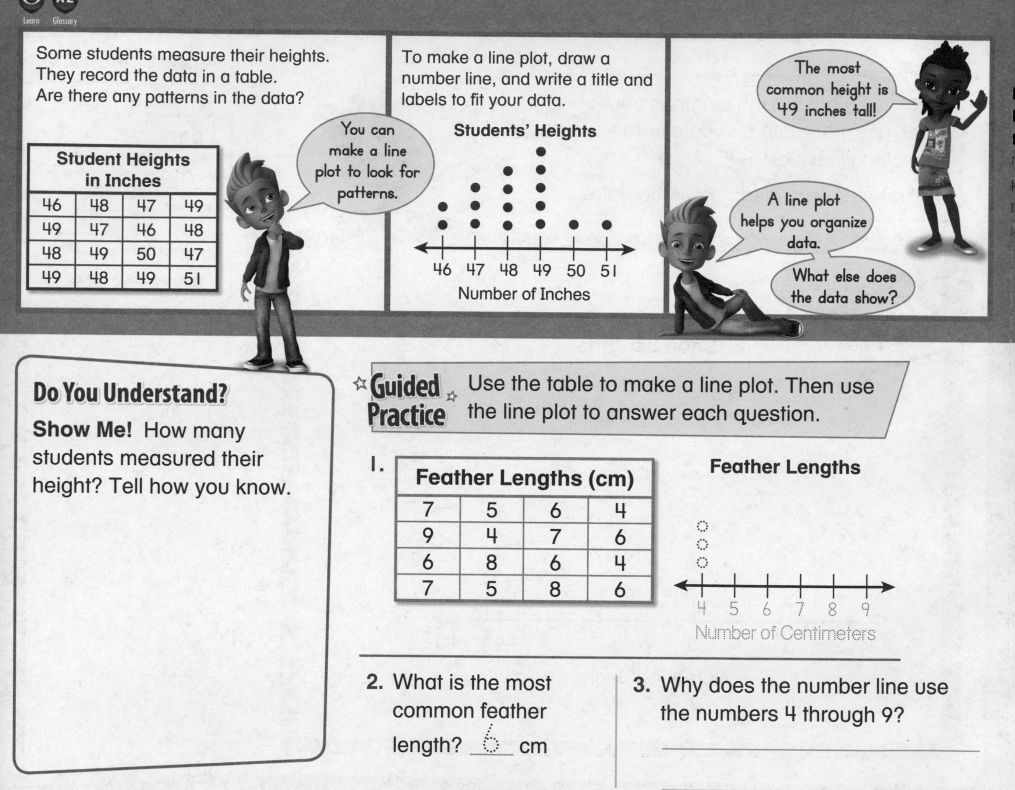

Number of Inches

The most common height is 49 inches tall!

A line plot helps you organize data.

What else does the data show?

Do You Understand?

Show Me! How many students measured their height? Tell how you know.

Guided Practice

Use the table to make a line plot. Then use the line plot to answer each question.

1.

Feather Lengths (cm)

7	5	6	4
9	4	7	6
6	8	6	4
7	5	8	6

Feather Lengths

4 5 6 7 8 9
Number of Centimeters

2. What is the most common feather length? __6__ cm

3. Why does the number line use the numbers 4 through 9?

© Pearson Education, Inc. 2

Independent Practice

Collect data and use the data to complete the line plot. Then use the line plot to solve the problems.

4. Measure the length of your pencil in centimeters. Collect pencil-length data from your classmates. Make a line plot with the data.

Title: _____

Make a line plot using the data you collect.

Label: _____

5. What is the length of the longest pencil?

_____

6. What is the length of the shortest pencil?

_____

7. What is the difference in length between the shortest and longest pencil?

_____

8. What is the most common pencil length?

_____

9. **A-Z** **Vocabulary** Use these words to complete the sentences.   **longest**   **line plot**   **order**

A _____ can help you see the data in _____.

A line plot makes it easy to see the shortest and _____ objects.

© **MP.4 Model** Use the data in the table to complete the line plot. Then use the line plot to solve the problems.

10.

Crayon Lengths in Centimeters			
6	7	5	6
7	5	7	6
7	8	6	5
5	6	7	6
8	8	6	8

Title: _____

What numbers will you use to make your line plot?

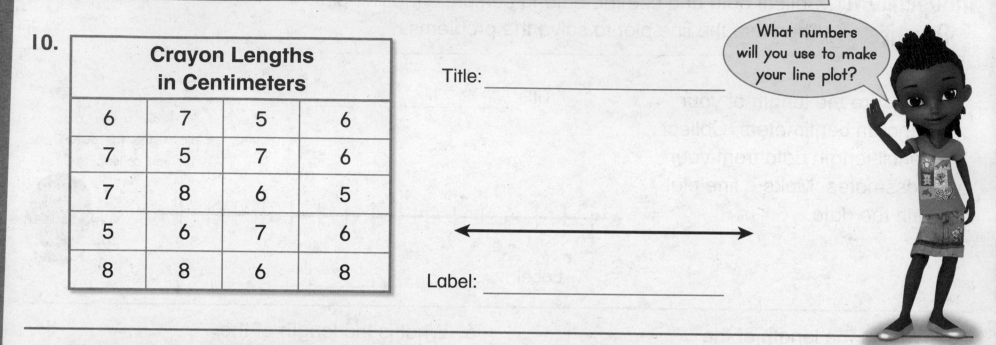

Label: _____

11. **Higher Order Thinking** How many crayons are longer than 5 centimeters? Explain.

_____

_____

_____

12. © **Assessment** Measure the length of the blue crayon to the nearest centimeter. Write the length below.

_____

Then record your measurement on the line plot above that you made in Item 10.

Name _____

Another Look! 7 students measured the length of the scissors to the nearest centimeter. The results are shown in the table below.

Length of Scissors in Centimeters			
8	7	7	6
7	6	7	7

Step 1 Measure the length of the scissors to the nearest centimeter.

Step 2 Write your measurement in the table above.

Step 3 Record your measurement on the line plot at the right.

HOME ACTIVITY Have your child measure the lengths of three windows in your home. The windows should have different lengths. Then ask your child to make a line plot of the data.

Length of Scissors

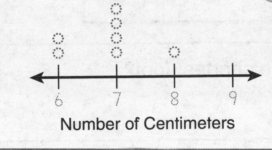

Number of Centimeters

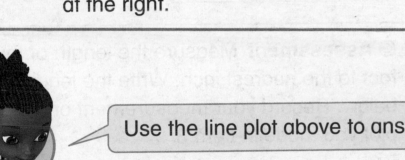

Use the line plot above to answer each question.

1. Which measurement of the length of the scissors is most common?

_____ centimeters

2. Why did people get different measurements? Write Yes or No.

_____ The object has a shape that is **NOT** flat.

_____ The measurement is halfway between two units.

_____ The ruler is not aligned with 0 when used.

© **MP.4 Model** Measure the foot length of 3 friends or family members. Write the measurements in the table below. Then use the data to complete the line plot.

3.

Foot Lengths in Inches			
8	7	8	7
6	9	6	7
10	7	9	10
7			

Foot Lengths

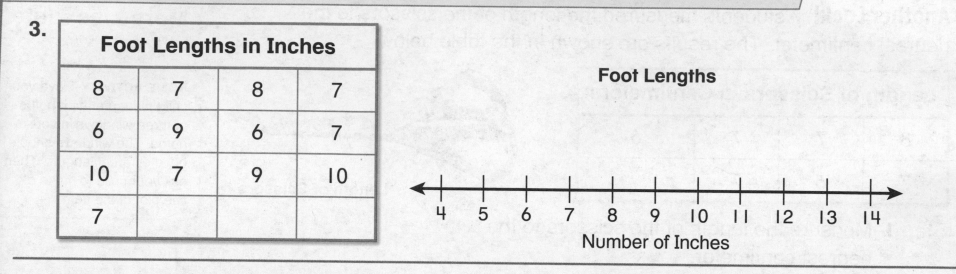

Number of Inches

4. How long is the shortest foot?

5. What is the most common foot length?

6. Higher Order Thinking How many people have a foot length that is an even number of inches? Explain.

7. © **Assessment** Measure the length of this foot to the nearest inch. Write the length below. Record your measurement on the line plot you made in Item 3.

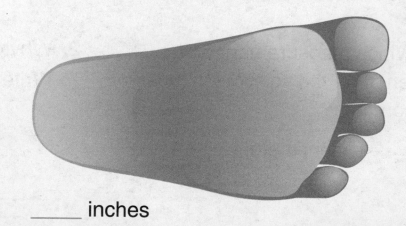

_____ inches

© Pearson Education, Inc. 2

Topic 14 | Lesson 2

Name _____

Solve & Share

The graph shows the number of birthdays in each season for a class.

How can you use the graph to write the number of birthdays in this table? Tell how you know.

I can ...
draw bar graphs and use them to solve problems.

© **Content Standard** 2.MD.D.10
Mathematical Practices MP.1,
MP.2, MP.4

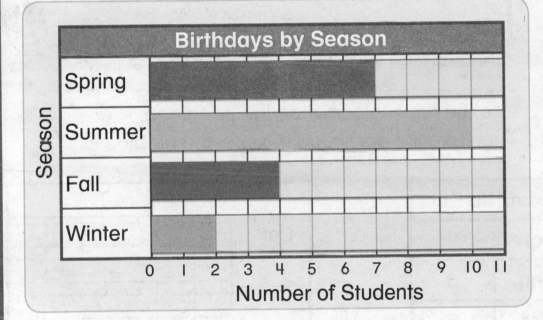

Birthdays by Season

Spring	
Summer	
Fall	
Winter	

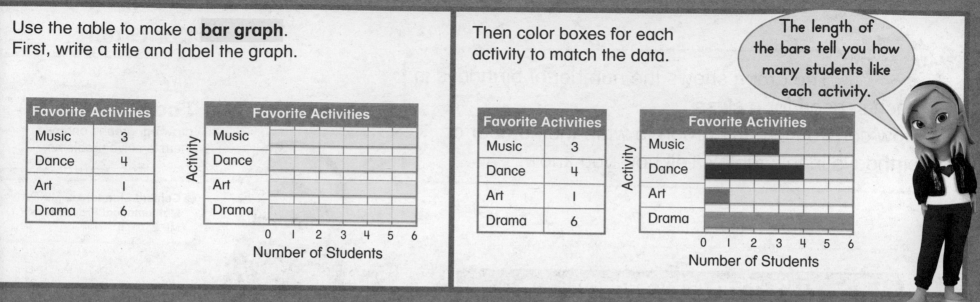

Use the table to make a **bar graph**.
First, write a title and label the graph.

Then color boxes for each activity to match the data.

The length of the bars tell you how many students like each activity.

Do You Understand?

Show Me! Which activity did the most students choose? Explain how you know.

★ **Guided** ★ Use the table to complete the bar graph.
Practice   Then use the bar graph to solve the problems.

Favorite Pet	
Cat	4
Dog	6
Bird	2
Turtle	3

1. How many students chose cat?

4

2. Which pet did the most students choose?

_____

© Pearson Education, Inc. 2
Topic 14 | Lesson 3

Independent Practice ⭐

Use the bar graph to solve the problems.

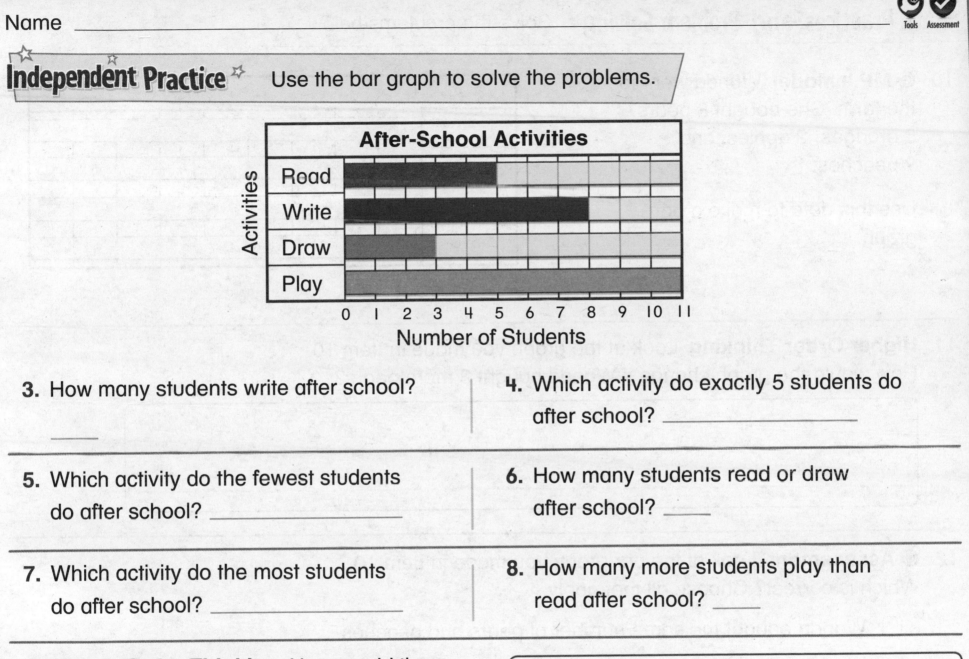

After-School Activities

Activities: Read, Write, Draw, Play

Number of Students (0 to 11)

3. How many students write after school?

_____

4. Which activity do exactly 5 students do after school? _____

5. Which activity do the fewest students do after school? _____

6. How many students read or draw after school? _____

7. Which activity do the most students do after school? _____

8. How many more students play than read after school? _____

9. Higher Order Thinking How would the graph be different if 2 students changed their after-school activity from Play to Read?

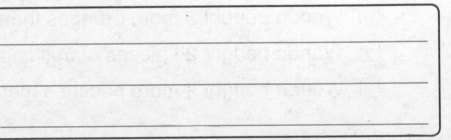

10. © **MP.4 Model** Wanda went to the farm. She bought 8 pears, 5 oranges, 2 apples, and 9 peaches.

Use this data to make a bar graph.

11. **Higher Order Thinking** Look at the graph you made in Item 10. How would the graph change if Wanda bought 3 more pears?

12. © **Assessment** Look at the bar graph you made in Item 10. Which is correct? Choose all that apply.

☐ Wanda bought the same number of pears and peaches.

☐ Wanda bought 3 more oranges than apples.

☐ Wanda bought 24 pieces of fruit in all.

☐ Wanda bought 4 more peaches than oranges.

Name _____

Another Look! The table shows how students voted to name the class goldfish.

Use the data from the table to make a bar graph.

Goldfish Names	
Flash	5
Goldie	3
Rocky	6
Bubbles	8

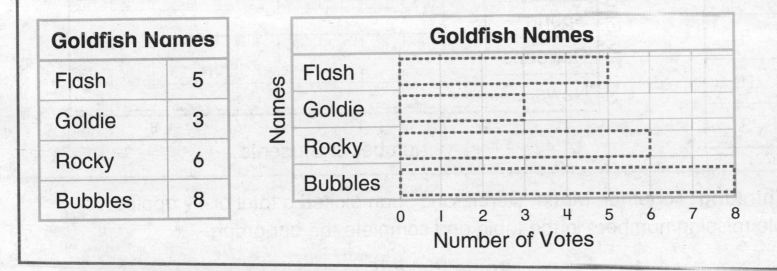

Goldfish Names

Names: Flash, Goldie, Rocky, Bubbles

Number of Votes: 0 1 2 3 4 5 6 7 8

Use the bar graph above to solve the problems.

1. How many students voted for the name Goldie or the name Rocky?

2. How many fewer students voted for the name Flash than voted for the name Rocky?

_____

3. Which name did the most students vote for? _____

4. Which name did the fewest students vote for? _____

Complete the bar graphs and solve the problems.

5. © **MP.4 Model** Use the data in the table to complete the bar graph.

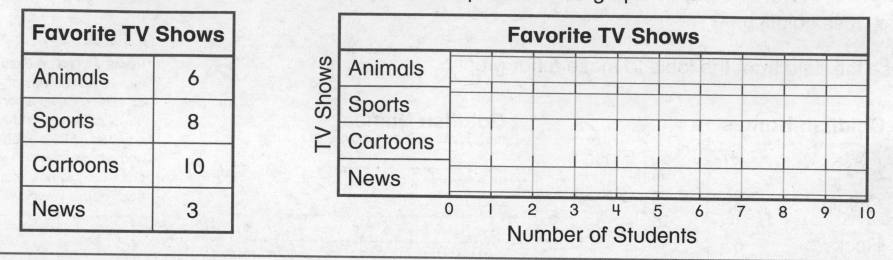

Favorite TV Shows	
Animals	6
Sports	8
Cartoons	10
News	3

6. Higher Order Thinking Together, Marla, Derek, and Juan picked a total of 19 apples. Write the possible missing numbers in the table and complete the bar graph.

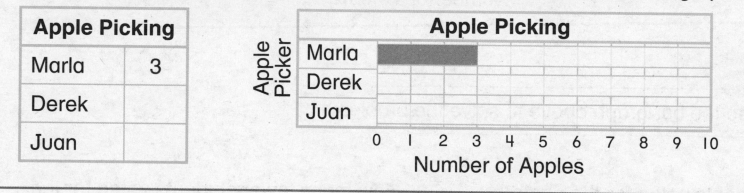

Apple Picking	
Marla	3
Derek	
Juan	

7. © **Assessment** Look at the bar graph in Item 5. Which statements are correct? Choose all that apply.

☐ 2 fewer students chose sports than animals.   ☐ 10 students chose news or animals.

☐ 5 more students chose sports than news.   ☐ 27 students in all were counted.

Name _____

Solve & Share

The graph shows the favorite subjects for a class. How can you use the graph to write the data in this table? Tell how you know.

I can …
draw picture graphs and use them to solve problems.

© **Content Standard** 2.MD.D.10
Mathematical Practices MP.2, MP.3, MP.4, MP.8

Favorite School Subject

	1	2	3	4	5	6	7	8
Reading	😊	😊	😊	😊				
Math	😊	😊	😊	😊	😊	😊		
Science	😊	😊	😊					
Social Studies	😊							

Number of Students

Favorite School Subject

Reading	
Math	
Science	
Social Studies	

The tally chart shows the favorite ball games of Ms. Green's class.

Favorite Ball Games

Favorite Ball Games	
Baseball	II
Soccer	THL III
Tennis	IIII

You can show the same data in another way.

Choose a **symbol** to represent the data.

The symbol will be 𝑋. Each 𝑋 represents 1 student.

A **picture graph** uses pictures to show data.

You can draw the symbols to show the data.

8 students chose soccer!

Favorite Ball Games	
Baseball	𝑋 𝑋
Soccer	𝑋 𝑋 𝑋 𝑋 𝑋 𝑋 𝑋 𝑋
Tennis	𝑋 𝑋 𝑋 𝑋

Each 𝑋 = 1 student

Do You Understand?

Show Me! How are the tally chart and picture graph for the favorite ball games of Ms. Green's class alike?

Guided Practice

Use the tally chart to complete the picture graph. Then use the picture graph to solve the problems.

Favorite Colors	
Blue	THL
Red	THL I
Purple	III

Favorite Colors	
Blue	╱ ╱ ╱ ╱ ╱
Red	
Purple	

Each ✏ = 1 vote

1. How many students like blue best?

5

2. Which color is the favorite of most students?

_____

Independent Practice Use the tally chart to complete the picture graph. Then use the picture graph to solve the problems.

3.

Favorite Season	
Spring	IIII
Summer	⊥⊥⊥⊥ ⊥⊥⊥⊥
Fall	⊥⊥⊥⊥ I
Winter	II

Favorite Season	
Spring	
Summer	
Fall	
Winter	

Each 🧍 = 1 vote

4. How many students like fall best?

_____

5. Which season do exactly 4 students like best? _____

6. Which season do the fewest students like?

_____

7. How many students like the season with the fewest votes? _____

8. Which season do the most students like?

_____

9. How many students like the season with the most votes? _____

10. **Higher Order Thinking** Look at the picture graph above. How would the graph change if 2 students changed their votes from Summer to Fall?

_____

_____

Use the tally chart to complete the picture graph.
Use the picture graph to solve the problems.

11. © **MP.4 Model** Bob made a tally chart to show the trees in a park.

Trees in the Park	
Birch	III
Oak	TTTT I
Maple	TTTT
Pine	II

Trees in the Park	
Birch	
Oak	
Maple	
Pine	

Each 🌲 = 1 tree

You can model data using a picture graph.

12. Math and Science Birch, oak, maple, and pine trees are common in North America. Which type of tree is most common in the park? _____

13. Higher Order Thinking How many birch and maple trees are there in all?

_____

14. © **Assessment** Draw a picture graph to show the data in the table.

Favorite Drink	
Milk	III
Juice	IIII
Water	I

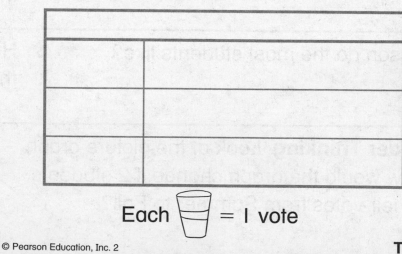

Each 🥛 = 1 vote

Name _____

Another Look! A picture graph uses pictures or symbols to show information.

The number at the right tells how many students chose each snack. Complete the picture graph.

There are 9 symbols for popcorn. So 9 students chose popcorn.

HOME ACTIVITY Tell your child which snack shown in the picture graph is your favorite. Ask him or her to explain how the Favorite Snacks picture graph would change if your response was added to the picture graph.

Favorite Snacks		
Popcorn	☺☺☺☺☺☺☺☺☺	9
Fruit Cup	☺☺☺☺	4
Yogurt	☺☺☺☺☺☺☺	7
Cheese and Crackers	☺☺☺☺☺☺☺☺☺☺	10

Each ☺ = 1 student

Use the picture graph above to solve the problems.

1. How many students like cheese and crackers best?

_____

2. How many students like yogurt best?

_____

3. Which snack is the least favorite?

4. Which snack is most students' favorite?

Solve each problem.

5. © **MP.4 Model** The tally chart shows how many tickets each student has. Use the tally chart to complete the picture graph.

Tickets We Have	
Denise	IIII
Steve	II
Tom	THL IIII
Lisa	THL I

Tickets We Have	
Denise	
Steve	
Tom	
Lisa	

Each [TICKET] = I ticket

6. **Higher Order Thinking** Lisa gives 2 tickets to Steve. How many tickets does Steve have now? Explain.

_____

_____

_____

7. © **Assessment** The tally chart shows the favorite pets of a class of second graders. Use the tally chart to draw a picture graph.

Favorite Pets	
Cat	THL I
Dog	THL II
Fish	THL
Hamster	II

♥ = I Vote

© Pearson Education, Inc. 2

Solve & Share

7 students voted for Turtle as their favorite pond animal.
10 students voted for Frog. 4 students voted for Fish.
Make a picture graph to show the data.
Write two things you notice about the data.

I can ...
draw conclusions from graphs.

© **Content Standards** 2.MD.D.10, 2.OA.A.1
Mathematical Practices MP.1, MP.3, MP.4, MP.7

Favorite Pond Animals

Turtle	
Frog	
Fish	

Each ★ = 1 vote

1. _____

2. _____

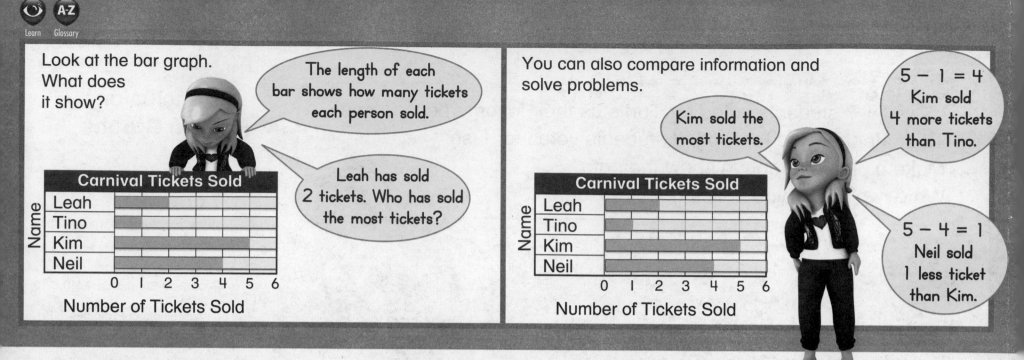

The length of each bar shows how many tickets each person sold.

Look at the bar graph. What does it show?

Leah has sold 2 tickets. Who has sold the most tickets?

Carnival Tickets Sold

You can also compare information and solve problems.

Kim sold the most tickets.

$5 - 1 = 4$
Kim sold 4 more tickets than Tino.

$5 - 4 = 1$
Neil sold 1 less ticket than Kim.

Carnival Tickets Sold

Do You Understand?

Show Me! Look at the graph above. How many tickets did Kim and Neil sell in all? How do you know?

☆ **Guided Practice** ☆ Use the bar graph to solve the problems.

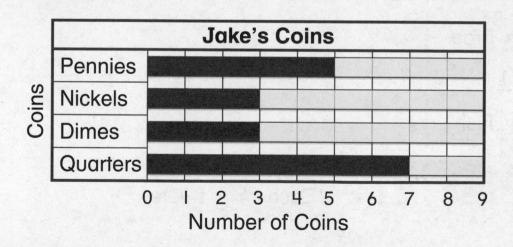

Jake's Coins

1. How many pennies does Jake have?

5

2. Jake spends 3 of his quarters. How many does he have left?

_____

© Pearson Education, Inc. 2

Independent Practice ☆ Use the bar graph to solve the problems.

3. How many students in all were absent on Tuesday and Thursday?

_____
_____

4. Were fewer students absent on Monday or Friday? How many fewer?

_____
_____

5. Three of the students absent on Friday were boys. How many girls were absent on Friday?

_____

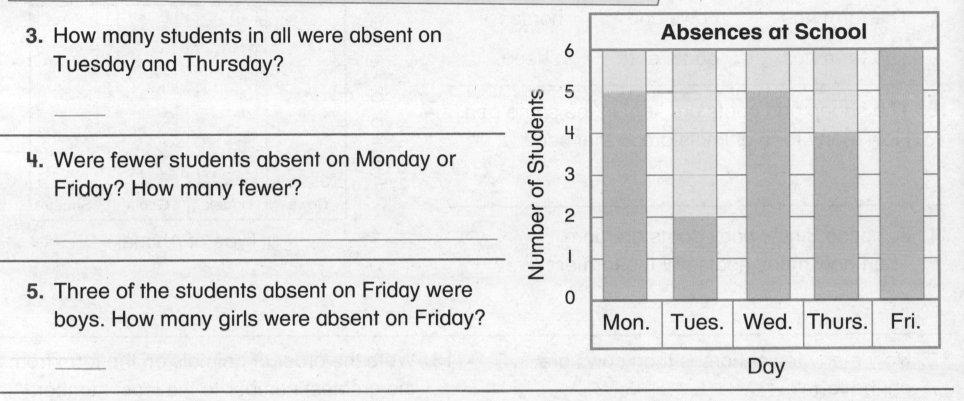

Absences at School

Number of Students
6
5
4
3
2
1
0

Mon. | Tues. | Wed. | Thurs. | Fri.

Day

6. On which two days were the same number of students absent?

_____

7. Were more students absent on Wednesday or Thursday? How many more?

_____

8. **Higher Order Thinking** The graph shows the number of students absent last week. This week, 19 students were absent. Compare the number of students absent this week to the number of students absent last week.

_____
_____
_____

9. © **MP.1 Make Sense** Complete each sentence.

The farm has _____ cows and _____ horses.

The farm has _____ goats and _____ sheep.

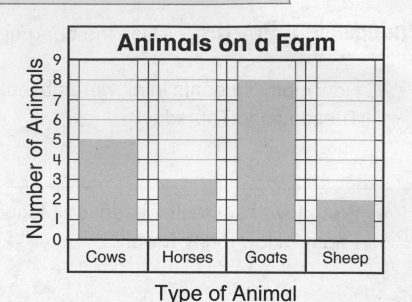

Animals on a Farm

Number of Animals

Cows   Horses   Goats   Sheep

Type of Animal

10. The sheep and goats are kept in the same pen. How many farm animals are in that pen?

____

11. Suppose 3 new baby goats are born. Then how many goats will the farmer have?

____

12. How many fewer horses than cows are on the farm?

____

13. Write the order of animals on the farm from the greatest number to the least number.

____

14. **Higher Order Thinking** Do you think the bars on a bar graph should all be the same color? Explain.

____

15. © **Assessment** The farmer wants to buy some sheep. He wants to have as many sheep as cows. How many more sheep should the farmer buy?

____

Name _____

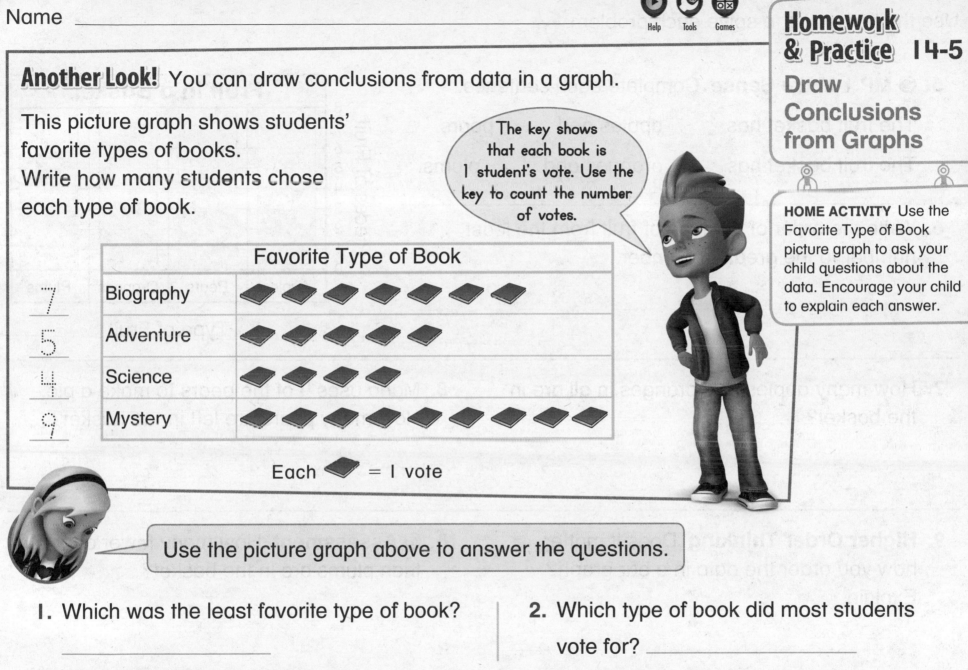

Help Tools Games

Another Look! You can draw conclusions from data in a graph.

This picture graph shows students' favorite types of books.
Write how many students chose each type of book.

The key shows that each book is 1 student's vote. Use the key to count the number of votes.

HOME ACTIVITY Use the Favorite Type of Book picture graph to ask your child questions about the data. Encourage your child to explain each answer.

Favorite Type of Book	
Biography	📖 📖 📖 📖 📖 📖 📖
Adventure	📖 📖 📖 📖 📖
Science	📖 📖 📖 📖
Mystery	📖 📖 📖 📖 📖 📖 📖 📖

7
5
4
9

Each 📖 = 1 vote

Use the picture graph above to answer the questions.

1. Which was the least favorite type of book?

_____

2. Which type of book did most students vote for? _____

3. How many more students voted for biography than for adventure?

_____

4. If each student voted one time only, how many students voted in all?

_____

5. © **MP.1 Make Sense** Complete each sentence.

The fruit basket has _____ apples and _____ pears.

The fruit basket has _____ oranges and _____ plums.

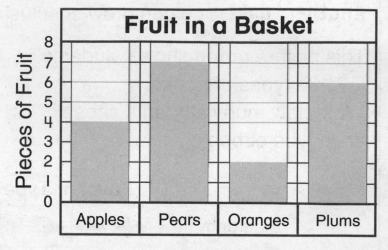

6. Write the order of the type of fruit from the least number to the greatest number.

_____

7. How many apples and oranges in all are in the basket?

_____

8. Maria uses 4 of the pears to make a pie. How many pears are left in the basket?

_____

9. **Higher Order Thinking** Does it matter how you order the data in a bar graph? Explain.

_____

_____

_____

10. © **Assessment** How many fewer apples than plums are in the basket?

_____

Name _____

Solve & Share

Make a picture graph to show how many connecting cubes, counters, and ones cubes you have. Then write and solve a problem about your data.

I can ...
reason about data in bar graphs and picture graphs to write and solve problems.

© **Mathematical Practices** MP.2 Also MP.1, MP.3, MP.4, MP.6, MP.8
Content Standards 2.MD.D.10, 2.OA.A.1

Math Tools	
Connecting Cubes	
Counters	
Ones Cubes	

Each _____ = 1 math tool

Thinking Habits
What do the symbols mean?

How are the numbers in the problem related?

_____

_____

_____

The bar graph shows the number of stamps each student has collected.

Write and solve a problem about the data in the bar graph.

Stamp Collections

How can I use reasoning to write and solve a problem?

I can look at the bars to see how many stamps each student has.

I can write a problem to compare the number of stamps two students have.

My Problem

How many more stamps does Lara have than Gail?

25 – 15 = 10

10 more stamps

Do You Understand?

Show Me! Use reasoning to write your own problem about the data in the graph. Then solve it.

☆ Guided Practice ☆

Use the bar graph to write and solve problems.

Meytal's Closet

Item		
Shorts		
Shirts		
Pants		
Skirts		

0 1 2 3 4 5 6 7 8 9 10 11 12 13 14 15 16
Number of Items

1. How many shirts and skirts are there in all?

10 (+) 4 = 14

2. _____

_____ ◯ _____ = _____

Tools   Assessment

Independent Practice ☆ Use the bar graph to write and solve problems.

3. _____

_____

_____

___ ◯ ___ = ___

4. _____

_____

___ ◯ ___ = ___

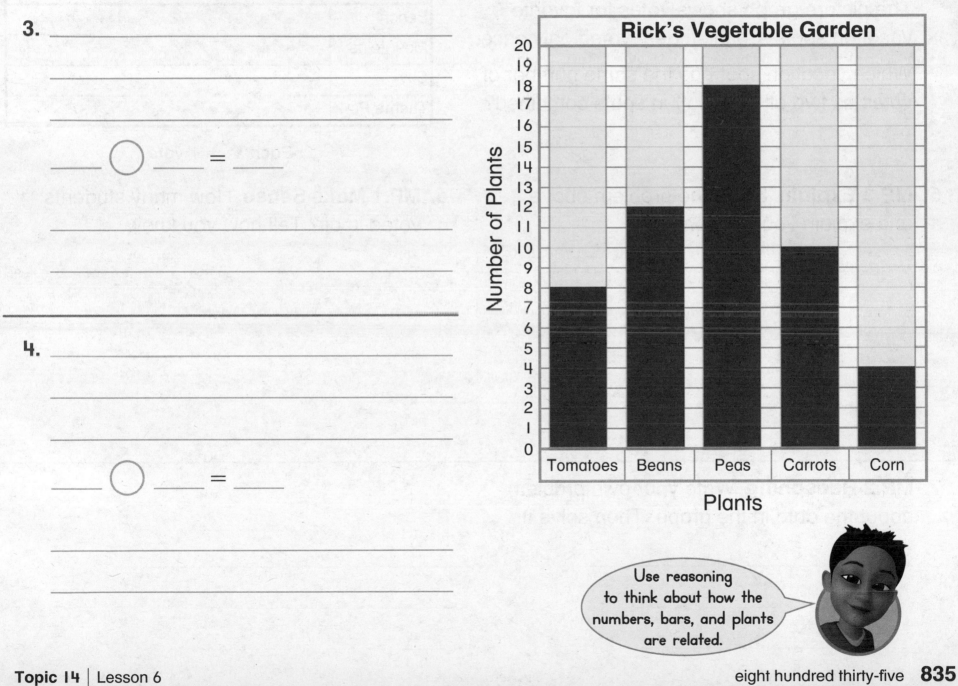

Rick's Vegetable Garden

Number of Plants

Plants

Tomatoes   Beans   Peas   Carrots   Corn

Use reasoning to think about how the numbers, bars, and plants are related.

Math Practices and Problem Solving

© **Performance Assessment** _____

Vacation Time!

The picture graph shows votes for favorite vacation spots. Each student voted only once.

Which vacation spot has the same number of votes as two other vacation spots combined?

Votes for Favorite Vacation Spot	
Beach	✔✔✔✔✔✔✔✔✔
Mountains	✔✔✔✔✔✔
City	✔✔✔✔
Theme Park	✔✔✔✔✔✔✔✔✔✔✔✔

Each ✔ = I vote

5. **MP.3 Explain** Solve the problem above and explain your reasoning.

_____

_____

_____

_____

6. **MP.1 Make Sense** How many students voted in all? Tell how you know.

_____

_____

_____

_____

7. **MP.2 Reasoning** Write your own problem about the data in the graph. Then solve it.

____ ◯ ____ = ____

_____

_____

_____

_____

© Pearson Education, Inc. 2

Name _____

Another Look! You can reason about data in the picture graph to write and solve problems.

How many more votes did the Tigers get than the Lions?

Votes for Team Name	
Wolves	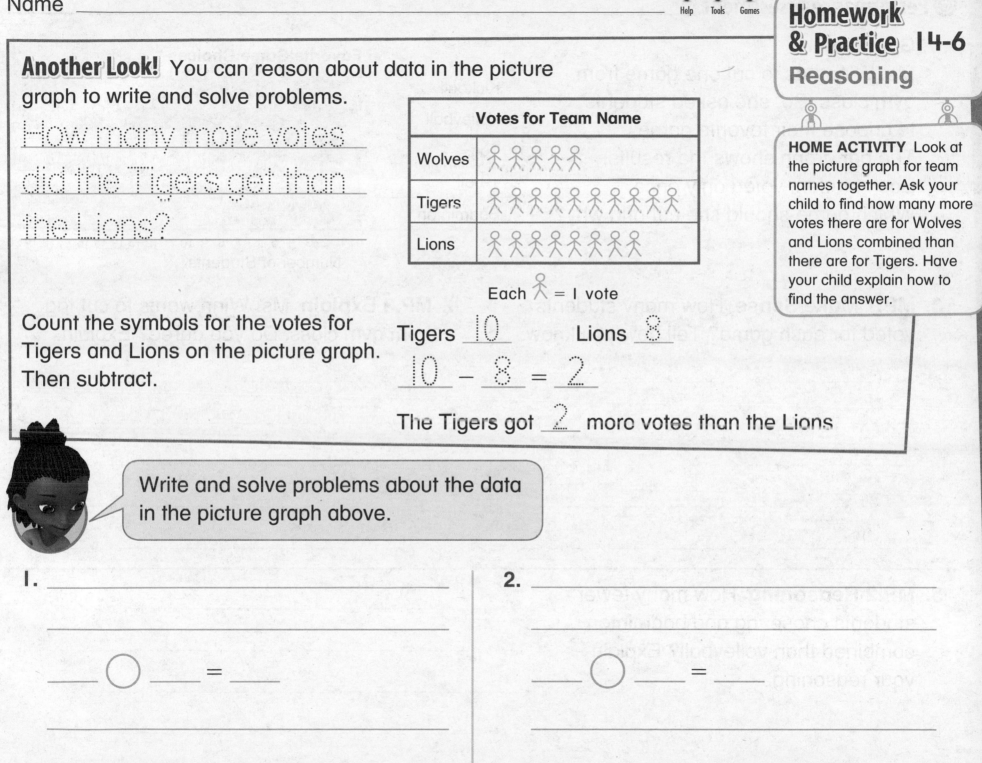
Tigers	
Lions	

Each 👤 = 1 vote

Count the symbols for the votes for Tigers and Lions on the picture graph. Then subtract.

Tigers __10__   Lions __8__

__10__ – __8__ = __2__

The Tigers got __2__ more votes than the Lions

HOME ACTIVITY Look at the picture graph for team names together. Ask your child to find how many more votes there are for Wolves and Lions combined than there are for Tigers. Have your child explain how to find the answer.

Write and solve problems about the data in the picture graph above.

1. _____

____ ◯ ____ = ____

2. _____

____ ◯ ____ = ____

Gym Games

Ms. Winn has to cut one game from gym class. So, she asked students to choose their favorite game. The bar graph shows the results. Each student voted only once. Which game should she cut and why?

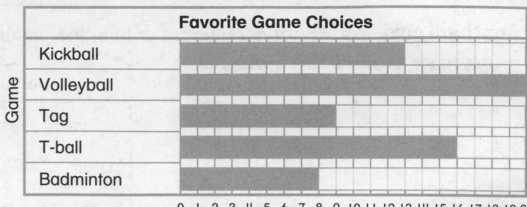

3. **MP.1 Make Sense** How many students voted for each game? Tell how you know.

4. **MP.3 Explain** Ms. Winn wants to cut tag from gym class. Do you agree? Explain.

5. **MP.2 Reasoning** How many fewer students chose tag and badminton combined than volleyball? Explain your reasoning.

Find a Match

Find a partner. Point to a clue. Read the clue.

Look below the clues to find a match. Write the clue letter in the box next to the match.

Find a match for every clue.

I can ...
add and subtract within 100.

© Content Standard 2.NBT.B.5

Clues

A The difference is less than 16.

B The sum equals 43 + 25.

C The difference equals 75 − 46.

D The sum equals 53 + 20.

E The difference equals 96 − 19.

F The sum equals 75.

G The sum is between 60 and 65.

H The difference is between 25 and 28.

☐ 39 + 24	☐ 81 − 52
☐ 33 + 42	☐ 35 + 38
☐ 73 − 59	☐ 67 − 40
☐ 88 − 11	☐ 17 + 51

Vocabulary Review

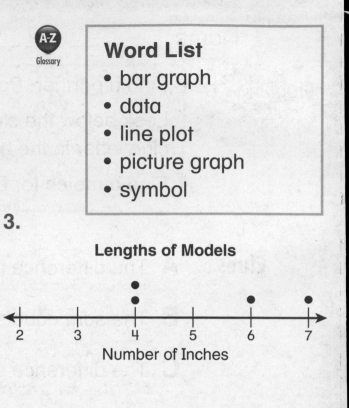

Word List
- bar graph
- data
- line plot
- picture graph
- symbol

Understand Vocabulary

Label each data display. Write *line plot, bar graph,* or *picture graph.*

1.

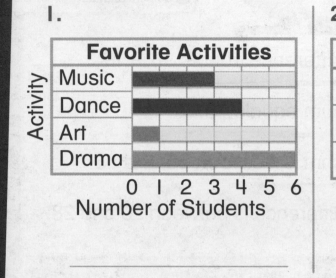

Favorite Activities

Activity
Music
Dance
Art
Drama

0 1 2 3 4 5 6
Number of Students

_____

2.

Favorite Ball Games	
Baseball	♀ ♀
Soccer	♀ ♀ ♀ ♀ ♀ ♀ ♀ ♀
Tennis	♀ ♀ ♀ ♀

Each ♀ = 1 student

_____

3.

Lengths of Models

← 2   3   4   5   6   7 →
Number of Inches

_____

Use Vocabulary in Writing

4. Look at the graph in Item 2. Use words to tell how to find which ball game is the most popular. Use terms from the Word List.

© Pearson Education, Inc. 2

Name _____

Set A

Line plots show and organize data.
Use an inch ruler. Measure the length of
the toy car. Then record the measurement
in the table.

Toy	Length in Inches
Car	3
Airplane	5
Doll	5
Block	1

Place a dot over the number that shows
the length of each toy.

Length of Toys

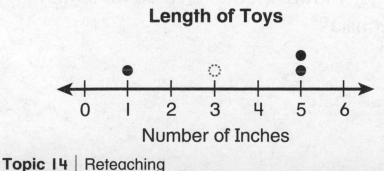

Number of Inches

Complete the table and show
the data on a line plot.

1. Use an inch ruler. Measure the length of
the pencil. Then record the measurement
in the table.

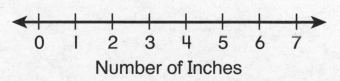

Object	Length in Inches
Pencil	
Stapler	6
Scissors	6
Eraser	3

2. Make a line plot to show each length.

Length of Objects

$\xleftrightarrow{\;\;0\quad1\quad2\quad3\quad4\quad5\quad6\quad7\;\;}$

Number of Inches

You can make a bar graph to show the data in a table.

Students voted for their favorite nut.
The table shows the number of votes.

Favorite Nut

Favorite Nut	
Peanut	7
Almond	4
Cashew	5

Color one space for each vote in the bar graph.
Then use the graph to solve the problem.

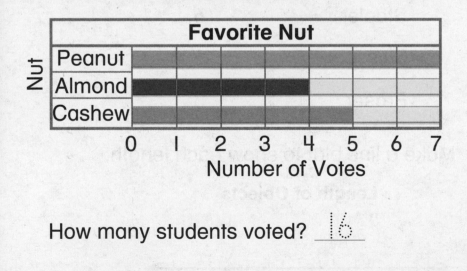

How many students voted? __16__

Use the table to complete the bar graph. Then solve each problem.

3.

Favorite Yogurt	
Lemon	3
Vanilla	7
Banana	6

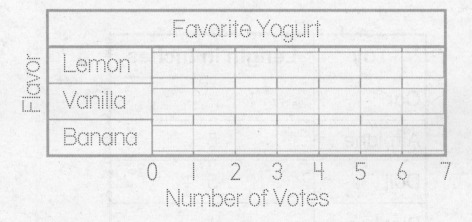

4. How many more students voted for vanilla than banana? ____

5. How many fewer students voted for lemon than vanilla? ____

Set C

Reteaching
Continued

A picture graph uses pictures or symbols to show data.

The tally chart shows votes for favorite sea animals.

Favorite Sea Animals	
Whale	卌 I
Dolphin	II
Seal	IIII

Use the data to make a picture graph.
Each 옷 stands for I vote.

Favorite Sea Animals	
Whale	옷옷옷옷옷옷
Dolphin	옷옷
Seal	옷옷옷옷

옷 = I vote

Which sea animal has the fewest votes?

dolphin

Use the tally chart to complete the picture graph.
Then solve each problem.

6.

Favorite Birds	
Blue Jay	卌
Robin	卌 III
Seagull	卌 卌

Favorite Birds	
Blue Jay	
Robin	
Seagull	

🐦 = I vote

7. How many votes did seagull get?

_____

8. Which bird had the fewest votes?

_____

Thinking Habits

Reasoning

What do the symbols mean?

How are the numbers in the problem related?

How can I write a word problem using the information that is given?

How do the numbers in my problem relate to each other?

How can I use a word problem to show what an equation means?

Use the picture graph to solve each problem. Each student voted once.

Favorite Winter Sport	
Skiing	❄❄❄❄❄❄❄
Snowboarding	❄❄❄❄❄❄❄❄❄❄
Skating	❄❄❄❄❄❄❄
Ice Fishing	❄❄❄❄

Each ❄ = I vote

9. How many fewer students chose ice fishing than snowboarding? _____

10. Write and solve your own problem about the data.

_____

_____

____ ◯ ____ = ____

Name _____

© Assessment

1. Pam has 5 pennies, 2 nickels, 8 dimes, and 9 quarters. Show this data in the bar graph below. Draw the bars.

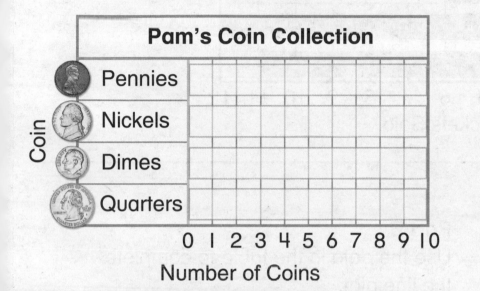

Pam's Coin Collection

Coin

Pennies

Nickels

Dimes

Quarters

0 1 2 3 4 5 6 7 8 9 10

Number of Coins

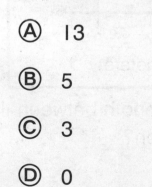

2. Use the bar graph you made above. Pam spends 5 of her dimes to buy an apple. Now how many dimes does Pam have left?

Ⓐ 13

Ⓑ 5

Ⓒ 3

Ⓓ 0

3. Is each sentence about the picture graph correct? Choose Yes or No.

Favorlte Camp Activity	
Crafts	🧍🧍🧍
Swimming	🧍🧍🧍🧍🧍
Archery	🧍🧍
Tennis	🧍🧍🧍🧍🧍🧍

Each 🧍 = 1 camper

7 students voted for tennis.   ○ Yes ○ No

16 students voted in all.   ○ Yes ○ No

2 more students voted for swimming than for crafts.   ○ Yes ○ No

3 fewer students voted for tennis than for crafts.   ○ Yes ○ No

4. How many more tickets did Kendra sell than Leon?

Ⓐ 5

Ⓑ 6

Ⓒ 11

Ⓓ 17

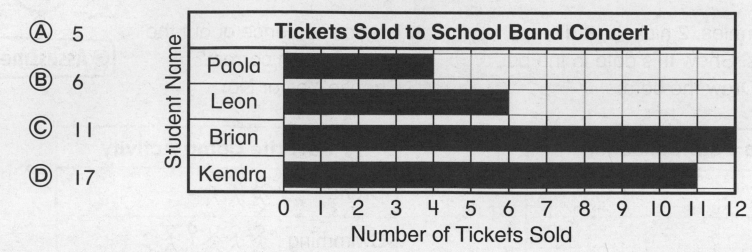

Tickets Sold to School Band Concert

Student Name: Paola, Leon, Brian, Kendra

Number of Tickets Sold: 0 1 2 3 4 5 6 7 8 9 10 11 12

---

5. Complete the table and the line plot.

Part A

Use a centimeter ruler. Measure the length of the crayon to the nearest centimeter. Write the length in the table below.

Crayon Lengths in Centimeters			
5	7	7	8
4	7	5	

Part B

Use the data in the table to complete the line plot.

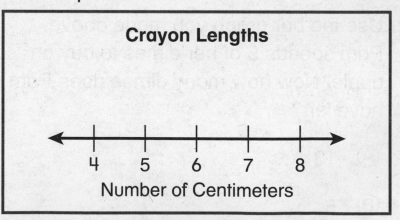

Crayon Lengths

4 5 6 7 8

Number of Centimeters

What is the difference in length between the shortest and longest crayon?

_____

Topic 14 | Assessment

6. Scott is making a picture graph from the data in the tally chart. How many symbols should he draw in the bottom row?

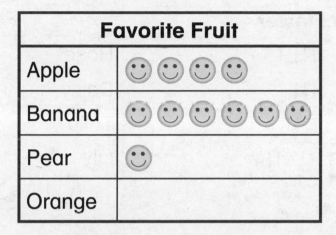

Favorite Fruit	
Apple	IIIII
Banana	||||| I
Pear	I
Orange	|||||

Favorite Fruit	
Apple	☺ ☺ ☺ ☺
Banana	☺ ☺ ☺ ☺ ☺ ☺
Pear	☺
Orange	

Each ☺ = I student

Ⓐ 3   Ⓑ 4   Ⓒ 5   Ⓓ 6

---

7. Mary gets new stamps every month. The bar graph shows the number of stamps she collects each month.

Which statements are true? Choose all that apply.

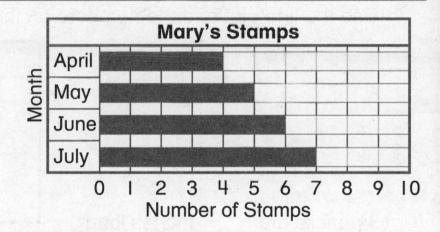

Mary's Stamps

☐ Mary collects I more stamp in May than she does in April.

☐ Mary collects 2 fewer stamps in June than she does in July.

☐ Mary collects a total of I I stamps in May and June.

☐ Mary collects one additional stamp each month from May to July.

8. Use the tally chart to complete the picture graph.
Then use the picture graph to solve the problems.

Favorite Flower	
Rose	卌 I
Daisy	III
Tulip	卌
Lily	卌 III

Favorite Flower	
Rose	
Daisy	
Tulip	
Lily	

Each 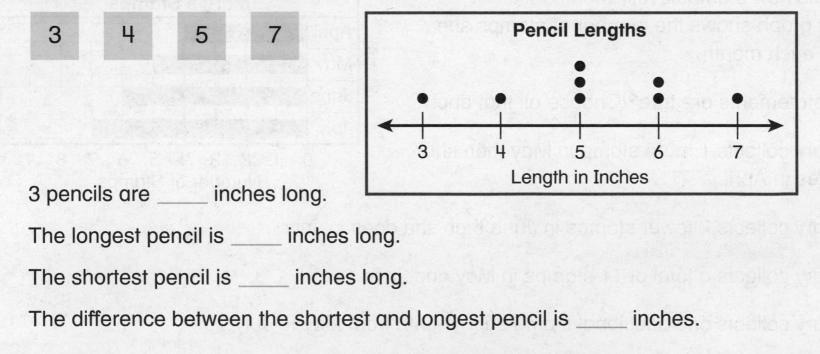 = I vote

How many students voted for Lily? _____

Which flower is the least favorite? _____

---

9. Use the line plot and the numbers on the cards to complete each sentence.

3	4	5	7

Pencil Lengths

```
                    •
                    •
        •           •           •
  •     •     •     •     •
  3     4     5     6     7
      Length in Inches
```

3 pencils are _____ inches long.

The longest pencil is _____ inches long.

The shortest pencil is _____ inches long.

The difference between the shortest and longest pencil is _____ inches.

     Topic I4 | Assessment

Name _____

School Surveys

Some students asked their classmates different questions.

George asked his classmates to vote on their favorite lunch. This table shows the results.

Favorite Lunch	
Taco	5
Pizza	8
Hamburger	9
Salad	6

1. Use the table to complete the bar graph.

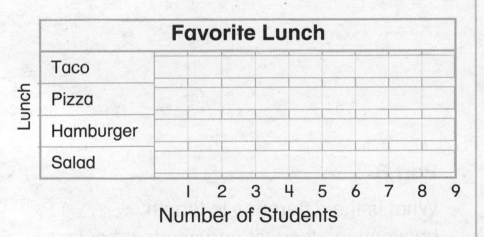

2. Use the Favorite Lunch table to complete the picture graph.

Favorite Lunch	
Taco	
Pizza	
Hamburger	
Salad	

Each ✔ = I student

3. Use the graphs you made to answer these questions.

How many students chose salad as their favorite lunch? _____

Which lunch is the favorite of the most students? _____

How would the bar graph change if two more students chose Taco?

_____

_____

4. Write and solve a math story about the Favorite Lunch graphs you made.

Part A

Use the bar graph or the picture graph about favorite lunches to write a math story problem. The problem should include addition or subtraction.

_____

_____

_____

_____

Part B

Solve your math story problem. Explain how you solved the problem.

_____

_____

_____

_____

5. Gina asked her classmates to measure the length of their favorite storybook in inches. She recorded their measurements in this table.

Lengths of Books in Inches			
12	9	8	10
6	10	11	9
10	9	9	12
12	10	7	7

Part A

Use the table to make a line plot.

Part B

What is the difference in length between the longest and shortest books?

_____ inches

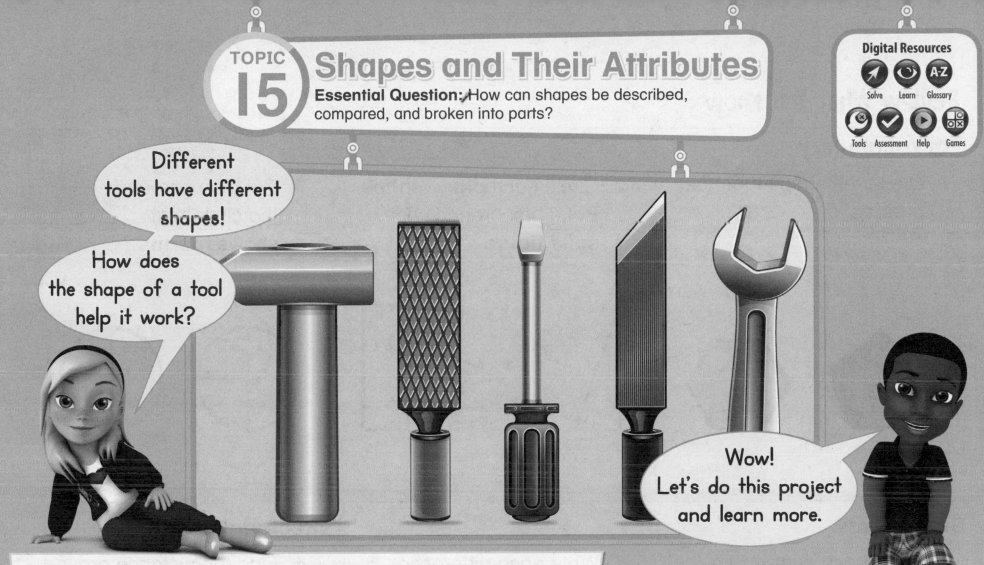

Shapes and Their Attributes

Essential Question: How can shapes be described, compared, and broken into parts?

Different tools have different shapes!

How does the shape of a tool help it work?

Wow! Let's do this project and learn more.

Math and Science Project: All About Shape

Find Out Draw pictures of tools used for gardening, cooking, or fixing. Describe the shape of each tool. Tell how the shape of each tool helps it work.

Journal: Make a Book Show your work in a book. In your book, also:

• Choose a tool that you use at school. Tell how the shape of the tool helps it work.

• Draw and describe polygon shapes.

Review What You Know

A-Z Vocabulary

1. Circle the shape that has 6 **sides**.

2. Circle each **plane shape**. Put a box around each **solid figure**.

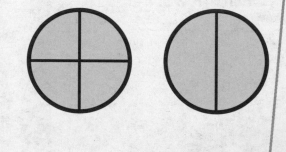

3. Put a box around the circle that shows **fourths**.

Basic Facts

4. Write each sum.

$$\begin{array}{r} 5 \\ +8 \\ \hline \end{array} \qquad \begin{array}{r} 7 \\ +7 \\ \hline \end{array} \qquad \begin{array}{r} 10 \\ +10 \\ \hline \end{array}$$

5. Write each difference.

$$\begin{array}{r} 17 \\ -9 \\ \hline \end{array} \qquad \begin{array}{r} 15 \\ -6 \\ \hline \end{array} \qquad \begin{array}{r} 12 \\ -8 \\ \hline \end{array}$$

Rectangles

6. Find the distance around.

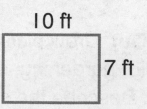

10 ft
7 ft

_____

My Word Cards

Study the words on the front of the card.
Complete the activity on the back.

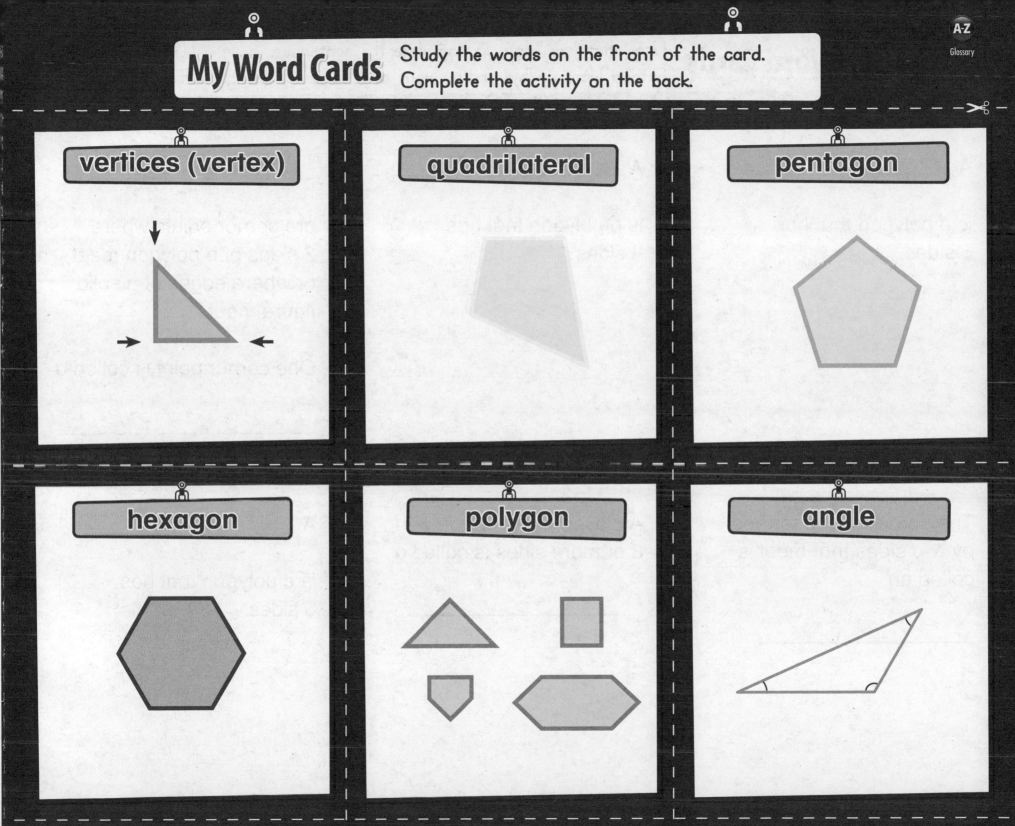

vertices (vertex)

quadrilateral

pentagon

hexagon

polygon

angle

My Word Cards

Use what you know to complete the sentences.
Extend learning by writing your own sentence using each word.

A _____

is a polygon that has
5 sides.

A _____

is a polygon that has
4 sides.

_____

are corner points where
2 sides of a polygon meet
or where edges of a solid
figure meet.

One corner point is called a

_____.

The corner shape formed
by two sides that meet is
called an

_____.

A closed plane shape with
3 or more sides is called a

_____.

A _____

is a polygon that has
6 sides.

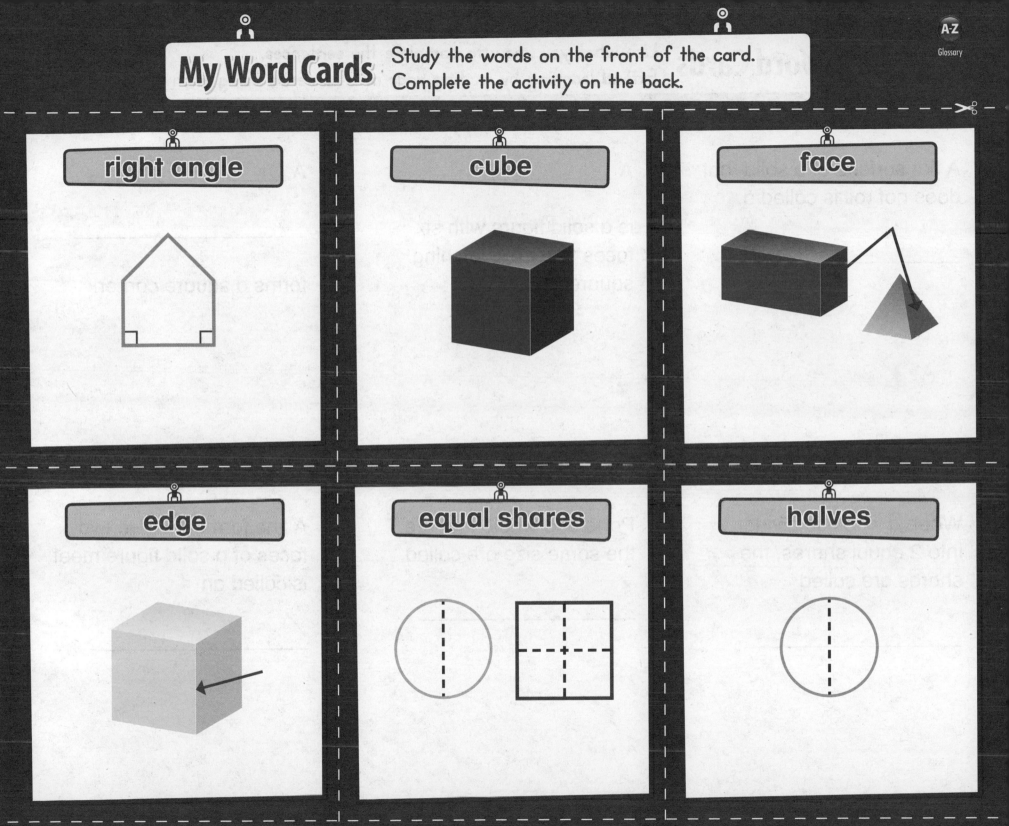

My Word Cards Study the words on the front of the card. Complete the activity on the back.

A-Z Glossary

right angle

cube

face

edge

equal shares

halves

Use what you know to complete the sentences.
Extend learning by writing your own sentence using each word.

A flat surface of a solid that does not roll is called a

_____.

A _____

is a solid figure with six faces that are matching squares.

A _____

_____

forms a square corner.

When a whole is divided into 2 equal shares, the shares are called

_____.

Parts of a whole that are the same size are called

_____.

A line formed where two faces of a solid figure meet is called an

_____.

My Word Cards Study the words on the front of the card.
Complete the activity on the back.

A-Z
Glossary

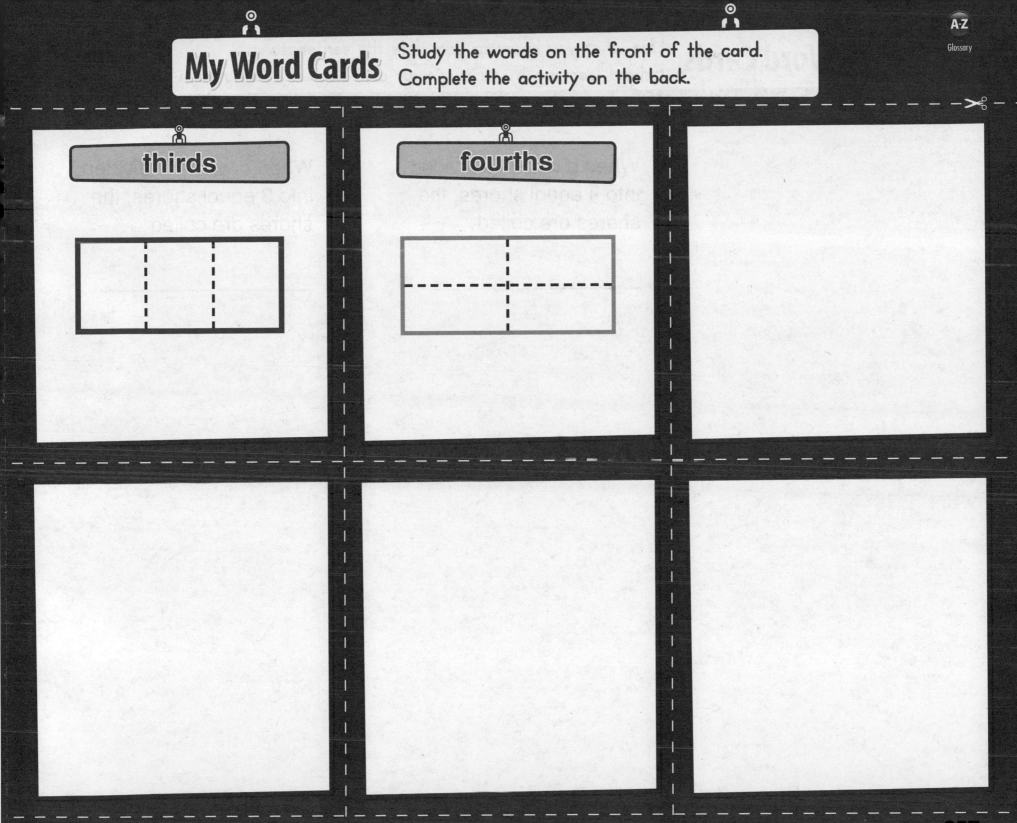

thirds

fourths

My Word Cards

Use what you know to complete the sentences.
Extend learning by writing your own sentence using each word.

When a whole is divided into 4 equal shares, the shares are called

_____.

When a whole is divided into 3 equal shares, the shares are called

_____.

Name _____

Solve & Share

Draw some closed plane shapes that have 3 vertices.
Write the name for one of your shapes.
Is this name correct for all of the shapes you made?

I can ...
recognize shapes by how they look.

© **Content Standard** 2.G.A.1
Mathematical Practices MP.3, MP.4, MP.6

3 vertices

Topic 15 | Lesson 1
Digital Resources at PearsonRealize.com
eight hundred fifty-nine **859**

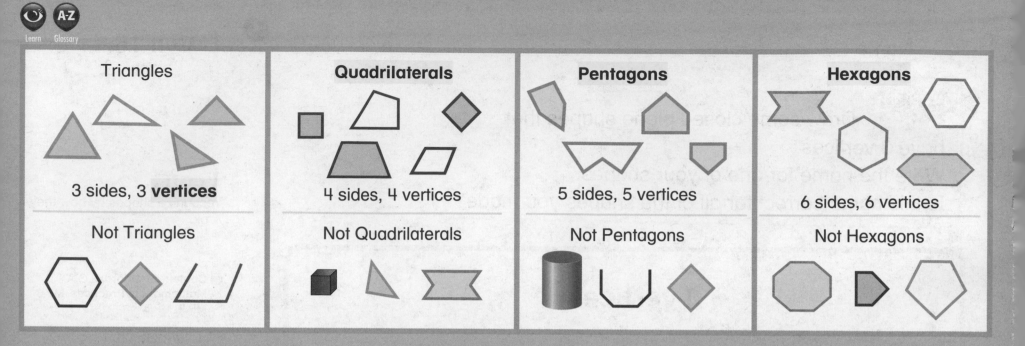

Triangles

3 sides, 3 **vertices**

Not Triangles

Quadrilaterals

4 sides, 4 vertices

Not Quadrilaterals

Pentagons

5 sides, 5 vertices

Not Pentagons

Hexagons

6 sides, 6 vertices

Not Hexagons

Do You Understand?

Show Me! How do sides and vertices help you name a plane shape?

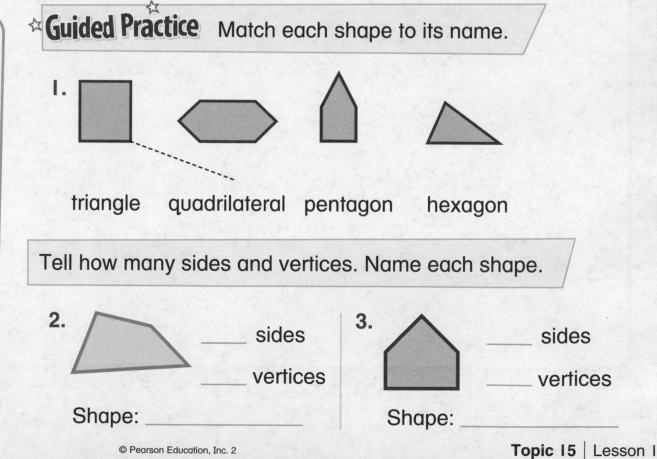

⭐ **Guided Practice** Match each shape to its name.

1.

triangle   quadrilateral   pentagon   hexagon

Tell how many sides and vertices. Name each shape.

2.

_____ sides

_____ vertices

Shape: _____

3.

_____ sides

_____ vertices

Shape: _____

© Pearson Education, Inc. 2

Name _____

Independent Practice ☆ Match each shape to its name.

4.

triangle   quadrilateral   pentagon   hexagon

5.

triangle   quadrilateral   pentagon   hexagon

Draw the shape. Tell how many sides and vertices.

6. Quadrilateral

_____ sides

_____ vertices

7. Hexagon

_____ sides

_____ vertices

8. Triangle

_____ sides

_____ vertices

9. Higher Order Thinking Bianca drew a triangle and a pentagon.
How many sides and vertices did she draw in all? Draw the shapes.

_____ sides   _____ vertices

10. © **MP.4 Model** Marcos has 4 toothpicks. He places them as shown. What shape can Marcos make if he adds one more toothpick?

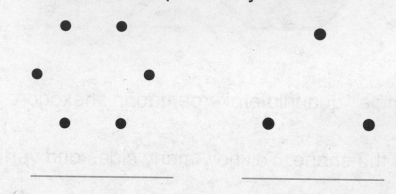

_____

11. **A-Z Vocabulary** Connect all the dots to make two shapes that have **vertices.** Name the shapes that you make.

•   •   •

•   •

•   •   •   •

_____   _____

12. **Higher Order Thinking** Randall said that a square is a quadrilateral. Susan said that a square is a square, so it is not a quadrilateral. Who is correct? Explain.

_____

_____

_____

_____

13. © **Assessment** Which polygon is **NOT** a hexagon?

Think: What do I know about hexagons?

Ⓐ

Ⓑ

Ⓒ

Ⓓ

Name _____

Help   Tools   Games

Another Look! You can name shapes by their number of sides and vertices.

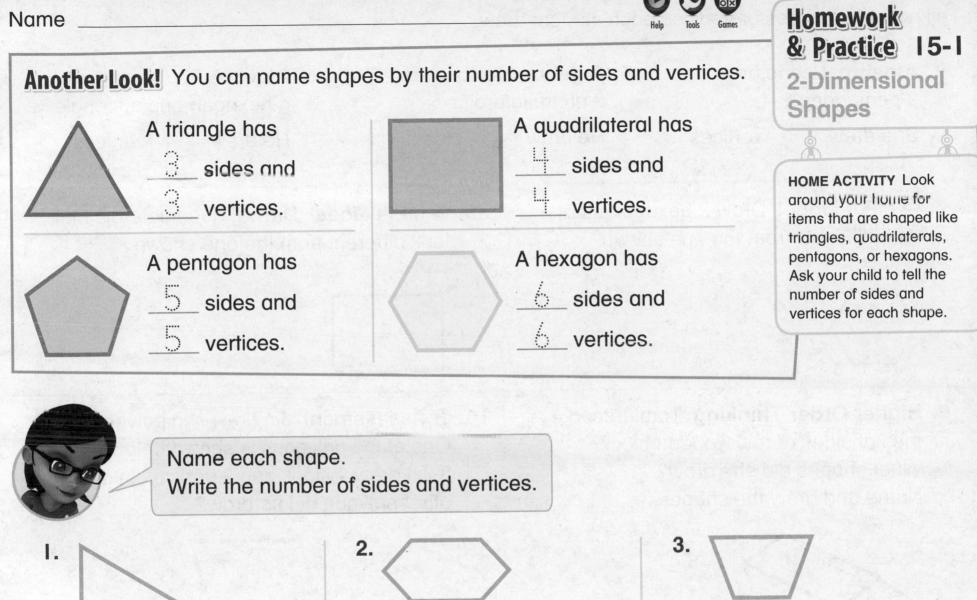

A triangle has
___3___ sides and
___3___ vertices.

A quadrilateral has
___4___ sides and
___4___ vertices.

A pentagon has
___5___ sides and
___5___ vertices.

A hexagon has
___6___ sides and
___6___ vertices.

HOME ACTIVITY Look around your home for items that are shaped like triangles, quadrilaterals, pentagons, or hexagons. Ask your child to tell the number of sides and vertices for each shape.

Name each shape.
Write the number of sides and vertices.

1.

Shape: _____
____ sides
____ vertices

2.

Shape: _____
____ sides
____ vertices

3.

Shape: _____
____ sides
____ vertices

4. **Algebra** Leona drew 2 pentagons.

She drew _____ vertices.

5. **Algebra** Nestor drew 3 quadrilaterals.

He drew _____ sides.

6. **Algebra** Kip drew a hexagon and a triangle.

He drew _____ vertices.

7. © **MP.4 Model** Draw 2 hexagons that look different from the one shown.

8. © **MP.4 Model** Draw 2 quadrilaterals that look different from the one shown.

9. **Higher Order Thinking** Tami traced the flat sides of this wooden block. What shapes did she draw? Name and draw the shapes.

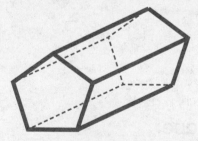

10. © **Assessment** Jin drew two polygons. One of the polygons is shown below. If Jin drew 9 sides and 9 vertices in all, which other polygon did he draw?

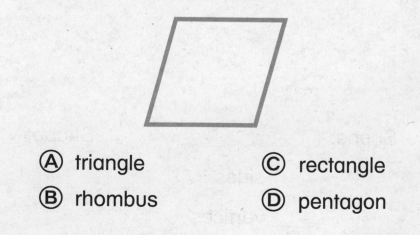

Ⓐ triangle

Ⓒ rectangle

Ⓑ rhombus

Ⓓ pentagon

Name _____

Solve & Share

Look at the two plane shapes below. How are they alike? How are they different? What is a name for both shapes?

I can ...
describe plane shapes by how they look.

© **Content Standard** 2.G.A.1
Mathematical Practices MP.2, MP.6, MP.7

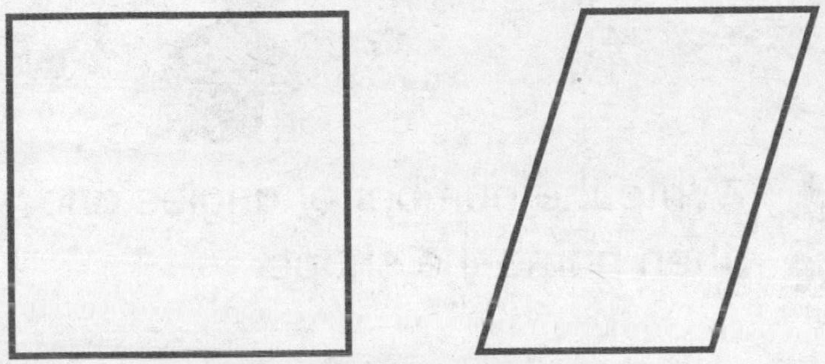

_____

_____

_____

_____

Polygon

A closed plane shape with 3 or more sides is called a polygon.

You know the names of these polygons.

Not Polygons

Polygons are not open shapes. Polygons do not have curved sides.

A circle is not a polygon.

Angle

Polygons have angles. They have the same number of angles as sides and vertices.

A triangle has 3 angles.

Right Angle

A right angle forms a square corner. A square has 4 right angles. The pentagon below has 2 right angles.

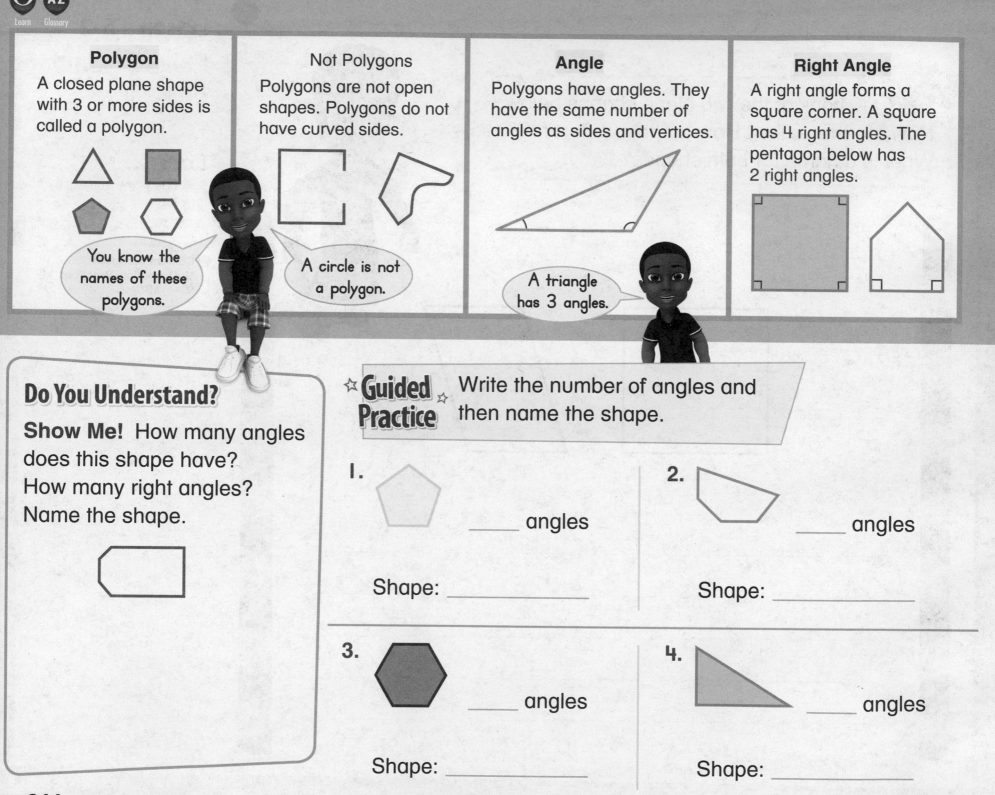

Do You Understand?

Show Me! How many angles does this shape have? How many right angles? Name the shape.

☆ Guided Practice ☆

Write the number of angles and then name the shape.

1.

_____ angles

Shape: _____

2.

_____ angles

Shape: _____

3.

_____ angles

Shape: _____

4.

_____ angles

Shape: _____

Name _____

Independent Practice   Write the number of angles and then name the shape.

5. 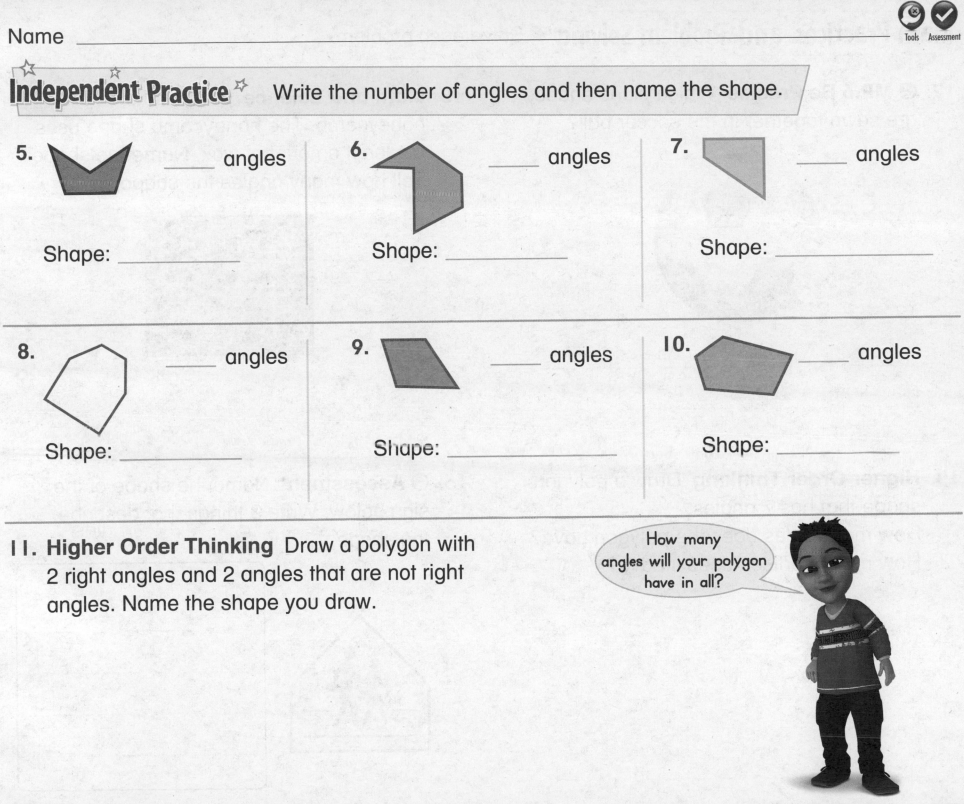 _____ angles

Shape: _____

6. _____ angles

Shape: _____

7. _____ angles

Shape: _____

8. _____ angles

Shape: _____

9. _____ angles

Shape: _____

10. _____ angles

Shape: _____

11. **Higher Order Thinking** Draw a polygon with 2 right angles and 2 angles that are not right angles. Name the shape you draw.

How many angles will your polygon have in all?

12. © **MP.6 Be Precise** Which plane shapes are sewn together in the soccer ball?

_____

_____

13. Math and Science Bees make honeycomb. The honeycomb shape uses the least amount of wax. Name the shape. Tell how many angles the shape has.

_____

_____

14. Higher Order Thinking Draw a polygon shape that has 7 angles.
How many sides does the polygon have?
How many vertices does it have?

15. © **Assessment** Name the shape of the sign below. Write 3 things that describe the shape.

_____

_____

_____

_____

Name _____

Another Look! Polygons are closed plane shapes with 3 or more sides. Polygons have the same number of angles and vertices as sides.

side

vertex   angle

An angle that forms a square corner is called a right angle.

HOME ACTIVITY Ask your child to find objects that have polygon shapes. Have your child name each shape and tell how many angles it has.

Name and describe this polygon.

Pentagon   5 sides   5 vertices   5 angles

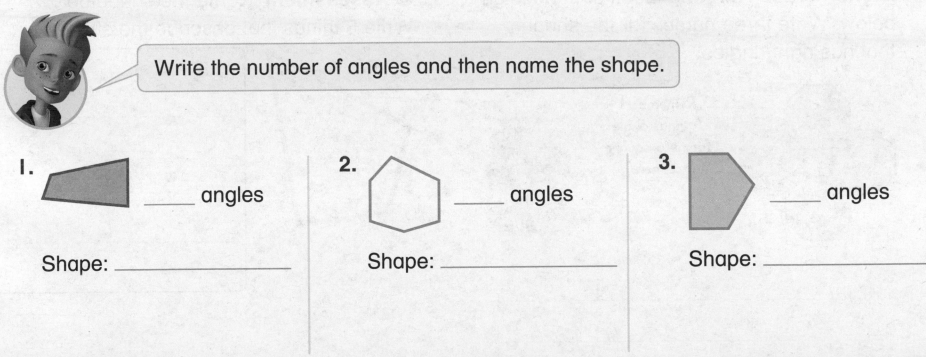

Write the number of angles and then name the shape.

1. _____ angles

Shape: _____

2. _____ angles

Shape: _____

3. _____ angles

Shape: _____

Solve each problem.

4. © **MP.6 Be Precise** The sign below tells drivers to yield. This means to wait for other cars or people to go first. Which polygon shape do you see in the sign?

_____

5. **A-Z Vocabulary** The outside edges of this nut for a bolt form a **polygon** shape. Name that shape.

_____

6. **Higher Order Thinking** Look at the design below. Write three names for the shape that has right angles.

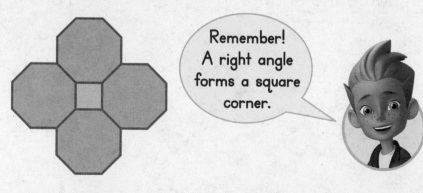

Remember! A right angle forms a square corner.

_____

7. © **Assessment** Name the shape below. Write 3 things that describe the shape.

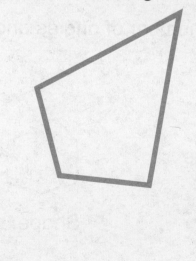

_____
_____
_____
_____

© Pearson Education, Inc. 2

Name _____

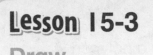
Solve & Share

Draw a polygon with 3 sides that are the same length.
Then draw a polygon with 3 sides that are different lengths.
Then tell 4 ways they are alike.

I can ...
draw polygon shapes.

© **Content Standard** 2.G.A.1
Mathematical Practices MP.1,
MP.6. MP.7

Sides: Same Length   **Sides: Different Lengths**

_____

_____

_____

_____

Learn Glossary

Draw a polygon with 5 vertices.

My polygon will have 5 vertices. That means it will have 5 sides, too!

I drew a pentagon!

Draw a polygon with 4 sides that are the same length.

My next polygon will have 4 sides, so I will draw a quadrilateral! The sides should be the same length.

I drew a quadrilateral!

Do You Understand?

Show Me! Draw a quadrilateral with 4 sides that are the same length and with 4 right angles. Write 2 names for the quadrilateral.

☆ Guided Practice ☆

Draw each shape. Complete the sentences.

1. Draw a polygon with 3 vertices.

The polygon also has ____ sides.

The polygon is a _____.

2. Draw a polygon with 6 sides.

The polygon also has ____ angles.

The polygon is a _____.

© Pearson Education, Inc. 2

Tools   Assessment

Independent Practice   Draw each shape. Complete the sentences.

3. Draw a polygon with 3 vertices and 1 right angle.

The polygon also has

_____ sides.

The polygon is

a _____.

4. Draw a quadrilateral with opposite sides that are the same length.

The polygon also has

_____ vertices.

The polygon is

a _____.

5. Draw a polygon with 4 sides that are the same length.

The polygon also has

_____ angles.

The polygon is

a _____.

6. Draw a polygon with 4 sides that are different lengths.

The polygon also has

_____ angles.

The polygon is

a _____.

7. Draw a polygon with 5 vertices and 3 sides that are the same length.

The polygon also has

_____ sides in all.

The polygon is

a _____.

8. Higher Order Thinking Can you draw a polygon with 3 vertices and 4 sides? Explain.

9. © MP.6 Be Precise Draw a rectangle with 4 equal sides.

What is another name for this shape?

_____

10. Draw 3 shapes. The first shape is a quadrilateral. The number of vertices in each shape increases by one.

Name the third shape. _____

11. Higher Order Thinking The owner of Joe's Fish Market wants a new sign. He wants the sign to have curved sides. Draw a sign for Joe's Fish Market.

Is the sign a polygon? Explain.

_____

_____

12. © Assessment David drew two different polygons. One of the polygons was a square. If David drew 9 sides and 9 vertices in all, what other polygon did David draw?

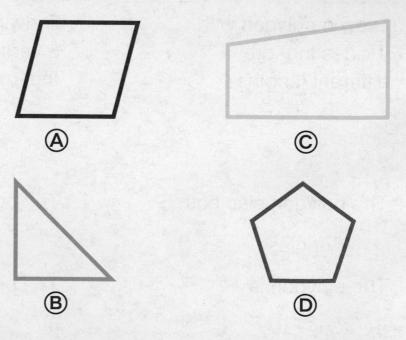

Ⓐ   Ⓒ

Ⓑ   Ⓓ

        Topic 15 | Lesson 3

Name _____

Help Tools Games

Another Look! The number of sides in a polygon is the same as the number of vertices and the number of angles.

Draw a polygon with 6 vertices.

The sides can be the same length.   The sides can be different lengths.

Each polygon has ___6___ vertices.

Each polygon also has ___6___ sides and ___6___ angles.

Both polygons are ___hexagons___.

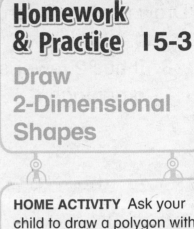

HOME ACTIVITY Ask your child to draw a polygon with 4 vertices. Then ask your child to tell you the name of the polygon and how many sides and angles it has.

What pattern do you see?

Draw two different polygons for each number of vertices.

1. 4 vertices

2. 5 vertices

Each polygon has ____ sides.

Both polygons are _____.

Each polygon has ____ angles.

Both polygons are _____.

Draw each polygon. Then complete the sentences.

3. It has 2 fewer sides than a pentagon.

The shape is a _____.

4. It has 3 more vertices than a triangle.

The shape is a _____.

5. © **MP.1 Make Sense** It has 1 less vertex than a hexagon and 2 more angles than a triangle.

The shape is a _____.

6. **Higher Order Thinking** Tanika has 7 toothpicks. She uses them all to create two polygons. Draw two polygons that Tanika could have created. Write the names of your shapes.

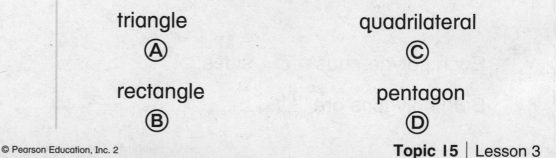

7. © **Assessment** Kit drew a polygon that has 4 vertices. Which could **NOT** be Kit's polygon?

quadrilateral
Ⓐ

rectangle
Ⓒ

triangle
Ⓑ

square
Ⓓ

8. © **Assessment** Reg drew a polygon with more sides than a square and fewer vertices than a hexagon. Which could Reg have drawn?

triangle
Ⓐ

quadrilateral
Ⓒ

rectangle
Ⓑ

pentagon
Ⓓ

Name _____

Solve & Share

Describe this shape in 3 or more ways.

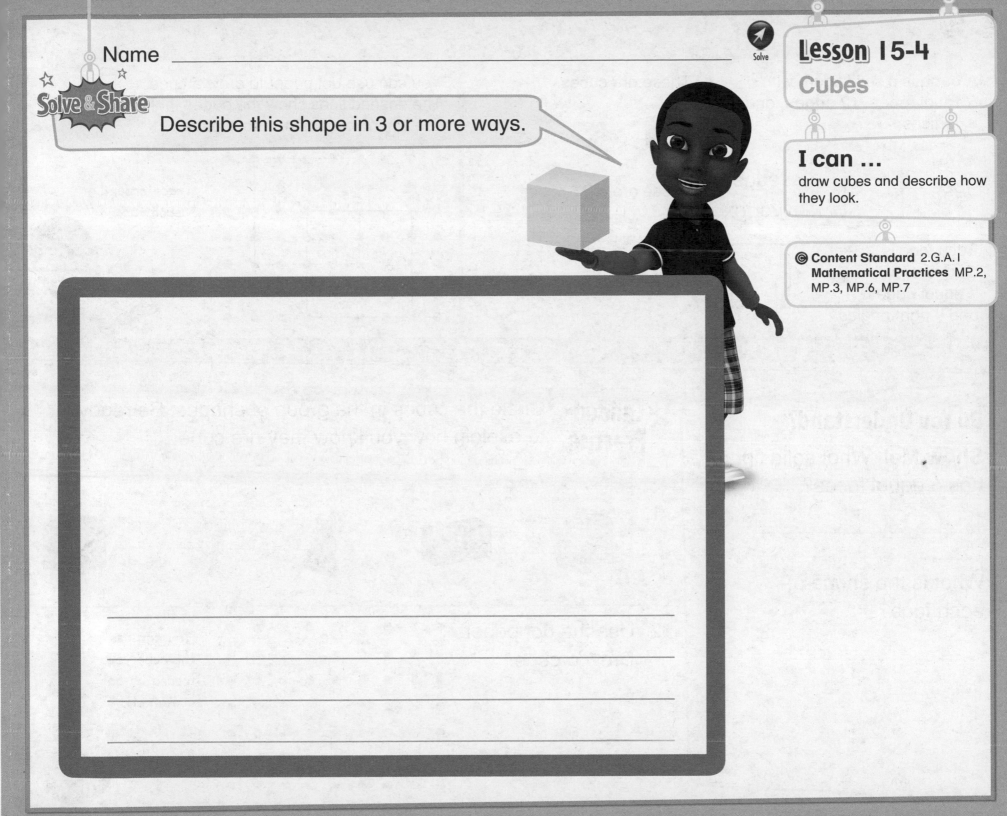

I can ...
draw cubes and describe how they look.

© **Content Standard** 2.G.A.1
Mathematical Practices MP.2,
MP.3, MP.6, MP.7

_____

_____

_____

_____

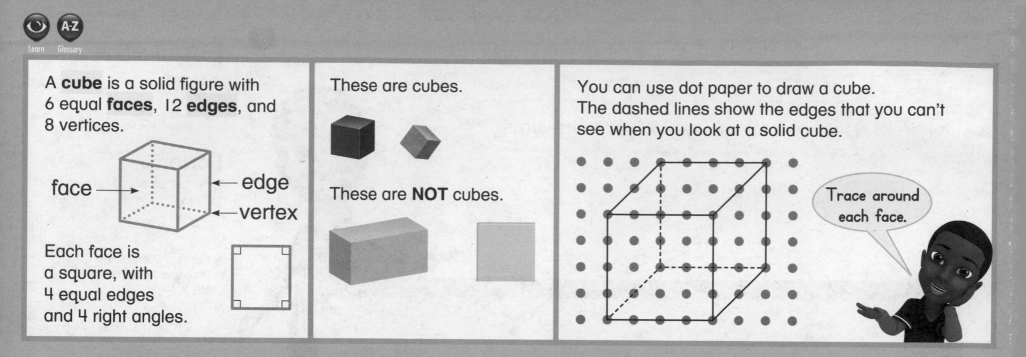

A **cube** is a solid figure with 6 equal **faces**, 12 **edges**, and 8 vertices.

face → ← edge
← vertex

Each face is a square, with 4 equal edges and 4 right angles.

These are cubes.

These are **NOT** cubes.

You can use dot paper to draw a cube. The dashed lines show the edges that you can't see when you look at a solid cube.

Trace around each face.

Do You Understand?

Show Me! What solid figure has 6 equal faces?

_____

What is the shape of each face?

_____

☆ **Guided** ☆
Practice
Circle the cubes in the group of shapes. Be ready to explain how you know they are cubes.

1.

2. Use the dot paper. Draw a cube.

You can use the cube you traced as an example.

Topic 15 | Lesson 4

Name _____

Independent Practice

Decide if the shape is a cube. Then draw a line from each shape to *cube* or **NOT** a cube.

3.

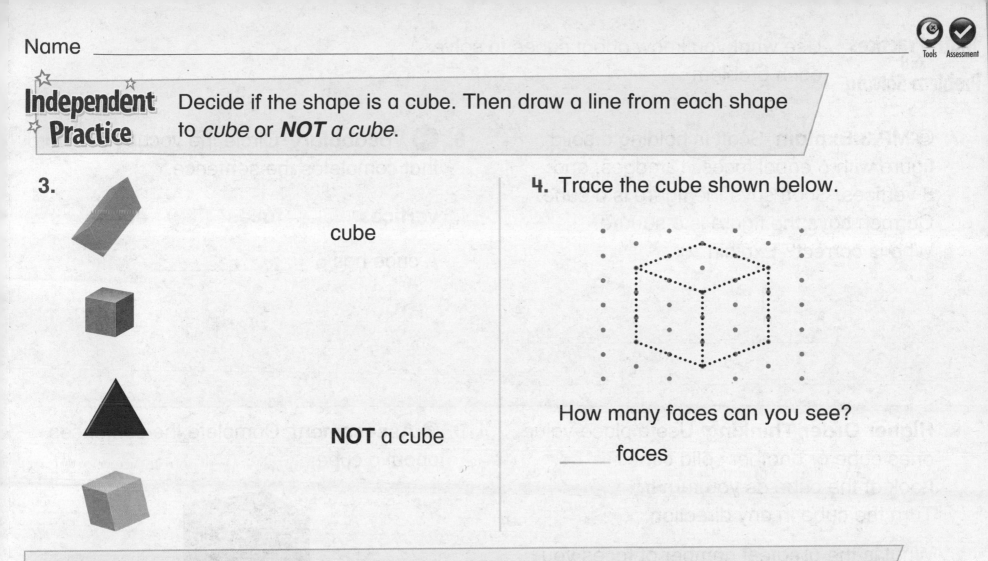

cube

NOT a cube

4. Trace the cube shown below.

How many faces can you see?

_____ faces

Algebra Use what you know about cubes to write an equation and solve each problem.

5. How many vertices do these two cubes have in all?

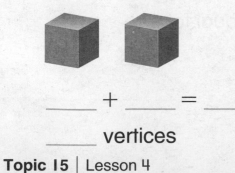

_____ + _____ = _____

_____ vertices

6. How many faces do these two cubes have in all?

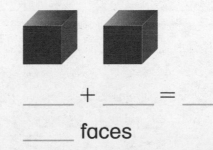

_____ + _____ = _____

_____ faces

Topic 15 | Lesson 4

eight hundred seventy-nine **879**

7. © **MP.3 Explain** Scott is holding a solid figure with 6 equal faces, 12 edges, and 8 vertices. Scott says the figure is a cube. Carmen says the figure is a square. Who is correct? Explain.

_____

_____

_____

8. **A-Z Vocabulary** Circle the vocabulary word that completes the sentence.

vertices   **faces**   **edges**

A cube has 6 _____.

9. **Higher Order Thinking** Use a place-value ones cube or another solid cube. Look at the cube as you turn it. Turn the cube in any direction.

What is the greatest number of faces you can see at one time? Explain.

_____

_____

_____

10. © **Assessment** Complete the sentences about a cube.

A cube is a solid _____.

A cube has _____ equal faces,

_____ vertices, and _____ edges.

     Topic 15 | Lesson 4

Name _____

Another Look! You can tell if a shape is a cube by counting its faces, vertices, and edges. Number cubes are examples of real-life objects that are cubes.

Every cube has 6 equal square faces, 8 vertices, and 12 edges.

HOME ACTIVITY Have your child find an object at home that has a cube shape. Ask your child to describe the object including the number of faces, vertices, and edges.

These real-life objects are **NOT** cubes.

Tell whether each shape or object is a cube. If it is not a cube, tell what shape it is. Then explain how you know.

1. ⬜ _____
_____
_____
_____

2.  _____
_____
_____
_____

Use what you know about cubes to solve each problem.

3. © **MP.7 Look for Patterns** You can make two squares to draw a cube.

1. Connect the 4 blue dots to make one square.
2. Connect the 4 green dots to make another square.
3. Connect each corner of the blue square to a like corner of the green square.

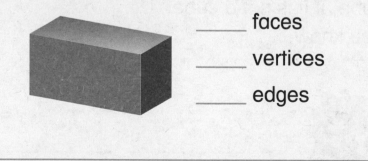

This is another way to draw a cube.

4. **Higher Order Thinking** Look at the solid figure below. Count the number of faces, vertices, and edges it has. Why is this figure **NOT** a cube?

_____ faces

_____ vertices

_____ edges

_____

_____

_____

5. © **Assessment** Circle the shapes that are **NOT** cubes. Explain how you know.

_____

© Pearson Education, Inc. 2

Solve & Share

How many equal squares cover this rectangle? How could you show this with an addition equation?

I can ...

divide rectangles into equal squares.

© **Content Standards** 2.G.A.2, 2.OA.C.4

Mathematical Practices MP.1, MP.3, MP.4, MP.5, MP.7

Columns

Rows

_____ equal squares

Equation: _____

How many red squares can cover this rectangle?

Begin like this:

NOT like this:

Count. Each row has 4 squares. You can add the squares by rows.

$4 + 4 + 4 = 12$

Count. Each column has 3 squares. You can add the squares by columns.

$3 + 3 + 3 + 3 = 12$

Do You Understand?

Show Me! Explain how you can divide a rectangle into equal squares.

☆ **Guided Practice** Solve.

1. Use square tiles to cover the rectangle. Trace the tiles. Column I is done for you.

2. Count and add. How many squares cover the rectangle?

Add by rows: _____ + _____ + _____ = _____

Add by columns:

_____ + _____ + _____ + _____ + _____ + _____ = _____

© Pearson Education, Inc. 2

Tools   Assessment

Independent Practice

Use square tiles to cover each rectangle. Trace the tiles. Count the squares.

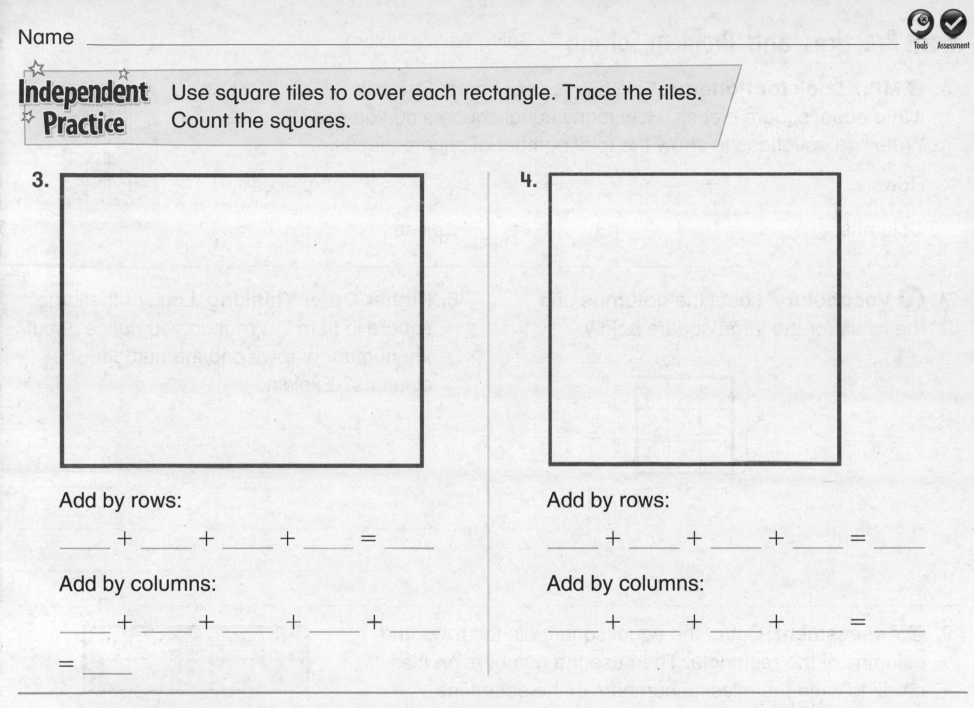

3.

Add by rows:

___ + ___ + ___ + ___ = ___

Add by columns:

___ + ___ + ___ + ___ + ___

= ___

4.

Add by rows:

___ + ___ + ___ + ___ = ___

Add by columns:

___ + ___ + ___ + ___ = ___

5. **Number Sense** Draw a rectangle that is divided into 6 equal squares.

Math Practices and Problem Solving   Solve each problem.

6. © **MP.7 Look for Patterns** Lisa bakes corn bread. She cuts it into equal square pieces. How many equal squares do you see? Write two equations to show the total number of square pieces.

Rows: _____ + _____ + _____ + _____ + _____ + _____ = _____ pieces

Columns: _____ + _____ + _____ + _____ = _____ pieces

7. **A-Z Vocabulary** Label the **columns** and the **rows** for the large square below.

8. **Higher Order Thinking** Look at the large square in Item 7. What do you notice about the number of rows and the number of columns? Explain.

_____

_____

_____

_____

9. © **Assessment** Count the equal squares in the rows and columns of the rectangle. Then use the numbers on the cards to write the missing numbers in the equations.

| 14 | 2 | 7 |

Rows: _____ + _____ = _____

Columns: _____ + _____ + _____ + _____ + _____ + _____ + _____ = _____

© Pearson Education, Inc. 2

Name _____

Another Look! How many squares cover this rectangle?

You can use square tiles to cover rectangles. Count the squares in the rows. Then count the squares in the columns.

Add the rows: $3 + 3 = 6$

Add the columns: $2 + 2 + 2 = 6$

HOME ACTIVITY Ask your child to draw a rectangular section of a floor made of square tiles. Then ask your child to count how many squares make up that rectangle.

Use square tiles to cover the rectangle. Trace the tiles. Count the squares.

1.

2. How many squares cover the rectangle?

Add by rows:

____ + ____ + ____ = ____

Add by columns:

____ + ____ + ____ + ____ + ____

= ____

Solve each problem.

3. **© MP.7 Look for Patterns** Mr. Cory puts square tiles on the kitchen floor. The square tiles are all the same size. How many equal squares are there? Write two equations to show the total number of square tiles.

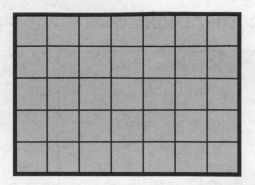

Rows:

____ + ____ + ____ + ____ + ____ = ____ tiles

Columns:

____ + ____ + ____ + ____ + ____ + ____ + ____ = ____ tiles

4. **Higher Order Thinking** 10 friends want to equally share a rectangular pan of granola bars. Show how to divide the rectangle into 10 equal pieces.

5. **© Assessment** Count the equal squares in the rows and columns of the rectangle. Then use the numbers on the cards to write the missing numbers in the equations.

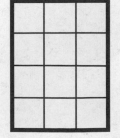

| 4 | 12 | 3 |

Rows: ____ + ____ + ____ + ____ = ____

Columns: ____ + ____ + ____ = ____

© Pearson Education, Inc. 2

Lesson 15-6
Partition Shapes

Solve & Share

Use one type of pattern block to cover this shape. Draw lines to show how you placed the pattern blocks. How many equal shares does the shape have now? What do you notice about the equal shares?

I can ...
divide circles and rectangles into halves, thirds, and fourths.

© **Content Standard** 2.G.A.3
Mathematical Practices MP.2, MP.4, MP.6, MP.8

_____ shares

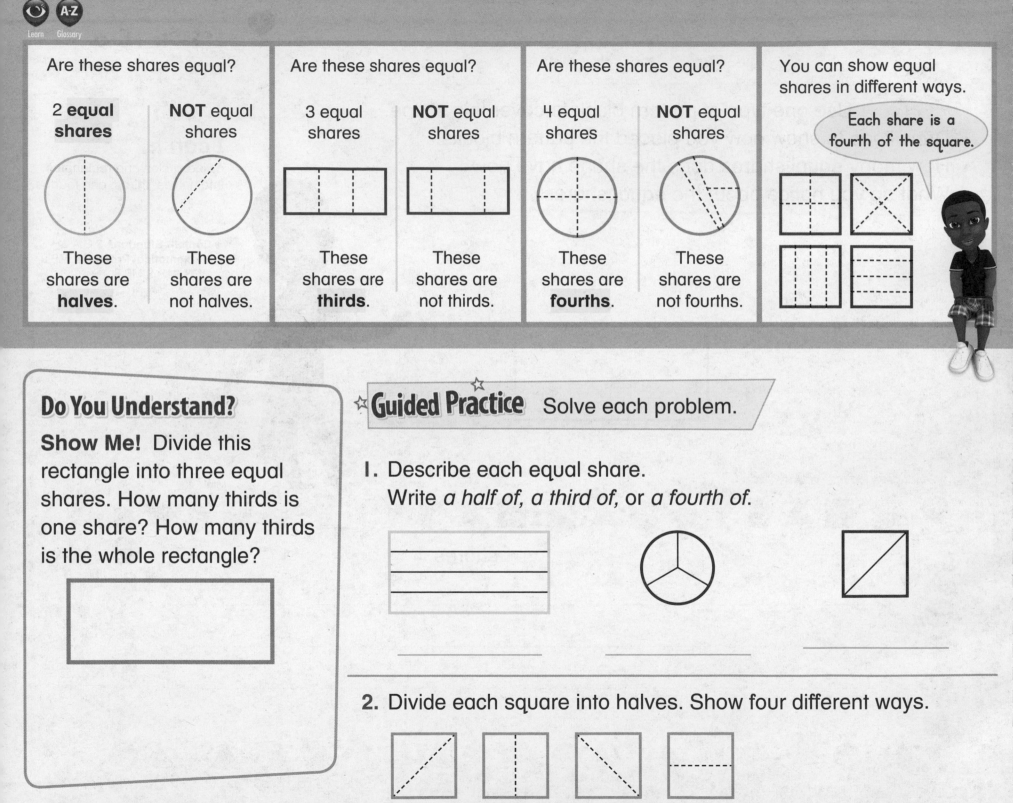

Are these shares equal?

| 2 **equal shares** | **NOT** equal shares |

These shares are **halves**.

These shares are not halves.

Are these shares equal?

| 3 equal shares | **NOT** equal shares |

These shares are **thirds**.

These shares are not thirds.

Are these shares equal?

| 4 equal shares | **NOT** equal shares |

These shares are **fourths**.

These shares are not fourths.

You can show equal shares in different ways.

Each share is a fourth of the square.

Do You Understand?

Show Me! Divide this rectangle into three equal shares. How many thirds is one share? How many thirds is the whole rectangle?

Guided Practice Solve each problem.

1. Describe each equal share.
   Write *a half of, a third of,* or *a fourth of*.

2. Divide each square into halves. Show four different ways.

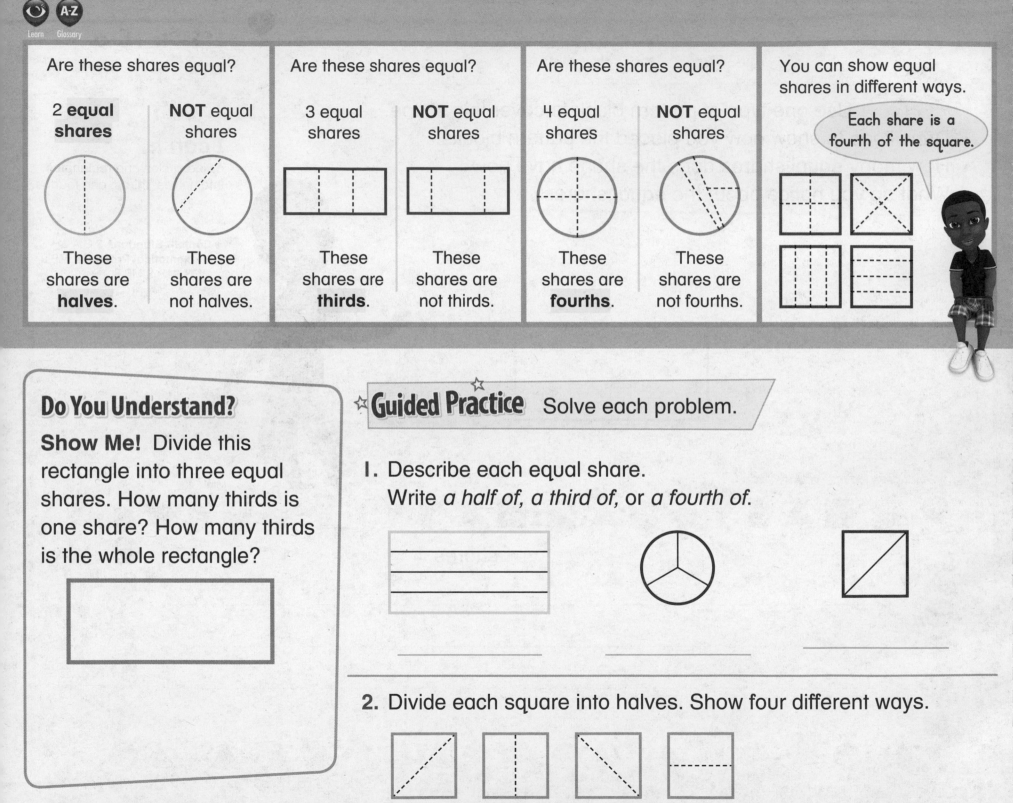

© Pearson Education, Inc. 2

Independent Practice   Divide each shape into the number of equal shares given. Show 2 ways. Then complete the sentences.

3. 3 equal shares

Each share is _____ the whole.

Each whole is _____ .

4. 4 equal shares

Each share is _____ the whole.

Each whole is _____ .

5. 2 equal shares

Each share is _____ the whole.

Each whole is _____ .

6. Higher Order Thinking Draw what comes next.

7. © MP.4 Model Leon cut a waffle into halves. Draw lines to show 3 different ways he could have cut the waffle.

8. Math and Science Tina is planting a garden. She wants to have equal parts for beans, for tomatoes, and for peppers. Draw a picture of how she could divide her garden.

9. Higher Order Thinking Draw lines on the picture to solve the problem.

4 friends want to share a watermelon. How could they cut the watermelon so each friend gets an equal share?

Each friend will get _____.

10. © Assessment Matt wants a flag that shows fourths. Which flags could Matt use? Choose all that apply.

Name _____

Another Look! Equal shares are the same size.

2 equal shares

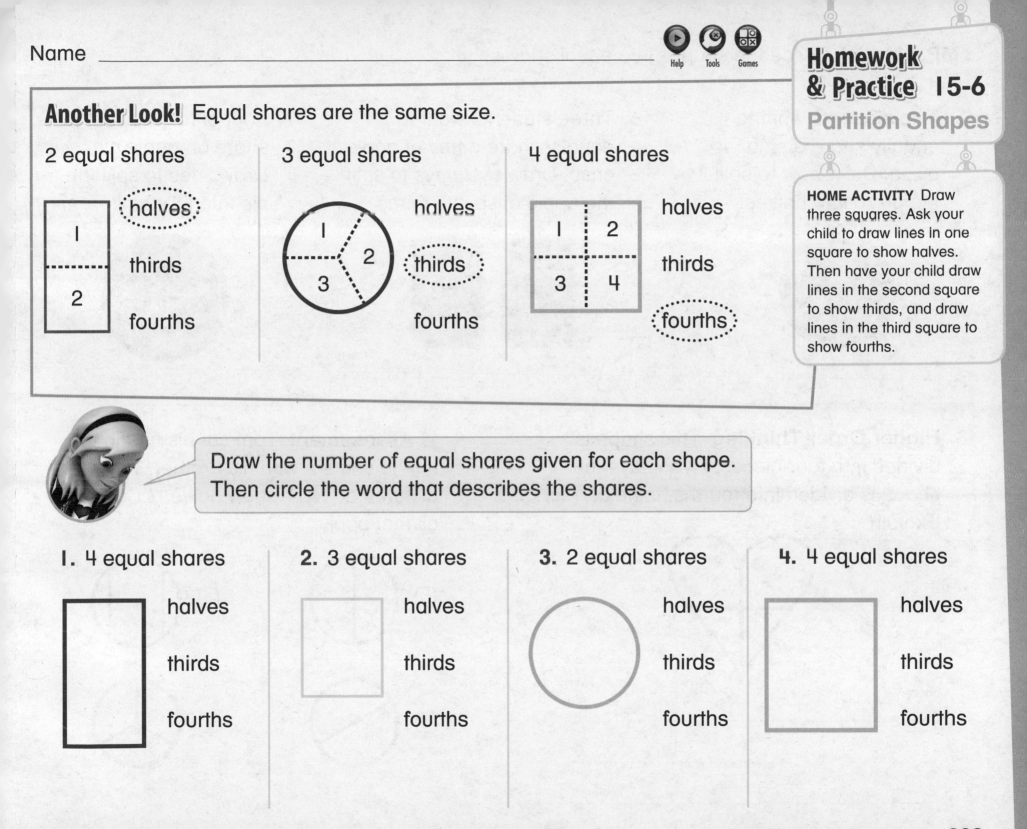

1	
2	

(halves)

thirds

fourths

3 equal shares

halves

(thirds)

fourths

4 equal shares

halves

thirds

(fourths)

Draw the number of equal shares given for each shape. Then circle the word that describes the shares.

1. 4 equal shares

halves

thirds

fourths

2. 3 equal shares

halves

thirds

fourths

3. 2 equal shares

halves

thirds

fourths

4. 4 equal shares

halves

thirds

fourths

5. Two students want to equally share a small pizza. Draw how to split the pizza into halves.

6. Three students want to equally share a tray of apple crisp. Draw two ways to split the apple crisp into thirds.

7. Four students want to share an apple pie. Draw lines to split the pie into fourths.

8. Higher Order Thinking This shape is divided into four pieces. Ryan says this shape is divided into fourths. Is he correct? Explain.

_____

_____

_____

9. © **Assessment** Tom cut his muffin in half to share it with his brother. Which pictures do **NOT** show halves? Choose all that apply.

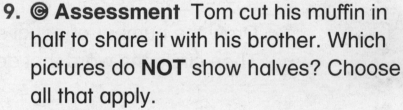

Name _____

Solve & Share

Divide this pizza into 4 equal shares. Compare your answer with a partner. Do you both have 4 equal shares? Did you both get the same answer?

I can ...
make equal shares that do not have the same shape.

© **Content Standard** 2.G.A.3
Mathematical Practices MP.1, MP.2, MP.3, MP.4, MP.7

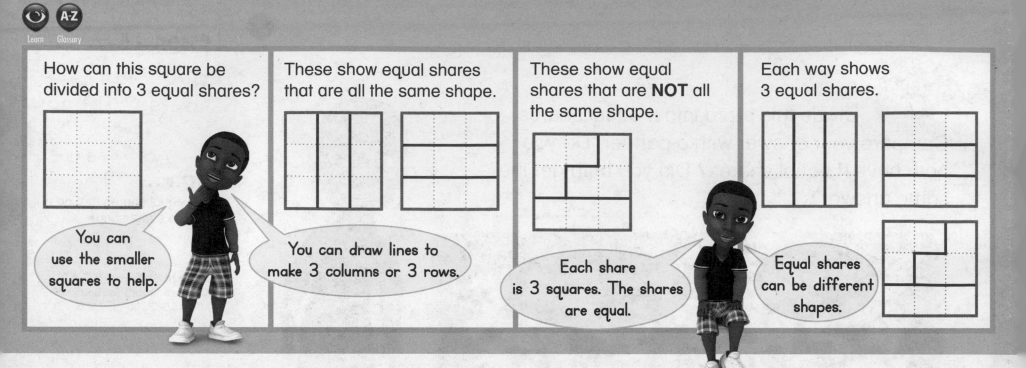

How can this square be divided into 3 equal shares?

You can use the smaller squares to help.

These show equal shares that are all the same shape.

You can draw lines to make 3 columns or 3 rows.

These show equal shares that are **NOT** all the same shape.

Each share is 3 squares. The shares are equal.

Each way shows 3 equal shares.

Equal shares can be different shapes.

Do You Understand?

Show Me! How can you check to make sure all of the shares are equal?

☆Guided Practice☆

Draw lines to show two different ways to divide the same rectangle into 2 equal shares.

1.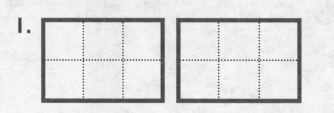

2. How many squares are in each equal share of the rectangles?

   _____

3. Describe the equal shares and the whole.

   Each share is ___a half of___ the whole.

   Each whole is ___two halves___.

© Pearson Education, Inc. 2   **Topic 15 | Lesson 7**

Name _____

Tools Assessment

Independent Practice   Draw lines to show two different ways to divide the same rectangle into 4 equal shares. Then answer the questions.

4. Show equal shares that are the **same shape**.   Show equal shares that are **different shapes**.

5. How many squares are in each equal share in Item 4? _____

6. Describe the equal shares and the whole in Item 4.

Each share is _____ the whole.

Each whole is _____ .

Draw lines to show two different ways to divide the same rectangle into 3 equal shares.

7.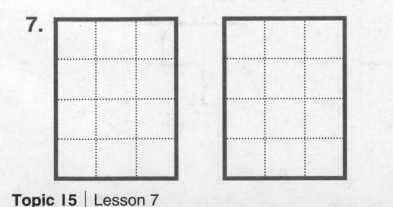

8. **Higher Order Thinking** How can equal shares in a rectangle have different shapes?

_____

_____

_____

9. Allen wants to share this pan of corn bread with 3 friends. Allen and his friends will each get an equal share.

How many pieces will be in each share?

_____ pieces

10. © **MP.3 Explain** Greg says that equal shares can be different in shape and size. Is Greg correct? Explain.

_____

_____

_____

11. Higher Order Thinking Donna drew the line in this rectangle to make 2 equal shares. Are the shares equal? Why or why not?

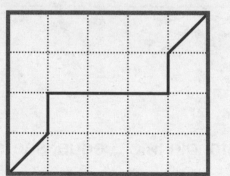

_____

_____

12. © **Assessment** Meg divides a rectangle into 3 equal shares that are **NOT** the same shape. Which could be Meg's rectangle?

Ⓐ

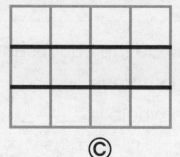

Ⓒ

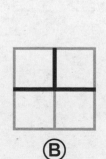

Ⓑ

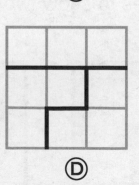

Ⓓ

Name _____

Another Look!

You can divide a rectangle into equal shares in different ways.

Each equal share has 5 squares.

Each rectangle has 3 equal shares. Each equal share has 5 squares.

HOME ACTIVITY Draw a rectangle. Ask your child to divide it into two equal shares that have different shapes.

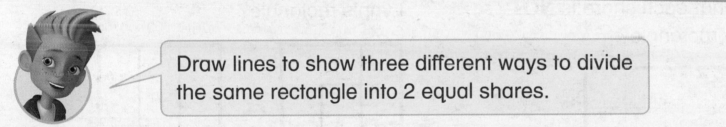

Draw lines to show three different ways to divide the same rectangle into 2 equal shares.

1.

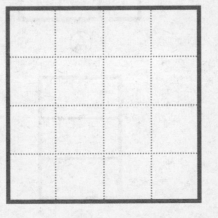

Can you divide a rectangle into equal shares that have DIFFERENT shapes?

Solve each problem.

2. © **MP.3 Explain** Lexi wants to share the sheet of tiger stickers with two friends. Are there enough stickers to make equal shares for Lexi and her two friends? Explain.

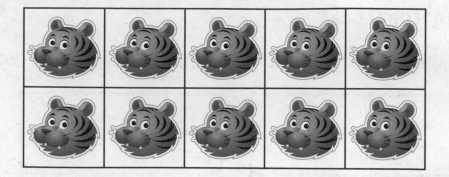

_____

_____

_____

3. **Higher Order Thinking** Corbin drew lines in this rectangle to make equal shares. How do you know that each share is **NOT** a third of the whole rectangle?

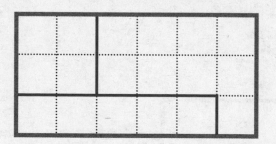

_____

_____

4. © **Assessment** Lynn divides a rectangle into 3 equal shares. Which could **NOT** be Lynn's rectangle?

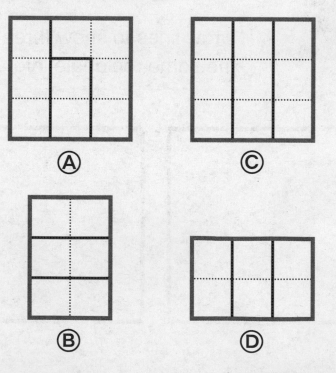

Ⓐ   Ⓒ

Ⓑ   Ⓓ

© Pearson Education, Inc. 2

Name _____

Solve & Share

Design a flag made of 15 equal squares. Use rows and columns. Draw two possible flag designs. Then write an equation for each flag to show the total number of squares.

Divide each flag to make three equal shares. Color each share differently.

Lesson 15-8
Repeated Reasoning

I can ...
use repeated reasoning to divide rectangles into rows and columns and to create designs with equal shares.

© **Mathematical Practices**
MP. 8 Also MP.1, MP.2, MP.3, MP.4, MP.7
Content Standards 2.G.A.2, 2.G.A.3 , 2.OA.C.4

My Flag Designs

Equation:

_____

Equation:

_____

Thinking Habits

Does something repeat in the problem?

How can the solution help me solve another problem?

Sam is designing a square quilt. The quilt must have 4 colors with an equal share for each color.

Help Sam make two designs.

How can I look for things that repeat in the problem?

I can count the small squares in each share in my first design. That will help me draw the shares in my second design.

Here, I used the same shape for each share. Each share is 4 small squares.

Design I

In both designs, each colored share is one fourth of the whole.

Here, I used different shapes for the shares.

Design 2

Do You Understand?

Show Me! How do you know each share in Design 2 is a fourth of the whole square?

☆ Guided Practice ☆ Solve the problem. Use crayons to color.

1. Hamal is painting a design. The design must have 3 colors with an equal share for each color. Create two possible designs for Hamal.

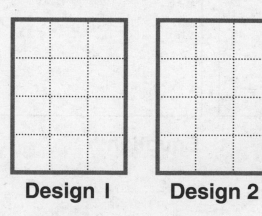

Design I   **Design 2**

Be ready to explain how you used repeated reasoning to help you solve the problem.

© Pearson Education, Inc. 2

Independent Practice ✫ Solve each problem. Use crayons to color. Explain your work.

2. Marie wants to put a rectangular design on a
T-shirt. The design must have 4 colors with an
equal share for each color. Create two possible
designs for Marie.

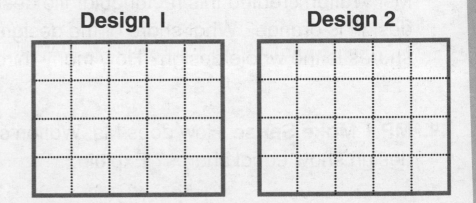

Design I   Design 2

_____

_____

_____

_____

3. Grant wants to put a circle design on his toy car.
The design must have 3 colors with an equal share
for each color. Create two possible designs for Grant.

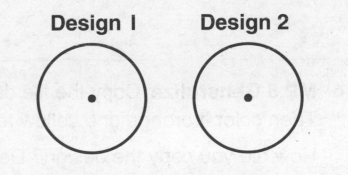

Design I   Design 2

_____

_____

_____

_____

Math Practices and Problem Solving

© **Performance Assessment** _____

Tile Design

Ms. Walton created this rectangular tile design. What share of the design is orange? What share of the design is yellow? How many shares is the whole design? How many thirds is the whole?

4. **MP.1 Make Sense** How does Ms. Walton's design show equal shares? Explain.

_____

_____

_____

5. **MP.2 Reasoning** What share of the design is orange? What share of the design is yellow? How many shares is the whole design? How many thirds is the whole?

_____

_____

_____

6. **MP.8 Generalize** Copy the tile design above onto this grid. Then color it orange and yellow to match the design shown above.

How did you copy the design? Describe one or two shortcuts you used.

_____

_____

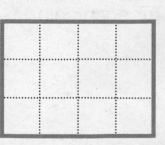

Help Tools Games

Another Look! Create two different designs for these squares that are the same size. Each design needs to have 2 colors with an equal share for each color.

I can draw a line down the center to make equal shares.

I can draw a line from opposite corners to make equal shares.

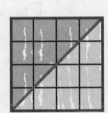

Design 2 also has equal shares that are the same shape.

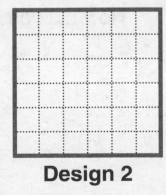

Design 1   **Design 2**

Solve the problem. Use crayons to color. Explain your solution.

1. Make two different designs. Each design must have 3 colors with an equal share for each color. One design should have shares that are NOT all the same shape.

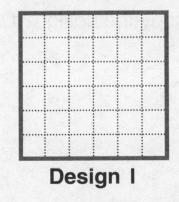

Design 1   **Design 2**

_____

_____

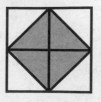

© Performance Assessment

A Design Repeated

Steven created this design on 4 squares of grid paper.
He wants to repeat this design 6 times on a larger grid.
Answer the questions to help Steven create the larger design.

2. **MP.7 Look for Patterns** Look at each small square of Steven's design. How are they alike? How are they different?

_____

_____

_____

3. **MP.3 Explain** Describe Steven's design. Explain what it looks like. Use *half of, a third of*, or *a fourth of* when you describe it.

_____

_____

_____

4. **MP.8 Generalize** Copy Steven's design 4 times.
Use 2 colors. Put 2 designs next to each other in each row.

How did you copy the design? Describe a shortcut you used.

_____

_____

Row 1

Row 2

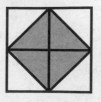

Name _____

Follow the Path

Find each sum or difference. Then color a path from **Start** to **Finish**. Follow the sums and differences that are even numbers. You can only move up, down, right, or left.

I can ...
add and subtract within 100.

© **Content Standard** 2.NBT.B.5

Start								
69 − 23	31 + 25	78 − 47	97 − 49	72 + 12	76 − 38	67 − 47	48 + 24	46 + 37
84 − 61	73 − 55	68 + 29	11 + 17	37 + 58	86 − 51	21 + 38	82 − 18	81 − 62
43 + 42	27 + 49	35 + 48	46 − 32	73 − 26	30 + 31	46 − 28	47 + 41	62 − 39
25 + 16	60 − 36	50 − 29	39 + 43	60 − 45	64 + 23	29 + 35	56 + 41	94 − 61
35 + 42	85 − 23	24 + 56	58 + 36	97 − 38	25 − 16	38 + 62	79 − 49	59 + 23

Finish

Vocabulary Review

A-Z Glossary

Word List
- angle
- cube
- edge
- equal shares
- face
- fourths
- halves
- hexagon
- pentagon
- polygon
- quadrilateral
- right angle
- thirds
- vertex

Understand Vocabulary

Write *always*, *sometimes*, or *never*.

1. A cube has exactly 4 faces. _____

2. A right angle forms a square corner. _____

3. Quadrilaterals are squares. _____

4. A solid figure with faces has edges. _____

Draw a line from each term to its example.

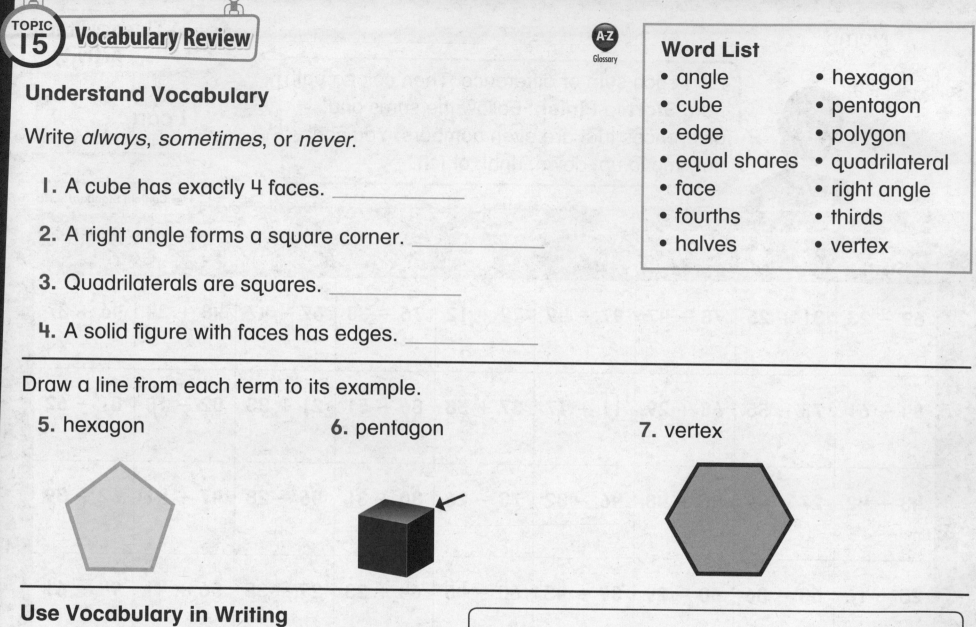

5. hexagon

6. pentagon

7. vertex

Use Vocabulary in Writing

8. Tell how you can divide a square into two equal shares. Then tell how you can divide that same square into 3 equal shares. Use terms from the Word List.

Name _____

Set A

You can name a plane shape by its number of sides and vertices.

vertex

side

_3_ sides

_3_ vertices

Shape: _triangle_

_4_ sides

_4_ vertices

Shape:

quadrilateral

Write the number of sides and vertices. Name the shape.

1. ____ sides

____ vertices

Shape: _____

2. ____ sides

____ vertices

Shape: _____

Set B

You can name a polygon by the number of its angles.

_5_ angles
pentagon

_6_ angles
hexagon

Write the number of angles. Then name the shape.

3. ____ angles

Shape: _____

4. ____ angles

Shape: _____

You can draw a polygon with a given number of sides, vertices, or angles.

Draw a polygon with 4 sides that are different lengths.

Draw a polygon with 5 vertices.

Draw a polygon with 3 angles. One angle is a right angle.

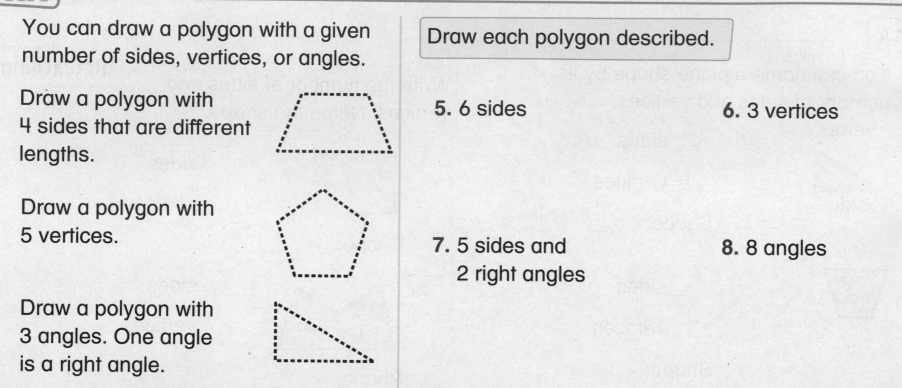

Draw each polygon described.

5. 6 sides

6. 3 vertices

7. 5 sides and 2 right angles

8. 8 angles

Set D

You can describe and draw cubes.

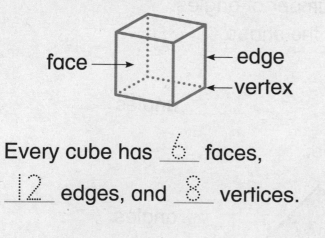

Every cube has __6__ faces, __12__ edges, and __8__ vertices.

9. Cross out the shapes that are **NOT** cubes.

10. Draw a cube. Use the dots to help you.

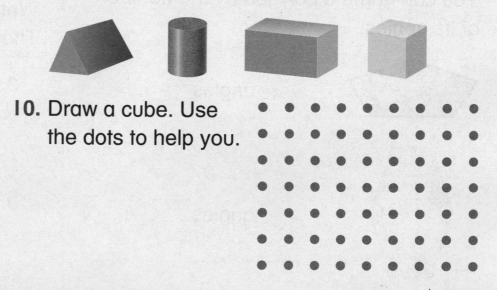

Set E

You can cover a rectangle with squares.

column

row →

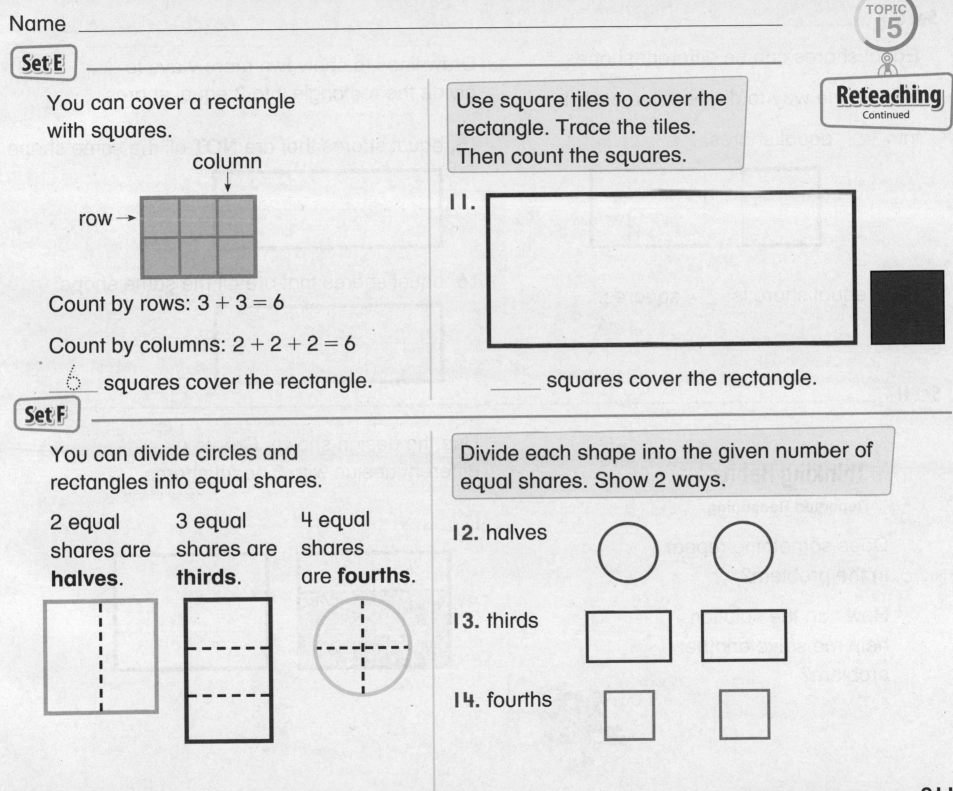

Count by rows: 3 + 3 = 6

Count by columns: 2 + 2 + 2 = 6

___6___ squares cover the rectangle.

Reteaching
Continued

Use square tiles to cover the rectangle. Trace the tiles. Then count the squares.

11.

_____ squares cover the rectangle.

Set F

You can divide circles and rectangles into equal shares.

2 equal shares are **halves**.

3 equal shares are **thirds**.

4 equal shares are **fourths**.

Divide each shape into the given number of equal shares. Show 2 ways.

12. halves

13. thirds

14. fourths

Equal shares can be different shapes.

This is one way to divide this rectangle

into __3__ equal shares.

Each equal share is __4__ squares.

Draw lines to show two more ways to divide the rectangle into 3 equal shares.

15. equal shares that are **NOT** all the same shape

16. equal shares that are all the same shape

Thinking Habits

Repeated Reasoning

Does something repeat in the problem?

How can the solution help me solve another problem?

Use the design shown. Create a different design with 3 equal shares.

17.

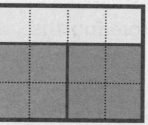 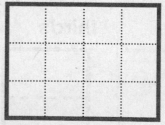

© Pearson Education, Inc. 2

Name _____

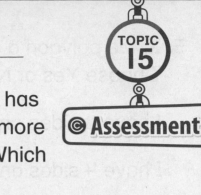
© **Assessment**

1. Which polygons are pentagons?
Choose all that apply.

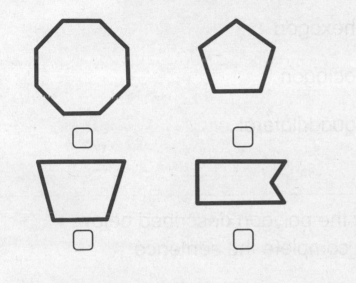

2. Rita draws a polygon. It has fewer than 8 sides and more angles than a square. Which shape did Rita draw?

Ⓐ triangle

Ⓑ rectangle

Ⓒ hexagon

Ⓓ quadrilateral

3. Which rectangles are divided into fourths?
Choose all that apply.

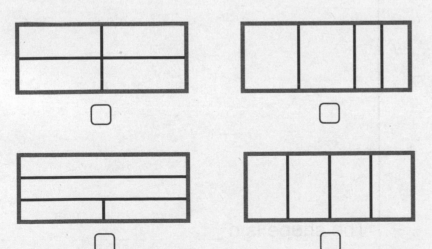

4. Draw a polygon with 4 angles.
Make one angle a right angle.
Then name the polygon.

Name: _____

5. Is the polygon a quadrilateral?
Choose Yes or No.

I have 3 sides and 3 angles. ○ Yes ○ No

I have 4 sides and 4 angles. ○ Yes ○ No

I am a square. ○ Yes ○ No

I am a rectangle. ○ Yes ○ No

6. Mandy draws a polygon with 6 sides and 6 angles. Which shape did she draw?

Ⓐ pentagon

Ⓑ hexagon

Ⓒ octagon

Ⓓ quadrilateral

7. Name the shape below. Write 3 things that describe the shape.

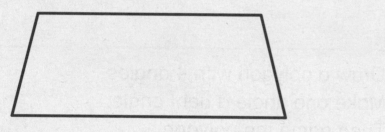

8. Draw the polygon described below. Then complete the sentence.

I have 2 fewer sides than a pentagon.
I have 1 less angle than a square.
I have one right angle.

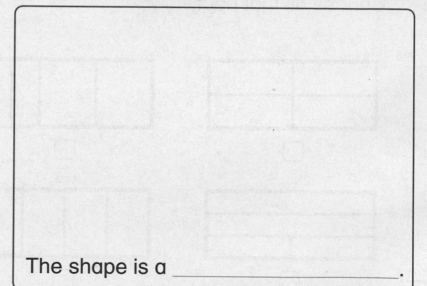

The shape is a _____.

9. Complete the sentence to name and describe the solid figure below.

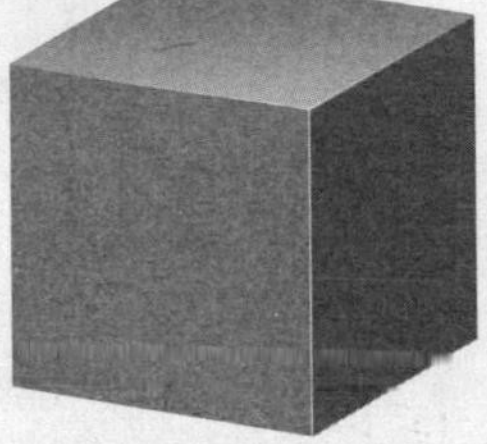

A _____ has _____ faces, _____ vertices, and _____ edges.

10. Divide the circle into 2 equal shares. Then complete the sentences.

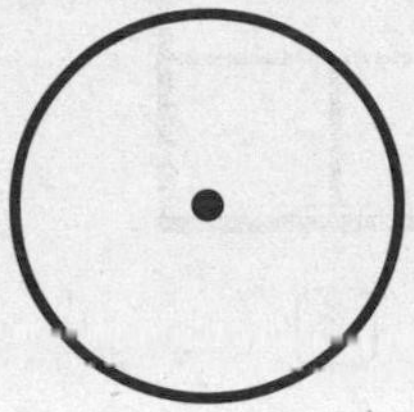

Each share is a _____ of the whole.

The whole is _____ halves.

11. Brad says there are only two ways to divide the same rectangle below into 3 equal shares. Do you agree? Use words and pictures to explain.

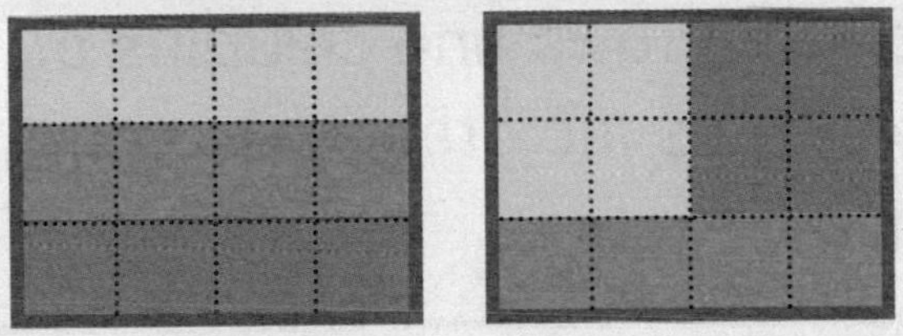

_____

_____

12. Count the number of squares in the rows and columns of the rectangle. Use the numbers on the cards to write the missing numbers in the equations.

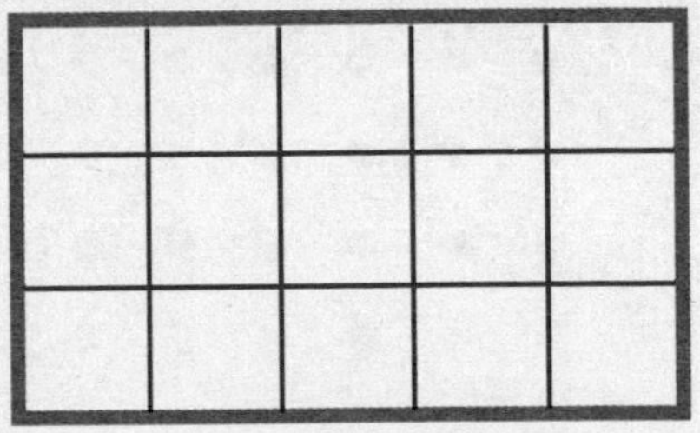

| 15 | 3 | 5 |

Rows: _____ + _____ + _____ = _____ squares

Columns: _____ + _____ + _____ + _____ + _____ = _____ squares

13. Kerry wants a design that shows thirds. Which designs could Kerry use? Choose all that apply.

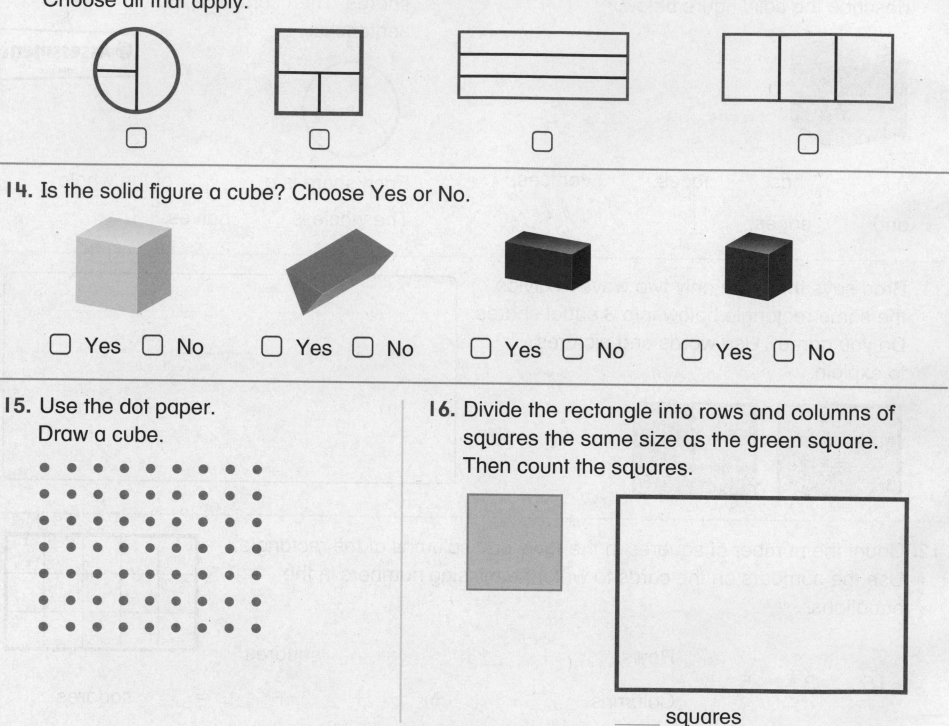

☐   ☐   ☐   ☐

14. Is the solid figure a cube? Choose Yes or No.

☐ Yes ☐ No   ☐ Yes ☐ No   ☐ Yes ☐ No   ☐ Yes ☐ No

15. Use the dot paper.
Draw a cube.

16. Divide the rectangle into rows and columns of squares the same size as the green square. Then count the squares.

_____ squares

Name _____

Happy Home

Tina and her family moved into a new home.
They bought different things for each room.

1. They hang pictures on the wall.
   Name the shape of each picture frame.

_____

_____

2. The rug in the kitchen has
   5 sides and 5 vertices.
   Draw the shape of the rug.

Name the shape. _____

3. The wallpaper uses this pattern.

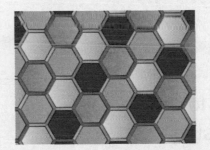

Name the shape in the pattern.

_____

Write the number of sides, vertices, and
angles in the shape.

_____ sides   _____ vertices   _____ angles

4. The living room has 2 end tables.

Circle the table that is a cube. Explain.

_____

_____

_____

_____

5. Tina has a new quilt for her bed.
Her quilt has this design.

What share is green? _____

What share is yellow? _____

6. Tina's mother is making a quilt made of
smaller squares. She wants the quilt to have
4 colors. Each color has an equal share.

Part A
Use 4 colors to make a possible quilt
design below. Make the equal shares
the same shape.

Design I

Part B
Use 4 colors to make a different quilt
design below. Make the equal shares have
different shapes.

Design 2

© Pearson Education, Inc. 2

STEP UP to Grade 3

Here's a preview of next year. These lessons help you step up to Grade 3.

Lessons

Grade 3 lessons
look different.
Rotate the pages
so your name is at
the top.

Name _____

Solve & Share

Lesson 1

Multiplication as Repeated Addition

Solve

Ms. Witt bought 3 boxes of paint with 5 jars of paint in each box. What is the total number of jars Ms. Witt bought? *Solve this problem any way you choose.*

I can ...
use addition or multiplication to join equal groups.

Ⓒ **Content Standards** 3.OA.A.1, 3.OA.A.3
Mathematical Practices MP.1, MP.2, MP.3, MP.4, MP.6

Make sense of this problem. Think about what you know and what you need to find.

Look Back! Ⓒ **MP.4 Model with Math** How can you use a picture to show the math you did in the problem?

How Can You Find the Total Number of Objects in Equal Groups?

A

Jessie used 3 bags to bring home the goldfish she won at the Fun Fair. She put the same number of goldfish in each bag. How many goldfish did she win?

I can use counters to show the groups.

8 goldfish in each bag

B

The counters show 3 groups of 8 goldfish.

You can use addition to join equal groups.

? goldfish →

3 bags →

| 8 | 8 | 8 |

8 goldfish in each bag

?

$8 + 8 + 8 = 24$

C

Multiplication is an operation that gives the total number when you join equal groups.

? goldfish →

3 bags →

| 8 | 8 | 8 |

8 goldfish in each bag

?

3 times 8 equals 24

$3 \times 8 = 24$

factor factor product

Factors are the numbers that are being multiplied. The product is the answer to a multiplication problem.

D

You can write equations.

Use a question mark for the unknown number that you find.

Addition equation:
$8 + 8 + 8 = ?$
$8 + 8 + 8 = 24$

Multiplication equation:
$3 \times 8 = ?$
$3 \times 8 = 24$

Jessie won 24 goldfish.

Convince Me! ⊚ MP.4 Model with Math Suppose Jessie won 5 bags of 8 goldfish. Draw a bar diagram and write an addition equation and a multiplication equation to represent the problem.

Name _____

☆ Guided Practice ☆

Do You Understand?

1. © **MP.2 Reasoning** Can you write
$3 + 3 + 3 + 3 = 12$ as a multiplication
equation? Explain.

2. © **MP.2 Reasoning** Can you write
$1 + 5 + 7 = 13$ as a multiplication
equation? Explain.

3. Write an addition equation and a
multiplication equation to solve this
problem.
Matt buys 3 bags of apples. There are
6 apples in each bag. How many apples
does Matt buy?

Do You Know How?

Complete **4** and **5**. Use the pictures
to help.

4.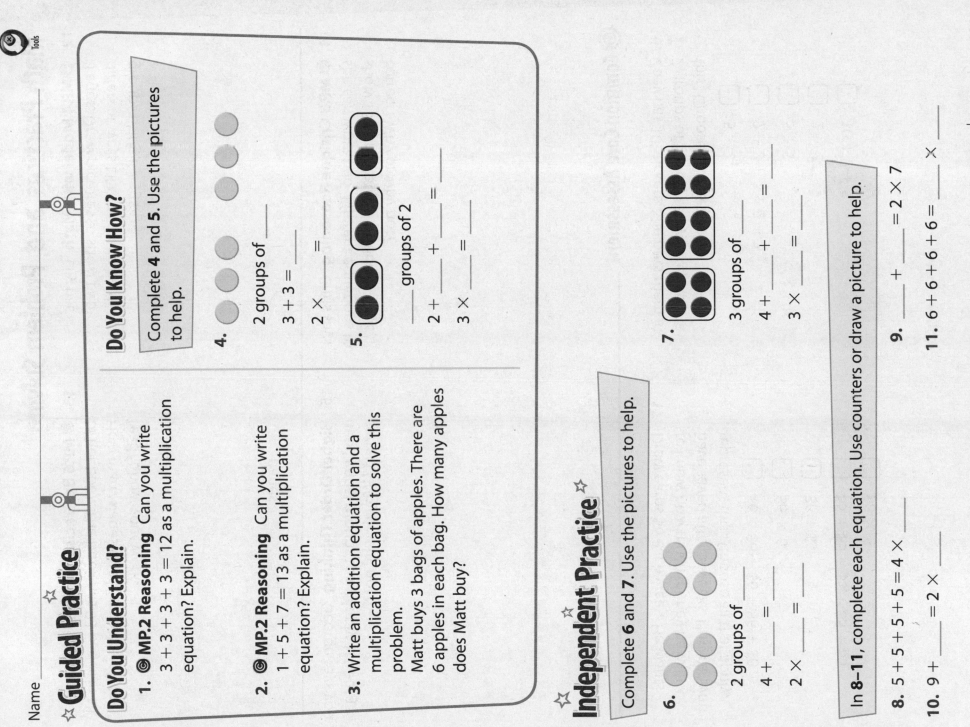

2 groups of _____

$3 + 3 =$ _____

$2 \times$ _____ = _____

5.

_____ groups of 2

$2 +$ _____ $+$ _____ $=$ _____

$3 \times$ _____ $=$ _____

☆ Independent Practice ☆

Complete **6** and **7**. Use the pictures to help.

6.

2 groups of _____

$4 +$ _____ $=$ _____

$2 \times$ _____ $=$ _____

7.

3 groups of _____

$4 + $ _____ $+$ _____ $=$ _____

$3 \times$ _____ $=$ _____

In **8–11**, complete each equation. Use counters or draw a picture to help.

8. $5 + 5 + 5 + 5 = 4 \times$ _____

9. _____ $+$ _____ $= 2 \times 7$

10. $9 +$ _____ $= 2 \times$ _____

11. $6 + 6 + 6 + 6 =$ _____ $\times$ _____

Math Practices and Problem Solving

12. © **MP.4 Model with Math** Lily has 8 eggs. Draw pictures to show two different ways Lily can make equal groups using 8 eggs.

13. © **MP.6 Be Precise** Erin reads 54 pages of her book. The book has 93 pages in all. How many pages does Erin have left to read? Show your work.

_____ pages

14. © **MP.3 Critique Reasoning** Chris says she can write two different equations to show 15 as repeated addition. Is Chris correct? Why or why not?

15. **Higher Order Thinking** George says you need equal groups to multiply. Is George correct? Why or why not?

© Common Core Assessment

16. Zoey has 10 stickers. She puts them in 2 groups of 5. How can you represent this? Choose all that apply.

☐ 5 + 2
☐ 2 + 2 + 2 + 2 + 2
☐ 5 + 5
☐ 2 × 5
☐ 10 + 2 + 5

17. Drew earns $6 each week. He wants to know how much money he will have saved after 5 weeks. How can you represent this? Choose all that apply.

☐ $6 + $6 + $6 + $6 + $6
☐ $6 × 6
☐ $6 + $5
☐ $5 + $5 + $5 + $5 + $5
☐ $6 × 5

Lesson 2

Arrays and Multiplication

I can...

use arrays to show and solve multiplication problems.

© Content Standards 3.OA.A.3, 3.OA.A.1
Mathematical Practices MP.1, MP.3, MP.5, MP.7

Solve

⭐ Solve & Share

Mark put sports cards in an album. He put 4 rows of cards on each page. He put 3 cards in each row. How many cards are on each page? *Solve this problem any way you choose.*

You can use tools. Sometimes using objects can help you solve a problem. Show your work in the space below!

Look Back! © MP.1 Make Sense and Persevere Will your answer be the same if Mark puts 3 rows of 4 cards on each page? Explain.

How Does an Array Show Multiplication?

A

Dana keeps her swimming medal collection in a display on the wall.

The display has 4 rows. Each row has 5 medals. How many medals are in Dana's collection?

The medals are in an array. An array shows objects in equal rows.

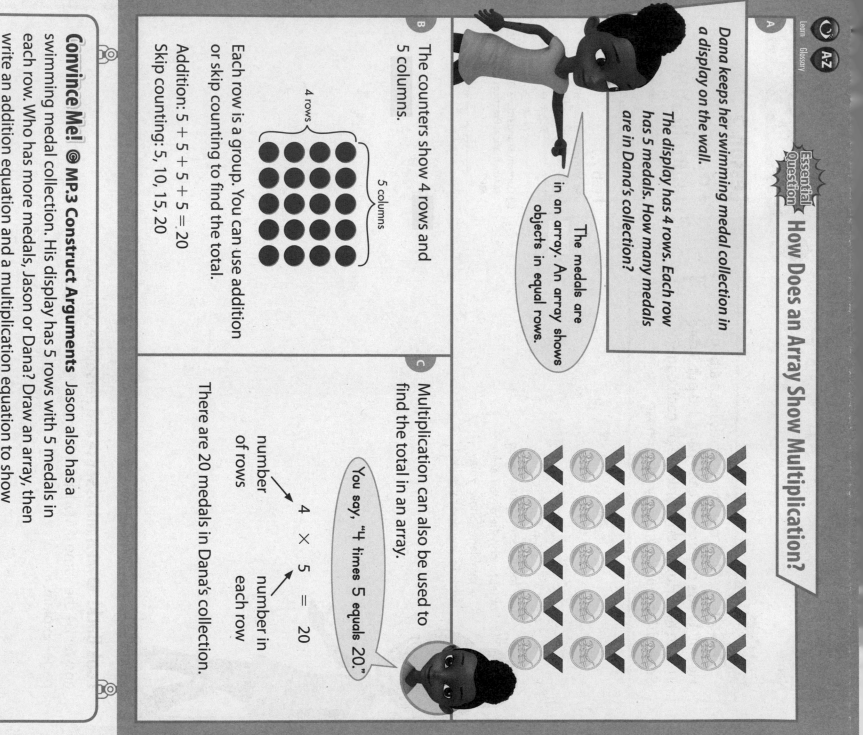

B

The counters show 4 rows and 5 columns.

4 rows

5 columns

Each row is a group. You can use addition or skip counting to find the total.

Addition: $5 + 5 + 5 + 5 = 20$
Skip counting: 5, 10, 15, 20

C

Multiplication can also be used to find the total in an array.

You say, "4 times 5 equals 20."

$$4 \times 5 = 20$$

number of rows → 4

number in each row → 5

There are 20 medals in Dana's collection.

Convince Me! © **MP.3 Construct Arguments** Jason also has a swimming medal collection. His display has 5 rows with 5 medals in each row. Who has more medals, Jason or Dana? Draw an array, then write an addition equation and a multiplication equation to show your work.

Name _____

☆ Guided Practice ☆

Do You Understand?

1. Look at page 926. What does the second factor tell you about the array?

2. Gina puts muffins in 4 rows with 8 muffins in each row. Draw an array to find the total number of muffins.

Do You Know How?

In **3** and **4**, write a multiplication equation for each array.

3.

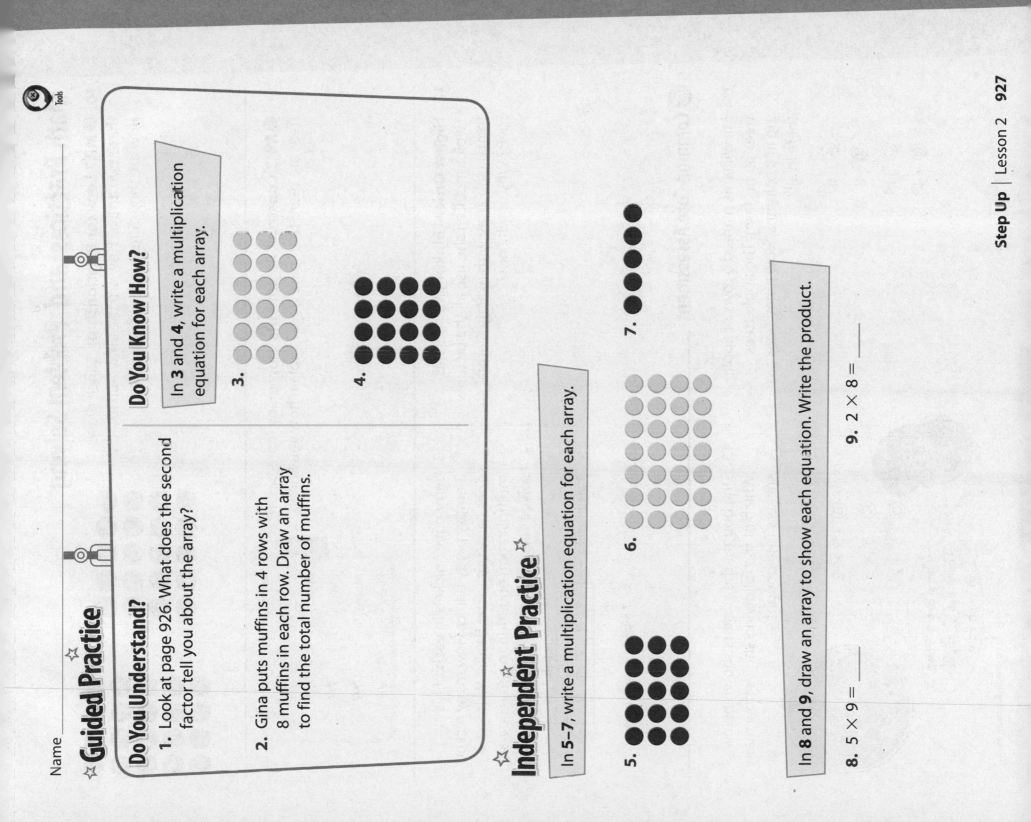

4.

☆ Independent Practice ☆

In **5–7**, write a multiplication equation for each array.

5.

6.

7.

In **8** and **9**, draw an array to show each equation. Write the product.

8. $5 \times 9 =$ _____

9. $2 \times 8 =$ _____

Math Practices and Problem Solving

10. © **MP.7 Look for Relationships** Lance draws these two arrays. How are the arrays alike? How are they different?

11. © **MP.3 Construct Arguments** How many more birch trees are there than pine trees? Explain how you know.

Trees in the Park	
DATA	
Birch	⧝⧝⧝ l
Oak	lll
Maple	⧝⧝⧝
Pine	ll

12. Higher Order Thinking Rachel has 19 pictures. Can she use all the pictures to make an array with exactly 4 equal rows? Why or why not?

13. Larry puts 7 nickels in each of his 3 empty piggy banks. How many nickels does Larry put in the banks? Write a multiplication equation to show how you solved the problem.

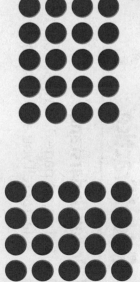

3 piggy banks → | 7 | 7 | 7 |

? nickels

7 nickels in each bank

© **Common Core Assessment**

14. Mr. Williams planted 6 rows of apple trees on his farm. The apple trees are in 8 columns. How many trees are there in all?

Ⓐ 6
Ⓑ 8
Ⓒ 14
Ⓓ 48

15. Tina bought the stickers shown below. Which of the following shows how many stickers Tina bought?

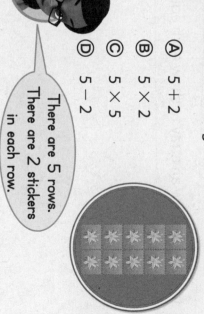

There are 5 rows. There are 2 stickers in each row.

Ⓐ 5 + 2
Ⓑ 5 × 2
Ⓒ 5 × 5
Ⓓ 5 − 2

928

Lesson 3
Division as Sharing

I can...
use objects or pictures to show how objects can be divided into equal groups.

Ⓒ Content Standards 3.OA.A.2, 3.OA.A.3
Mathematical Practices MP.1, MP.3, MP.4, MP.5, MP.5

Solve

Name _____

Solve & Share

Four friends picked 20 apples. They want to share them equally. How many apples should each person get? **Solve this problem any way you choose.**

Model with math. Drawing a picture that represents the problem can help you solve it. Show your work!

Look Back! Ⓒ **MP.5 Use Appropriate Tools** Can you use counters to help you solve this problem? Explain.

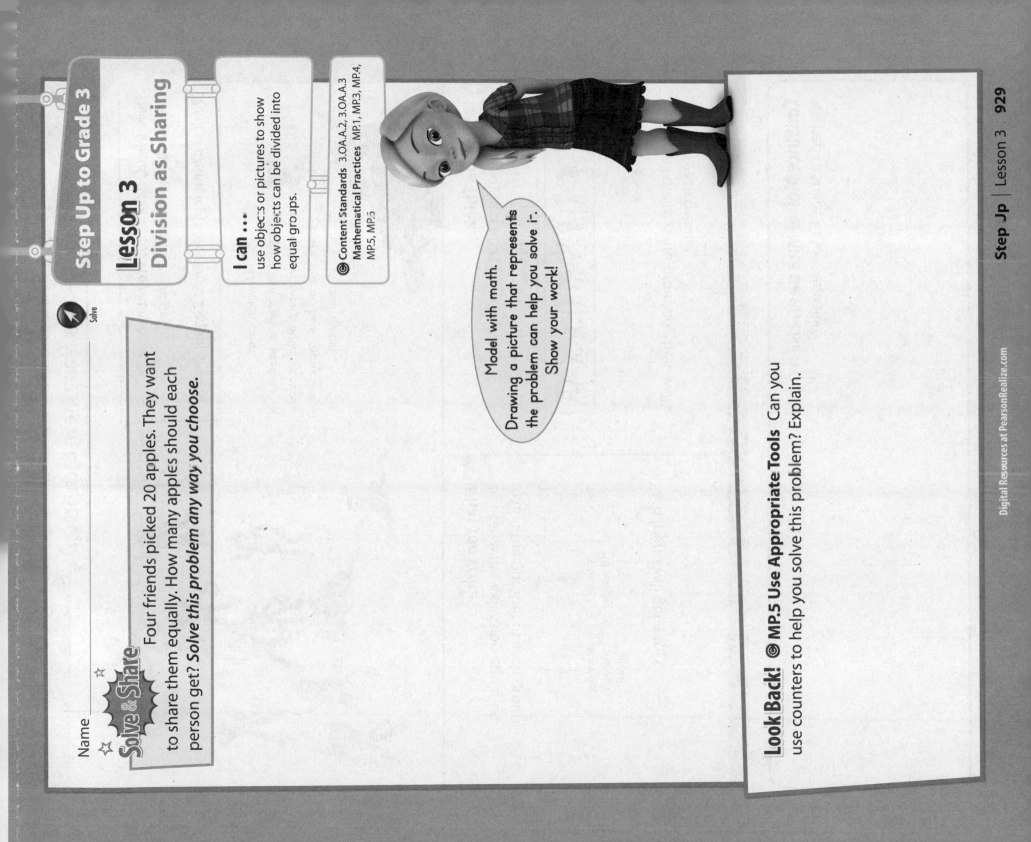

How Many Are in Each Group?

A

Three friends have 12 toys to share equally.
How many toys will each friend get?

Think of arranging 12 toys into 3 equal groups.

> Division is an operation that is used to find how many equal groups there are or how many are in each group.

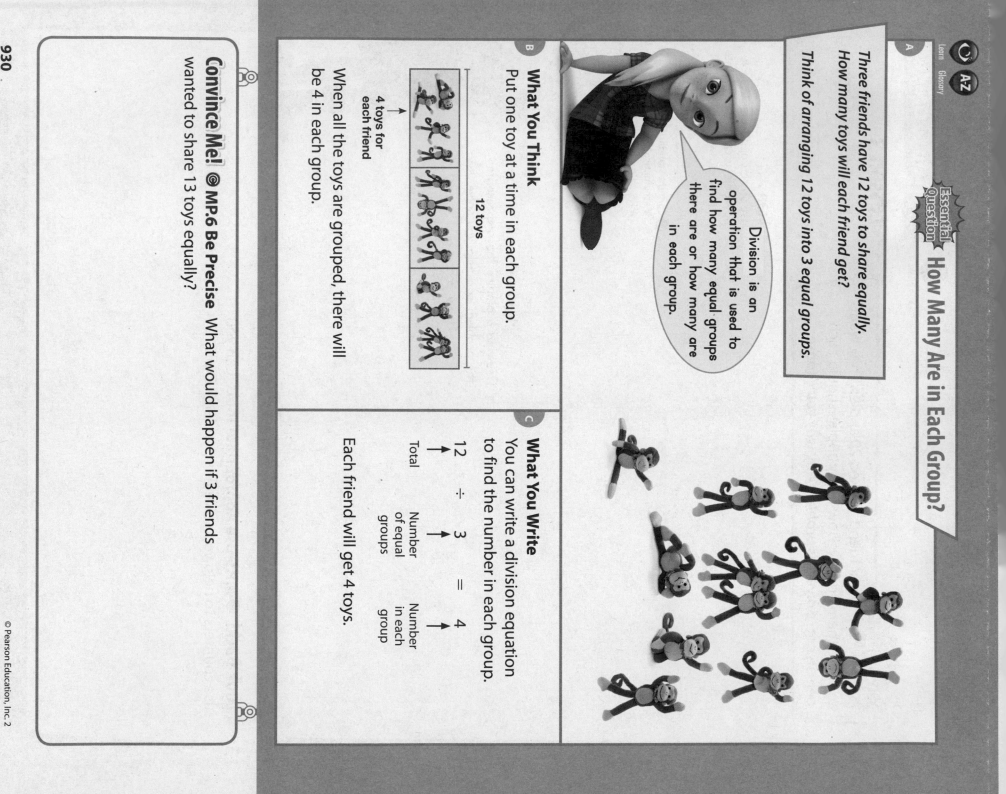

B

What You Think

Put one toy at a time in each group.

12 toys

4 toys for each friend

When all the toys are grouped, there will be 4 in each group.

C

What You Write

You can write a division equation to find the number in each group.

$$12 \div 3 = 4$$

Total → Number of equal groups → Number in each group

Each friend will get 4 toys.

Convince Me! © **MP.6 Be Precise** What would happen if 3 friends wanted to share 13 toys equally?

☆ Guided Practice ☆

Do You Understand?

1. 15 blocks are divided into 3 rows. How many blocks are in each row? Use the bar diagram to solve.

15

?	?	?

$15 \div 3 = $ _____ blocks

2. © MP.6 Be Precise Can 11 apples be shared equally among 4 children with no apples remaining? Explain.

Do You Know How?

In **3** and **4**, draw a picture to solve.

3. 16 bananas are shared equally by 4 monkeys. How many bananas does each monkey get?

4. 21 marbles are divided equally into 3 jars. How many marbles are in each jar?

☆ Independent Practice ☆

In **5** and **6**, draw a picture to solve.

5. 24 sandwiches are divided equally into 6 bags. How many sandwiches are in each bag?

6. 12 pencils are shared equally by 2 people. How many pencils does each person have?

In **7–10**, complete each equation.

7. $14 \div 2 = $ ☐

14

?	?

8. $24 \div 8 = $ ☐

24

?	?	?	?	?	?	?	?

9. $12 \div 4 = $ _____

10. $28 \div 7 = $ _____

Math Practices and Problem Solving

☆ ☆ ☆ ☆

11. © **MP.3 Critique Reasoning** Dean is putting 16 pens into equal groups. He says if he puts them into 2 equal groups he will have more pens in each group than if he puts them in 4 equal groups. Is Dean correct? Explain.

12. © **MP.1 Make Sense and Persevere** Ms. Baker's second grade class is divided into 4 teams. Each team has an equal number of students. Do you have enough information to find how many students are on each team? Explain.

13. Lily draws a rectangle. Sarah draws a pentagon. Who draws the shape with more sides? How many more sides does that shape have?

14. © **MP.4 Model with Math** The jazz band in a parade marches in 9 rows with 6 members in each row. Write an equation to show how many members there are.

15. Number Sense Joan equally shares 30 grapes with some friends. Is the number of grapes that each friend gets greater than 30 or less than 30? Explain.

16. Higher Order Thinking Lacie has 16 shells. She gives 6 shells to her mom. Then she and her sister share the other shells equally. How many shells does Lacie get? How many shells does her sister get? How do you know?

© **Common Core Assessment**

17. Darren has the 12 stickers shown at the right. He wants to put an equal number of stickers on each of 2 books. Draw circles in each box to represent the stickers Darren puts on each book.

Book 1

Book 2

x

932

© Pearson Education, Inc. 2

Lesson 4
Division as Repeated Subtraction

I can...
use repeated subtraction to understand and solve division problems.

© Content Standards 3.OA.A.2, 3.OA.A.3
Mathematical Practices MP.2, MP.4, MP.5, MP.8

Solve

Solve & Share

Li made 12 tacos. He wants to give some of his friends 2 tacos each. If Li does not get any of the tacos, how many of his friends will get tacos? *Solve this problem any way you choose.*

You can use reasoning. How can what you know about sharing help you solve the problem? Show your work in the space below!

Look Back! © MP.5 Use Appropriate Tools How can counters or other objects help you show your work?

AZ

How Can You Divide Using Repeated Subtraction?

Essential Question

A

June has 10 strawberries to serve to her guests.
If each guest eats 2 strawberries, how many
guests can June serve?

10 strawberries ⟶

2 strawberries
for each guest ⟶ | 2 |

| 10 |
? guests

B

You can use repeated
subtraction to find how many
groups of 2 are in 10.

$10 - 2 = 8$
$8 - 2 = 6$
$6 - 2 = 4$ ⎫ You can subtract 2 five times.
$4 - 2 = 2$ ⎬ There are five groups of 2 in 10.
$2 - 2 = 0$ ⎭ There are no strawberries left.

June can serve 5 guests.

C

You can write
a division equation to find the
number of groups.

Write: $10 \div 2 = ?$

Read: Ten divided by 2 equals what
number?

Solve: $10 \div 2 = 5$

June can serve 5 guests.

Convince Me! ⓒ MP.4 Model with Math In the example above, what
if each guest eats 5 strawberries? Use the math you know to represent
the problem and find how many guests June could serve.

Name _____

☆ Guided Practice ☆

Do You Understand?

1. Show how you can use repeated subtraction to find how many groups of 5 there are in 25. Then write a division equation to solve the problem.

Do You Know How?

In **2** and **3**, use counters or draw a picture to solve.

2. The basketball team has 14 shoes. There are 2 shoes in each pair. How many pairs of shoes are there?

3. Maya has 18 cat toys. She gives each of her cats 6 toys. How many cats does Maya have?

☆ Independent Practice ☆

In **4** and **5**, complete the equations.

4. Tanya picks 18 pears. She places 9 pears in each bag. How many bags does Tanya have?

$18 - 9 = $ _____

___ $- 9 = $ _____

___ $\div 9 = $ _____

Tanya has ___ bags.

5. The workers on a farm have 7 keys each. There are 21 keys. How many workers are on the farm?

$21 - 7 = $ _____

___ $- 7 = $ _____

___ $- $ ___ $ = $ _____

___ $\div$ ___ $ = $ _____

There are ___ workers.

In **6** and **7**, use counters or draw a picture to solve.

6. Shawna bought 36 markers that came in packages of 4 markers each. How many packages did Shawna buy?

7. James has 16 pencils. He puts 2 pencils on each desk. How many desks are there?

Math Practices and Problem Solving ☆ ☆ ☆ ☆

8. © MP.8 Generalize The chart shows the number of pennies each of three friends has in her pocket. Each friend divides her money into piles of 4 coins. Write division equations to show how many equal piles each friend can make. Explain what repeats in the equations and how it helps you solve.

> Does something repeat in the problem?

DATA

Money in Pockets

Paige	20 pennies
Lexi	16 pennies
Nancy	12 pennies

9. If Lexi makes 8 columns of pennies, how many rows does she make? Write an equation to model and solve the problem.

11. Higher Order Thinking A bakery plans to make 8 new muffins each year. How many years will it take for the store to make 40 new muffins? Write and solve an equation.

10. © MP.4 Model with Math Tim has $45. He spends $21, then finds $28. How much money does Tim have now? Use math to represent the problem.

© Common Core Assessment

12. Andy writes the following:

$$8 - 4 = 4$$
$$4 - 4 = 0$$

Which equation could Andy use to represent the same problem?

- (A) $4 \times 4 = 16$
- (B) $8 \div 8 = 1$
- (C) $8 \div 4 = 2$
- (D) $4 \div 2 = 2$

13. Rae writes the following:

$$27 - 9 = 18$$
$$18 - 9 = 9$$
$$9 - 9 = 0$$

Which problem is Rae trying to solve?

- (A) $27 \div 9$
- (B) $27 \div 3$
- (C) $27 - 9$
- (D) 27×3

Name

Solve & Share

Find the sum of 327 + 241. Think about place value. *Solve this problem any way you choose.*

Solve

I can...
add numbers using partial sums.

© Content Standard 3.NBT.A.2
Mathematical Practices MP.2, MP.3, MP.4

You can use reasoning to make a plan. Part of your plan for solving this problem could be to show each of the numbers in expanded form. Show your work in the space below!

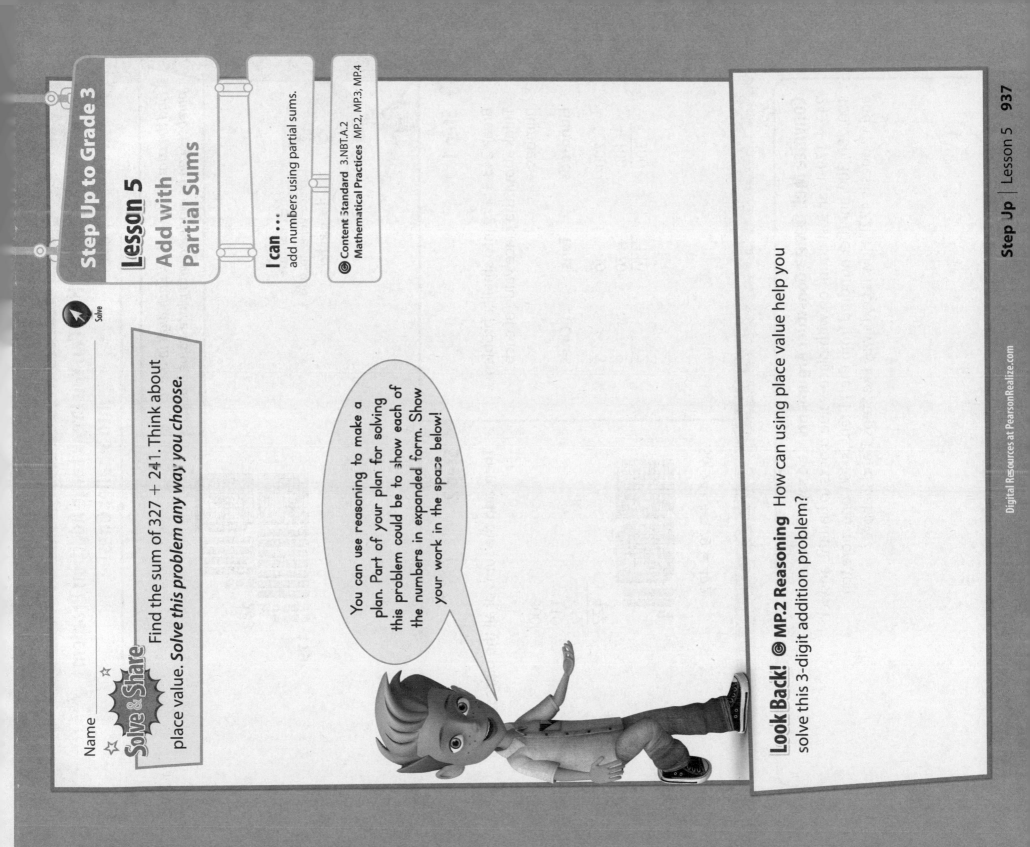

Look Back! © **MP.2 Reasoning** How can using place value help you solve this 3-digit addition problem?

How Can You Break Large Addition Problems into Smaller Ones?

A

Find the sum of 243 + 179. Each digit in the numbers can be modeled with place-value blocks.

You can use place value to add the numbers.

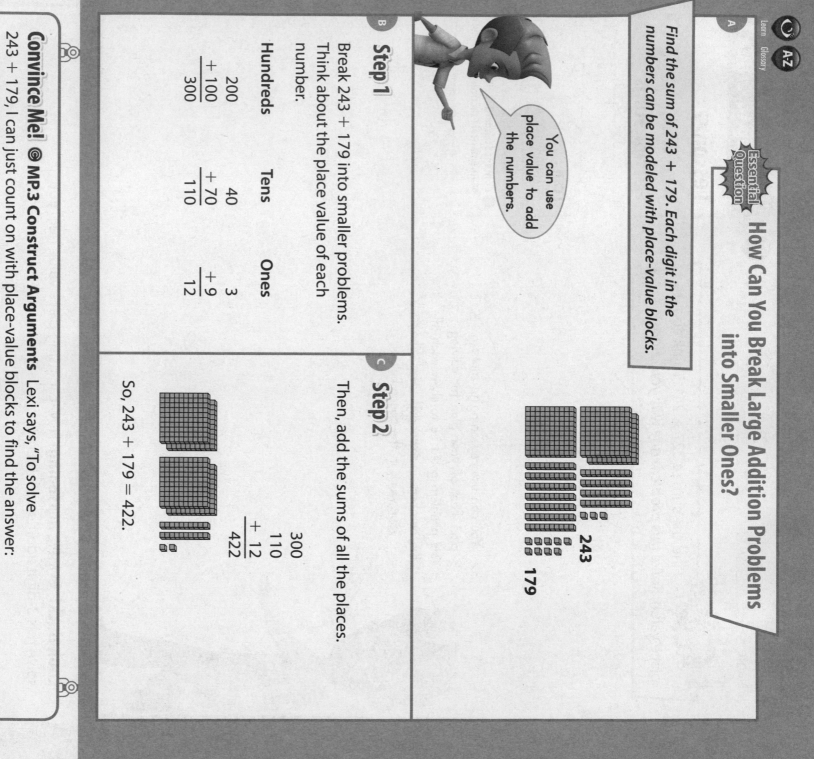

243

179

B

Step 1

Break 243 + 179 into smaller problems. Think about the place value of each number.

Hundreds	Tens	Ones
200	40	3
+100	+70	+9
300	110	12

C

Step 2

Then, add the sums of all the places.

```
  300
  110
+  12
  422
```

So, 243 + 179 = 422.

Convince Me! © MP.3 Construct Arguments Lexi says, "To solve 243 + 179, I can just count on with place-value blocks to find the answer: 100, 200, 300, another hundred from the 11 tens is 400, one more ten and 12 ones is 422!" How is Lexi's way like Steps 1 and 2 above?

☆ Guided Practice

Do You Understand?

1. © MP.2 Reasoning Suppose you are adding 824 + 106. What would the tens problem be? Why?

2. Write the smaller problems you could use to find 512 + 362. What is the sum?

Do You Know How?

In **3**, use place value to find the sum.

3.

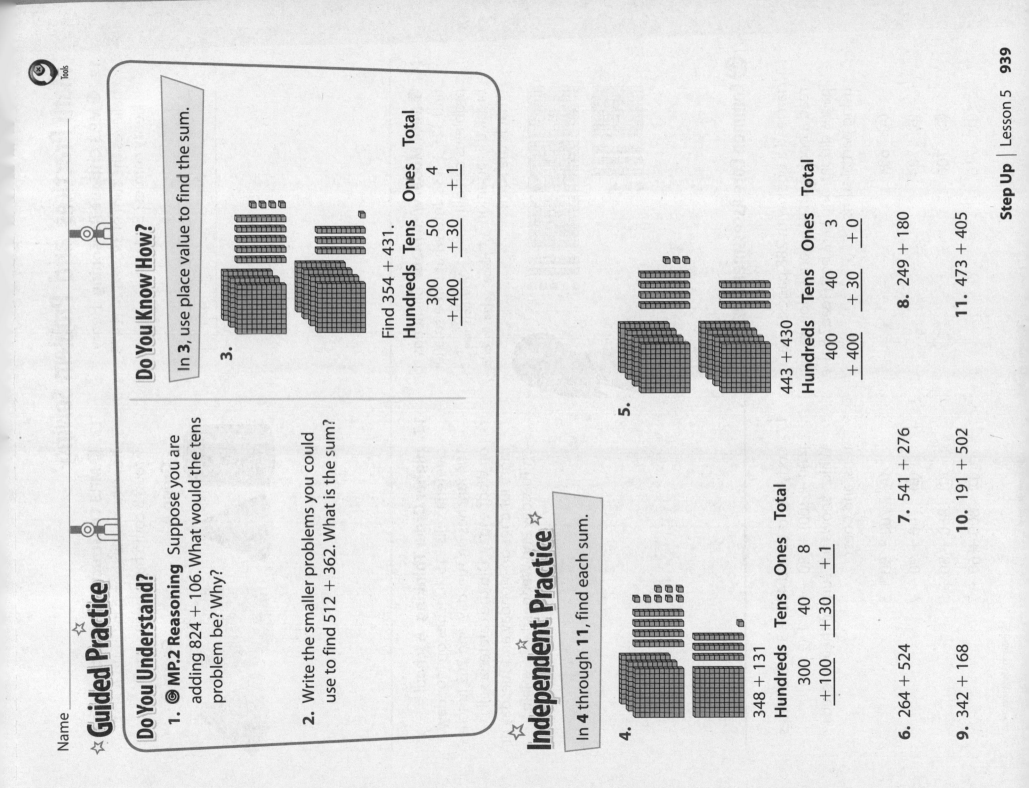

Find 354 + 431.

Hundreds	Tens	Ones	Total
300	50	4	
+ 400	+ 30	+ 1	

☆ Independent Practice ☆

In **4** through **11**, find each sum.

4.

348 + 131

Hundreds	Tens	Ones	Total
300	40	8	
+ 100	+ 30	+ 1	

5.

443 + 430

Hundreds	Tens	Ones	Total
400	40	3	
+ 400	+ 30	+ 0	

6. 264 + 524

7. 541 + 276

8. 249 + 180

9. 342 + 168

10. 191 + 502

11. 473 + 405

12. ◎ MP.3 Critique Reasoning Henry believes the sum of 345 + 124 is 479. Is Henry correct? Explain.

345	124

?

13. ◎ MP.3 Construct Arguments Explain how the solids shown in Group A and Group B could have been sorted.

Group A   Group B

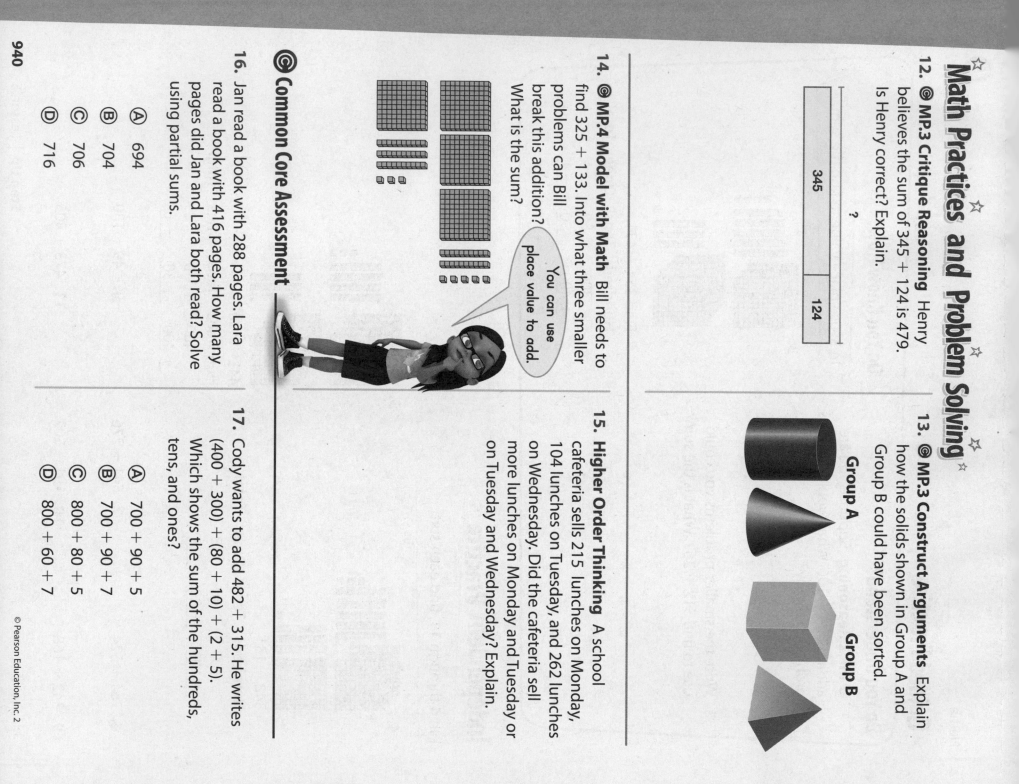

14. ◎ MP.4 Model with Math Bill needs to find 325 + 133. Into what three smaller problems can Bill break this addition? What is the sum?

You can use place value to add.

15. Higher Order Thinking A school cafeteria sells 215 lunches on Monday, 104 lunches on Tuesday, and 262 lunches on Wednesday. Did the cafeteria sell more lunches on Monday and Tuesday or on Tuesday and Wednesday? Explain.

◎ Common Core Assessment

16. Jan read a book with 288 pages. Lara read a book with 416 pages. How many pages did Jan and Lara both read? Solve using partial sums.

Ⓐ 694

Ⓑ 704

Ⓒ 706

Ⓓ 716

17. Cody wants to add 482 + 315. He writes (400 + 300) + (80 + 10) + (2 + 5). Which shows the sum of the hundreds, tens, and ones?

Ⓐ 700 + 90 + 5

Ⓑ 700 + 90 + 7

Ⓒ 800 + 80 + 5

Ⓓ 800 + 60 + 7

Name _____

Solve & Share

Find the sum of 146 + 247.
Solve this problem any way you choose.

Lesson 6
Models for Adding 3-Digit Numbers

➤ Solve

I can ...
add 3-digit numbers using models, drawings, and place value.

Ⓒ Content Standard 3.NBT.A.2
Mathematical Practices MP.3, MP.4, MP.5, MP.8

Model with math. You can use place-value blocks and draw pictures of the blocks to show how you found the sum. Show your work!

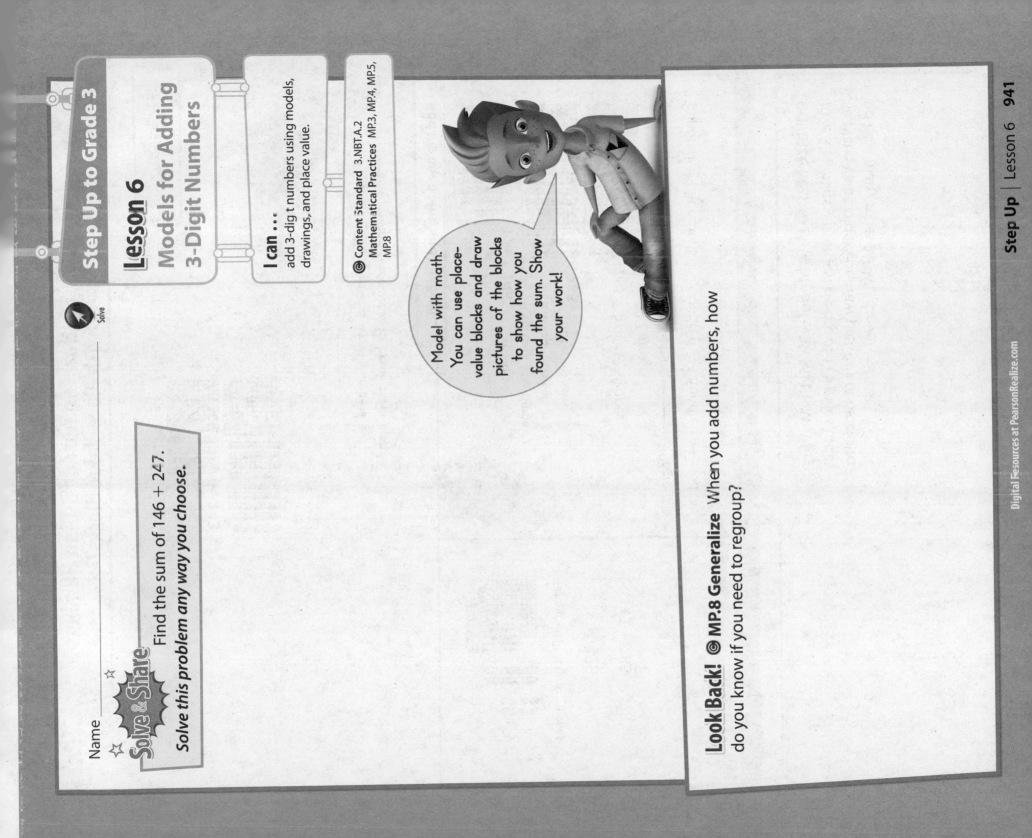

Look Back! Ⓒ **MP.8 Generalize** When you add numbers, how do you know if you need to regroup?

How Can You Add 3-Digit Numbers with Place-Value Blocks?

A

Find 143 + 285.

You can add whole numbers by using place value to break them apart.

143

285

B

Add the ones, tens, and hundreds.

143

285

When you regroup, you name a whole number in a different way.

3 ones + 5 ones = 8 ones

4 tens + 8 tens = 12 tens

12 tens = 1 hundred 2 tens ← Regroup.

1 hundred + 2 hundreds + 1 hundred = 4 hundreds ← Add the hundreds.

C

4 hundreds 2 tens 8 ones

428

143 + 285 = 428

Convince Me! © **MP.4 Model with Math** Mr. Wu drove 224 miles yesterday. He drove 175 miles today. Use place-value blocks or draw pictures of blocks to find how many miles Mr. Wu drove.

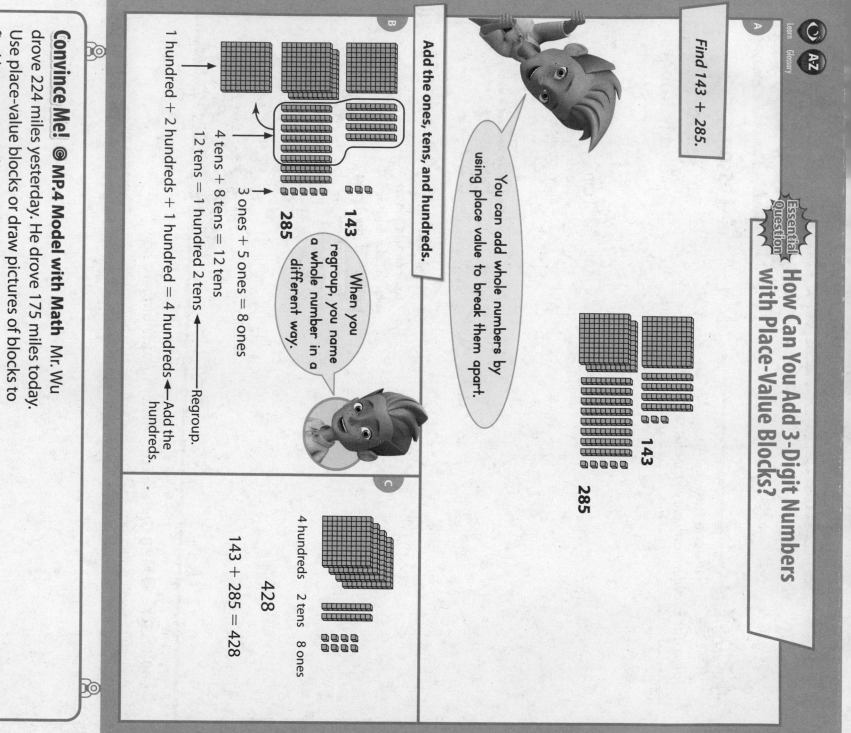

Name _____

Another Example!

You may have to regroup twice when you add. Find 148 + 276.

Step 1

Add the ones.

8 ones + 6 ones = 14 ones

Regroup.

14 ones = 1 ten 4 ones

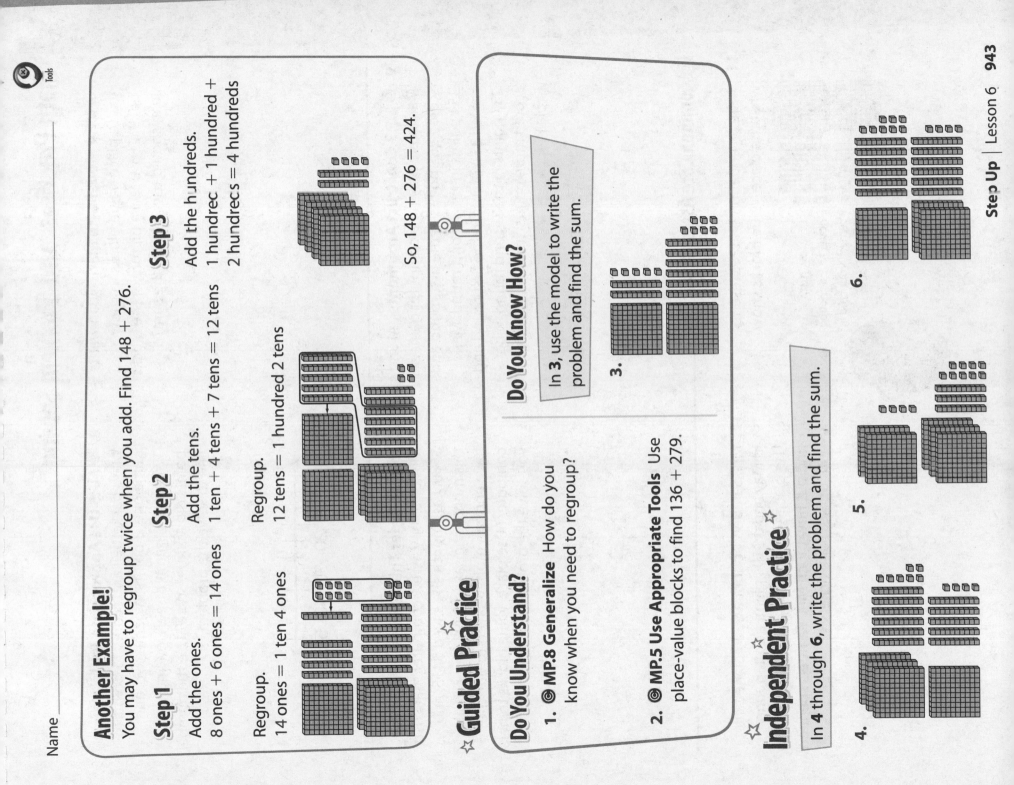

Step 2

Add the tens.

1 ten + 4 tens + 7 tens = 12 tens

Regroup.

12 tens = 1 hundred 2 tens

Step 3

Add the hundreds.

1 hundred + 1 hundred + 2 hundreds = 4 hundreds

So, 148 + 276 = 424.

☆ Guided Practice ☆

Do You Understand?

1. © MP.8 Generalize How do you know when you need to regroup?

2. © MP.5 Use Appropriate Tools Use place-value blocks to find 136 + 279.

Do You Know How?

In **3**, use the model to write the problem and find the sum.

3.

☆ Independent Practice ☆

In **4** through **6**, write the problem and find the sum.

4.

5.

6.

Step Up | Lesson 6   **943**

7. ⓒ MP.4 Model with Math Juan wants to use place-value blocks to show $148 + 256$. Draw a picture of the blocks Juan should use. What is the sum?

8. ⓒ MP.5 Use Appropriate Tools Manuel plays basketball and scores 15 points in game one, 8 points in game two, and 17 points in game three. How many points did Manuel score? Use the number line to solve the problem.

0 10 20 30 40 50

9. ⓒ MP.3 Construct Arguments Al and Mark were playing a computer game. Al scored 265 points in the first round and scored 352 points in the second round. Mark scored 352 points in the first round and 237 points in the second round. Who scored more points and won the game? Explain.

10. Higher Order Thinking Paula is saving money to buy a new computer that costs $680. Last month she saved $415, and this month she saved $298. Does Paula have enough money saved to buy the computer? Use place-value blocks to help you solve the problem. Explain.

ⓒ Common Core Assessment

11. Write an equation that represents what the place-value blocks show.

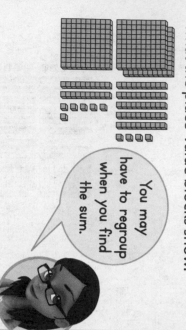

You may have to regroup when you find the sum.

12. Mrs. Samuels bought a $526 plane ticket in May and a $194 plane ticket in June. Use place-value blocks or draw pictures to find out how much Mrs. Samuels spent on both of the plane tickets.

944

Lesson 7

Subtract with Partial Differences

I can...

subtract numbers using partial differences.

© **Content Standard** 3.NBT.A.2
Mathematical Practices MP.2, MP.3, MP.4, MP.5, MP.7

Solve

Solve & Share

Find the difference of 534 − 108. Think about place value. *Solve this problem any way you choose.*

You can use reasoning. How could you break this problem into smaller subtraction problems? Show your work in the space below!

Look Back! © **MP.2 Reasoning** How can using place value help you solve this subtraction problem?

Essential Question

How Can You Break Large Subtraction Problems into Smaller Ones?

A

At the end of the fourth round of a game of Digit Derby, Marco's score was 462 points. During the fifth round of the game, Marco loses points. What is Marco's score at the end of the fifth round?

Find 462 − 181.

End of Round 4
Marco has 462 points.

End of Round 5
Marco loses 181 points.

Place value can help you break a subtraction problem into smaller problems.

B

Step 1

Start with 462.

Subtract the **hundreds**.

462 − 100 = 362

So far, 100 has been subtracted.

C

Step 2

Next, start with 362.

Subtract the **tens**.

You need to subtract 8 tens, but there are not enough tens. So, subtract the 6 tens.

362 − 60 = 302

Then, subtract the 2 tens that are left.

302 − 20 = 282

So far, 100 + 60 + 20 = 180 has been subtracted.

D

Step 3

That leaves just 1 to subtract.

Subtract the **ones**.

282 − 1 = 281

100 + 60 + 20 + 1 = 181 has been subtracted.

At the end of the fifth round, Marco's score is 281 points.

Convince Me! ⊙ MP.7 Use Structure Find 453 − 262. Use place value to help break the problem into smaller problems. Show your work.

Name _____

☆ Guided Practice ☆

Do You Understand?

1. © MP.3 Construct Arguments Why do you need to record the numbers you subtract at each step?

2. © MP.2 Reasoning Carmella is trying to find 784 − 310. She decides to start by subtracting 10 from 784. Do you agree with Carmella? Explain.

Do You Know How?

In **3** and **4**, use place value to help break the problem into smaller problems.

3. Find 564 − 346.

564 − 300 = _____

264 − 40 = _____

224 − 4 = _____

220 − 2 = _____

4. Find 769 − 375.

769 − 300 = _____

469 − 60 = _____

409 − 10 = _____

399 − 5 = _____

☆ Independent Practice ☆

In **5** through **10**, follow the steps to find each difference. Show your work.

5. 728 − 413

First, subtract 400.

_____ − _____ = 328

Then, subtract 10.

_____ − _____ = _____

Then, subtract 3.

_____ − 3 = _____

6. 936 − 524

First, subtract 500.

936 − _____ = _____

Then, subtract 20.

_____ − 20 = _____

Then, subtract 4.

_____ − _____ = _____

7. 854 − 235

First, subtract 200.

_____ − 200 = _____

Then, subtract 30.

_____ − 30 = _____

Then, subtract 4.

_____ − _____ = _____

Then, subtract 1.

_____ − 1 = _____

8. 955 − 283

9. 946 − 507

10. 984 − 356

Math Practices and Problem Solving

11. © MP.5 Use Appropriate Tools
Write the time shown on the clock in
2 different ways.

_____

12. © MP.7 Use Structure There are
96 boys and 83 girls in the school
lunchroom. Near the end of lunch,
127 students leave. How many
students are left in the lunchroom?
Show how you can break part of the
problem into smaller problems.

13. © MP.4 Model with Math Yuki had a necklace
with 131 beads. The string broke, and she lost
43 beads. How many beads does Yuki have left?

	131 beads
43	?

43 beads lost   ? beads left

14. Higher Order Thinking Which weighs
more, two adult male Basset Hounds
or one adult male Great Dane? Show
the difference in pounds between the
two Basset Hounds and the Great Dane.
Draw bar diagrams to represent and
help you solve the problem.

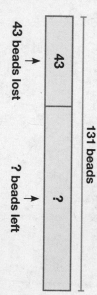

Great Dane   Basset Hound

145 pounds   66 pounds

© Common Core Assessment

15. Karl's book has 416 pages. He read 50 pages last week. He
read another 31 pages this week. How many more pages
does Karl have left to read?

Ⓐ 125
Ⓑ 245
Ⓒ 335
Ⓓ 345

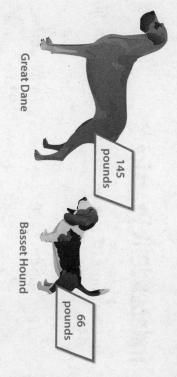

You can
break the problem
into smaller problems
to solve.

Lesson 8

Models for Subtracting 3-Digit Numbers

I can ...
subtract 3-digit numbers using models, drawings, and place value.

© Content Standard 3.NBT.A.2
Mathematical Practices MP.1, MP.4, MP.8

Solve

Name _____

Solve & Share

Find the difference of 246 − 153.
Solve this problem any way you choose.

Model with math.
Drawing pictures of place-value blocks is one way to represent this problem and help you solve it. Show your work!

Look Back! © **MP.8 Generalize** How can you check your answer for 246 − 153?

AZ

How Can You Subtract 3-Digit Numbers with Place-Value Blocks?

A

Fish caught near the Hawaiian Islands can be very large. How many more pounds does a broadbill swordfish weigh than a blue marlin?

Find 237 − 165.

Wild Hawaiian Fish Weights	
Type of Fish	**Weight (in lb)**
Blue Marlin	165
Broadbill Swordfish	237

DATA

Use place value to subtract the ones first, the tens next, and then the hundreds.

Show 237 with place-value blocks.

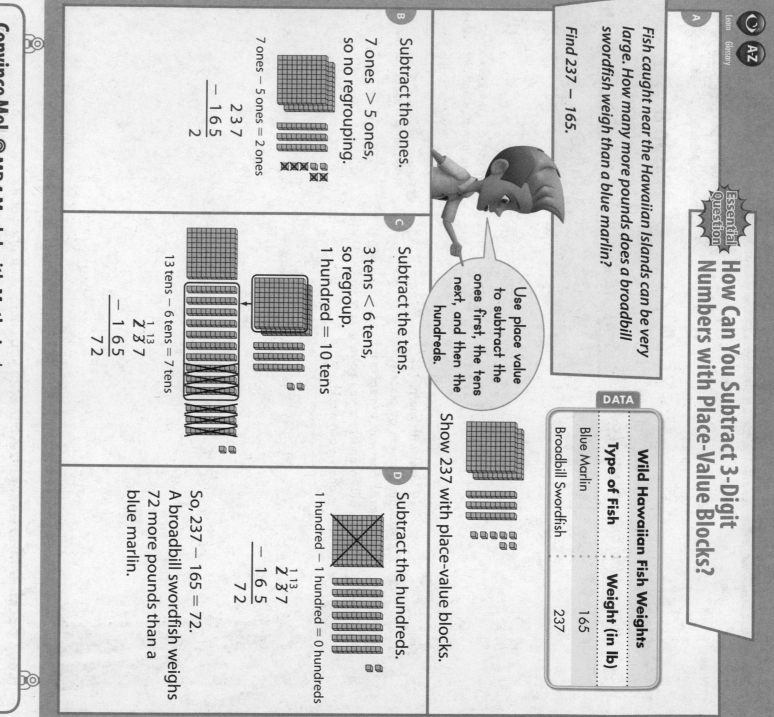

B

Subtract the ones.

7 ones > 5 ones, so no regrouping.

7 ones − 5 ones = 2 ones

$$\begin{array}{r} 237 \\ -165 \\ \hline 2 \end{array}$$

C

Subtract the tens.

3 tens < 6 tens, so regroup.

1 hundred = 10 tens

13 tens − 6 tens = 7 tens

$$\begin{array}{r} ^{1\ 13}2\cancel{3}7 \\ -165 \\ \hline 72 \end{array}$$

D

Subtract the hundreds.

1 hundred − 1 hundred = 0 hundreds

$$\begin{array}{r} ^{1\ 13}2\cancel{3}7 \\ -165 \\ \hline 72 \end{array}$$

So, 237 − 165 = 72. A broadbill swordfish weighs 72 more pounds than a blue marlin.

Convince Me! Ⓜ **MP.4 Model with Math** Anderson needs $231 to buy a new bike. He saved $144 from his summer job. How much more does Anderson need to save to buy the bike? Write a subtraction equation that models the problem. Use place-value blocks to help you solve the problem using the same steps shown above.

950

© Pearson Education, Inc. 2

Name _____

☆ Guided Practice ☆

Do You Understand?

1. ⓒ MP.8 Generalize In the example on page 950, for 237 − 165, why do you need to regroup 1 hundred into 10 tens?

2. ⓒ MP.4 Model with Math Gary saved $287 doing jobs in his neighborhood. He bought a computer printer for $183. How much money did Gary have left? Draw a picture of place-value blocks to help you subtract.

Do You Know How?

In **3** through **10**, use place-value blocks or draw pictures to subtract.

3.　859
　−768

4.　361
　−124

5.　285
　− 49

6.　684
　−482

7. 384 − 358

8. 352 − 214

9. 512 − 101

10. 999 − 889

☆ Independent Practice ☆

You can draw squares to show hundreds, lines to show tens, and dots to show ones. This picture shows 123.

□ | | | ∴

In **11** through **22**, use place-value blocks or draw pictures to subtract.

11.　651
　−543

12.　492
　−138

13.　690
　−481

14.　508
　−137

15.　168
　− 39

16.　618
　−476

17.　419
　− 59

18.　192
　−108

19.　573
　−468

20.　596
　−128

21.　819
　−124

22.　438
　−283

Math Practices and Problem Solving

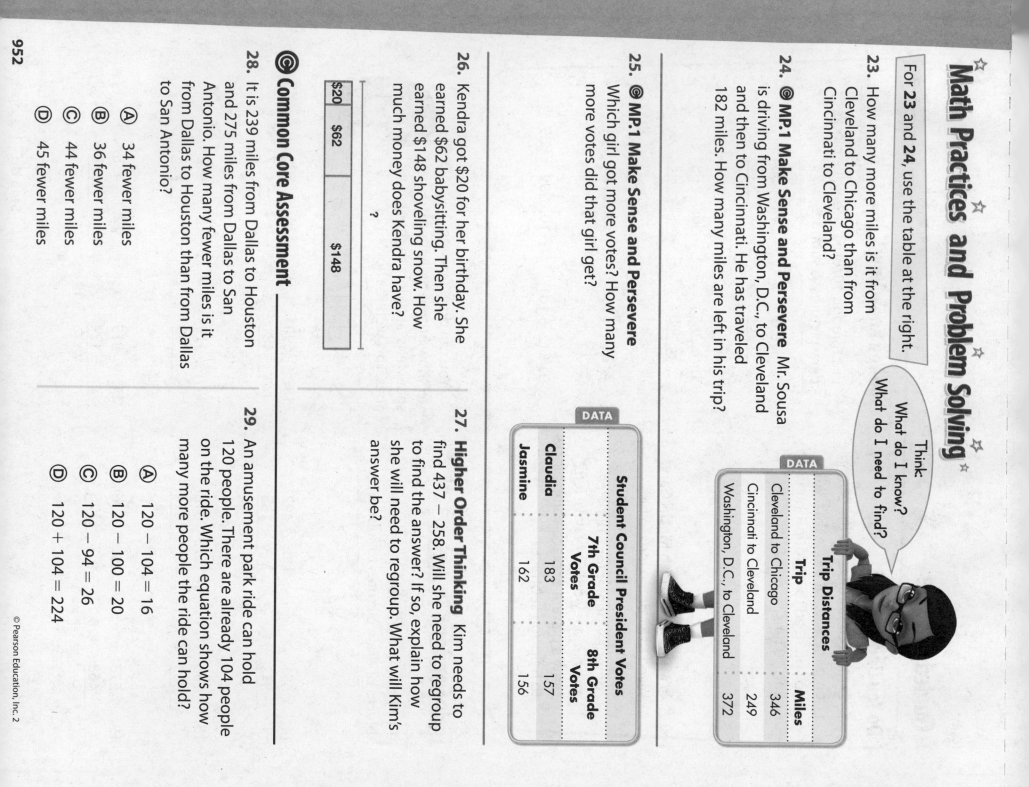

For **23** and **24**, use the table at the right.

Think:
What do I know?
What do I need to find?

Trip Distances

DATA

Trip	Miles
Cleveland to Chicago	346
Cincinnati to Cleveland	249
Washington, D.C., to Cleveland	372

23. How many more miles is it from Cleveland to Chicago than from Cincinnati to Cleveland?

24. © **MP.1 Make Sense and Persevere** Mr. Sousa is driving from Washington, D.C., to Cleveland and then to Cincinnati. He has traveled 182 miles. How many miles are left in his trip?

25. © **MP.1 Make Sense and Persevere** Which girl got more votes? How many more votes did that girl get?

Student Council President Votes

DATA

	7th Grade Votes	8th Grade Votes
Claudia	183	157
Jasmine	162	156

26. Kendra got $20 for her birthday. She earned $62 babysitting. Then she earned $148 shoveling snow. How much money does Kendra have?

$20	$62	$148

?

27. **Higher Order Thinking** Kim needs to find $437 - 258$. Will she need to regroup to find the answer? If so, explain how she will need to regroup. What will Kim's answer be?

© **Common Core Assessment**

28. It is 239 miles from Dallas to Houston and 275 miles from Dallas to San Antonio. How many fewer miles is it from Dallas to Houston than from Dallas to San Antonio?

Ⓐ 34 fewer miles

Ⓑ 36 fewer miles

Ⓒ 44 fewer miles

Ⓓ 45 fewer miles

29. An amusement park ride can hold 120 people. There are already 104 people on the ride. Which equation shows how many more people the ride can hold?

Ⓐ $120 - 104 = 16$

Ⓑ $120 - 100 = 20$

Ⓒ $120 - 94 = 26$

Ⓓ $120 + 104 = 224$

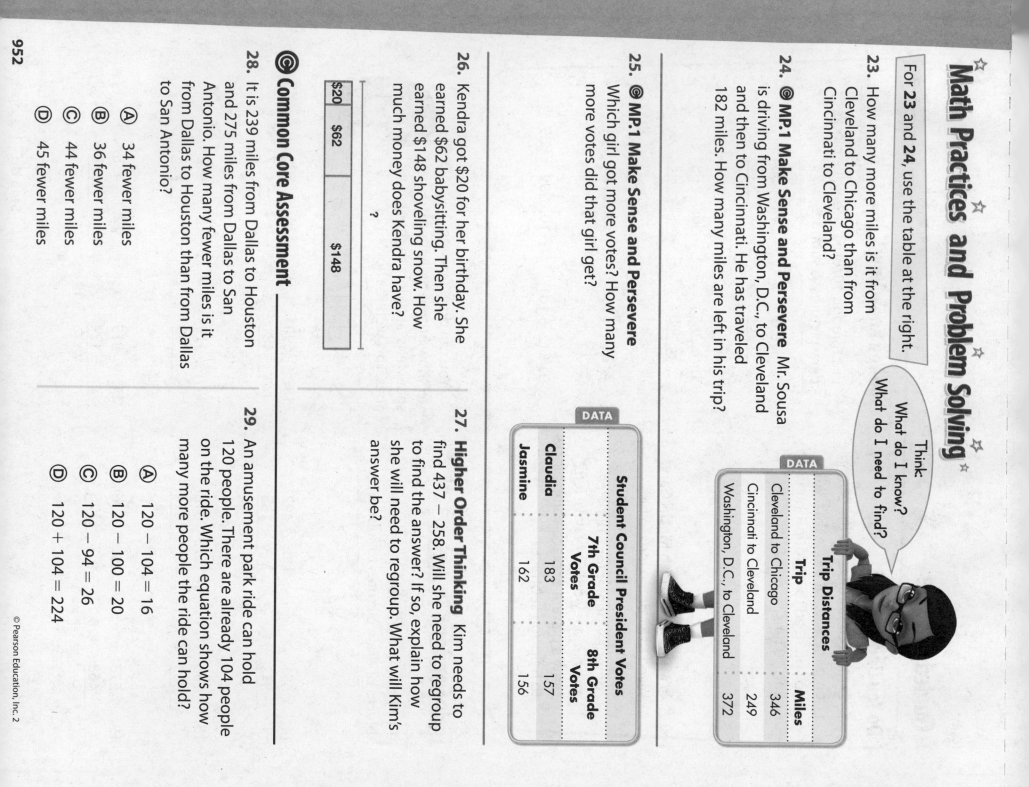

952

© Pearson Education, Inc. 2

Lesson 9

Divide Regions into Equal Parts

I can ...

read and write a unit fraction.

© Content Standards 3.NF.A.1, 3.G.A.2
Mathematical Practices MP.4, MP.6, MP.7

Name

Solve & Share

Show two different ways to divide a 2 × 6 region into 6 equal parts. Color the 6 parts of each region a different color. How do you know the parts are equal?

Solve

Be precise. Think about each part as you divide the regions.

Look Back! © MP.7 Use Structure How are the parts of the regions alike? How are they different?

How Can You Name the Equal Parts of a Whole?

A

Divide a whole into halves. What fraction can you write to represent one half of a whole?

A fraction is an equal part of a whole.

B

one half

one half

Each part is made up of 6 unit squares. Both parts have equal areas.

C

$\frac{1}{2}$

$\frac{1}{2}$

Each part is **one half** of the area of the whole shape.

This fraction can be written as $\frac{1}{2}$.

$\frac{1}{2}$ is a unit fraction. A unit fraction represents one of the equal parts.

D

The number above the bar in a fraction is called the numerator.

The numerator shows the number of equal parts represented by that fraction.

numerator $\longrightarrow$ 1
denominator $\longrightarrow$ 2

The number below the bar in a fraction is called the denominator.

The denominator shows the total number of equal parts in that whole.

Convince Me! © MP.6 Be Precise Divide the grid at the right into thirds. Label each third using a unit fraction. Explain how you knew which fraction to write.

Name _____

⭐ Guided Practice

Do You Understand?

1. In the examples on page 954, explain how you know the two parts are equal.

In **2** and **3**, tell if each shows equal or unequal parts. If the parts are equal, label one of the parts using a unit fraction.

2.

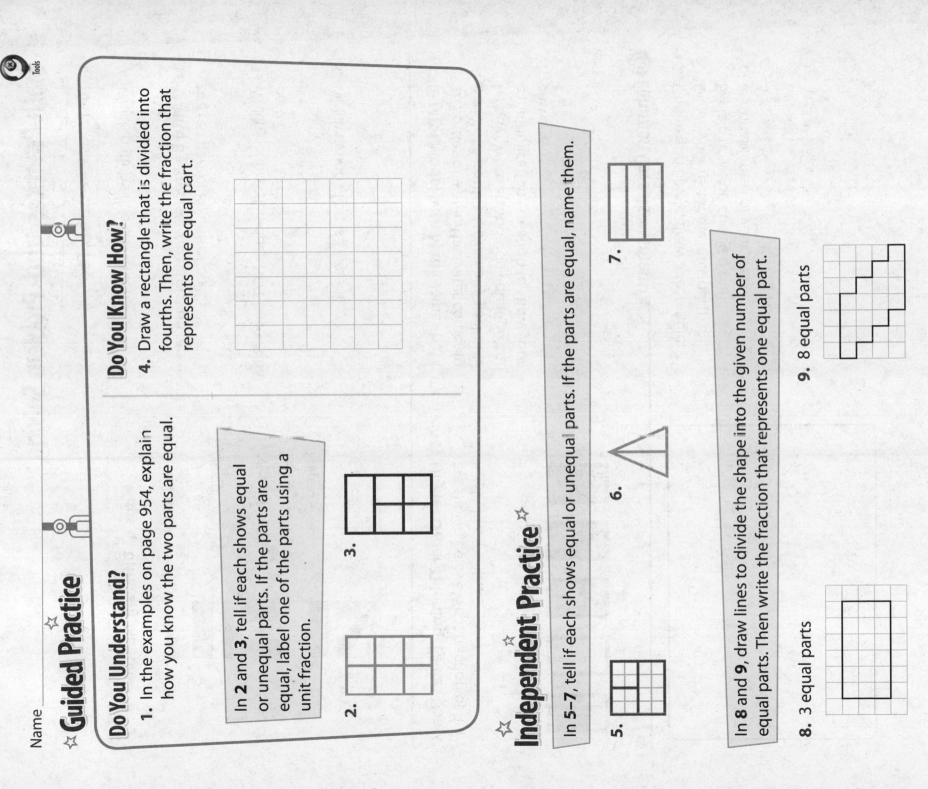

3.

Do You Know How?

4. Draw a rectangle that is divided into fourths. Then, write the fraction that represents one equal part.

⭐ Independent Practice ⭐

In **5–7**, tell if each shows equal or unequal parts. If the parts are equal, name them.

5.

6.

7.

In **8** and **9**, draw lines to divide the shape into the given number of equal parts. Then write the fraction that represents one equal part.

8. 3 equal parts

9. 8 equal parts

☆ ☆ Math Practices and Problem Solving ☆ ☆

In **10–13**, use the table of flags.

10. Which nation's flag is $\frac{1}{3}$ white?

11. ⓒ **MP.6 Be Precise** What fraction represents the red part of Poland's flag?

12. Which nation's flag does **NOT** have equal parts?

13. Which nation's flag is $\frac{1}{4}$ green?

Flags of Different Nations

Nation	Flag
Mauritius	
Nigeria	
Poland	
Seychelles	

14. ⓒ **MP.4 Model with Math** James buys 18 bottles of water. The water comes in packs of 6 bottles. How many packs did he buy? Write an addition equation and a multiplication equation to show your answer.

15. Higher Order Thinking Laura's books are shown below. What fraction of her books has a yellow cover?

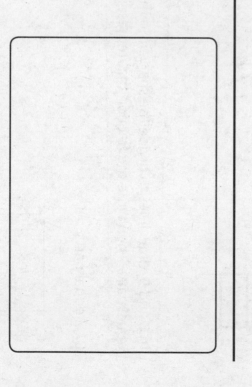

ⓒ Common Core Assessment

16. On the grid below, draw a rectangle. Divide your rectangle into fourths. Explain how you checked the reasonableness of your work.

Name _____

Solve & Share

Solve

Pat made a garden in the shape of a rectangle and divided it into 4 same-size parts. She planted flowers in one of the parts. Draw a picture of what Pat's garden might look like.

You can make sense of the given information to plan your drawing of Pat's garden.

Lesson 10
Fractions and Regions

I can ...
show and name part of a region.

© Content Standards 3.NF.A.1, 3.G.A.2
Mathematical Practices MP.1, MP.2, MP.3, MP.4

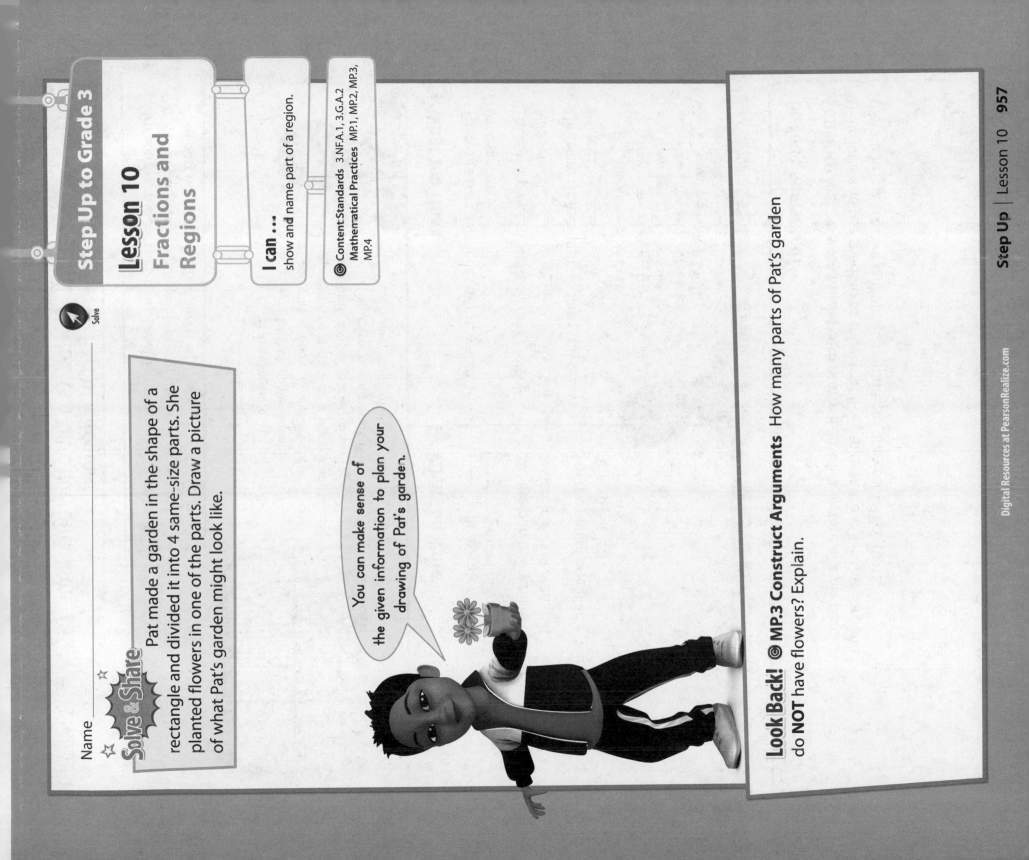

Look Back! © MP.3 Construct Arguments How many parts of Pat's garden do **NOT** have flowers? Explain.

How Can You Show and Name Part of a Region?

A

Mr. Peters served part of a pan of enchilada casserole to a friend. What does each part of the whole pan of casserole represent? What part was served? What part is left?

A fraction is a symbol that names equal parts of a whole. A unit fraction represents one part of a whole that has been divided into equal parts. A unit fraction always has a numerator of 1.

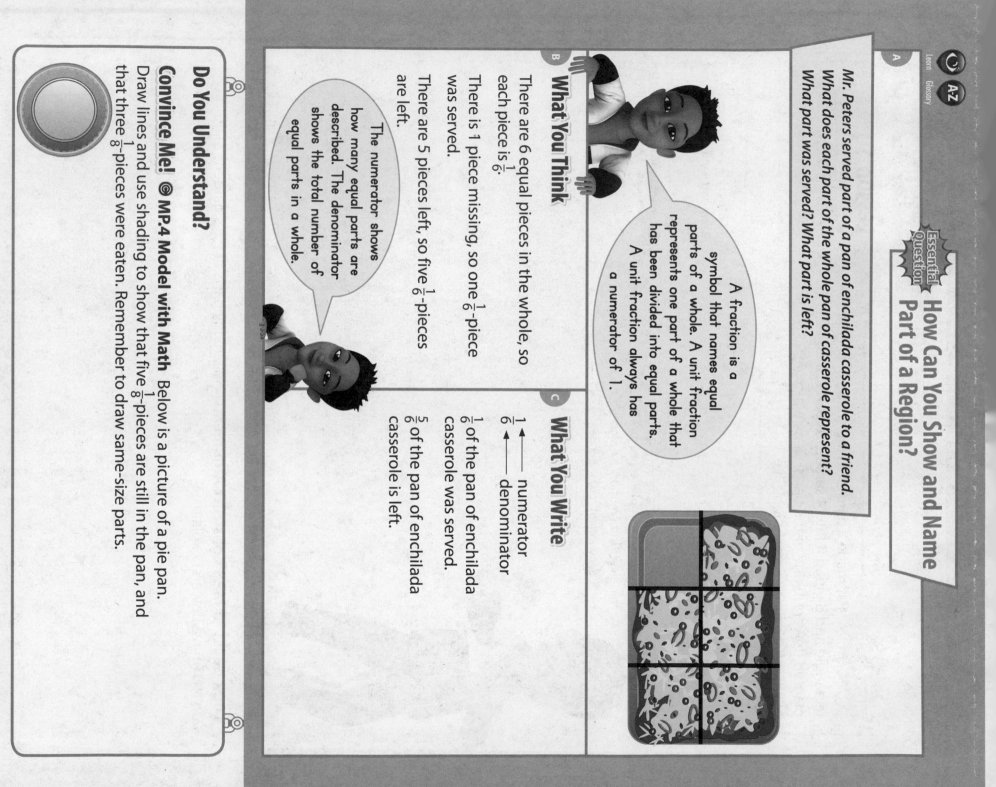

B

What You Think

There are 6 equal pieces in the whole, so each piece is $\frac{1}{6}$.

There is 1 piece missing, so one $\frac{1}{6}$-piece was served.

There are 5 pieces left, so five $\frac{1}{6}$-pieces are left.

The numerator shows how many equal parts are described. The denominator shows the total number of equal parts in a whole.

C

What You Write

$$\frac{1}{6} \quad \begin{array}{l} \leftarrow \text{numerator} \\ \leftarrow \text{denominator} \end{array}$$

$\frac{1}{6}$ of the pan of enchilada casserole was served.

$\frac{5}{6}$ of the pan of enchilada casserole is left.

Do You Understand?

Convince Me! © MP.4 Model with Math Below is a picture of a pie pan. Draw lines and use shading to show that five $\frac{1}{8}$-pieces are still in the pan, and that three $\frac{1}{8}$-pieces were eaten. Remember to draw same-size parts.

958

Name _____

☆ Guided Practice ☆

Do You Understand?

1. In the problem at the top of page 958, what fraction names all of the pieces in the casserole?

2. © MP.4 Model with Math Mrs. Rao made a cake. What fraction of the whole cake does each piece represent?

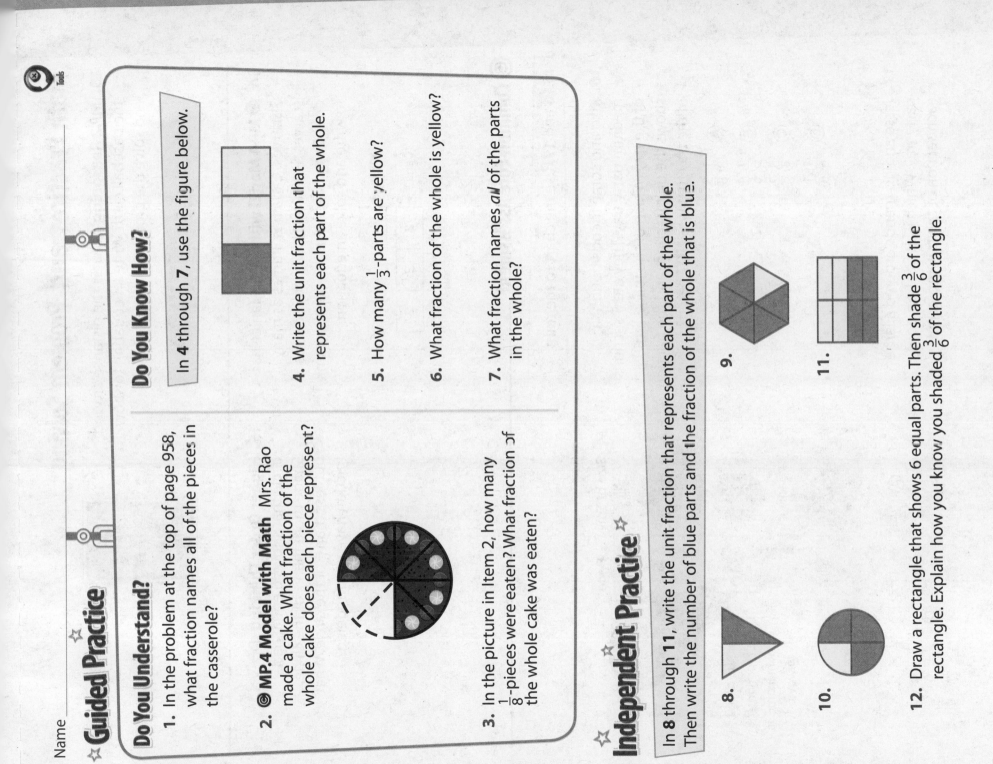

3. In the picture in Item 2, how many $\frac{1}{8}$-pieces were eaten? What fraction of the whole cake was eaten?

Do You Know How?

In **4** through **7**, use the figure below.

4. Write the unit fraction that represents each part of the whole.

5. How many $\frac{1}{3}$-parts are yellow?

6. What fraction of the whole is yellow?

7. What fraction names *all* of the parts in the whole?

☆ Independent Practice ☆

In **8** through **11**, write the unit fraction that represents each part of the whole. Then write the number of blue parts and the fraction of the whole that is blue.

8.

9.

10.

11.

12. Draw a rectangle that shows 6 equal parts. Then shade $\frac{3}{6}$ of the rectangle. Explain how you know you shaded $\frac{3}{6}$ of the rectangle.

Math Practices and Problem Solving ☆

13. MP.2 Reasoning What is the distance around the baseball card? Write an equation to show and solve the problem.

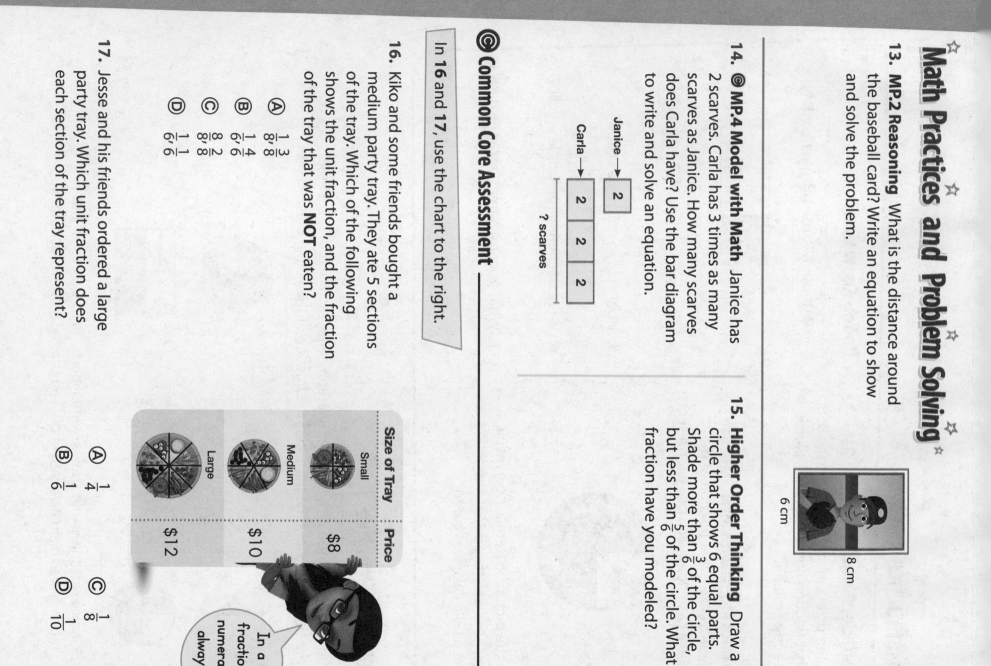

6 cm

8 cm

---

14. ◎ MP.4 Model with Math Janice has 2 scarves. Carla has 3 times as many scarves as Janice. How many scarves does Carla have? Use the bar diagram to write and solve an equation.

Janice → | 2 |

Carla → | 2 | 2 | 2 |

? scarves

15. Higher Order Thinking Draw a circle that shows 6 equal parts. Shade more than $\frac{3}{6}$ of the circle, but less than $\frac{5}{6}$ of the circle. What fraction have you modeled?

◎ Common Core Assessment

In **16** and **17**, use the chart to the right.

16. Kiko and some friends bought a medium party tray. They ate 5 sections of the tray. Which of the following shows the unit fraction, and the fraction of the tray that was **NOT** eaten?

Ⓐ $\frac{1}{8}, \frac{3}{8}$

Ⓑ $\frac{1}{6}, \frac{4}{6}$

Ⓒ $\frac{8}{8}, \frac{2}{8}$

Ⓓ $\frac{1}{6}, \frac{1}{6}$

Size of Tray	Price
Small	$8
Medium	$10
Large	$12

In a unit fraction the numerator is always 1.

17. Jesse and his friends ordered a large party tray. Which unit fraction does each section of the tray represent?

Ⓐ $\frac{1}{4}$

Ⓑ $\frac{1}{6}$

Ⓒ $\frac{1}{8}$

Ⓓ $\frac{1}{10}$

Glossary

A

add

When you add, you join groups together.

$$3 + 4 = 7$$

addend

numbers that are added

$$2 + 5 = 7$$

addends

after

424 comes after 423.

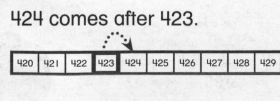

a.m.

clock time from midnight until noon

7:10 PM

angle

the corner shape formed by two sides that meet

array

a group of objects set in equal rows and columns that forms a rectangle

B

bar diagram

a model for addition and subtraction that shows the parts and the whole

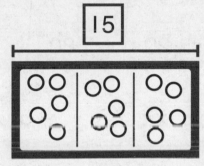

15

bar graph

A bar graph uses bars to show data.

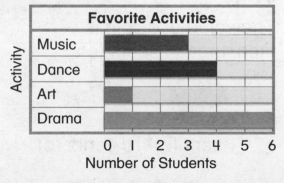

Favorite Activities

Music
Dance
Art
Drama

Activity

0 1 2 3 4 5 6
Number of Students

before

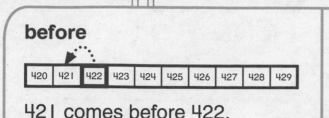

421 comes before 422.

break apart

You can break apart a number into its place value parts.

$$27 \; + \; 35 = ?$$

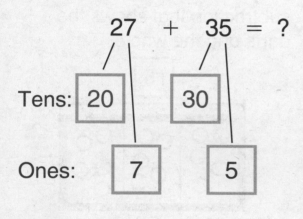

Tens: 20   30

Ones: 7   5

cents

The value of a coin is measured in cents (¢).

1 cent (¢)   10 cents (¢)

centimeter (cm)

a metric unit of length that is part of 1 meter

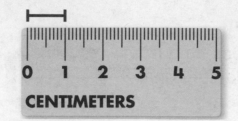

CENTIMETERS

coins

money that is made out of metal and that can have different values

1¢   5¢   10¢   25¢   50¢

column

objects in an array or data in a table that are shown up and down

 column

1	2	3	4	5
11	12	13	14	15
21	22	23	24	25
31	32	33	34	35

compare

When you compare numbers, you find out if a number is greater than, less than, or equal to another number.

$$147 \; \textgreater \; 143$$

147 is greater than 143.

compatible numbers

numbers that are easy to add or subtract using mental math

$$8 + 2$$
$$20 + 7$$
$$53 + 10$$

compensation

a mental math strategy you can use to add or subtract

$$38 + 24 = ?$$
$$+ 2 \quad - 2$$

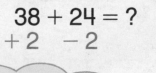

You add 2 to 38 to make 40. Then subtract 2 from 24 to get 22. 40 + 22 = 62. So, 38 + 24 = 62.

cone

a solid figure with a circle shaped base and a curved surface that meets at a point

cube

a solid figure with six faces that are matching squares

cylinder

a solid figure with two matching circle shaped bases

 D

data

information you collect and can be shown in a table or graph

Favorite Fruit	
Apple	7
Peach	4
Orange	5

decrease

to become lesser in value

$$600 \longrightarrow 550$$

600 decreased by 50 is 550.

denominator

the number below the fraction bar in a fraction, which shows the total number of equal parts

$$\frac{3}{4} \longleftarrow \text{denominator}$$

difference

the answer in a subtraction equation or problem

$$14 - 6 = 8$$

↑

difference

digits

 43

Numbers are made up of 1 or more digits. 43 has 2 digits.

dime

10 cents or 10¢

division

an operation that tells how many equal groups there are or how many are in each group

$$12 \div 3 = 4$$

divided by

what you say to read a division symbol

$$18 \div 3 = 6$$

↙ divided by

dollar

One dollar equals 100¢.

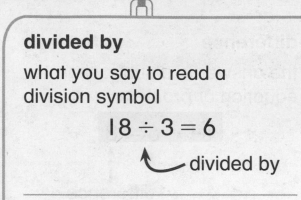

dollar bills

paper money that can have different dollar values, such as $1, $5, $10, or $20

dollar sign

a symbol used to show that a number represents money

$37

↑
dollar sign

doubles

addition facts that have two addends that are the same

$$4 + 4 = 8$$

↑   ↑
addend addend

E

edge

a line formed where two faces of a solid figure meet

edge

eighths

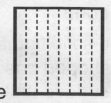

When a whole is separated into 8 equal shares, the parts are called eighths.

equal groups

groups that have the same number of items or objects

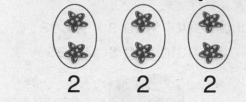

2   2   2

equal shares

parts of a whole that are the same size

All 4 shares are equal.

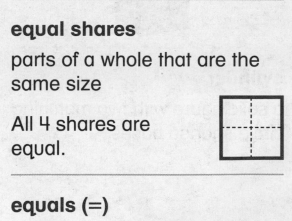

equals (=)

has the same value

$$36 = 36$$

36 is equal to 36.

equation

a math sentence that uses an equal sign (=) to show that the value on the left is equal to the value on the right

$$3 + ? = 7$$

$$14 - 6 = 8$$

estimate

When you estimate, you make a good guess.

This table is about 3 feet long.

even

a number that can be shown as a pair of cubes.

8 is even.

F

expanded form

a way of writing a number that shows the place value of each digit

$$400 + 60 + 3 = 463$$

face

a flat surface of a solid figure that does not roll

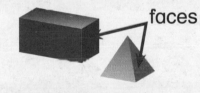

faces

fact family

a group of related addition and subtraction facts

$$2 + 4 = 6$$

$$4 + 2 = 6$$

$$6 - 2 = 4$$

$$6 - 4 = 2$$

factors

numbers that are multiplied together to give a product

$$7 \times 3 = 21$$

factors

flat surface

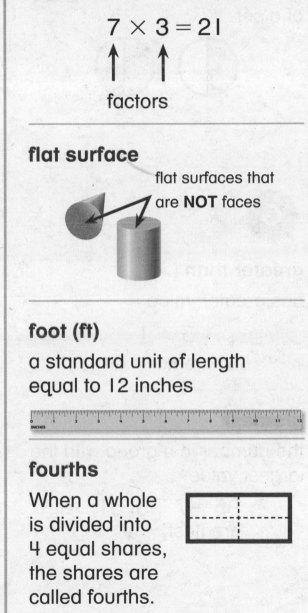

flat surfaces that are **NOT** faces

foot (ft)

a standard unit of length equal to 12 inches

fourths

When a whole is divided into 4 equal shares, the shares are called fourths.

fraction

a number, such as $\frac{1}{2}$ or $\frac{3}{4}$, that names part of a whole or part of a set

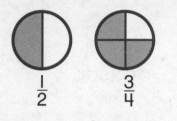

$\frac{1}{2}$ $\frac{3}{4}$

greater than (>)

has greater value

$$5 > 1$$

5 is greater than 1.

greatest

the number in a group with the largest value

35   47   58   (61)

greatest

---

greatest value

The coin that has the greatest value is the coin that is worth the most.

The quarter has the greatest value.

half-dollar

50 cents or 50¢

half past

30 minutes past the hour

It is half past 9.

---

halves (half)

When a whole is divided into 2 equal shares, the shares are called halves.

height

how tall an object is from bottom to top

heptagon

a polygon that has 7 sides

hexagon

a polygon that has 6 sides

hour

An hour is 60 minutes.

hundred

10 tens make 1 hundred.

I

inch (in.)

a standard unit of length that is part of 1 foot

INCHES

increase

to become greater in value

$$550 \longrightarrow 600$$

550 increased by 50 is 600.

L

least

the number in a group with the smallest value

35 47 58 61
└─ least

least value

The coin that has the least value is the coin that is worth the least.

The dime has the least value.

length

the distance from one end to the other end of an object

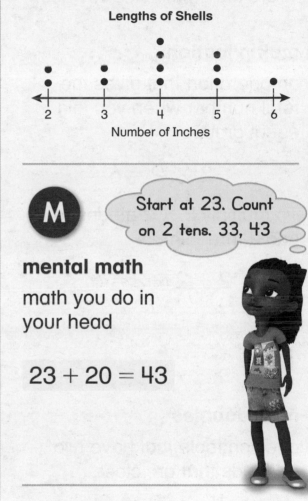

less than (<)

has less value

$$2 < 6$$

2 is less than 6.

line plot

A line plot uses dots above a number line to show data.

Lengths of Shells

2 3 4 5 6

Number of Inches

M

Start at 23. Count on 2 tens. 33, 43

mental math

math you do in your head

$$23 + 20 = 43$$

meter (m)

a metric unit of length equal to 100 centimeters

A long step is about a meter.

minute

a standard length of time

There are 60 minutes in 1 hour.

multiplication

an operation that gives the total number when you join equal groups

$$3 \times 2 = 6$$

To multiply 3×2 means to add 2 three times.

$$2 + 2 + 2 = 6$$

near doubles

addition facts that have two addends that are close

$$4 + 5 = 9$$

addend   addend

nearest centimeter

The whole number centimeter mark closest to the measure is the nearest centimeter.

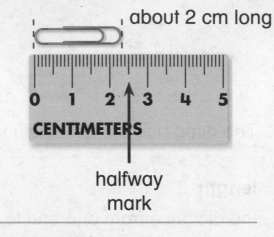

about 2 cm long

CENTIMETERS

halfway mark

nearest inch

The whole number inch mark closest to the measure is the nearest inch.

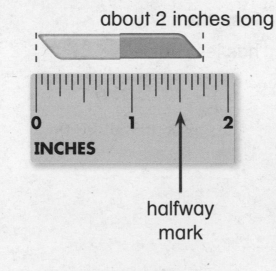

about 2 inches long

INCHES

halfway mark

next ten

the first ten greater than a number

30 is the next ten after 27.

nickel

5 cents or 5¢

nonagon

a polygon that has 9 sides

number line

a line that shows numbers in order from left to right

1 2 3 4 5 6 7 8 9 10

numerator

the number above the fraction bar in a fraction, which shows how many equal parts are described

$\dfrac{3}{4}$ ←—— numerator

octagon

a polygon that has 8 sides

odd

a number that can **NOT** be shown as pairs of cubes

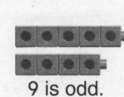

9 is odd.

ones

digits that shows how many ones are in a number

$$54 + 14 = 68$$

↑   ↑   ↑

open number line

An open number line is a tool that can help you add or subtract. It can begin at any number.

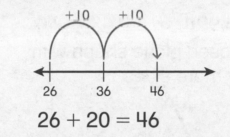

$$26 + 20 = 46$$

order

to place numbers from least to greatest or from greatest to least

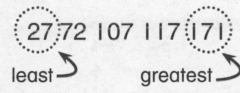

least →   greatest →

P

parallelogram

a quadrilateral that has 4 sides and opposite sides parallel

part

a piece of a whole or of a number

2 and 3 are parts of 5.

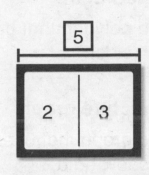

partial sum

When you add numbers, the sum of one of the place values is called a partial sum.

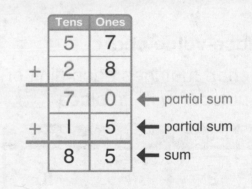

penny

I cent or I¢

pentagon

a polygon that has 5 sides

picture graph

a graph that uses pictures to show data

Favorite Ball Games	
Baseball	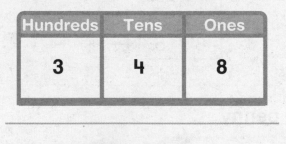
Soccer	
Tennis	

Each 👤 = 1 student

place-value chart

a chart matches each digit of a number with its place

Hundreds	Tens	Ones
3	4	8

plane shape

a flat shape

circle · rectangle · square · triangle

p.m.

clock time from noon until midnight

7:10 PM

polygon

a closed plane shape with 3 or more sides

product

the answer to a multiplication problem

$$4 \times 2 = 8$$

↑ product

pyramid

a solid figure with a base that is a polygon and faces that are triangles that meet in a point

Q

quadrilateral

a polygon that has 4 sides

quarter

25 cents or 25¢

quarter past

15 minutes after the hour

4:15

It is quarter past 4.

quarter to

15 minutes before the hour

3:45

It is quarter to 4.

R

rectangular prism

a solid figure with bases and faces that are rectangles

regroup

to name a number or part in a different way

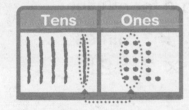

10 ones can be regrouped as 1 ten. 1 ten can be regrouped as 10 ones.

related

Addition facts and subtraction facts are related if they have the same numbers.

$$2 + 3 = 5$$
$$5 - 2 = 3$$

repeated addition

adding the same number repeatedly

$$3 + 3 + 3 + 3 = 12$$

right angle

an angle that forms a square corner

row

objects in an array or data in a table that are shown across

1	2	3	4	5
11	12	13	14	15
21	22	23	24	25
31	32	33	34	35

← row

S

separate

to subtract or to take apart into two or more parts

$$5 - 2 = 3$$

side

a line segment that makes one part of a plane shape

side

solid figure

a shape that has length, width, and height

These are all solid figures.

sphere

a solid figure that looks like a ball

standard form

a way to write a number using only digits

436

subtract

When you subtract, you find out how many are left or which group has more.

$$5 - 3 = 2$$

sum

the answer to an addition equation or problem

$$3 + 4 = 7$$

$$\begin{array}{r} 4 \\ + 3 \\ \hline 7 \end{array}$$

sum → 7

symbol

a picture or character that stands for something

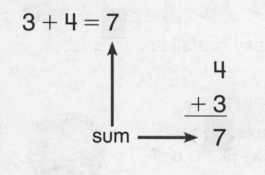

The symbol will be ☆.
Each ☆ represents 1 student.

 T

tally mark

a symbol used to keep track of each piece of information in an organized list

Ways to Show 30¢			
Quarter	Dime	Nickel	Total
I		I	30¢
	III		30¢
	II	II	30¢
	I	IIII	30¢
		⊞ I	30¢

tens

the digit that shows how many groups of ten are in a number

238
↑

thirds

When a whole is divided into 3 equal shares, the shares are called thirds.

thousand

10 hundreds make 1 thousand.

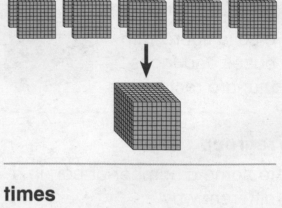

times

another word for multiply

times
$$7 \times 3 = 21$$

trapezoid

a polygon with 4 sides and one pair of sides are parallel

triangular prism

a solid figure that has two triangle shaped bases and three faces that have rectangle shapes.

U

unequal

Unequal parts are parts that are not equal.

5 unequal parts

unit

You can use different units to measure.

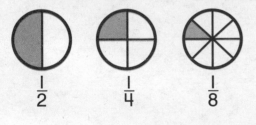

about 12 inches
about 1 foot

unit fraction

a fraction that reperesents one equal part of a whole or a set

$\frac{1}{2}$ $\qquad$ $\frac{1}{4}$ $\qquad$ $\frac{1}{8}$

unknown

a symbol that stands for a number in an equation

$$34 + ? = 67$$

↑

unknown

V

vertices (vertex)

corner points where 2 sides of a polygon meet or where edges of a solid figure meet

vertex

W

whole

a single unit that can be divided into parts

The two halves make one whole circle.

width

the distance across an object

word form

a way to write a number using only words

The word form for 23 is twenty-three.

Y

yard (yd)

a standard unit of length equal to 3 feet

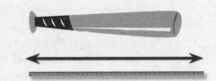

A baseball bat is about a yard long.

Photographs

Every effort has been made to secure permission and provide appropriate credit for photographic material. The publisher deeply regrets any omission and pledges to correct errors called to its attention in subsequent editions.

Unless otherwise acknowledged, all photographs are the property of Pearson Education, Inc.

Photo locators denoted as follows: Top (T), Center (C), Bottom (B), Left (L), Right (R), Background (Bkgd)

F13C Pearson Education;**F13CL** Pearson Education;**F13CR** Pearson Education;**F13L** Pearson Education;**F13R** Pearson Education;**001BL** Lori Martin/Shutterstock;**001BR** An Nguyen/Shutterstock;**001C** Africa Studio/Fotolia;**001L** Africa Studio/Fotolia;**001R** karandaev/Fotolia;**077BL** michaklootwijk/Fotolia;**077BR** Jitka Volfova/Shutterstock;**077L** Charles Brutlag/Shutterstock;**077R** Erni/Fotolia;**119L** FiCo74/Fotolia;**119R** Antonio Scarpi/Fotolia;**189** Beboy/Shutterstock;**253** Deborah Benbrook/Fotolia;**321** GlebStock/Shutterstock;**389** Paylessimages/Fotolia;**435** Ambient Ideas/Shutterstock;**456** Pearson Education;**494C** Pearson Education;**494** Pearson Education;**494B** Pearson Education;**494T** Pearson Education;**503** Es0lex/Fotolia;**504B** Pearson Education;**504BL** Pearson Education;**504BR** Pearson Education;**504C** Pearson Education;**504CL** Pearson Education;**504CR** Pearson Education;**504T** Pearson Education;**504TC** Pearson Education;**504TL** Pearson Education;**583** kalafoto/Fotolia;**635** Klagyivik Viktor/Shutterstock;**675** Nagel Photography/Shutterstock;**678** Optionm/Shutterstock;**687** Ant Clausen/Fotolia;**759** Bonita R. Cheshier/Shutterstock;**788** Lledó/Fotolia;**790** Ivan Kruk/Fotolia;**799L** Karichs/Fotolia;**799R** Ivonne Wierink/Fotolia;**845B** Pearson Education;**845BC** Pearson Education;**845CT** Pearson Education;**845T** Pearson Education;**851** Yurakr/Shutterstock;**868** StudioSmart/Shutterstock;**932** Pearson Education;**934** Pearson Education;**G2L** Pearson Education;**G2R** Pearson Education;**G3L** Pearson Education;**G3R** Pearson Education;**G4B** Pearson Education;**G4C** Pearson Education;**G4CB** Pearson Education;**G4CT** Pearson Education;**G4T** Pearson Education;**G6BL** Pearson Education;**G6BR** Pearson Education;**G6TC** Pearson Education;**G6TL** Pearson Education;**G6TR** Pearson Education;**G7C** Pearson Education;**G7L** Pearson Education;**G7R** Pearson Education;**G8L** Pearson Education;**G8R** Pearson Education;**G9L** Pearson Education;**G9R** Pearson Education;**G10L** Pearson Education;**G10R** United State Mint.